The Wonderland of Nature

written and illustrated by

NURI MASS, M.A.

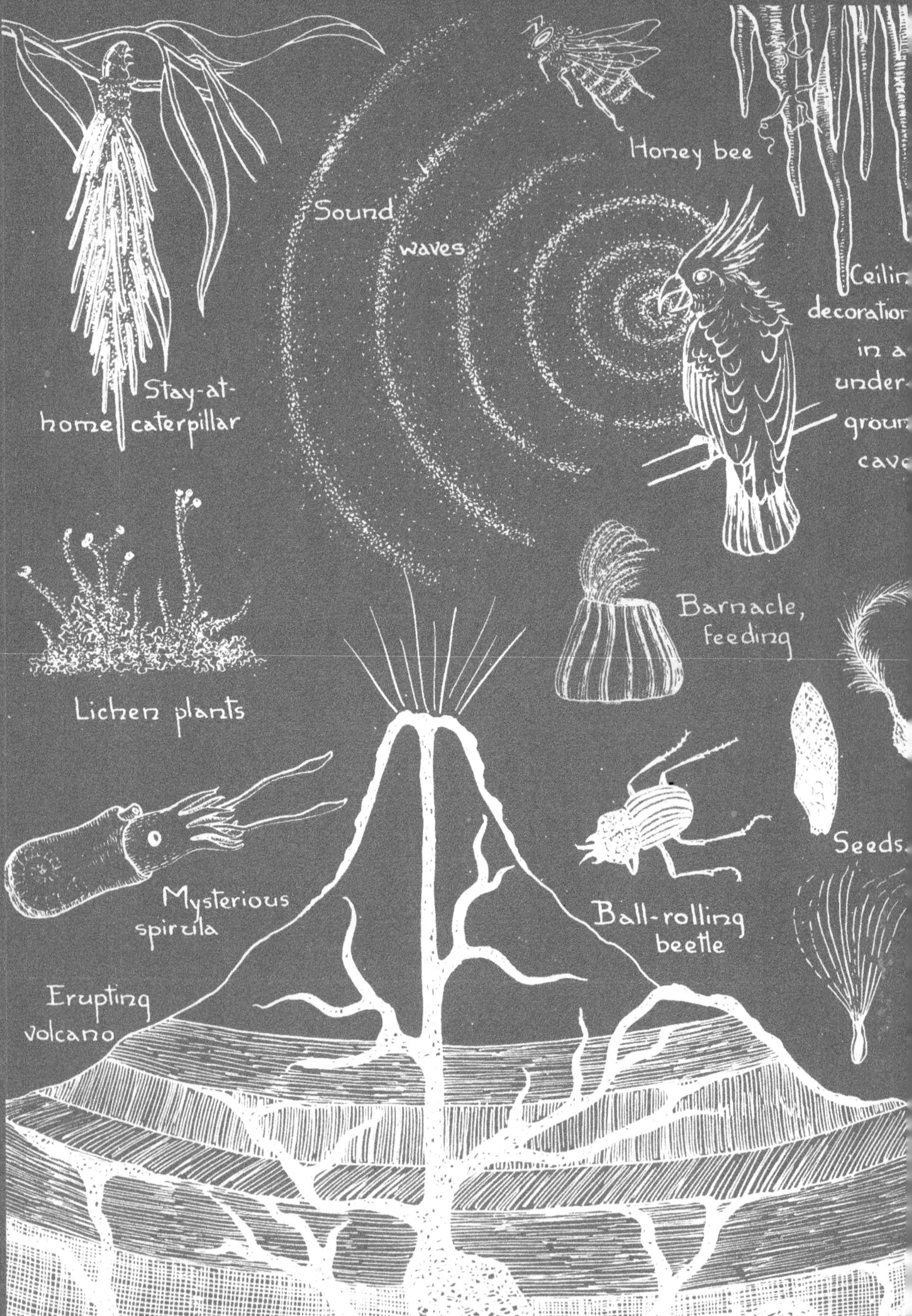

Honey bee

Sound waves

Stay-at-home caterpillar

Ceiling decoration in a underground cave

Lichen plants

Barnacle, feeding

Mysterious spirula

Ball-rolling beetle

Seeds

Erupting volcano

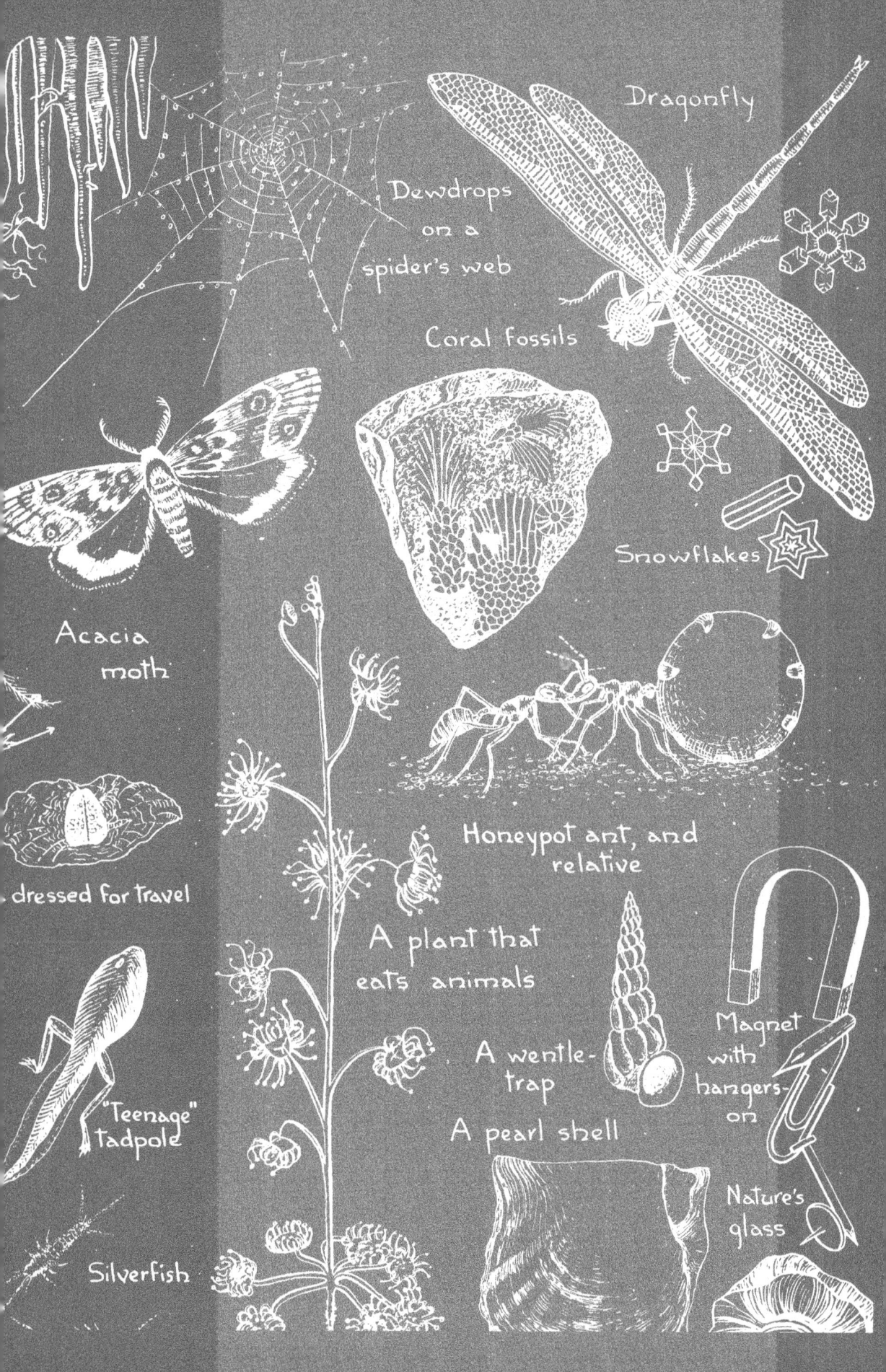

OTHER BOOKS BY THE SAME AUTHOR:

The Little Grammar People *China the Waking Giant*
The Wizard of Jenolan *Australian Wildflower Magic*
Magic Australia *Flowers of the Australian Alps*
The Silver Candlestick *The Gift*
Where the Incas Trod *Donna Roon*
Randy Blair *As Much Right To Live*
Australian Wildflower Fairies *Don't Kill It - It's Me*
Many Paths - One Heaven *Just Give Us Time*

Virginia Woolf, The Novelist (M.A. Thesis, Sydney Univ. 1942)
Magazine Features, published under Tina Banks nom-de-plume;

Magic Circle *Spotlight Getaway*
Babe in the Woods *Russian Mystery*
Such Little Things *His Happiness*
The Visit *The Parcel*
Neighbour-Wise *Foxy and I*
The Uninvited *Fallen Leaf*
Article - Virginia Woolf *The Reason Why*
Review - Tomorrow is Theirs *There Was, Once Upon a Time...*
It Couldn't Fail

Cover Artwork by EDWARD BINDER
Artwork by NURI MASS *with two 2019 additions by* TESS HORWITZ.
Additional 2019 text by TESS HORWITZ *and* CHRIS HORWITZ.

This edition published 2019
By Living Book Press

Copyright © The Estate of Nuri Mass 1964, 2019

1st edition; The Writers' Press 1964, reprinted 1964
2nd edition; The Writers' Press 1965, reprinted 1966, 1968
3rd edition; Ure Smith 1973
4th edition (condensed); Downunder Literature 2007, reprinted 2013
Braille edition; St. Lucy's School for Blind and Visually Handicapped Children (6 volumes)

ISBN: 978-1-925729-47-4 (softcover)
       978-1-925729-48-1 (hardcover)
       978-1-925729-49-8 (ebook)

All rights reserved. No part of this publication may be reproduced, stored in a retrieval system, or transmitted in any other form or means – electronic, mechanical, photocopying, recording or otherwise, without the prior permission of the copyright owner and the publisher or as provided by Australian law.

A catalogue record for this book is available from the National Library of Australia

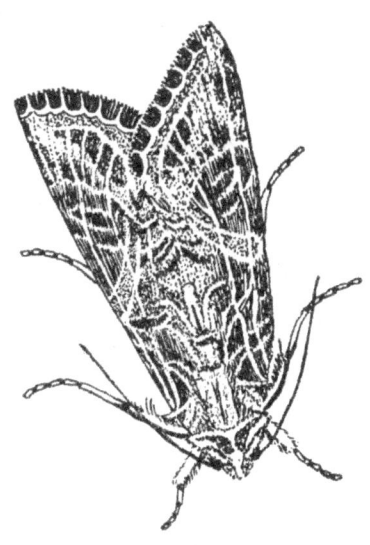

To

dearest Gray,

with all our love —

Tess

Chris

Gouri

A NOTE FROM TESS HORWITZ AND CHRIS HORWITZ
- the two children featured in this book.

Our mother Nuri Mass spent many months researching, writing and drawing for this book. We loved helping her find the specimens that decorated our house in Sydney, all in jars with mesh tops, with favourite foods for the insects inside.

When a moth or butterfly was about to come out of its case, we all gathered around to watch while our mother drew the event so expertly. Investigating nature with our mother was an important part of the happiness of our childhood and we are thrilled that so many others have shared in these experiences, through all the editions of this book over the years.

Today we remain in awe of the amazing powers of nature, and in this edition have expanded several sections to show newly discovered features of the complex world around us. We continue to delight in nature, and hope that this delight will keep expanding and deepening in all of our young—and not so young—readers.

December 2018.

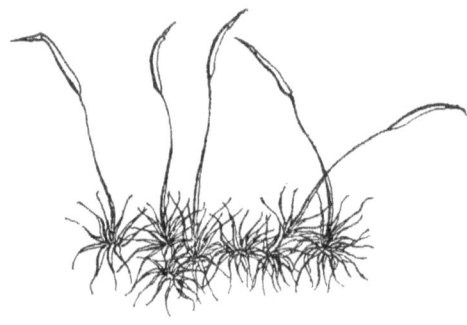

... Long ago, a little girl named Alice fell asleep — and, in her magical dream, she walked through a looking-glass into Wonderland. Today, we know that Wonderland is all around us every moment of our lives, and that we can pass into it, wide awake, whenever we like — through a magnifying glass.

Contents

Insects

What Makes an Insect an Insect?	7
Ladybird, Ladybird, Don't Fly Away!	10
The Mantis—A Very Special Insect	13
The Kindly Cicada	15
Tiny Mischief-Makers	19
Busy Little Silverfish	23
Insect "Cows"	25
The Tiny World of Ants	28
The Acrobatic Grasshopper	37
Tiny Musician—Underground	41
Beetles — Friends and Foes	44
Bugs—Not Beetles	51
Lacewings—and Their Terrible Children	54
The Large Family of Flies	58
How Ichneumons (Mis)Behave	64
Insect Phantoms	66
Jewel of the Pond	70
The Honey-Makers	73
Galls—and Other Oddities	80
It Eats Everything—and is Paper-thin	84
Those "Waspish" Fellows!	86
A Moth Without Wings	91
Caterpillars That Decorate Their Homes	94
The Caterpillar That Became a "Hawk"	97
Caterpillar With a Sting	100
A "Twig" That Loops	102
Caterpillars That Eat Their Home	104
A Moth Emperor	106
A Blue Triangle from a Green Caterpillar	109
The "Twig" with a Butterfly Inside	112
World Travellers on Fragile Wings	115

A Few Other Small Animals

The Changeable Frog	122
Forty-six Legs	126
Slugs and Snails...	127
Spiders, and Their Webs	130
Spider With a Cross	134
Spider in a Leaf	136
Our Friend the Worm	138

Plants

The Story of Plants	142
Plants That Are Never Green	143
Four Plants That Look Like One	150
A Plant Pioneer	153
Those Lovely Carpets of Moss	155
The Magic of Ferns	157
Plants That Have Cones	160
Flowers—and the Clever Things They Do	165
How Seeds Travel	175
Plants That Pretend	180
That "Taker", the Mistletoe	186
Plants That Eat Animals	189

The Seashore

What ARE Shells?	194
Shells Made of One Piece	197
Shells Like Butterflies, and Fans	205
Roly-Poly Molluscs—and Inside-Out Ones	212
One Rock Pool	216

Remarkable Everyday Things—and Rocks

Light—The Fastest Thing There Is	224
Sound Is Never Still	234
Mysterious Magnetism	240
Where and What Is Electricity?	248
Air and Weather	261
The Wonderful Story of Rocks	277
Opal—and Other Treasures in Australia	293
Pictures in Stone	301

Index

306

Before we begin, I should like you to meet . . .

CHRIS and TESS . . .

who have explored the Wonderland of Nature with me, and found new treasures in it day by day.

They have enjoyed every exciting moment of it. They have searched, and observed, and asked all of the questions that most other children would ask.

In short, I couldn't have done without them in the writing of this book.

Insects

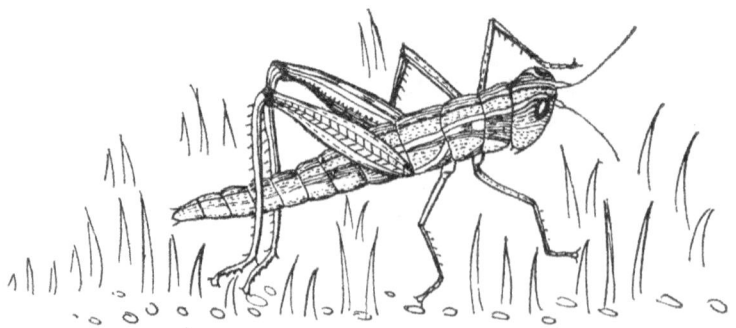

What Makes an Insect an Insect?

IT is possible that there are more insects on this Earth than all the other animals put together, so we really should know something about them, shouldn't we? And the first thing to know is, what makes them insects instead of something else?

First, an insect always has six legs.

Next, an insect's body has three parts to it—head, chest (or thorax) and abdomen. Mostly these three parts show out quite clearly, but sometimes there doesn't seem to be much difference between them at all.

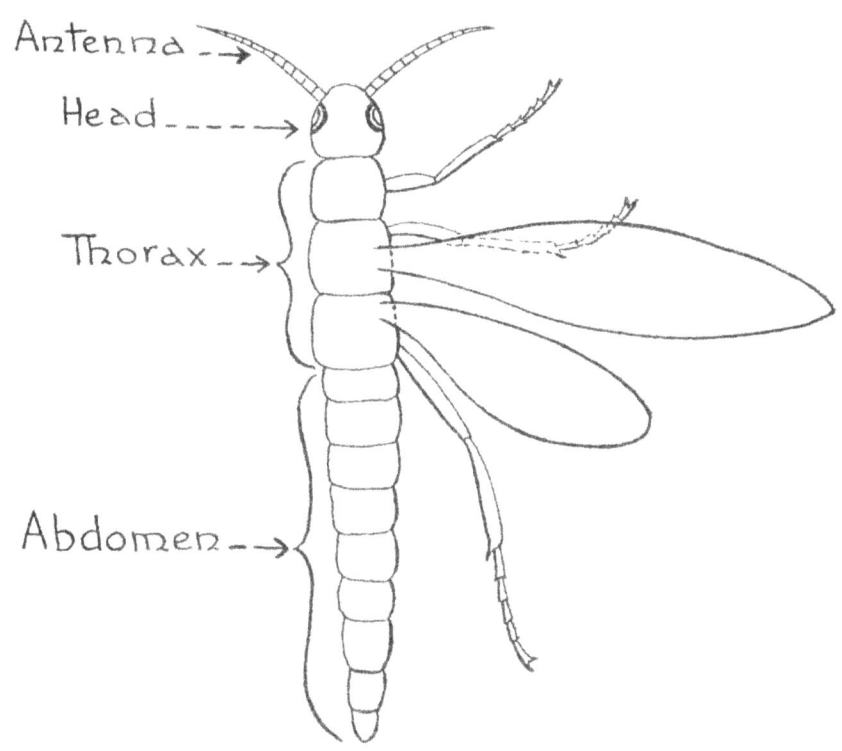

Next, an insect has two feelers (or antennae) on its head—very sensitive, like the antenna of your TV set. Also, most insects have wings at some stage during their life histories. These are always attached to the thorax—the same as the legs. Mostly there are four wings, but the large fly family have only two.

Some groups of insects have wings that are smooth, papery and transparent, with lovely patterns of veins showing clearly. But the

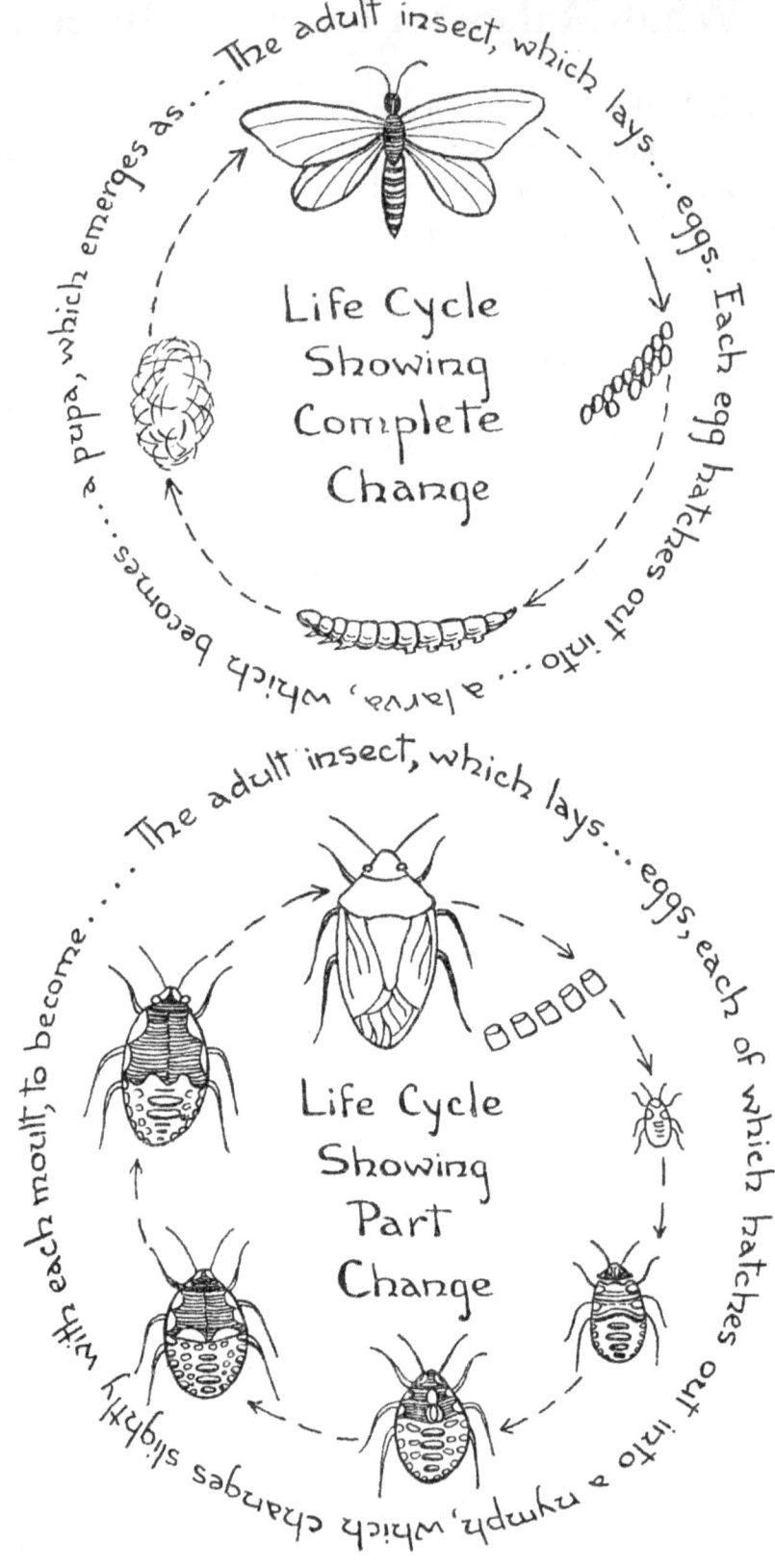

wings of moths and butterflies are covered with tiny scales, and sometimes they have soft silky hairs on them, too.

Then, there is something funny about an insect's skin. Even though it may seem to be soft, it isn't. It is quite hard, and cannot grow as the animal inside it does. So of course, there keeps coming a time when it is too small. Then it splits open, and the insect wedges out of it, in a new, larger skin. This is called moulting, and insects moult their skins quite a number of times before they are fully grown.

Another thing about an insect's growth is that it often brings about great changes—and all of these, taken together, are called its life cycle. Insects like moths, butterflies and beetles change completely during their lives. They start off as eggs. Each of these hatches out into a caterpillar (which is called the larva). When the caterpillar has had enough to eat, it folds itself away out of sight and nobody sees what it is up to for a while. Sometimes it makes a little case for itself, called a cocoon or chrysalis—other times it just curls up under the ground somewhere, without any covering—and at this stage, it is called a pupa.

A pupa does not eat, and many people think that it is resting. Well it is, too, in a way, but *while* it rests, Nature is busy making great changes in it, so that when it wakens again at last, and comes out into the open, it is a moth, butterfly, beetle, fly, wasp, or some such, which lays eggs to begin the life cycle all over again.

But insects do not always change completely in this way. Some—like bugs, mantids and grasshoppers—change only partly. Again, they start off as eggs, but out of each egg that hatches comes a tiny creature that looks *rather* like what it will be when it grows up. As it grows and moults, it often changes the colour or pattern of its skin, until at last it is full grown—and all the time it is doing this, it is called a nymph.

Then of course, there are a few insects, like the silverfish, that do not change at all. They come out of their eggs as tiny versions of what they will be like when they are grown up. Look at a baby silverfish under a magnifying glass, and you will see a grown-up silverfish.

Now, if you read on, you will learn about some of the insects that you meet most often in bush and gardens.

Ladybird, Ladybird, Don't Fly Away!

WHEN Chris and Tess first saw a certain kind of little grub running around on a plant covered with aphids, and stopping to eat a few now and then, they didn't think for a moment that it had anything to do with ladybirds or beetles.

But then, on the back of a leaf, they found another of these grubs, looking the same as the first one, but behaving differently. Its little brown-and-orange body was bent over into a hoop, and it was so still that it reminded us of caterpillars when they turn into pupae. And that's exactly what was happening—it was becoming a pupa.

We decided to watch this one, and see what would happen.

Soon it had become a perfect little dome, with dark spots arranged in a pretty pattern—and so it remained for a few days quite still, on the back of its leaf.

Then, one morning, its outer skin broke open, and out walked a very shiny, pale-yellow ladybird beetle, with no markings at all. But gradually its colour changed to bright orange, and the tiny black patches appeared that we all know so well.

Chris touched it gently, and it rose up in a little flight, showing the pretty gauzy wings that lay protected underneath its black-and-orange ones. It didn't go far, though, because—the same as the little grub that it used to be—it was very interested in a branch covered with aphids. So it soon came back and got really busy amongst them, for an aphid is a ladybird's favourite dish.

People often destroy ladybirds, thinking that they are eating their plants—but in reality, they are one of the best friends a garden could have. Only one of their many different kinds is a plant eater—the one with twenty-eight spots on its back. The others eat only those bad little creatures known as "blight", which ruin plants by swarming all over them and sucking out their juices.

So, instead of reciting that old rhyme, "Ladybird, ladybird, fly away home, Your house is on fire and your children are gone," we should sing,

> Ladybird, ladybird, don't fly away!
> Our plants need a friend, and would like you to stay.
> And we like you, too, with your colours so bright.
> Welcome, dear ladybird—gay little mite!

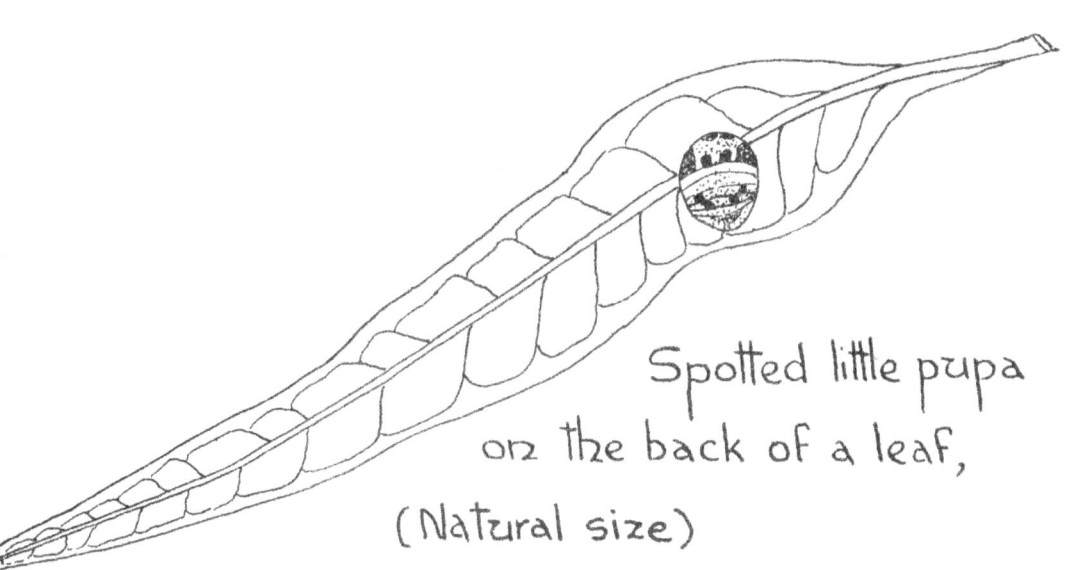

Greedy little aphid-eater, dark brown and orange

Spotted little pupa on the back of a leaf, (Natural size)

A few hours after it emerged from its pupal "sleep" — flame-coloured, with black marks

A little "visitor" — yellow and black

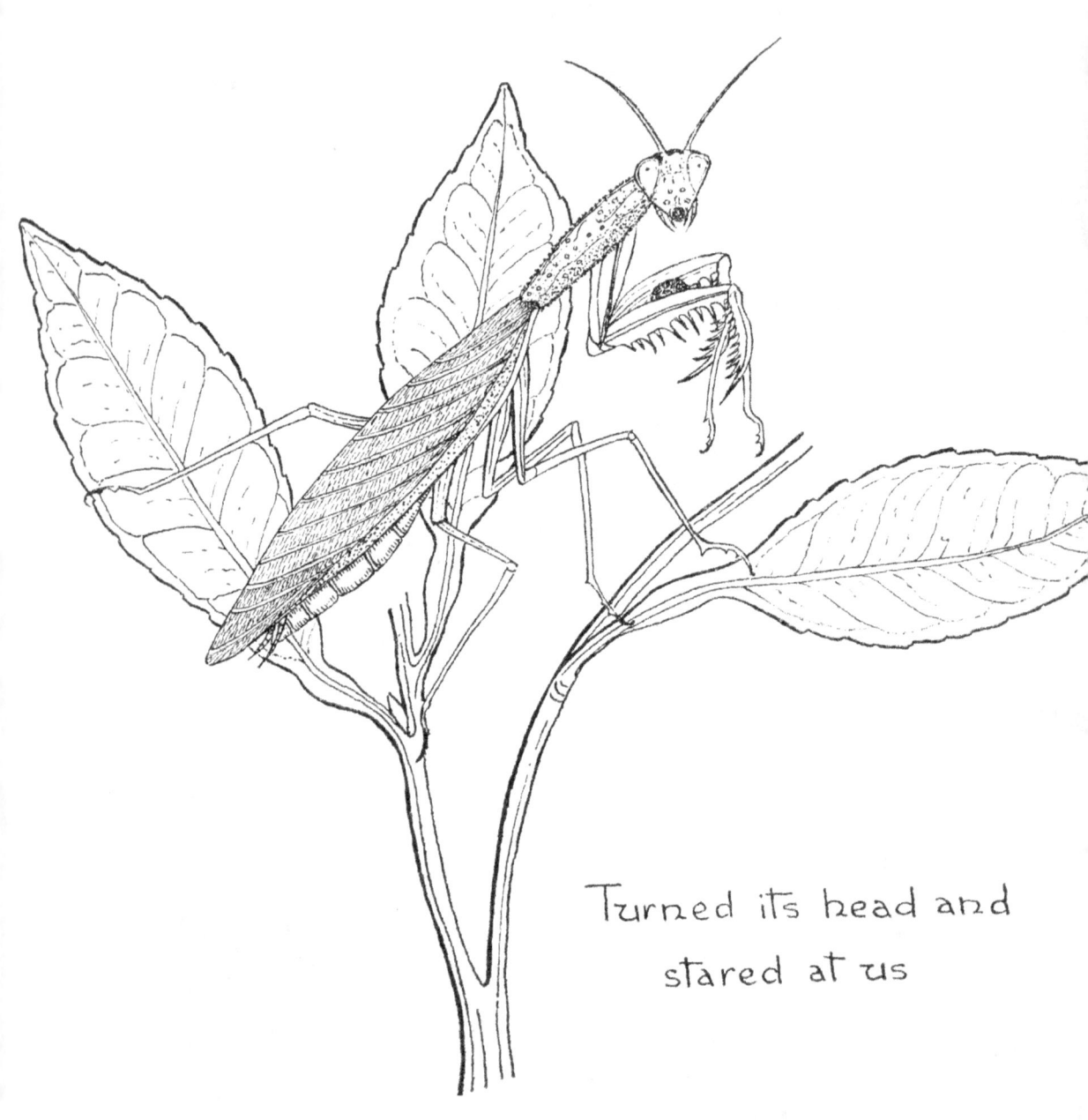

Turned its head and stared at us

The Mantis—A Very Special Insect

IF ever you should find a praying mantis in your garden, stop and have a good look at it, because it's one of the most entertaining insects in the world.

We found one in our orange-tree the other day, and it was rather a wonder that we did find it, because it was exactly the same colour as the leaves, and standing perfectly still, and if you looked away for a minute it was difficult to find again.

Then, as we watched, it did all kinds of funny things. First, it changed leaves, swaying and balancing on its four back legs while stretching forward and "pawing" at the air with its two front ones, very prettily, like a dog begging. Then it drew one of its back legs forward and ran its tiny mouth up and down, cleaning it. Next, it rubbed one of its front legs over its face and right round the back of its head, just like a cat washing *its* face.

When this was over, suddenly it swivelled its head around and stared at us.

Tess said, "Oh, look, Mummie, what a darling!"

Chris said, "That's funny! I don't remember any other insect doing that."

And he was right. That's one of the queerest things about the whole family of mantids. They can twist their heads around the way we do—and no other insect can.

Tess was also right, about its looking a darling, with its funny little head shaped like a triangle, and its big bulging eyes, and endless antics. But if she had been a fly, she wouldn't have been so pleased, because the mantis would probably have eaten her.

You see those fierce-looking front legs with all their spines? Those are to catch flies and other small insects with, and to hold them tightly while the mantis eats them. But lady mantids don't stop at other kinds of insects. They quite often eat their own husbands, as well.

The one on our orange-tree was rather small—about 50mm long—but there are other kinds much bigger, and sometimes they are brown instead of green.

You'll be delighted if you ever find one of the little cases in which mother mantis lays her eggs. It's very delicate-looking-brown or pale green—and *so* pretty. But even prettier are the baby mantids themselves when they are first "born".

Each of them has to struggle out of a tight skin sheath before it can take its first look at the world—and then, you can't help loving this tiny creature which looks and behaves so exactly the same as the big grown-ups.

Do you know why it is called a praying mantis? Just watch it and see how often it folds its front legs up against itself in an attitude of prayer! Of course, considering the way it hunts and eats insects, it should be called *preying* mantis, shouldn't it? But we shouldn't think of it too unkindly for this, since it relieves us of so many flies and other insect pests.

Actually, a praying mantis is as useful to us as it is entertaining.

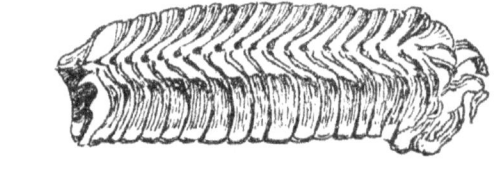

A little brown egg-case, papery thin

The Kindly Cicada

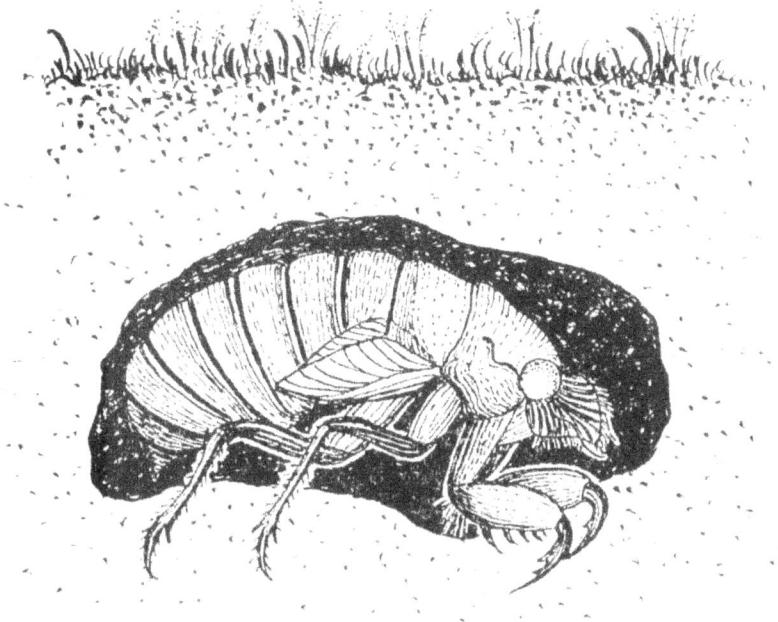

THIS looks like the kind of thing you wouldn't like to meet in the dark. Perhaps you wouldn't like to meet it at all. Yet it is quite harmless in spite of its looks—and when grown-up, it is actually very handsome. Strange as it may seem—this youngster (or nymph) will one day be a long-winged, loudly-singing, summer-loving cicada.

You do not often see a cicada at this stage, for while it is like this, it lives under the ground, as though it didn't want to be seen looking so ugly. Sometimes it goes to extremes, and lives very far under the ground indeed—about 6m—and it stays there for several years, in the dark, with nothing to eat except a bit of sugary sap out of the roots of plants.

Then, one night, after it has had enough of this kind of life, it makes its way up to the surface of the soil, climbs on to something and clings there waiting for its skin to split open. When it does split open, wedging and pushing movements can be seen, and at last a beautiful creature comes out of it, with long transparent wings.

It doesn't look very beautiful at first—just pale, soft, and rather shapeless. But by morning it is already straightening out, and a few hours later—with darkened colour and strengthened wings—it is a full-grown cicada bug. And you know what fine creatures they are.

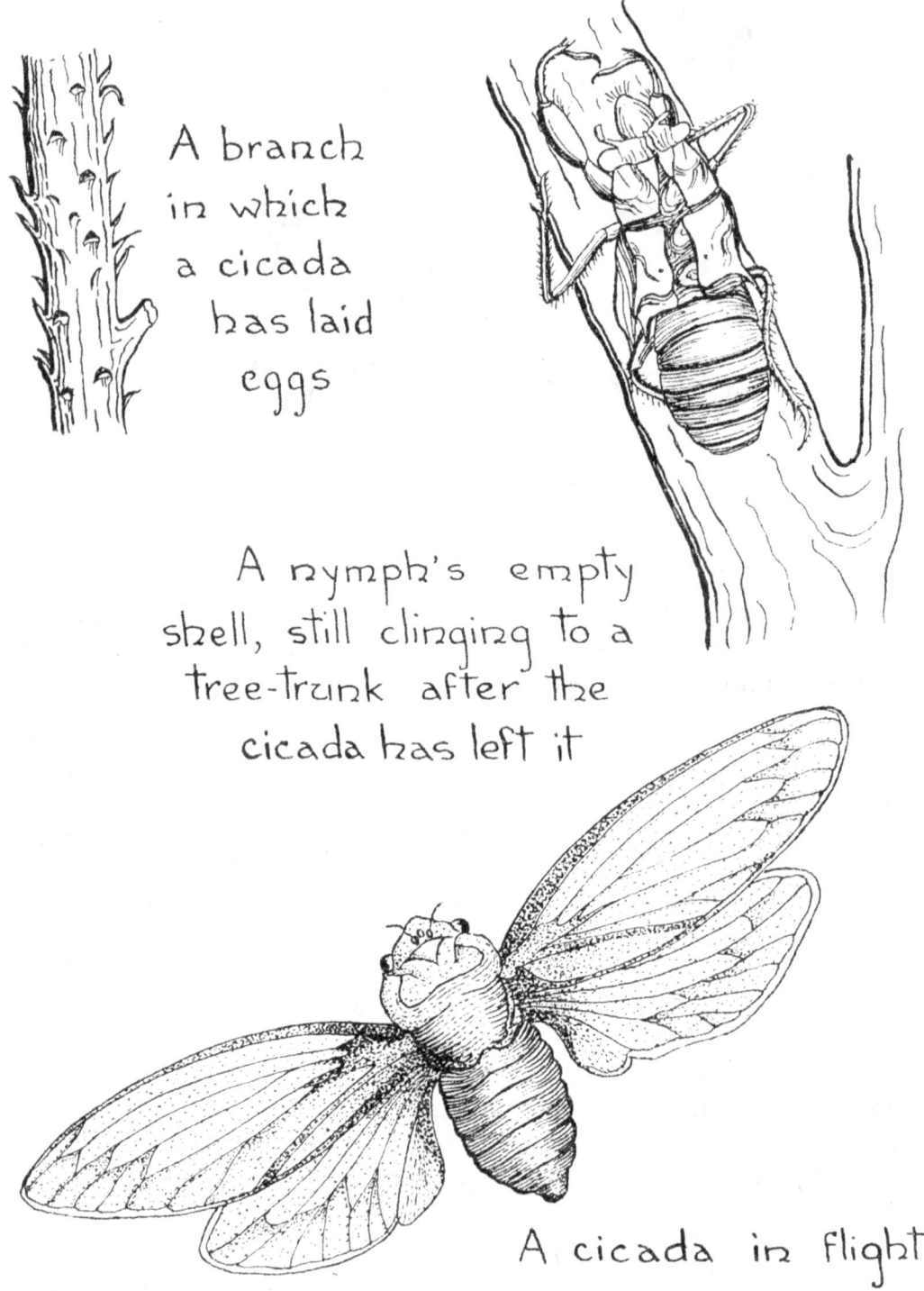

A branch in which a cicada has laid eggs

A nymph's empty shell, still clinging to a tree-trunk after the cicada has left it

A cicada in flight

You also know how noisy they can be, on summer days and evenings. And, considering how long they have been living here, it is possible that their singing was the first sound made by any animal on Earth. Why, there are fossils of our Australian cicadas which prove that they were here 200 million years ago—looking just the same as they do today.

There are many strange things about a cicada's singing. First, the lady is quite silent—it is only the male who sings. The next strange thing is that the whole idea of the song is to attract the lady's attention—yet cicadas have no ears, so you may think that they are quite deaf. The third is that the sound is made with a sort of little drum on the cicada's abdomen. But instead of being tapped, this drum is crinkled in and out by movements of the cicada's muscles—and as it crinkles, it makes a surprisingly loud noise.

Although the lady cicada doesn't hear this "song" with ears like ours, she feels it. She feels the vibrations it makes, and she likes them so much that she agrees to marry the clever "singer". Then, after a while, when she has eggs to lay, she chooses a suitable branch on a gumtree, and cuts a lot of little slits in its bark, until it looks quite fuzzy. Into each of these slits she places a few eggs, and when the baby cicadas hatch out, you would never guess what they were going to be, for they are black and very small, like fleas.

Also, you would be really lucky to see them at all, for as soon as they come out of their eggs, they can think of only one thing—getting underground as fast as possible. They do not even waste time climbing down the tree. They just let themselves drop to the ground—and the next moment they have disappeared, to begin their long life as nymphs in the little dark and silent room they dig for themselves below the earth's surface.

Slowly, as the years go by, they grow bigger, and moult their skins, and grow bigger again, until at last they come up for a few weeks of summer sunshine in the glory of their final, winged form.

But now, as well as sunshine, they find danger, for birds and other animals go after them hungrily, and children are always catching them—quite often hurting them, also, I am sorry to say. Yet of all insects, cicadas least deserve to be hurt, for they themselves do no harm to anything, and cannot even defend themselves against their enemies. They do not bite or sting, they do not burrow in the branches of plants or eat their leaves—and the small amount of plant juice that they suck, does no damage at all.

Since cicadas have no defences against being eaten, they come out of the ground in huge numbers all at once so that it is hard for other animals to eat all of them, so some will survive to lay eggs for the next generation.

If you have ever hurt a cicada in the past, you never would again, would you? Knowing how good-natured it is, and how long it has lived underground in the darkness, I am sure that you would never wish to rob it of one precious moment in the light and warmth and joy of the sun. You might gently lift it off a branch to admire it, of course, but then, quickly, you would let it go again, marvelling at this strange, bright insect who lives peacefully amongst its enemies, and whose song has resounded on our Earth through almost endless time.

> Ah, welcome, dear cicada,
> To the summer and the sun!
> When you shrill your deafening music,
> You are always lots of fun—
> and you never do the slightest
> Bit of harm to anyone.

Tiny Mischief-Makers

NEARLY everyone in Australia knows about white ants, because—although they are blind and very small, they are one of our greatest pests. They live in huge communities, and when they go out looking for food, people are in trouble. White ants eat all sorts of important things like furniture, houses, paper, and telegraph poles—which goes to show how much damage even the tiniest of creatures can do, if there are enough of them.

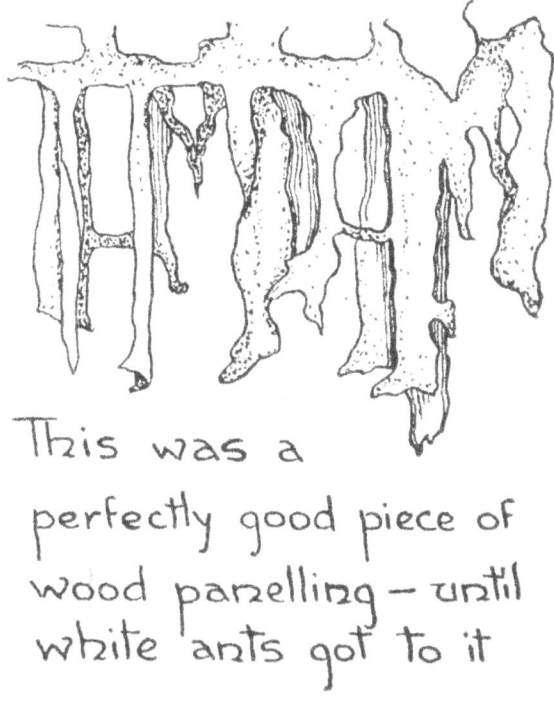

This was a perfectly good piece of wood panelling — until white ants got to it

They work silently in dark places, so that, unless you are on the watch for them, they can go right ahead without your even knowing that they are there.

Strange to say, white ants are not really ants at all. They are quite different in almost everything except the way they live in groups.

Insects that live alone do everything for themselves, but those that live in groups spend their whole lives doing one special job. The biggest section of the white ant population is the workers, another important section is the soldiers, and at the centre of the whole group is the queen. Her job is to lay eggs—and she lays thousands of them a day—while her ladies-in-waiting fuss around doing everything for her.

Another name for white ants is termites. That's why their large community nest is called a termitarium. In the north of Australia, these homes may be great towering brown masses of clay after they have taken over a tree, six metres high. Some of them are like half of a disk poking out of the ground, about 1 or 2m high, with flattened sides and with their sharp ends pointing north and south. That's rather wonderful, isn't it? Then, there are white ants whose homes are down under the ground, so that you don't see them at all. Sometimes a termitarium is a knobbly mound way up in the fork of a tree. Other times it is one of those brown or reddish "anthills" that you often see in the bush.

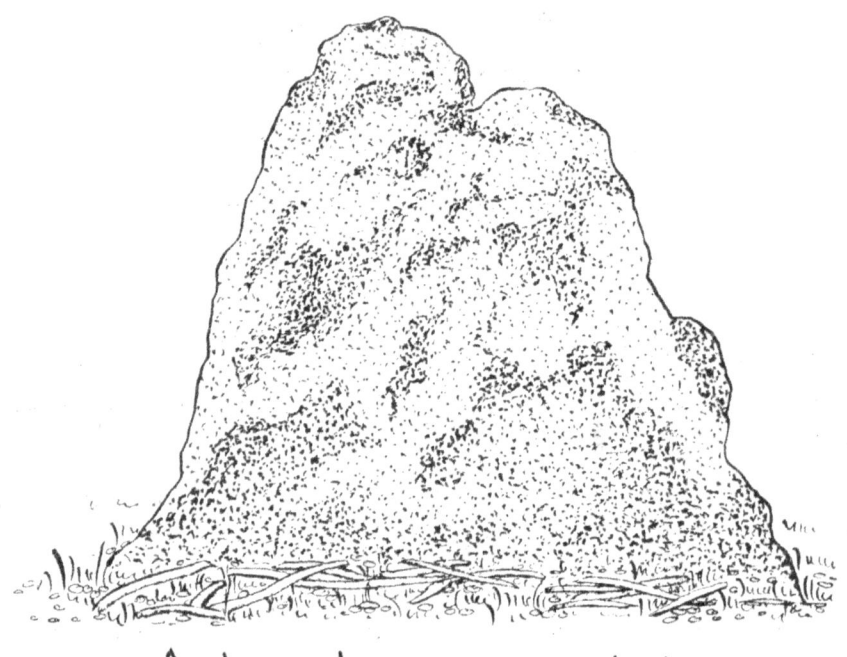

A termitarium of red clay

But wherever it is or whatever it looks like, an enormous amount of work has been put into it. Inside, it is a whole maze of passageways leading to the nursery, store-houses, cemeteries, the queen's chamber, and so on. This is all made of tiny pieces of wood which the workers have chewed thoroughly before building with them. Then, the thick clay covering, outside, is put together grain by grain from the earth round about. Just think of that!

As you can imagine, the workers are very important members of the white ant community. But the termitarium also has to be defended against enemies, and this is the job of the soldiers, with their hard-plated heads and strong pincers.

Man, of course, is their chief enemy, and the fierce little soldiers can't do anything against *him*. But they do wage battles against true ants quite often, which, strange to say, are another of their deadliest enemies.

Sometimes, though, the ants invade a nest so secretly that, by the time the white ants wake up to what is happening, the invaders have outnumbered them and are killing them off right and left—between one and two million of them.

Another occasion on which they are killed off in great numbers starts off as the most exciting day of their lives. This is how it happens:

There is a section of the white ant colony, quite different from where the workers and soldiers live. This is made up of males and females which actually have eyes, whilst the others are all blind. Also, to begin with, they have pretty little wings, and on a certain hot day in the year, the attention of the whole colony is upon them, for this is *their* day.

The workers get busy cutting holes right through the thick clay walls of the nest, while the soldiers stand around keeping close guard. Then at last the great moment arrives, and streams of the little winged creatures come pouring out through the openings prepared for them.

It's all very exciting, but for most of the adventurers it doesn't have a happy ending, for there are swarms of enemies lying in wait for them, and only a very few escape being eaten. These divide up into pairs, then do what seems like a strange thing. They shake their fragile wings right off—as a sign that the flighty part of their life is over, and that they are ready to settle down to the serious business of starting a new colony.

At first, of course, there is no nest or termitarium, but soon the new mother (or queen) starts laying eggs. These hatch out into baby white ants, which are soon old enough to take up their duties as workers and soldiers. First, the workers build a dome-shaped room around their queen. Then they get busy with the other parts of the nest. It's a huge job, as we have seen—but the queen keeps laying more eggs, which hatch out into helpers by the thousand, and the work goes steadily on until the nest is full-size and its population about two million.

Now, here is a very strange thing. People had lived on earth for many centuries before they began to grow crops and live a settled home life, yet there are some kinds of white ants which actually cultivate crops of "mushrooms" in special little garden plots near the nursery. These are not real mushrooms, but the soft masses of thread which would grow into toadstools. By constantly pruning these, the workers keep them down to just the right size for the nest's tiny inhabitants.

So you see, even though white ants are such a nuisance to us, many of the things they do are really interesting and wonderful.

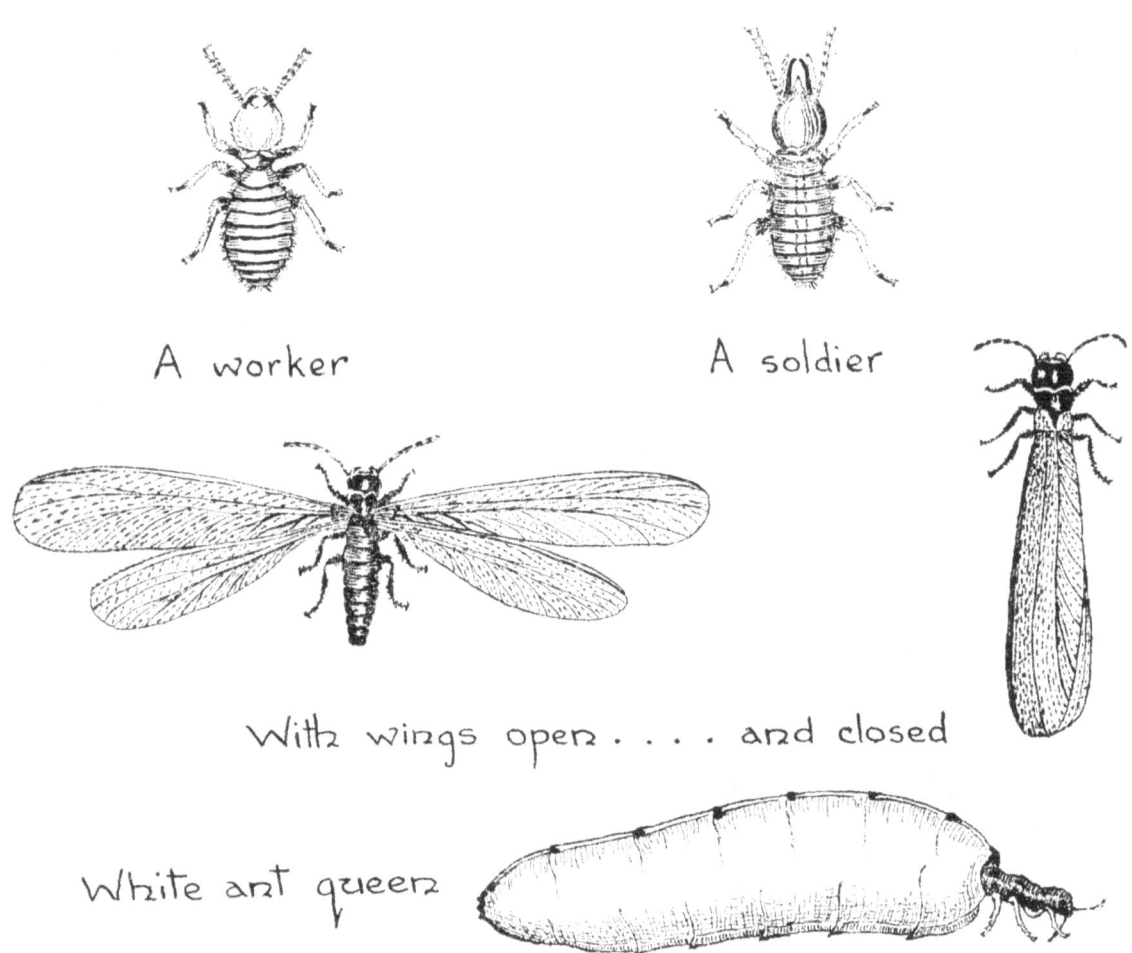

A worker

A soldier

With wings open .... and closed

White ant queen

Busy Little Silverfish

IT'S funny how many things are given the wrong names. The rock lily, for instance, is an orchid that prefers to live on trees, the sea anemone is not a flower but an animal, the white ant is not an ant, and the silverfish is certainly not a fish. But perhaps, if you half-close your eyes, it may look like one—a very tiny one.

Have you got silverfish in your home? If so, you will know all about it, because your wallpaper will start to look chewed, and your pictures and book-covers, and even some of your clothing, especially if it has been starched—for silverfish are particularly fond of starch. When they nibble at wallpaper and so on, they're not so much interested in the paper, as in the paste sticking it to the wall, because this is made of starch. So, if you paste pictures in scrap-books, be sure that the silverfish don't know about it, otherwise they'll most likely make a meal of your pretty cut-outs.

They also eat the dead bodies of other insects, as well as their own skins when they cast them off for bigger ones. Worst of all, they sometimes even eat one another. So what is another name for them? Cannibals.

Perhaps you have already noticed that silverfish have no wings—and it's very few insects that haven't, at some stage in their life-histories. But then, as far as we know, silverfish are the most primitive of the insects. Probably they existed on Earth before any of the others did. And perhaps that has something to do with their winglessness.

They are different from other insects in another way, too. When they come out of their eggs, they are already tiny silverfish as we know them. They are not grubs or caterpillars, and they don't change their colours and markings the way bugs do. The only way they change, as time goes on, is that they grow bigger. And they take several years to become fully grown, while most of the other insects take only weeks or months.

Then, they never go to sleep as pupae, the way many other insects do. They're on the move for the whole of their lives, resting in the day and running around eating at night.

Have you ever wondered about their shining silver coats? These are made up of the tiniest scales, ever so delicate, and beautifully formed. Here, then, is another of those countless tiny things in which we see Nature's genius for lovely design, and for making every detail perfect. Yet the silverfish is one of our humblest and most despised insects.

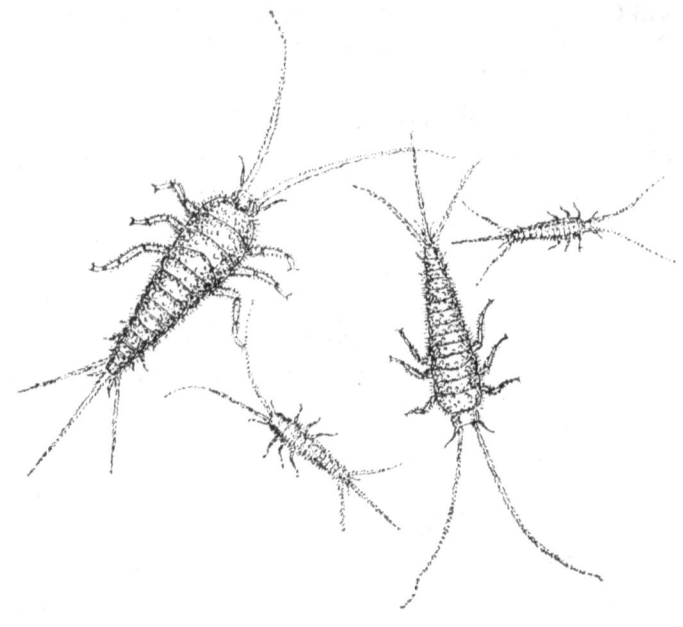

Hungry little silverfish,
Please don't come to tea
'Cause your table manners
Are the worst I ever see.

Others eat politely
What is served upon a plate,
But you are so impatient
That you never sit and wait.

You nibble clothes and papers,
Books, and pictures on the wall
So that is why we'd like you
Not to visit us at all.

Tell me, little fellow,
Would you think it very cute
If I should start to nibble
At your pretty silver suit?

Insect "Cows"

NO matter how troublesome certain things might be in your garden—like aphids, for instance—you only have to look at them closely to realise how beautiful they are.

We have a native cotton plant in our garden—the one with the orange-coloured flowers—and there's a little yellow aphid that seems to like this more than anything. It swarms over its leaves and stems in thousands, and when this happens to a plant, people say that it is covered with blight.

Since aphids suck the juices out of a plant and would end up by killing it if they were allowed to, gardeners do everything possible to get rid of them. But the other day we put a few of our yellow aphids under a microscope, and found that they are as pretty as can be.

They are like little golden globules. They have six long, delicate legs, the tiniest black eyes, and a black honey-tube on either side of their backs. Some of them have wings, too—big beautiful ones so fragile that you can see right through them. But these winged aphids are particularly villainous, for they fly to other plants, and start up new colonies far and wide.

There's a very strange thing about aphids. For the greater part of the year all of them are female. They are called stem mothers, and during their short lives they produce many baby aphids which quickly grow to full size and themselves become stem mothers. Only coming up towards winter do a few male aphids appear. After this, the females lay eggs in some protected spot—perhaps in the cracks of bark—and these are able to live right through the colder months.

When warm weather comes again, they hatch out into young aphids, which soon become stem mothers—and you know the rest of the story.

Have you ever heard aphids called "ant cows"? That is because ants "milk" them—though, of course, they don't get actual milk from them, but honey-dew.

Ants are so fond of this delicacy that they often "raise" aphids and tend them, much the same as we raise herds of cattle. They even carry

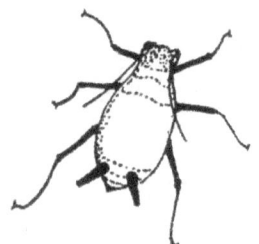

Wingless aphid

Wild-cotton leaf infested with aphids (Natural size)

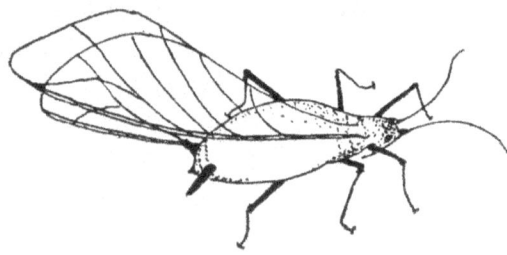

Aphid with wings

Little black relative off the lemon-tree

An ant "milking" an aphid

aphid eggs down into their own nurseries, and look after them together with their own eggs. When at last the baby aphids hatch out, the ants carefully carry them out and place them on the right kind of food plant. Sometimes they build a little mud shelter over them, as well—and all so that they themselves can go on enjoying their honey-dew.

If you have any aphids in your garden, there will most likely be a lot of ants amongst them. I'd suggest that you take a magnifying glass and watch them for a while. Every now and then you will see the ants stroking the aphids with their feelers. This is called "milking", because it encourages the aphids to give up their honey-dew.

So you see, here's this giving-and-taking arrangement again. In lichen plants, one part gives water and the other part gives food. Many orchids also give food to the tiny fungi from which they receive water. And aphids give delicious honey-dew to the ants from which they accept protection and caresses.

The other day, Tess found a group of black aphids on the back of a leaf on our orange-tree—just in time for one of them to have itself drawn. As you can see, it's the same as the yellow ones, except for its colour—and its legs have pretty little bands of pale yellow and black.

The Tiny World of Ants

IF you were an ant, you would be one of the busiest creatures in the world. You would work practically all day and all night, scarcely ever stopping to sleep. Then, when you did snatch a little sleep, you would have it standing up, or perhaps you would just roll over wherever you happened to be. And what you would be working at so hard would be—gathering food, looking after ant eggs and babies, caring for the queen or queens in every possible way, building additions to the nest, tending aphid "cows", keeping the ant city clean, and so on.

Also, if you were an ant, you would most likely be a girl, for there are only ever a few hundred boys in an ant community, whereas there are many thousands of girls.

The boys are all princes, but the girls are divided into different groups—princesses, nurses, workers, and even soldiers. And very fierce soldiers they can be, too. Just look at this bulldog ant, for instance, with her long curved pincers toothed like saws, and imagine how you would like to be another ant having an argument with her!

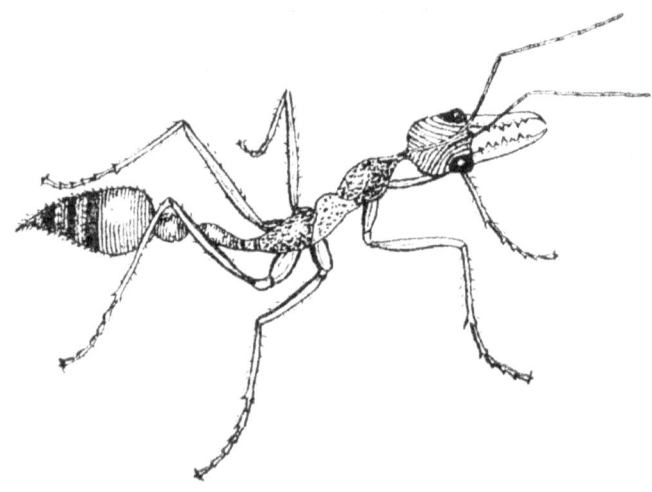

The race of ants is very ancient indeed. They were on earth, running their great cities, many millions of years before people appeared. And they do not seem to have changed through all those thousands of centuries, whereas most of the other living things on Earth have changed quite a lot. Take another special look at our bulldog ant up there, for of all the different kinds of ants, she is perhaps the most ancient.

Well, as you know, ants live together in huge communities, like bees and termites. Also, like bees and termites, they have an egg-laying queen, and they take great care of their young, and in some ways ant and termite cities are rather alike. But you could never mistake a city of ants for one of bees.

Ants are intelligent builders, for they are able to use all kinds of materials in the making of their cities—earth, wood, leaves, packed mud, gravel. Perhaps their favourite kind of city is one that has its entrance beside a rock, and then delves underground with many branching passageways, with rooms at different levels, and with the rock as the city's main roof.

A prince and... princess

Everybody in an ant city is busy except the princes and princesses. These royal brothers and sisters have everything done for them as long as they live. They are fed, combed, cleaned and generally fussed over. It is easy to pick them out from the workers and soldiers, because they are the only ones with wings in the whole ant city, and the only ones who are utterly carefree. Right up to that exciting day when they fly off to get married, these princes and princesses have nothing to do except play around and enjoy themselves.

Then, when the time comes, a remarkable thing happens. The princes and princesses in all the nests over quite a distance prepare for their marriage flight on exactly the same day—and we of the human race are *still* wondering how they all know one another's intentions.

Anyway, off they go on their great adventure, flying up into the air for the first and only time in their lives. And if any of them are afraid to leave the nest, the workers push and hustle them out.

Once in the air, the princes from each nest forget all about their sister princesses with whom they have grown up and played until this very day, and can think only of the princesses from other nests. To these, they feel very much attracted, and way up in the air many of them marry. But after this, the poor little princes do not live more than a few days, for they cannot even feed themselves.

For the princesses, things are very different. Each one is now a young queen who—if all goes well—will begin a new ant colony. When she lands on the ground again, she immediately pulls off her wings, for she will never need them again. Then she finds a sheltered spot, digs a little hole, creeps into it, seals it up with earth, and waits until her first eggs arrive.

Many young queens die during this time, for they have no food except that which they absorb from their own fat wing muscles.

At last, sometimes after months, the first eggs appear. These are very tiny, as the young queen has had so little food for them. But she watches over them like a good mother, and when they hatch out into tiny larvae, she feeds them with her own saliva. Very soon now they become true ants, and immediately go out to find some food for their mother. Then they get busy "around the house". They start digging passages and rooms. They tend their mother the queen in every possible way—and from now on, she will never again be lonely. She will live for many years, surrounded by her enormous family, for she will lay many thousands of eggs.

During her lifetime she will see her nest grow from the tiny hole she first dug, into a large rambling city. And as time goes on, more and more queens will become established in it until there are perhaps hundreds of them.

In an ant nest, nothing is by chance. Everything is carefully planned, and has a good reason for being there. There are royal quarters, nurseries, store-houses, "cattle" pens where aphids are kept and tended for their precious honey-dew, which the ants enjoy so much. Sometimes there are even mushroom gardens very much like those that termites grow.

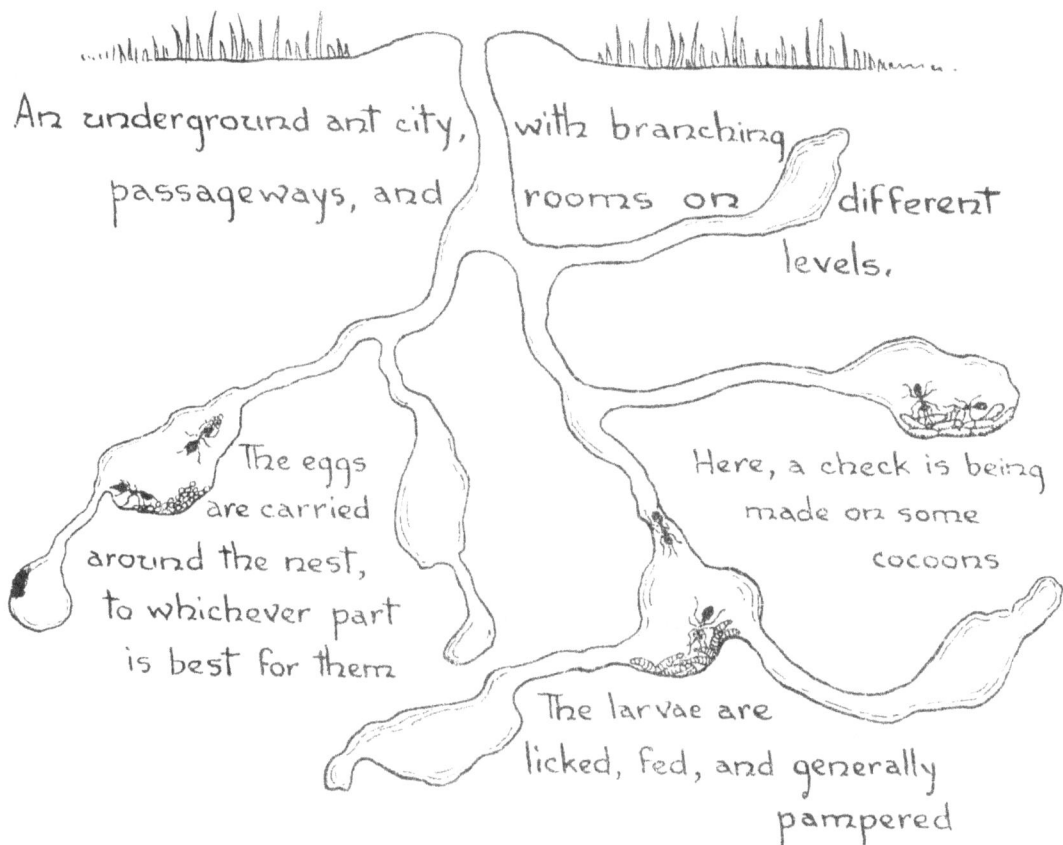

The rooms, built at different levels, have different degrees of warmth and dampness, and this is very important in the rearing of ant babies. For instance, the larvae are kept in a damp nursery so that the moisture won't dry out of their skins. And the workers are always carrying the eggs around to the best places—up towards the top of the nest to get warm... down again to stop them from growing too warm. The looking-after of eggs and larvae would be a full-time job in itself, yet the tireless ants do so much more besides.

The moment the eggs are laid, workers carry them away to a nursery, and lick them all over until they stick to one another. Then they can be carried around in groups instead of one at a time. After about three weeks, tiny white larvae hatch out of the eggs, and these—in their separate nursery—receive special attention, for there is an oiliness on their skins which the nurses love to lick. They are also generously fed until they are big enough to become pupae. Then, they spin little silken cocoons for themselves, and stay tucked away in these for another three weeks or so.

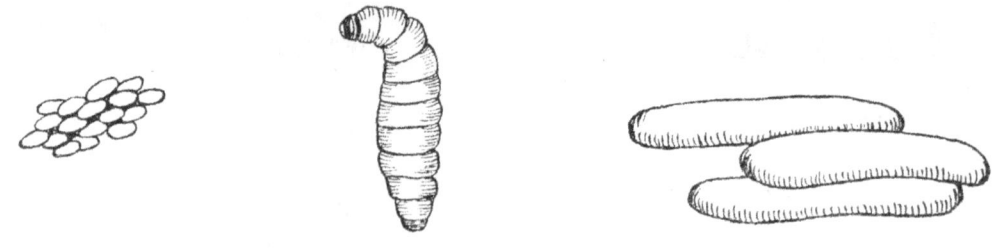

Eggs... a larva, and... cocoons

Of course, inside their cocoons they gradually change into ants as we know them—and the wonderful thing is that, when their change is complete, the nurses know about it, and arrange for them to be "born". They cut a hole in each cocoon, and carefully ease it off. But the new ant is not yet free, for she still has a tight skin around her. The nurses lick this off, then wash her, straighten out her legs, and welcome her into the nest with every possible attention.

She now has the ant shape that we all know well, but is still very pale in colour, and doesn't go outside to start her "work" life for a week or two, until her colour has darkened. Of course, if it is a royal ant, it doesn't go out to work at all, but settles down for a life of luxury.

At first, when she goes out food-hunting, the young worker ant may get lost, but she soon learns how to find her way home by the position of the sun, as well as by following the smell of other ants from the same nest. Also, at first, she may mistake a tiny pebble for a seed, and carry it all the way home just to have the gatekeeper take it and throw it away. But very soon she corrects this sort of mistake too, and makes a perfect job of everything she has to do.

She knows that she mustn't wander into the hunting-grounds of other nests, because these are defended by very stern guardians, who would kill her right away without asking any questions if they found her there. She in turn guards against strangers as she goes hurrying around, but she enjoys meeting others from her own nest. When this happens, the "sisters" recognise each other by their "nest" smell, and they stop to say a word or two in passing. They do this by tapping on each other's heads with their feelers—and it is remarkable how accurately they can give messages with this "feeler" talk.

Each little worker also learns how to help keep the nest clean by carrying rubbish out of it and throwing it on the garbage tip. She learns the happy task of looking after ant babies and the royal members of the nest, the sad task of burying her dead sisters in the cemetery, and the unpleasant task of fighting her enemies with bites, stings, and sprays of poison.

In her spare time, she may amuse herself with the herds of aphids that ants keep as men keep herds of cattle. She may help to carry them from a worked-out feeding ground to a new one. She may help to build little mud shelters over them to protect them from enemies, she will look after aphid eggs as lovingly as if they were her own, and she will certainly sip the delicious honey-dew which is aphid "milk".

There is no end to the cleverness of ants. We have only to look at their homes to realise this. Not all of them are built underground or in mounds of earth. The fierce little green tree ants of northern Australia build their nests in trees. Great numbers of leaves have to be drawn up and bound together in some way, to make a home large enough for a whole tribe. But ants do not make thread, as spiders do, so they put their own babies to work on the job. Larvae about to spin their cocoons are carried out of their nursery and moved backwards and forwards over the leaves so that their small amount of cocoon silk helps to make a shelter for the whole nest instead of one for themselves alone.

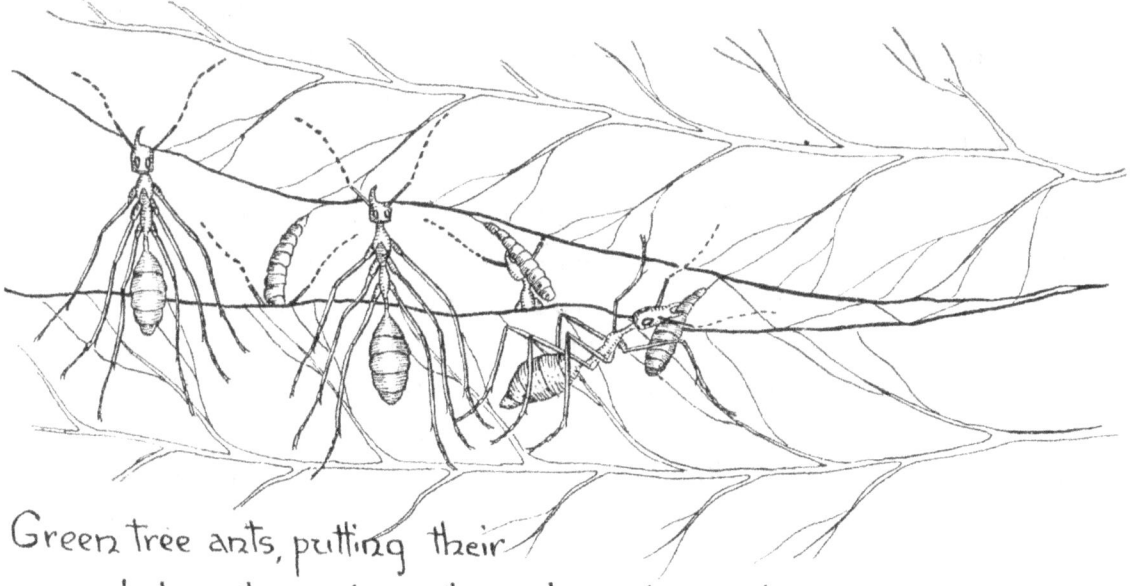

Green tree ants, putting their babies to work in their clever home-building scheme

Then, as they have to become pupae without cocoons, the nurses take very special care of them.

Another wonderful kind of ant home is to be found in tropical jungles, high up in trees. It is a great mud ball, pressed together grain by grain with endless patience and industry. But as this kind of home would be quickly washed away by heavy rains, its clever little builders gather seeds and plant them in it. These soon grow into sturdy plants, whose roots bind the mud together so firmly that rain will not harm it—and when at last they produce flowers, you can imagine what a beautiful garden those ants live in, high above the ground.

So you see, ants can find an intelligent way around every difficulty. Have you ever heard of the honeypot ants, for instance? These live in Central Australia, and in other desert parts of the world where it is hot and dry, and food is scarce. Now, all ants have two stomachs—a tiny one for themselves, and a bigger one for their brothers and sisters. In this bigger one they hold a little honey-dew or some other ant delicacy, so that when they visit the larval nursery or meet a prince, princess or queen, or even one of their fellow workers, they can bring some of this "community" food up into their mouths and hand it over. But the honeypot ants store so much food in their community stomachs that they look like marbles with absurdly tiny legs and heads. They spent their whole lives clinging to the ceiling and walls of a special storeroom in the nest, ready to feed any of their hungry family who come to them for a snack—and if it were not for this wonderful, unselfish service, the desert ant tribes would have scarcely any chance of survival.

Ants that grow "mushrooms" actually feed their gardens with the bodies of dead caterpillars, and with leaves that they have cut from orange- and lemon-trees, and thoroughly chewed. And the harvester ants gather seeds which they sometimes drop around their nests. Here, the seeds grow into plants, so that the ants have their own little fields. Also, they gather certain grains, which they chew up and mix with saliva. They shape this dough into tiny loaves, place them outside on the warm earth to bake—and in no time they have a batch of tasty ant-bread.

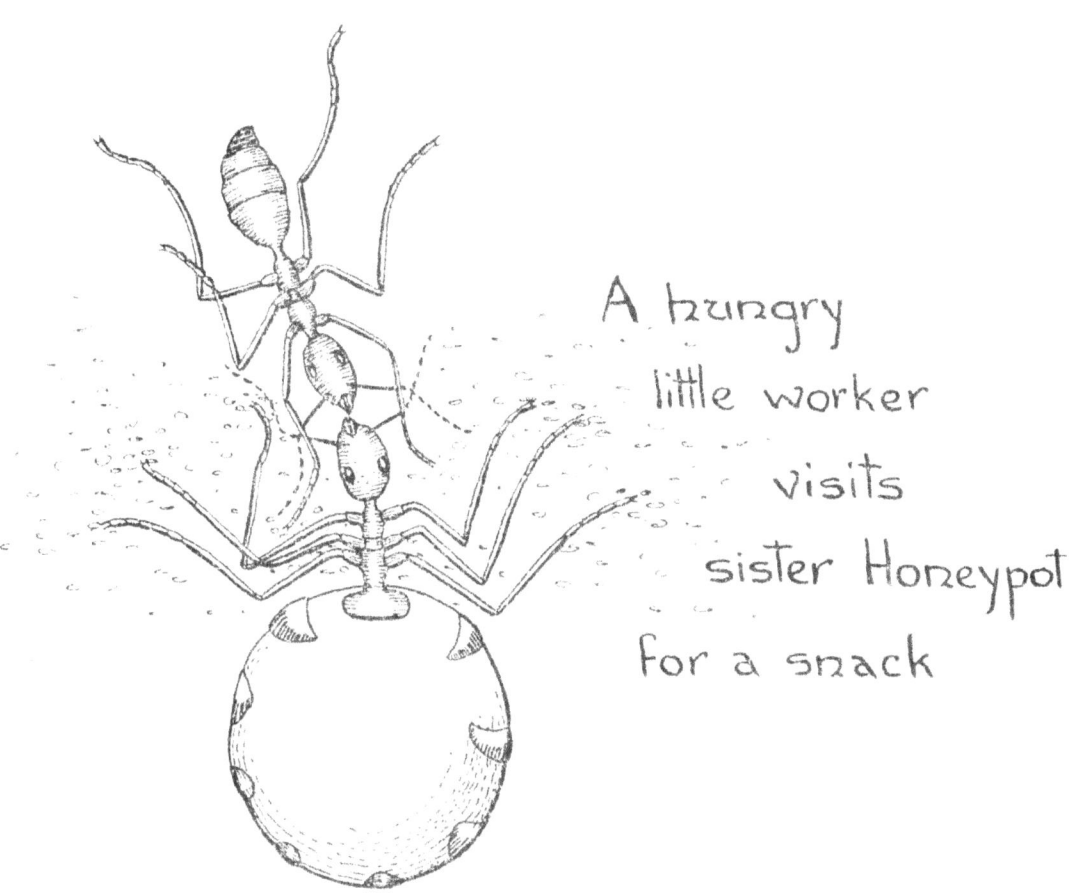

A hungry little worker visits sister Honeypot for a snack

This is all great fun, but ants are not always good-natured and peaceful. They will always fight if they have to, to defend their homes and hunting-grounds, but there are some kinds that spend their whole lives warring. Fortunately these grim killers, known as army ants, are not found in Australia, but in the tropical jungles of Africa and America they are terrible indeed. They have no settled home. They are almost always out marching, and destroying everything in sight. Other insects and animals flee from them in terror, and even a sleeping man can be killed when thousands of them attack him at once.

Then, in America and Europe, there is another dreadful race of ants, called the amazons. These have cruel jaws which can snap other ants in two, but which are useless for the simplest jobs of housework or even for eating. So the amazons set out on marches to the nests of other ants, and steal as many cocoons as they can carry. The kidnapped babies have no idea of what has happened to them, of course—and when they come out of their cocoons as perfect ants, they think they are in their own home. So they hurry about doing everything that needs to be done in the nest, and feeding the big bullies who have made them their slaves. If only they knew that, without them, those bullies would soon starve to death!

No doubt you have thousands of ants living in your own garden, but not mean or cruel ones like the armies or amazons. So when you come across them, just stop a few minutes to watch them going about the important business of living their tiny lives, which in many ways are so much like our own. And as you watch them moving around busily in their tiny world, you might also think of how tiny our world is, among all the millions of other worlds in space. Thinking of it like that, we ourselves seem almost as tiny as the ants, don't we?

The Acrobatic Grasshopper

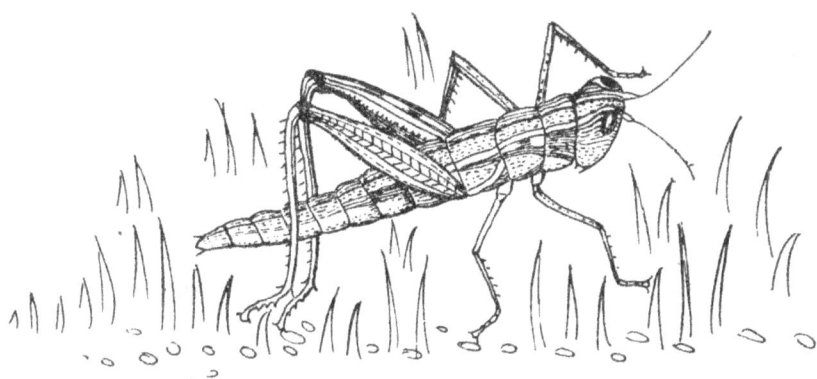

HAVE you ever tried to catch a grasshopper? If so, you know how cunning you have to be, for there is nothing more expert than a grasshopper at springing away when you come anywhere near it.

Tess and Chris often catch them, just for the fun of it, and to have a good look at them, but it's never an easy matter, especially as they are so careful not to hurt the 'hoppers' delicate feet, legs and feelers.

Next time you have a chance, look carefully at a grasshopper, and see how beautifully Nature has built it for all the jumping and springing around that it does. Look at its hind legs—ever so long, and broad with muscles up towards the top. These muscles, of course, give it the strength to spring with. And its feet have tiny cushiony pads on them, so that when it lands from a huge jump, it won't be badly jolted. Nature never forgets anything, it seems.

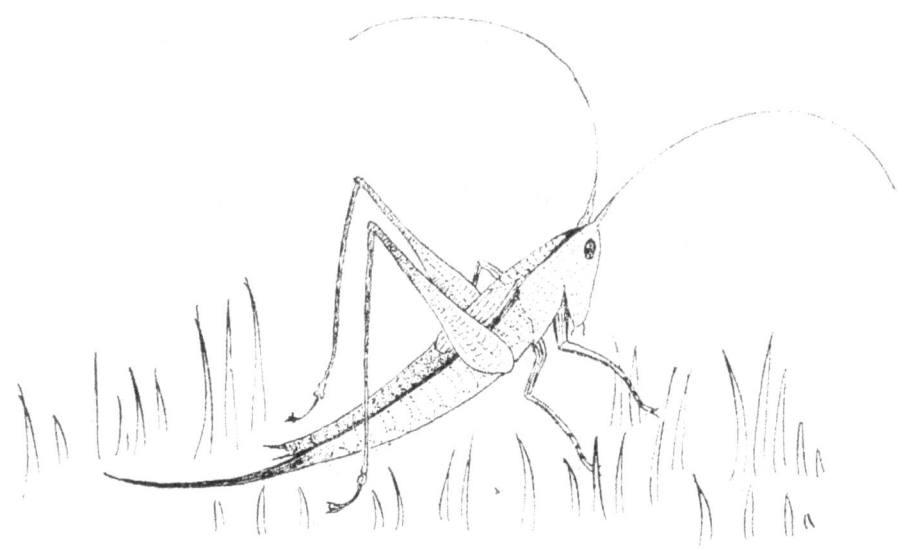

Then, as well as jumping, many grasshoppers can also fly. They have lovely big, gauzy wings that fold away like fans when not being used, underneath the top wings, which are narrower and tougher. But grasshoppers do not all have wings—and even those that do have them when they are grown-up, do not have them while they are nymphs, or youngsters. So it's often a bit puzzling to know what you are looking at. When you find a grasshopper without wings, it might really be a wingless kind, or it might be a nymph of a winged kind—for nymphs and adults look very much alike. And right from babyhood a grasshopper is an excellent jumper.

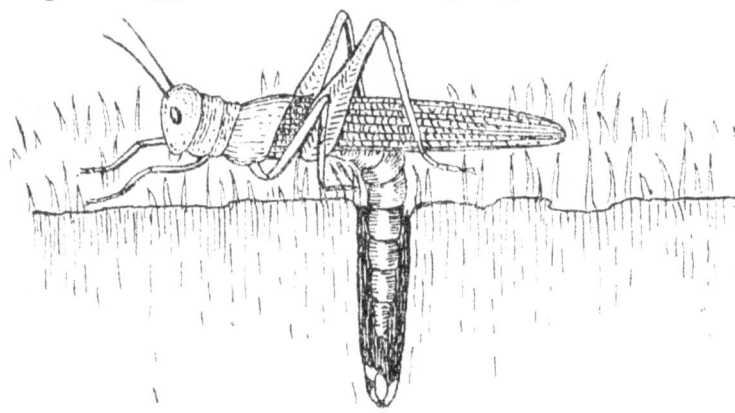

When you find one with a long pointy tail, like this, you know that it is a lady 'hopper, and that the "tail" is what she uses to dig burrows and deposit eggs with. She digs these burrows in the earth, and places her eggs neatly inside them, where they are well protected until they hatch. Some lady 'hoppers do not have these long pointed "egg placers", but they dig burrows quite well just the same, with the ends of their bodies.

If all the baby 'hoppers that hatched out of their eggs lived and grew, there wouldn't be much room on Earth for anything else. But they have so many enemies among birds and insects that they are killed off in great numbers. People have also declared war on grasshoppers, for they do a lot of damage to his crops and pastures—and when a plague of them comes swarming over the landscape in thousands of millions, they eat everything in sight.

Have you ever seen such a swarm? Tess and Chris haven't, but I have. There were so many of them that, as they flew towards us, they looked like a huge, dark, moving cloud. For a while they blotted out the sun and, although it was only midday, it looked as if night was coming. Then they settled—one great seething, crawling, chewing mass—and a few hours later, when they rose into the air again and travelled farther on, there was no living thing left except people and animals—not a sign of a plant anywhere, except the bare branches of a few trees.

These plague grasshoppers have short feelers, but there are others with extremely long antenna feelers. Sometimes they come into the house, and they'll bite if you're not careful. But you don't have to worry about this, as they have no poison.

Some long-feelered grasshoppers live in trees, and their wings look so much like leaves that you can be right next to one of them and not realise that you are looking at an insect.

Have you ever wondered about a grasshopper's song? The short-feelered kind keeps his "musical instrument" on the inside of his hind leg. It's a row of little pegs which make a rattling, rasping sound when he rubs them against a hard vein in his wings. The long-feelered kind makes *his* music by scraping one of his front wings over the other, where he has a sharp file. But wherever his song comes from, it is meant as a call to the lady grasshoppers—a sort of proposal of marriage. And the ladies hear it with "ears" which are little holes either in their front legs, or at the base of their hind ones. Insects keep things in funny places, don't they?

Of course, as with most other insects, there are many different kinds of grasshoppers—some very large, and others so small that they can live happily in ant nests. Some are brown and others green, and while most of them have squat faces, there's one kind with a long pointy one.

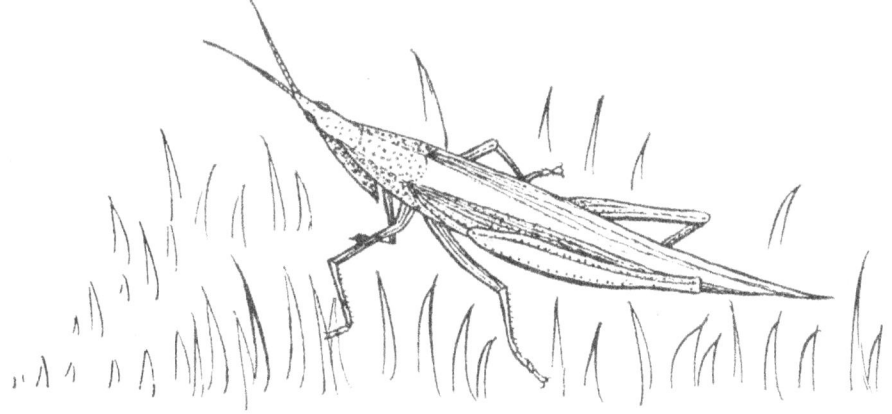

This one lives in grassy fields, and is so much like a grassblade in shape and colour that it's very hard to find it unless it moves. Then if you disturb it, it flies off quickly, on the prettiest light-green wings.

One day last summer, Chris and Tess had some friends in to play. Suddenly they were deafened with noise. It sounded as if hundreds of cicadas were "singing" all at once. One little girl said, "Heavens! Those locusts!" And Chris said, "That's where you're wrong. They're not locusts—they're cicadas."

"Well, then, what *are* locusts?" the little girl wanted to know.

"Locusts are grasshoppers," he told her.

"Are you sure?" she asked.

"Of course I'm sure," he said. "They're grasshoppers, all right."

But he told only part of the story. Actually, it's the long-feelered grasshoppers that are locusts, yet nearly everybody calls the plague grasshoppers "locusts", and these have short feelers. So the name "locust" seems to be given to the wrong insect nearly always.

We needn't do that, need we? We can all be clever enough to give the name "locust" only to grasshoppers with long feelers. And we would never, never dream of giving it to a cicada.

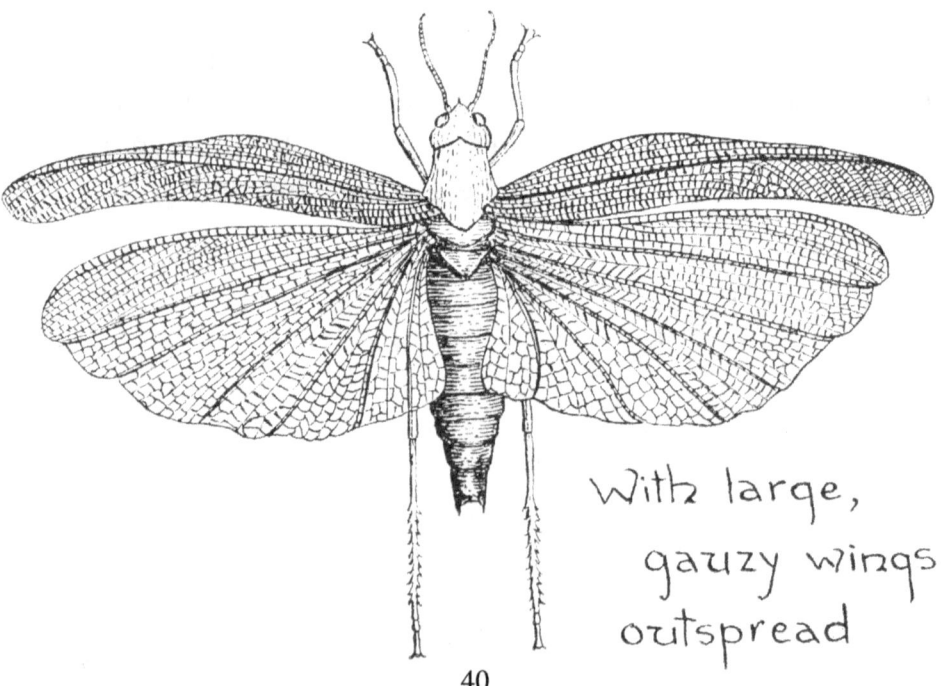

With large, gauzy wings outspread

Tiny Musician—Underground

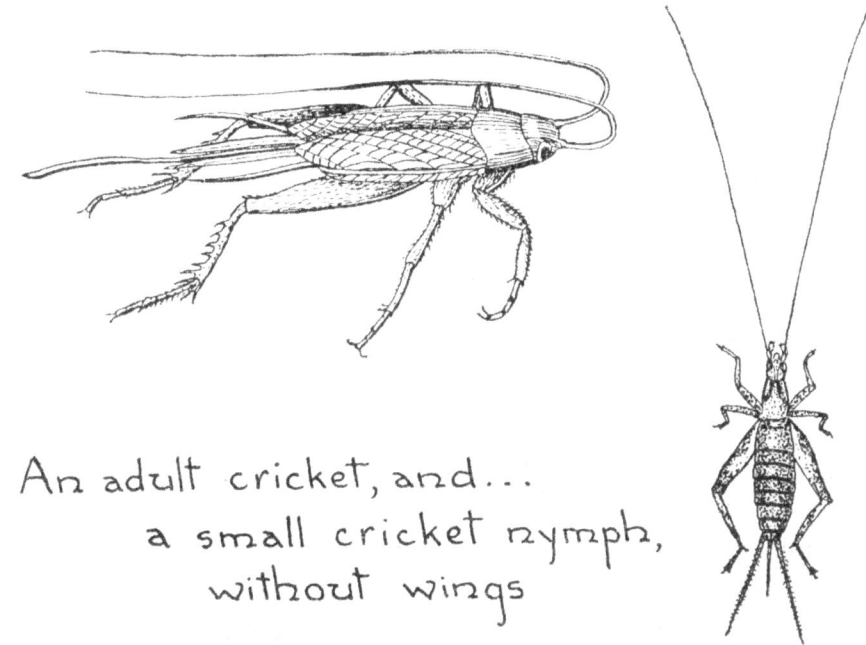

An adult cricket, and... a small cricket nymph, without wings

CRICKETS are those nice little creatures whose "song" is very much like the sound of their name—"Crii—crii—crii!" But of course they do not sing the way we do. Instead—like grasshoppers, cicadas and some other insects—they play on a musical instrument.

With crickets, this instrument is a sort of file on each upper wing, which they rub against a hard vein on the other upper wing.

And on each of these wings there is also a large section of tightly stretched skin which makes the sounds ring out loudly. People make things called amplifiers to do this job, but crickets just grow them.

Because of their amplifiers, you may hear the chirping of crickets from quite a distance, but you don't very often see them, for most of them hide away in burrows and under stones during the day, and come out foraging for food at night.

Don't be worried if any of them wander into your home, because they won't eat anything of value to you, as silverfish and cockroaches do. But it is always a kindness to put them out again where they *can* get food, provided you handle them carefully, for nothing loses a leg as easily as a cricket does. Pick one up a bit roughly, and he might well spring off, way out of reach, leaving one of its precious little legs in your hand. So do be careful, won't you?

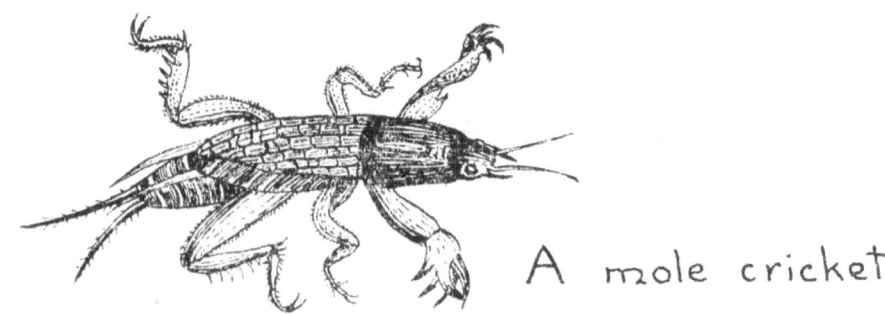

A mole cricket

Perhaps the most interesting of all the crickets are the large brownish ones called mole crickets, because their whole bodies are built for underground burrowing, especially their shield-like chest cover, and their front legs. These front legs and feet are enormous, and ever so strong, and they are broadened out into a wonderful kind of tool which is like a spade and a set of shears combined.

It's amazing how quickly a mole cricket can dig itself an underground tunnel even through hard soil and tangled plant roots with these clipping and shovelling front feet. Then it settles down to enjoy life in the safety and comfort of its queer little home.

Sometimes, from inside the tunnel, you will hear a gentleman mole cricket playing quite a musical note by rubbing his two upper wings together. Then, if you listen carefully, you just might hear the very soft answer of a lady mole cricket, who has heard the call and liked it. Her answer tells the gentleman that she will almost certainly become his wife. The two little creatures talk to each other with their wings, and listen to each other with their front legs, because, as with many of the grasshoppers, it is in their front legs that they keep their ears.

Then, if they do marry, there comes the time when, at the end of her burrow, the little lady lays about two hundred eggs. These are very lucky eggs compared with those of most other insects, for their mother really seems to love them. She doesn't leave them alone in a world that may be either kind or unkind to them. She watches over them and protects them from when they are merely eggs to when the baby crickets are old enough to look after themselves.

There is something particularly lovable about the sound that crickets make. One of these days you must read that beautiful little story by Charles Dickens called "The Cricket on the Hearth". *He* thought them lovable, too.

One evening when we had visitors, we brought a pot-plant inside and stood it on the sideboard. Evidently a little garden cricket had made his home in it, for after a while a short musical note came from the pot, followed by another—and another. It sounded so pretty. We all stopped our conversation to listen, and our tiny unseen musician gladdened the silence with his one happy little note. It was like having an elf in the room—and some day, if you hear of a story called "Cricket on the Sideboard", you will know how it all started.

Beetles — Friends and Foes

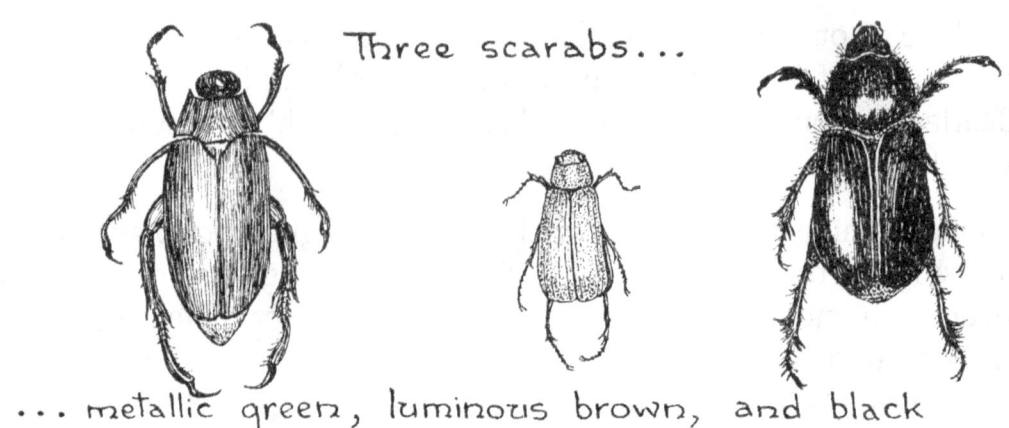

Three scarabs... ... metallic green, luminous brown, and black

WE have already met one beetle in this book. Do you remember its name? The ladybird. But there are thousands upon thousands of other kinds. In fact, there are more beetles than any other kind of animal in the world, but you do not notice them as often as you might, because they are not noisy as cicadas are, and while they are larvae they mostly live underground or buried away in wood.

You will also find them in flour, nuts and other foods at certain times of the year—and aren't they a nuisance then! And of course, there are many that live underwater in ponds and streams. It would be difficult to find anything, anywhere, in which a beetle could not live at some stage of its life.

You do know the quickest and easiest way to recognise a beetle, don't you? By its wings. It has four of these; the under ones for flying, and the upper ones for covering and protecting the flying ones. These upper wings may be smooth, grooved or knobbly, dull or shiny, but they are nearly always hard, and they come neatly together right down the centre of the beetle's back. Whenever you find an insect with two stiff little cover wings meeting in a straight line down its back, you will know that it is some kind of beetle.

Apart from the ladybird, I suppose the one that everybody knows and loves best is the Christmas beetle—that large, beautifully coloured beetle that comes around at the end of the year as though it would like to be used as a decoration on our Christmas-trees.

Looking at its lovely colours, you would never guess that, as a larva, it was one of those large curl-grubs that you sometimes find when you dig in soft earth. They are not very intelligent-looking grubs, and do not move around much. They just stay there eating decaying vegetable matter and plant roots, and growing fat. Then, when they change into grown-up beetles, they do a fair bit of damage to gumtrees by eating too many of their leaves. But they look so pretty that we just have to forgive them.

They belong to a very large group of beetles, called the scarabs. So does the big brown-and-black cowboy beetle, which also comes zooming around in the summer months, and whose larva has the peculiar habit of wriggling around on its back.

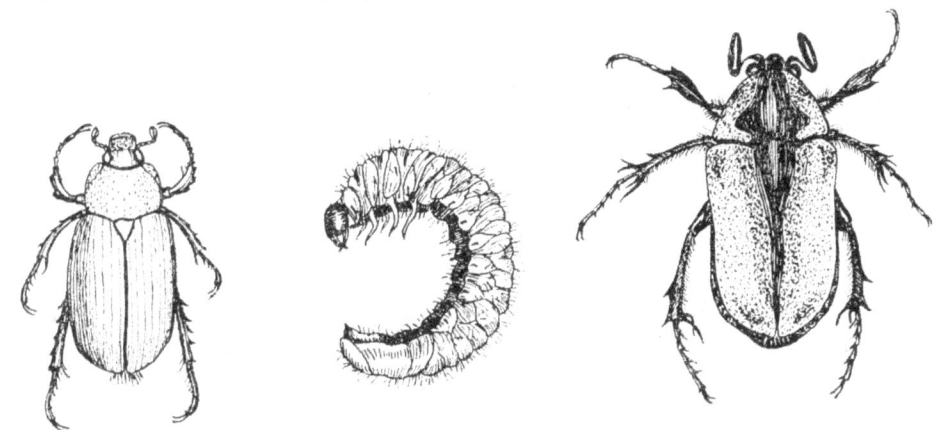

Christmas beetle... a curl grub... and a cowboy beetle

The scarabs are *such* a large group that you could spend years studying them, and still not come to the end of them.

Of course, Christmas beetles and ladybirds are not the *only* ones with lovely colours. There are the jewel beetles, as beautiful as their name—but destructive, too, for their hard-headed, broad-chested larvae live in tunnels inside the branches of trees and bushes—and that never does any good to trees and bushes.

Then, there's that lovely little beetle—ever so small at less than 6mm long, but shining like a bright blue light—that you'll sometimes find on swamp plants. When you see a lot of them together, they're as pretty as can be.

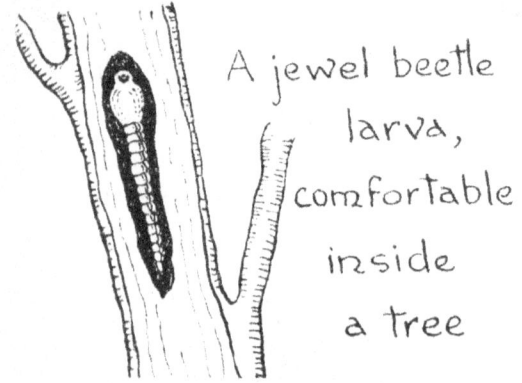
A jewel beetle larva, comfortable inside a tree

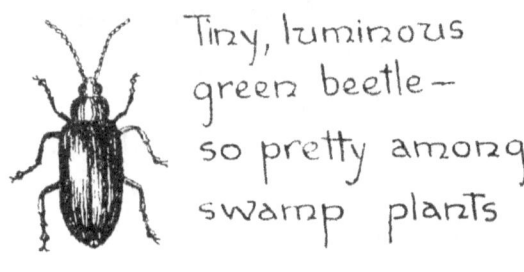
Tiny, luminous green beetle— so pretty among swamp plants

People with farms and forests look upon certain beetles as friends—tiger ones, for instance, whose larvae catch many insects on their way to do mischief to crops and trees. These queer little grubs live in tunnels in the ground, but with their heads right up at the surface, where they can see everything without being seen themselves. Along comes another insect, hurrying by for a feed, when it is suddenly grabbed by the tiger beetle larva—and before it has had a chance to get over its shock, the larva has killed and eaten it.

Does that remind you of any other insect in this book? What about the ant lion?

Then, at last, the larva becomes a grown-up tiger beetle with wings—and it's even busier than before. It still eats other insects, but it does a lot of running around as well, and its green and gold colours are so beautiful that it, too, could easily be called a jewel beetle.

But, as a rule, beetles are not liked very much by the human race, for they do more harm than good. How often do you see valuable furniture, and the wooden parts of buildings, riddled with tiny holes? These are the work of powder-post beetles, which bore into wood and eat it right down to powder. They are real villains.

And the weevils are no better. There are such enormous numbers of them—mostly long-snouted, with a ridgy look—and it's a real disgrace the way some of them eat the leaves and roots of plants, bore into their stems, and invade fruits, nuts and packets of prepared foods. Both as larvae and as full-grown beetles, the weevils are a problem indeed. But there are quite a lot of shabby-looking ground weevils that do not seem to do much harm.

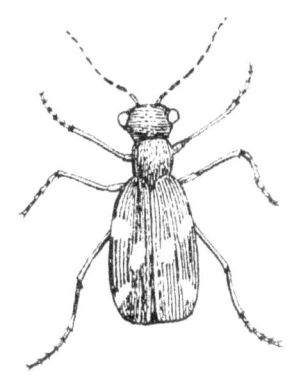 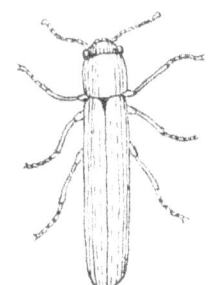 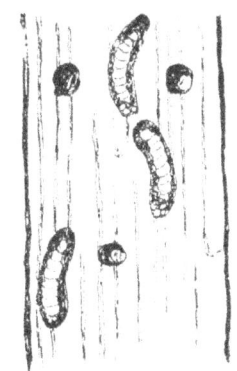

A tiger beetle, bright and alert   A powder-post beetle... and some of its larvae at home

Once, we kept one of them almost as a pet for some time. We had it in a box, with soil and some grass plants, and a few pieces of bark. During the day we never saw it, but at night it would come out and wave its little hand-like feelers around as though it was trying to talk to us. And apparently it was one of the kinds that can go long periods without eating, for the grass went on growing quite happily, and didn't look the least bit chewed, the whole of the time we had it with us.

A grain weevil, its larva, and... our ground weevil "pet"

Whenever we picked it up, it was really funny. In would go its head and feelers so that it looked as if it didn't have any at all, and it would roll over and stay quite still, pretending to be dead—as is the way with so many weevils. Then, after a few minutes, it would get up and move around again, in its slow, clumsy way.

Weevils are mostly a drab-looking lot, yet a few of them are quite the opposite, like the one drawn here—as beautiful as you could wish for. It is black, with bright blue markings—the kind of blue that you see in gems called turquoises. So it is rather puzzling to find that its common name is diamond or sapphire beetle. If you want to find this beetle, look for it on wattle-trees.

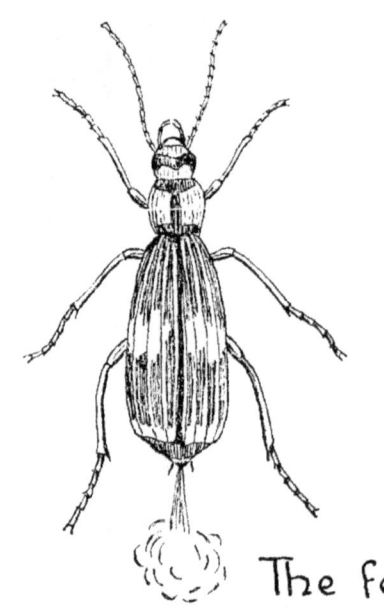

The fearsome bombardier

The beautiful diamond beetle — black with bright blue markings

Well, what with the long snouts that they usually have, and feelers that bend like elbows, weevils are queer little creatures indeed. But there are many other beetles even queerer—in looks or in habits. Think of the bombardier, for instance—a black beetle with large orange spots who shelters under rocks and fallen trees, and very much dislikes being interfered with. If anyone or anything does interfere, it lets out a small explosion, together with a puff of white "smoke"— and this is often quite enough to scare any enemies away.

Then there's the fierce-looking rhinoceros beetle with his strange horns. Such a big, dark, lumbering beetle it is. And another odd-looking little beetle, with something like a coronet on its head, has very odd habits as well. It likes eating horse and cow manure, so it rolls some of that manure into a ball, and buries it, like a dog burying a bone. Then it goes underground with that ball, to enjoy a nice leasurely meal. And at a certain time of year, female beetles lay their eggs in balls like this, so that when the little grubs hatch out, they will have plenty to eat. Fancy—a cradle and dinner, all in one!

Other real oddities are the click beetles which sometimes find their way right into our homes on summer evenings. Aren't they queer little things, the way they snap and crack, and look as if they are trying to turn themselves inside-out? They behave very much the same as a double-jointed person can, for the front part of their thorax is so

A horned rhinoceros beetle, and... a little ball-roller

loosely attached to the rest of their body that they can do remarkable bending exercises, and the clicking sound comes when they straighten up again—when they "snap" back into position.

Next time you meet a click beetle, turn it over on to its back, and see what happens. See how it bends over in two, and leaps up into the air as its own special way of turning itself right-way-up again.

As a larva, this beetle is a thin wriggly little grub that lives in the earth and is often called a wire worm. Then, when the time comes, it settles down in a tiny earth cell—as so many other beetle larvae do—to become a pupa and at last a full-grown beetle.

But beetles are not *all* land dwellers. Quite a number of them prefer the water—and those that do are excellent swimmers. Also, both as larvae and as beetles, they are greedy eaters of other insects. In fact, one of them has such a fierce larva that it is called the water tiger.

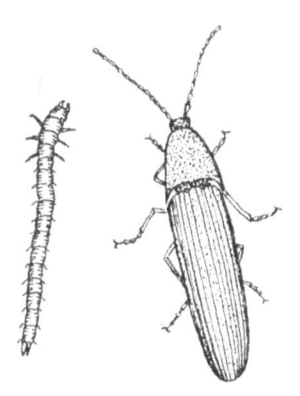

A click beetle, with its larva, the "wire worm"

A whirligig and its larva

But the one you are most likely to find when you go out searching in ponds and creeks is the whirligig beetle—called that because of its swift darting movements, backwards and forwards, round in circles, all over the place.

Its back legs are like little flat oars, and it has special kinds of eyes, like bifocal glasses. This is because it swims near the surface of the water, and Nature has made it possible for it to see perfectly in two different places at once. While the upper part of its eyes is looking at everything above the water, their lower part is keeping a good watch on everything under the water. So altogether, it doesn't miss much. Its larva is a busy little swimmer too, with hairy gills all the way up its body.

Although there are about a quarter of a million types of beetles in the world, there is still a good deal to be learnt about many of them. So whenever you find what looks like an interesting specimen, try to study its habits as closely as possible. And—you never know—you might discover something quite new. Wouldn't that be fun?

Bugs—Not Beetles

WE visited some friends the other day, in a suburb quite near the city—and we found, to our surprise, that their garden was filled with the most interesting insects. There were grasshoppers, case moths, aphids and aphid-lions, butterflies, an enormous green emperor caterpillar, and the odd-looking creatures you see here.

These were strangers to the children, and they were most excited about them. "Look, Mummie, have you ever seen this kind of beetle?" Tess asked. And she was about to pick it up in her fingers when one of our friends called out and told her not to, because quite often this rather unfriendly creature lets out a nasty bad-smelling fluid when it is disturbed.

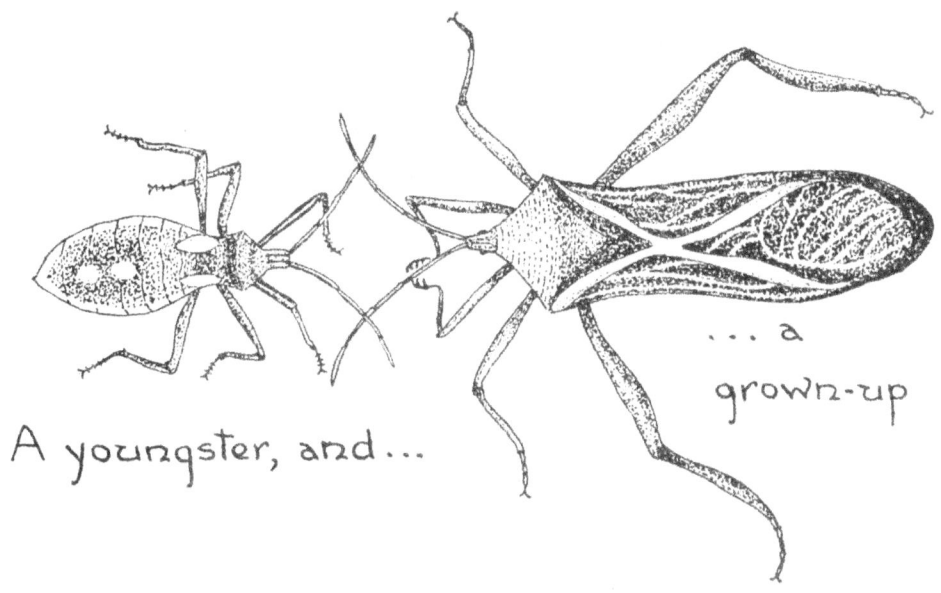

A youngster, and... ...a grown-up

The next thing to find out about it was that it wasn't a beetle at all, but a bug. And because of the cross on its back, formed by the placing of its wings, it is called the crusader bug.

Actually, it is quite well known in gardens, but very seldom liked, because it does a lot of damage to fruit-trees and other plants, piercing into the branches and sucking out the juices that the plants need for themselves.

So, do you remember another word for it? A parasite.

This particular one was on a cassia bush, and as we looked around we found several more. Then Chris said, "Look, here's another kind!" And he pointed to a smaller one, much lighter in colour than the one with the cross on its back, and with different markings, although its head was the same shape. Actually, it wasn't a different kind at all, but a young crusader bug without its "adult" colours and markings.

Tess asked, "What makes them bugs instead of beetles?" And perhaps you are wondering that, too.

To begin with, they have long sucking beaks which they hold tucked back underneath their chests (or thorax) when they're not using them. Also, they often have half of their front wings thickened, so as to protect their frail little back wings. And when they first hatch out of their eggs—which are like tiny boxes with lids on them—they already look like tiny bugs, whereas beetles come out of their eggs as grubs. So in this, beetles are more like moths and butterflies, aren't they? Cicadas, which we have met earlier, are a type of bug also. However they have their own different lifecycle with a different-looking larva, and don't usually damage the plants they feed from.

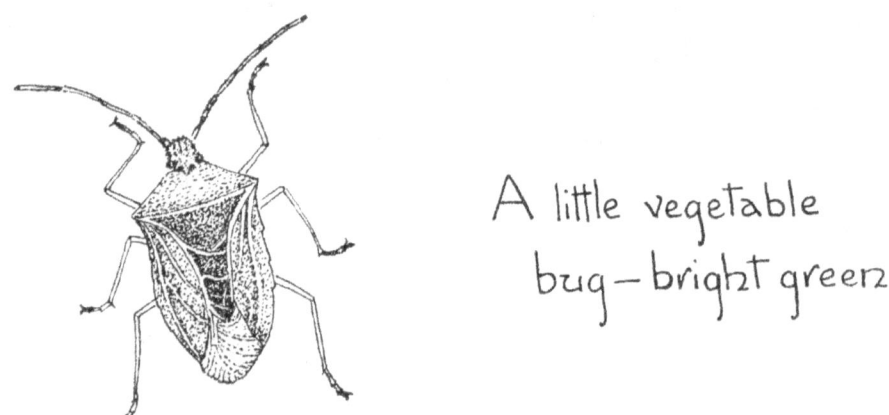

A little vegetable bug — bright green

Now, here is another little bug, that you must have seen quite often wandering over your vegetables, and sometimes finding its way on to your curtains by mistake. It's a pretty shade of green, like young leaves, but gardeners do not approve of its appetite for their pet vegetables.

Like the crusader bug, this bug has more or less the same shape when it is young as when he is fully grown, but its colourings and markings are quite different. As a youngster, it is decorated with a rich pattern of browns, yellows and reds, and this pattern changes every time it moults one skin to get a new one, until finally it becomes an all-over green.

How would *you* like to keep changing your colour every little while? It might be a bit confusing, but think of what fun it would be, always wondering what you might look like a few days from now!

Lacewings—and Their Terrible Children

EVEN as a little two-and-three-year-old, toddling around the garden, Tess used to chatter happily whenever she found a group of those tiny bead-like things suspended lightly on the ends of frail silky threads attached to a leaf, perhaps, or a stem, or even a fence-post or a window-frame. "Mummie, look—look! Tessie found!" she would cry excitedly. And I always felt excited, too, even though I had seen them so many times already—for there is always a newness about the things of Nature, no matter how often they are repeated.

You, also, must have seen these tiny swaying "beads" many a time, and wondered about them. Perhaps you have even found out the secret of where they come from and what they lead to—and if so, you already know one of the strangest of all insect stories.

To begin with, they are not beads, of course, but eggs, laid by a small dainty insect known as a lacewing. It goes by this name because its wings are so beautifully patterned with a "lacework" of delicate veins. And do you know why she places her eggs like this, on the tops of swaying, silky threads? Because the tiny grubs or larvae that hatch out of them are real cannibals, as fierce as they are hungry. If they were to hatch out side by side—on a stem or a leaf—instead of snuggling up together for a few moments in a happy family circle before going their separate ways, they would set to work and eat one another. But as it is, their first job in the world is to climb down from the tops of their stalks—and these are far enough apart to give them all a fair chance of survival.

Well now, as they haven't been able to eat one another, they must go out hunting for something else. They are busy, impatient little grubs, with bristly coats—and they're hungry, as well. They run around quickly, and before long they find their very favourite dish—a collection of aphids.

If only those aphids had known! But now it's too late, and they have no way of escaping. A lacewing larva pierces into one after another of them with its needle-sharp mandibles, and, holding them up in front, sucks them dry. Then it has a most curious habit of attaching these empty skins on to its own bristles, instead of just dropping them.

It rather reminds you of a head-hunter collecting heads, doesn't it? Perhaps it does this to hide itself, as though it feels that somebody might start paying it back, some day.

Of course, when it moults its decorated skin and gets a new one, it must begin all over again, attaching the bodies of more and more victims. Then at last, right there on one of the stems in his hunting-ground, it spins a little white silk cocoon, and later, when it comes out of this, you wouldn't recognise it. Instead of a bristly grub covered with dead skins, it is a lovely, delicate-looking little creature with long fragile wings—the very same lacewing that our story started with.

As you can imagine, gardeners give these insects a big welcome, since they help to get rid of aphids. But there are many different kinds of lacewings, and they are not *all* aphid-eaters. The larvae of some of them eat ants—and because of the way they lie in wait for their victims and then pounce on them, they are called ant-lions.

Ant-lion lacewings lay their eggs in the earth, and in due time these hatch out into tiny grubs with big ferocious-looking jaws. Immediately, each one gets busy building its own special ant trap. It goes round in circles, drilling out a cone-shaped hole in the loose earth, and when this is finished, it himself takes up position at the bottom of the hole—the narrow end of the "cone"—and waits for dinner to drop in. This seems too extraordinary to be true, yet it is exactly what happens.

In a little while, sure enough, an ant happens along. Perhaps it is thinking of other things and not looking where it is going—or perhaps it sees the hole in the ground and decides to examine it more closely. But whatever the reason, down it goes tumbling. The earth is so soft, and the sides of the hole are so steep, that the ant cannot keep its footing—and of course, down at the bottom of the hole, the lacewing larva crouches waiting. This is what it has been hoping for. This is working out exactly as planned, and—with a leap of triumph—it grabs the hapless little ant in those strong jaws. It gobbles that ant up with relish, then lies in wait for another one—and it's amazing how many ants fall into that trap. Some days, it has ants for breakfast, lunch and dinner, and it grows big and fat, moulting its skin several times before finally settling down in a cocoon—still at the bottom of that hole. Small grains of earth or sand cling to the outside of the cocoon

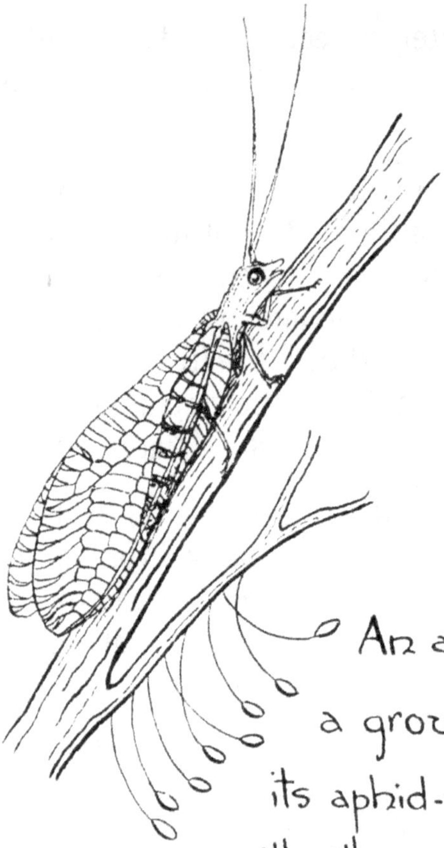

An adult lacewing, a group of its eggs, and its aphid-eating larva covered with the skins of its victims

An ant-lion at home — waiting for his dinner

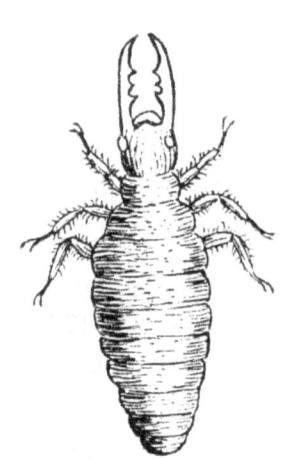

An ant-lion

while, inside it, our rather ugly-looking little larva is changing into a lacewing—one of the daintiest of insects.

These delicate creatures often fly into our houses on summer evenings, attracted by the lights, as moths are. They are small, fragile, and rather helpless-looking, and you would never imagine that they had been such little terrors in their "childhood".

The Large Family of Flies

NOBODY likes flies very much—and for quite good reasons. Considering all the mess and garbage that they seem to enjoy so much, their feet are none too clean—then, if you give them a chance, they stand all over your food.

Because of their dirty habits, they are great spreaders of disease. Some of them ruin our nicest fruit—and some of them, like March flies, also bite. So, as a general rule, they are not friendly insects to man. But look at them closely, and you will see they are no less beautiful than other insects.

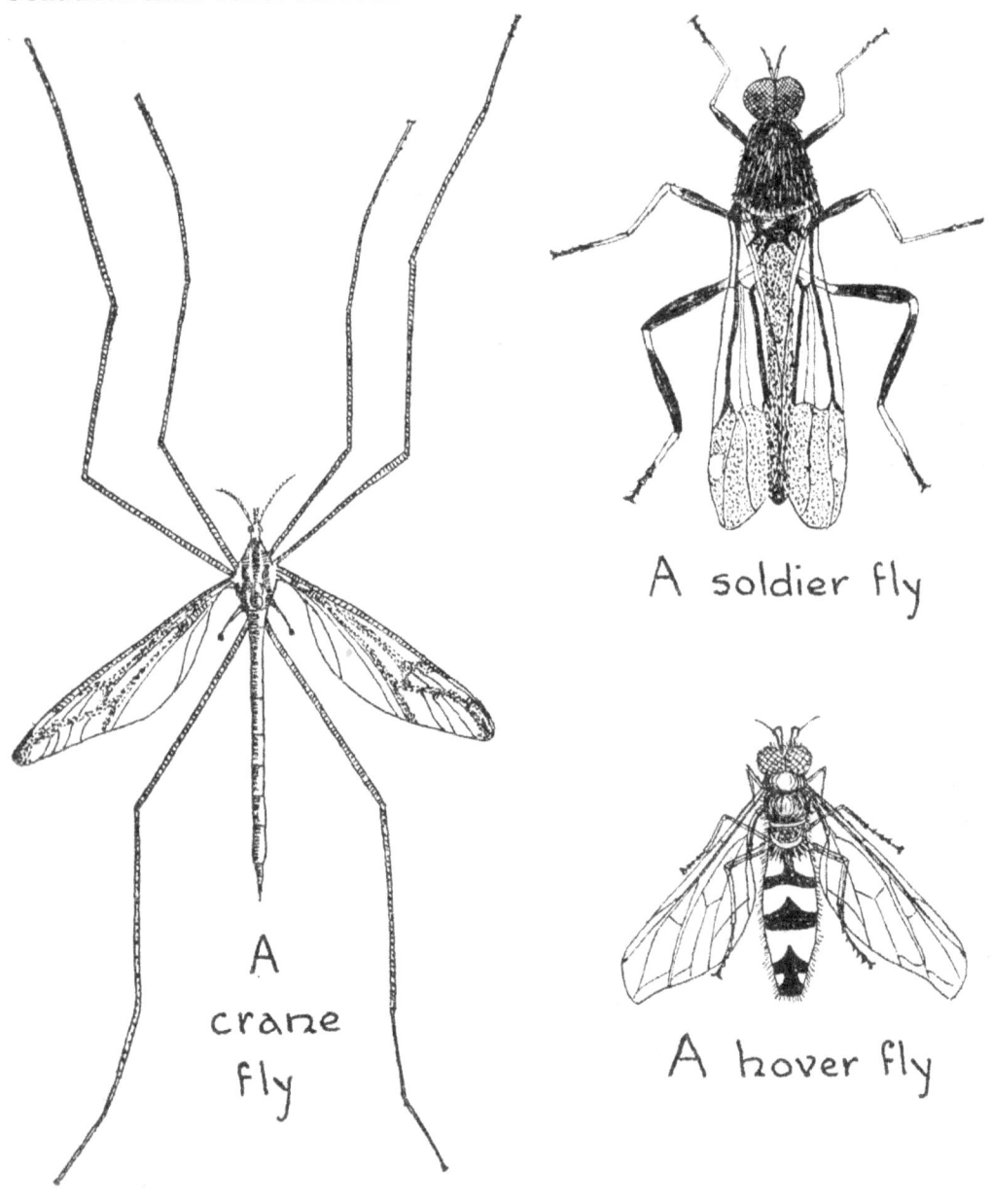

A soldier fly

A crane fly

A hover fly

Sometimes their colours shine like jewels, and their wings are very daintily veined. Also, their large eyes—which are made in such a way that they can see in all directions at once—have a lovely frosted look about them. So you see, we can admire a fly's appearance even if we can't approve of its behaviour.

Some flies look very much like bees, and others like wasps. But there is one easy way of telling them apart. Do you know it? Flies have only two wings—and they are the only insects that have only two. So you see, a "wasp" or a "bee" with two wings must be a fly.

Mostly, when people speak of flies, they mean the ones that so often come into houses. But of course, there are ever so many different kinds apart from these—far too many, considering what a nuisance they are.

Some are very tiny, and others are very large. Some have no wings at all, and others have enormously long legs. The long-legged ones are called crane flies. Perhaps you have seen one of them fluttering against your own windows now and then, and wondered what on earth it could be. Before it gets its wings and long legs, it lives under the ground in the form of a very thin worm-like larva (or maggot), and eats the roots of plants. Then, of course, it becomes a pupa—still underground—and works its way up into the open air only when it wakens out of its "sleep" as a fly.

Then, there are the prettily coloured hover flies. The one here has bands of bright yellow and black, and a dark red head. These flies have a queer habit of hovering in mid-air with their wings fluttering so quickly that you can scarcely see them. Go up near to them, and they dart off, then start their hovering again just a short distance away. Now, why would a fly want to do a thing like that? As a larva, this fly is a green and yellow maggot that feeds on aphids, so it actually does some good in the garden.

Soldier flies look altogether different, with their long narrow bodies. Some time or other, you are sure to see at least one kind of soldier fly walking over your windows. It will probably be like the one we have drawn, with the ends of its wings smoky-grey, a shiny black head and body, and four spines finishing off the top part of the body, or thorax.

Soldier flies don't do much harm, but fruit flies certainly do. Here in Australia they are one of our worst pests. We all know how horrid it is to cut open a beautiful-looking peach, for instance, and find the inside of it all brown and soggy, and crawling with white maggots. These maggots are the larvae of the fruit fly. By the time the fruit—or what is left of it—drops to the ground to rot away, the maggots are just about ready to become pupae, and then finally they come awake again as flies with thin little waists and round bodies ending in a point. The one drawn here is yellow and brown, and doesn't look a bit like the villain that it actually is, for it will very soon get busy laying eggs just under the skin of young fruit, and these will hatch out into maggots, and the trouble will start all over again—unless we get busy first with sprays.

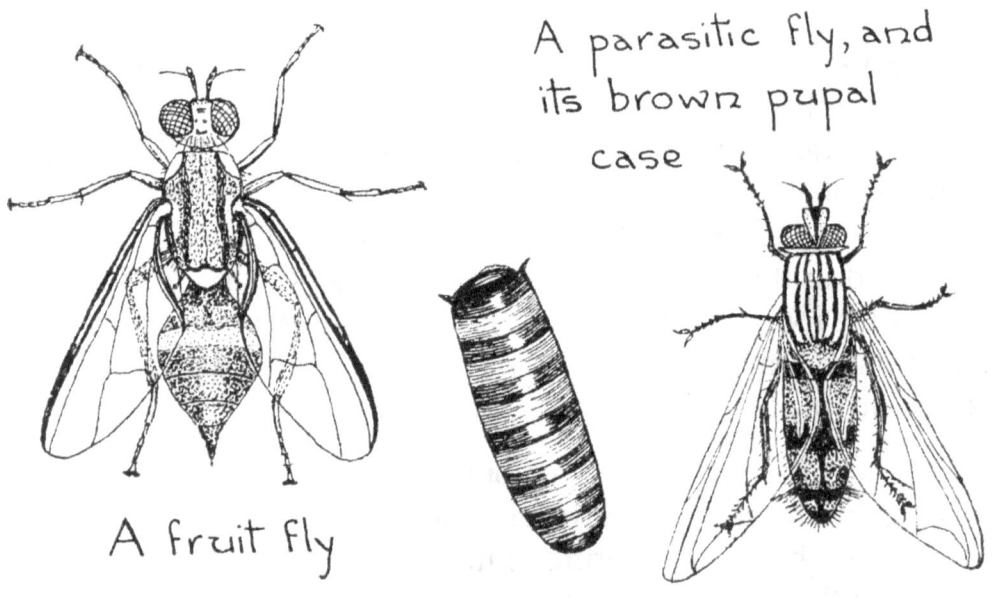

A fruit fly

A parasitic fly, and its brown pupal case

Tess was so annoyed with the next fly, that she didn't want anything to do with it. For weeks we had kept a dark-brown woolly caterpillar in a jar, feeding it on grasses and wondering what sort of moth it would turn into. At last it spun a light-brown cocoon around itself, and we set it aside to wait. Then, after a few weeks, what came out of it was not a moth, but two flies like the one in our drawing—mostly black and grey in colour. We opened the cocoon, and there, sure enough, were the little dark brown cases they had come out of—together with the remains of our caterpillar. So you see, the maggots of these flies had lived inside the caterpillar as parasites, and had ended up by killing it.

Then they themselves became pupae inside its cocoon. It isn't a very nice story, is it?

And another nasty story can be told about robber flies. There are several different kinds of these—some real giants in the fly family, others of only medium size. But they are all fierce killers of other insects—even of insects larger than themselves, like dragonflies. Honey bees are often killed by them, and Christmas beetles, and ever so many smaller insects. Robber fly larvae live in rotten wood or damp earth, and eat any other larvae that they fancy. Then, as adult flies, they dash around grasping one victim after another with their strong hairy legs, piercing into them with their sharp beaks, and sucking out their blood. If you disturb one of them at its meal, it will fly off with an angry buzz, probably carrying its victim away, even when it is larger.

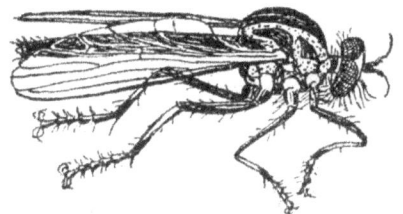

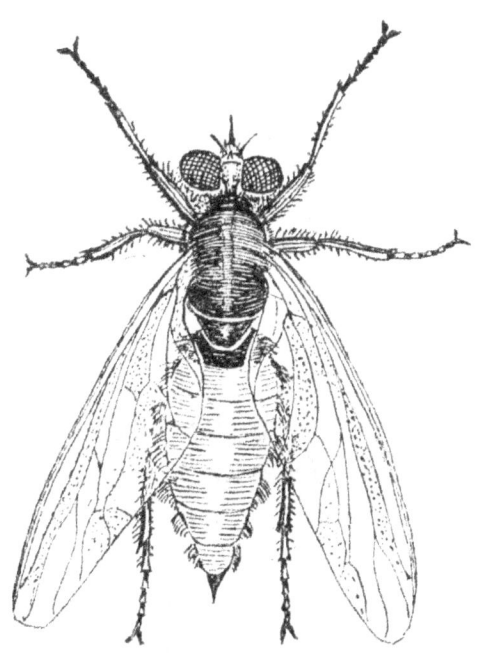

Two robber flies — one large and showy, with a bright-orange abdomen ... the other with a slender abdomen and a bulging thorax

Apart from their hairy legs, robber flies have thick "beards", and sometimes hairy bodies as well. One huge specimen that we saw once in a collection case had what looked like a full-length fur coat—and it was actually 50mm long. Fancy running into *this fly* if you were a juicy insect!

As you can see, the two kinds of robber flies sketched on the previous page are quite different in shape and in size. One has a thin abdomen and a bulging thorax—and this is the kind you are most likely to find. The other is so beautiful to look at, with its bright orange abdomen and tufts of brown hair, that you cannot help admiring it, and wishing that it weren't so murderous.

Did you know that mosquitoes are flies? Yes, they are one of the many groups in the large fly family, and everyone knows what a nuisance they can be to man. Some of them are dangerous, too, as they spread serious diseases. But it's only the female mosquitoes that bite, and suck blood. The males are not nearly so vicious. Their main foods are plant juices, and the nectar of flowers.

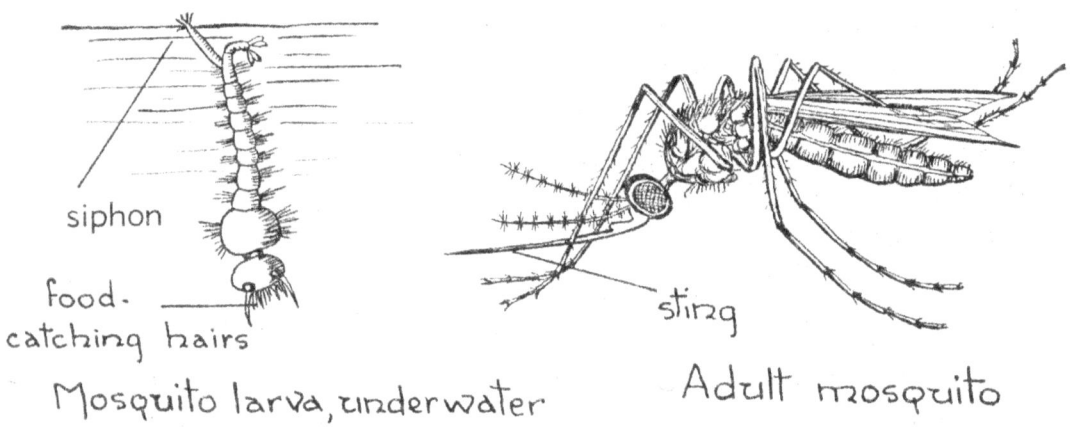

Mosquito larva, underwater   Adult mosquito

While they are larvae and pupae, most other flies live under-ground or in soft, decaying things, but mosquitoes are different. They live in water. Their larvae are the "wrigglers" that you see so often in pools, or in any water that is stale, even in flower vases. But they are not water creatures the way fish are, for they need to have contact with the outside air, so—while they hang head-downwards underwater—a little siphon at the end of their bodies reaches up above the surface, and through this the "wrigglers" receive air. Meanwhile, they are busily eating tiny forms of water life which they actually sweep into their mouths with hairy brushes.

While they are "resting" as pupae, they keep on receiving air—through two little horns near their heads. And then, after all this, when they come out of their pupal state as full-grown mosquitoes, they leave the water for the first time, and start pestering the race of man.

Well, the fly family are not *all* villainous, but most of them still have a lot to learn about living peacefully with their fellow creatures, haven't they?

How Ichneumons (Mis)Behave

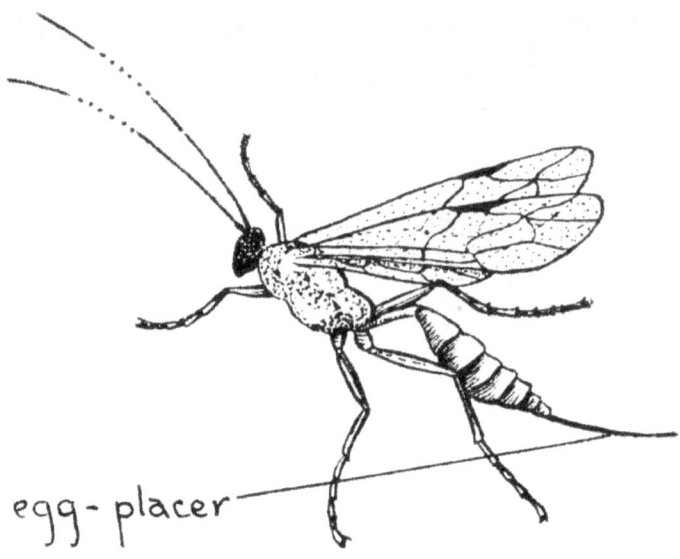

egg-placer

YOU will often see little wasps like these, darting about in your garden, and they're some of the prettiest little creatures on wings.

Tess went out in the garden the other day, with a jar in each hand, looking for anything new, and she soon came in again, quite excited. "Look, Mummie," she said, "these are different kinds of flies all together."

I said, "Thank you, dear, I'm glad to have them. We'll certainly put them in our book. But why do you call them flies?"

"Well, *aren't* they, Mummie?" she asked. "Flies do sometimes have waists, the same as wasps—and these have only two wings—so doesn't that make them flies?"

I told her that it certainly would if they did have only two wings, but that these creatures had four. To be sure, it didn't look as if they had, until we examined them very closely with magnifying glasses, then the two extra wings showed out quite clearly.

The two wasps she had caught were quite different in colour. One was bright orange and the other black with white markings. But both of them were ichneumon wasps.

When I told Tess about them, she turned away in disgust, because she cannot stand parasites—and ichneumons are parasites. With their needle-sharp egg-placers, they puncture the flesh of caterpillars that, in time, would change into moths or butterflies.

These eggs soon hatch out into little grubs, which spend their lives eating parts of the caterpillars' insides. Finally, of course, they eat too much, and the caterpillars die.

Sometimes this happens after they have spun their cocoons, and sometimes before—but whenever it happens, it makes a very ugly story, doesn't it. Of course, garden-lovers, farmers and orchardists do not think it an ugly story. *They* think of ichneumons as friends, for these wasps destroy many of the insects which would otherwise be eating their plants. But it's the fact of their being parasites that seems so nasty.

Safe and comfortable inside a caterpillar, the tiny ichneumon grubs, or larvae, have it all their own way. They live a life of luxury, with all the food they could wish for. Then they spin their own tiny cocoons, and become pupae inside them.

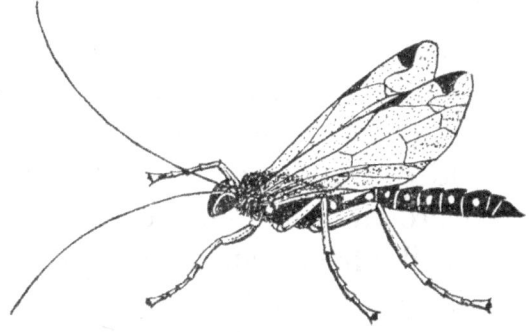

The dainty little ichneumons that emerge from these cocoons soon take up the activities of their parents before them; The males fly around enjoying themselves among flowers and other pretty things in the garden, most of the time—and the females set to work laying their eggs in caterpillars.

> Ichneumon, you're one of the prettiest things
> That dart round our garden on four gauzy wings.
> But why do you have to be so impolite
> As to go and lay eggs in a grub? Is that right?

Insect Phantoms

FROM time to time through the years, we have found a kind of stick insect in our garden that you simply cannot tell apart from twigs and branches. They have no wings, and their legs and bodies are long, thin and brown. They rest among bushes for long periods at a time without moving, and if you glance away for a moment, you have trouble finding them again. This is why stick insects are called phasmids, because—like phantoms—they just seem to disappear into their surroundings.

But they are not *all* like sticks. Some of them—real giants of the insect world, maybe 150mm long are green in colour, and have legs that look like big leaves with serrated edges, so they should really be called leaf insects. Once, in a museum, we saw an enormous stick insect over 400mm long, and we were glad that we hadn't come upon it unawares in any of our bush wanders, for it would have given us an awful shock.

But recently, in the beautiful bush around Yarrangobilly Caves, we met hundreds of stick insects quite different from the ones at home, yet not nearly so fierce-looking as the leafy-legged giants. Their bodies were about 100mm long, but of course, with their great sprawling legs, they looked a lot longer. The first ones we saw were slender and brown, very much like the branches around them, and as far as we could see, they had no wings. But then one of them took a little flight, and to our surprise—folded away like fans down the length of its body, underneath narrow brown covers—were the loveliest heliotrope wings, transparent like cellophane, and prettily veined. Somehow, they didn't quite suit it. They were so fanciful, and the rest looked so woody and gaunt.

The next day we found another kind of stick insect, different from the brown one with heliotrope wings, so of course we thought at first that it was a separate species. But actually it was the female of this same species. She was fatter than the lean, brown male, and green in colour. Also, her wings were quite small—two gauzy, pale pink ones folded away underneath two green cover ones.

Of course, we brought her inside, to watch her and draw her—and while she strolled over the branch of gum-leaves we had picked for her, she laid quite a number of eggs—just dropped them around

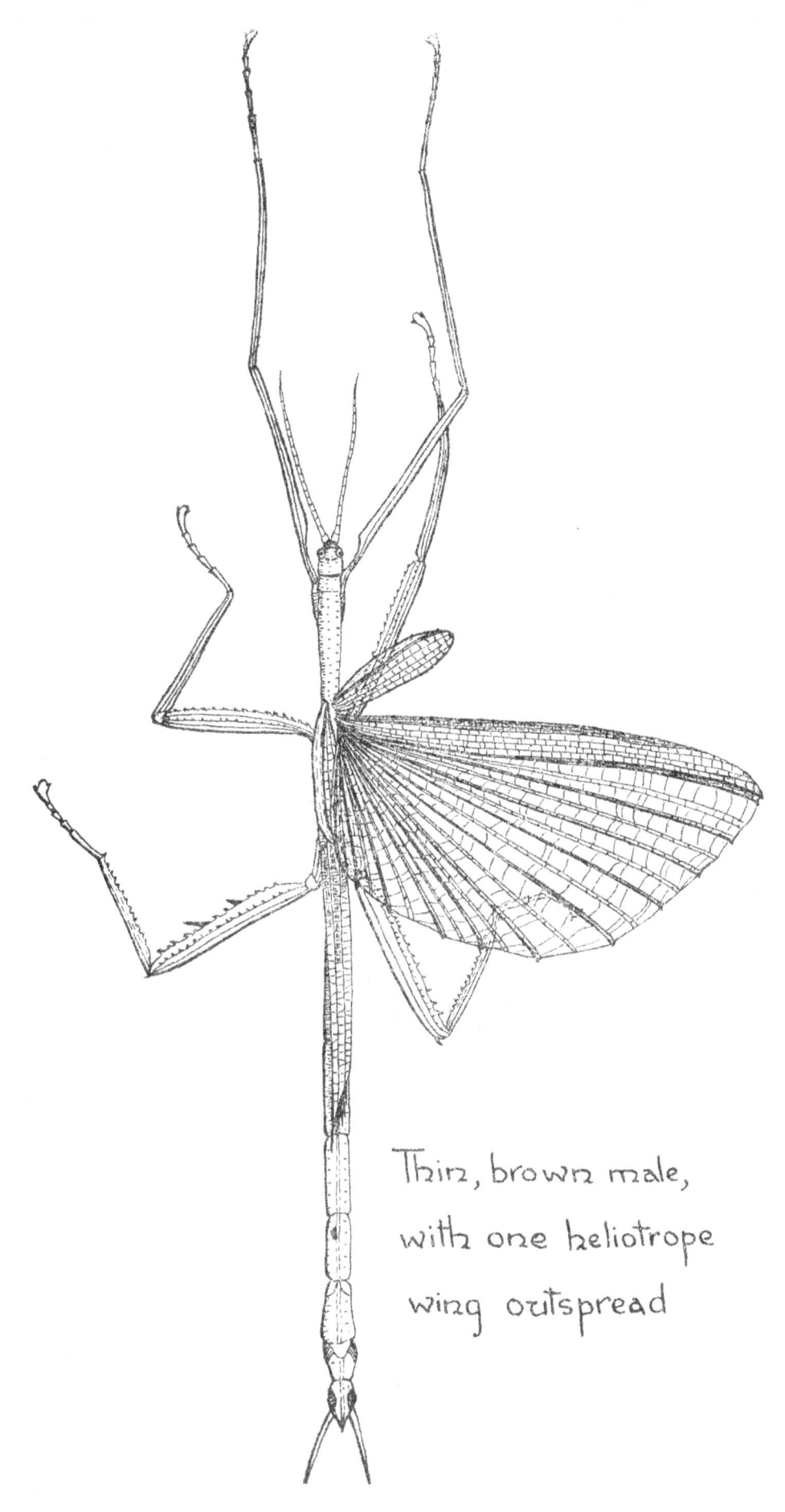
Thin, brown male, with one heliotrope wing outspread

carelessly, wherever she happened to be. So you see, a stick insect (or phasmid) is not a very thoughtful mother.

Once, we were lucky enough to see one of these green ladies moult her skin. She wedged out of it gradually, with great effort, stopping every now and then for a rest—as you would have to, if you were getting out of clothes that were far too tight for you. Then, after she had worked quite free from it, she set to work and ate it. But that is the nearest that a stick insect would come to eating "meat", for they are quite harmless to themselves or to other insects. They do not bite, either, even though some of them look so fierce.

When it comes to gum-leaves, though, they have enormous appetites. A sapling gum, on which we found several phasmids, looked quite ragged, with scarcely a leaf that hadn't been thoroughly nibbled. Sometimes entire trees can be killed by these phasmids eating all of its leaves.

Phasmids have eyes that are very different from our own eyes. When they are young, they have very simple eyes that see light coming from only a few directions. Each time they moult however, their eyes become more complex and can see more and more detail all around them, and even put dark chemicals into their eyes when the light is bright – rather like having removable sunglasses built into their own eyes! Some male stick insects also have spots on their skin that can detect light, although these spots can't easily tell what direction the light is coming from.

You should try to find some of these interesting and graceful insects for yourselves. But if you *are* going to find any, you will have to have very sharp eyes, for they hide so cleverly—hanging limp and motionless among foliage when in danger—that even birds don't see them. And you know how sharp the eyes of birds are.

If we could hide ourselves so well, think of the fun we would have!

> Where *are* you, dear phasmid?
> I *would* like to know.
> At rest among branches,
> You simply don't show.
>
> You *were* here right now,
> And I think it's most queer,
> How you sit without moving
> And just disappear.

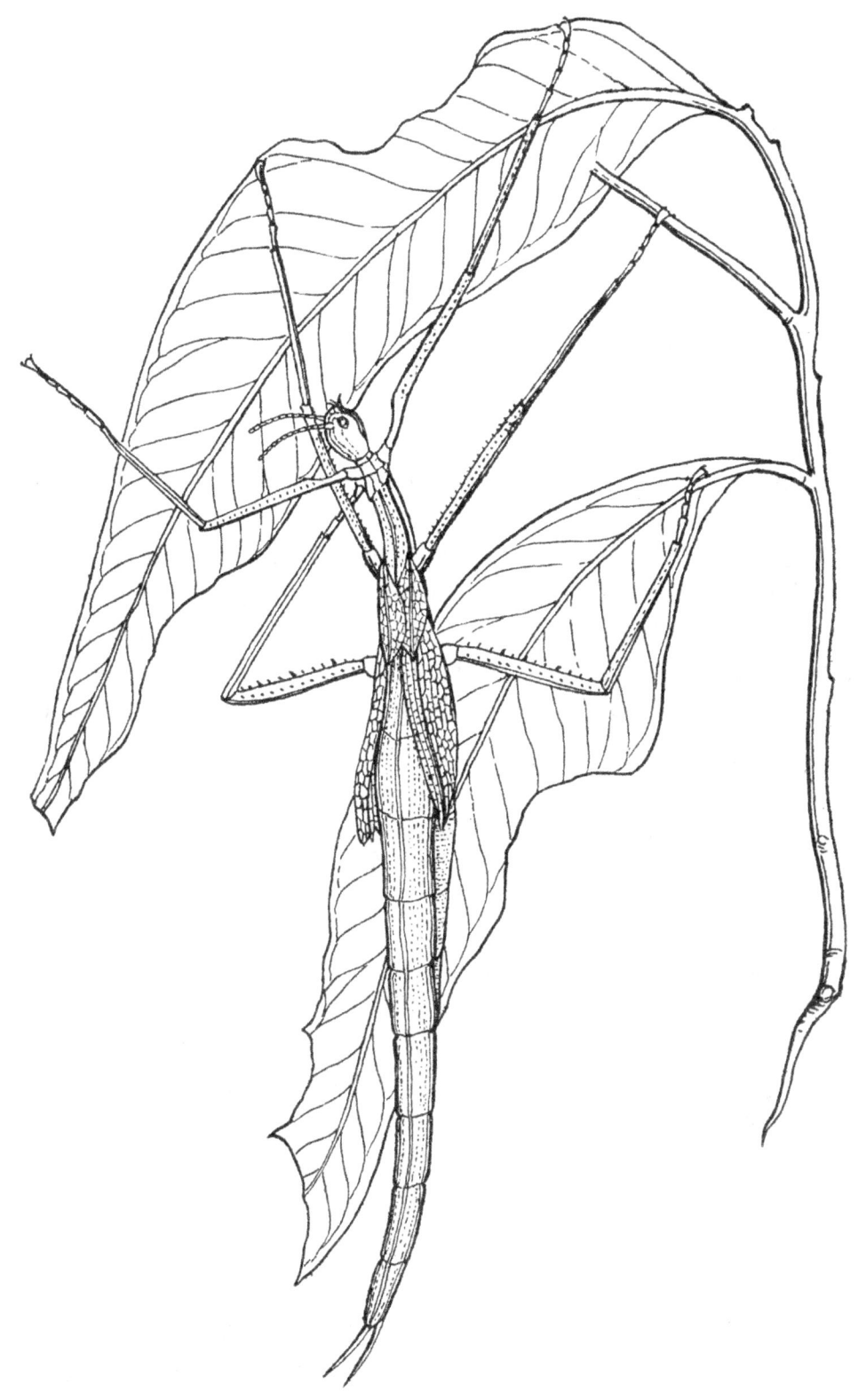

A lady phasmid, green, with tiny wings

Jewel of the Pond

DID you ever see a prettier thing than a dragonfly? Then perhaps it was a damsel-fly, which is very much the same, only smaller and daintier.

It is hard to understand why so many people are frightened of dragonflies, calling them horse-stingers and a few other unkind names, for they are quite harmless. They sting neither horses nor humans, and the only things they eat—like flies and mosquitoes—are not particularly nice to have around, anyway.

Perhaps they get their name for fierceness from the earlier parts of their lives, when they live underwater and hunt almost everything in sight. The young nymph is a very ferocious creature indeed. It has a huge lower lip which is called a mask, because it folds up over part of its face until there is something good to eat—most likely the larva or nymph of some other insect. Then, the mask springs open into the most fearsome-looking claw-like grasper, and the victim hasn't a hope of escaping.

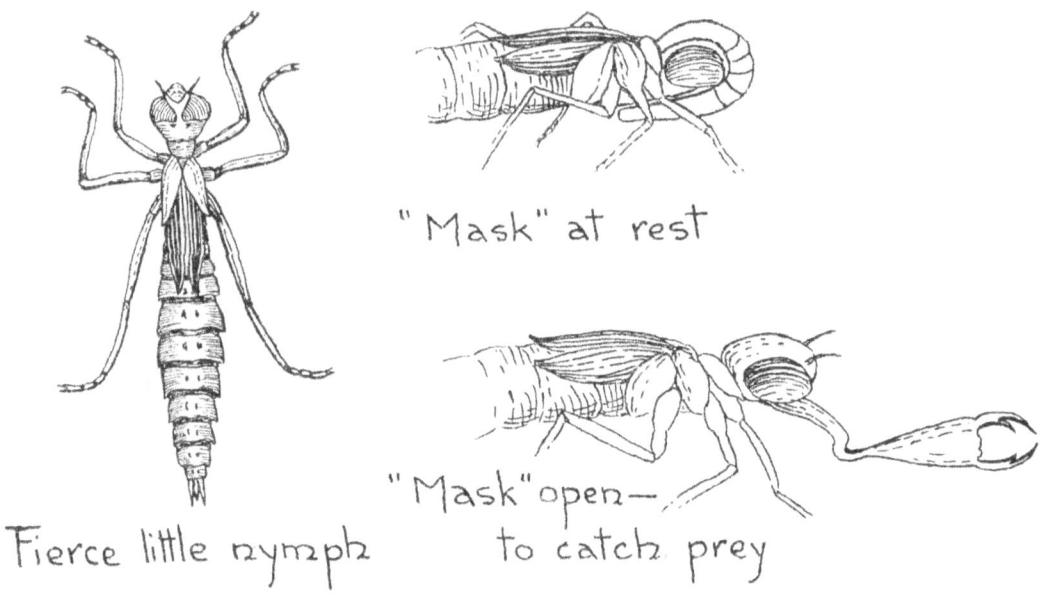

Fierce little nymph

"Mask" at rest

"Mask" open—to catch prey

This terror grows bigger, and moults its skin many times, before it is a full-sized nymph, with wing-pads. Then one day—perhaps after several years—something tells it that a great change is about to come, much greater than any since it first hatched out of that egg as a tiny, frail creature.

To be ready for this change, it leaves the water for the first time in its life. Almost timidly it climbs up the stem of one of the water-plants among which it has lived and grown, and then grips on to it tightly with those little claws while a wonderful new creature inside heaves and pushes to free itself from the rather ugly shell of the nymph.

Do try to watch this marvellous happening for yourself, some day. The frail shell slits open down the back, and—bit by bit—out comes a long, delicate little form with shiny, crumpled wings. The outside world is quite new to it, and it has no one to look after it until it becomes used to the strange place. It is utterly alone. Its legs and wings feel anything but strong. It holds on to the water-plant's stem

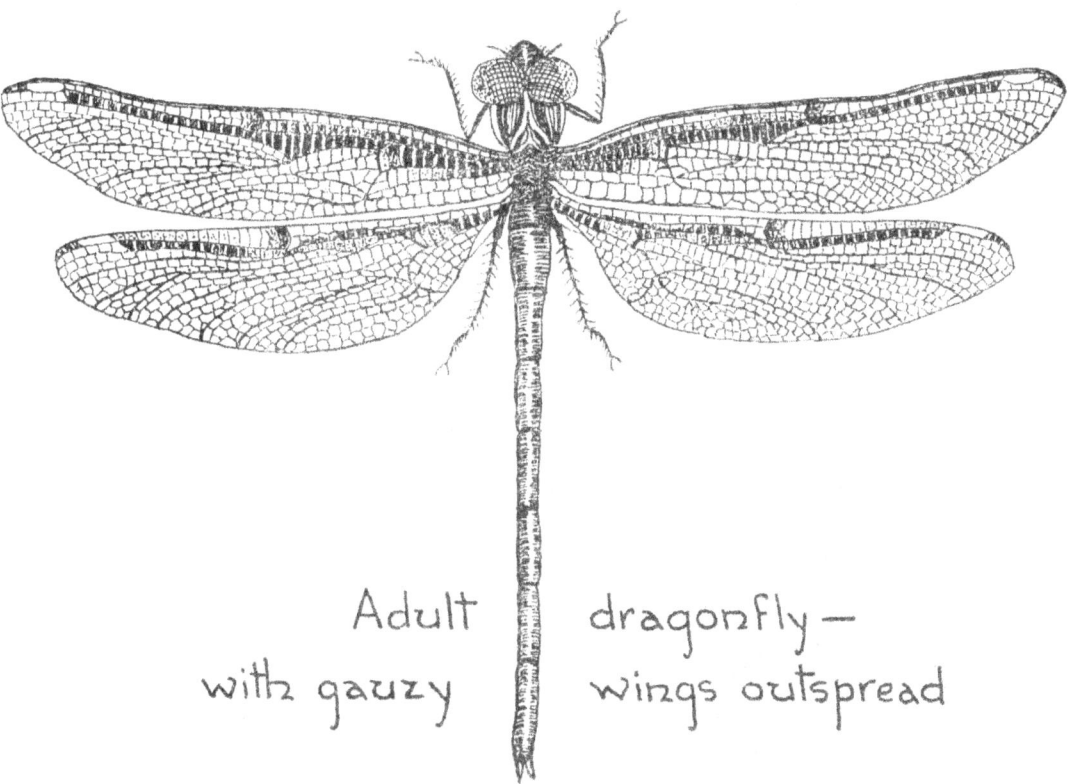

Adult dragonfly — with gauzy wings outspread

for a few moments, just above where its old skin is still clinging, then it flutters off rather weakly to a safe place, where its enemies will not find it while it dries off, rests, and grows stronger.

You have often seen dragonflies darting around over ponds and swamps, and no doubt you have tried to catch one, too. But have you ever succeeded? The dragonfly is one of the fastest insects on wings. If it wants to, it can dart around at 100 kilometres an hour. It can also swerve in any direction at great speed, or suddenly fly backwards if it sees danger. So a bird—or a human—has to be very smart indeed if it wants to catch one.

And another thing that you cannot capture is a dragonfly's beautiful colours. As it flies and hovers, they flash like the brightest opals—but if it is killed and placed in an insect collection, they fade completely, leaving it a dull uninteresting brown.

We were talking about all this one day while watching a beautiful one flitting about over a pond in one of the city parks. "Isn't it big!" said Tess.

"That's nothing," Chris answered. "I've read about dragonflies in a library book—and you know, Tess, in prehistoric days, they used to be enormous. Their wings used to be 700mm across when they were spread out. Think of that! And look, Tess," he went on, scarcely pausing for breath—"you see how its wings are arranged? They're straight out, and one behind the other. The back ones aren't sort of tucked underneath the front ones, the way they are in moths and butterflies." And he had a lot more to say, too.

Then our dragonfly darted into a ray of sunlight like a flashing jewel, and the next moment it disappeared.

Tess said, "Nature just didn't *mean* dragonflies to be captured, did she? They move so quickly, for one thing, and for another thing, you can't even keep their colours. They just *have* to be alive and free!"

I think she was right, don't you?

> Dragonfly nymph, how your fellows must fear you!
> You gobble up any who dare to come near you.
> And I'm sure you have one of the funniest faces
> Ever to goggle in watery places.
>
> But once you have wings, you are just like a jewel,
> Darting and hovering over a pool,
> Eating mosquitoes and having great fun,
> But never attempting to sting anyone.
>
> I love you, dear dragonfly. Please understand,
> And come for a moment to sit on my hand!

The Honey-Makers

MOST likely you know a lot about bees already, because such an enormous amount has been written about them. But every time I go around looking for something new and interesting, a bee seems to come along before anything else, as if to say, "You simply can't leave me out of your book!" So, let us talk a little, right away, about just a few of the things that make bees so wonderful.

It will have to be only a few of these wonders, because people have

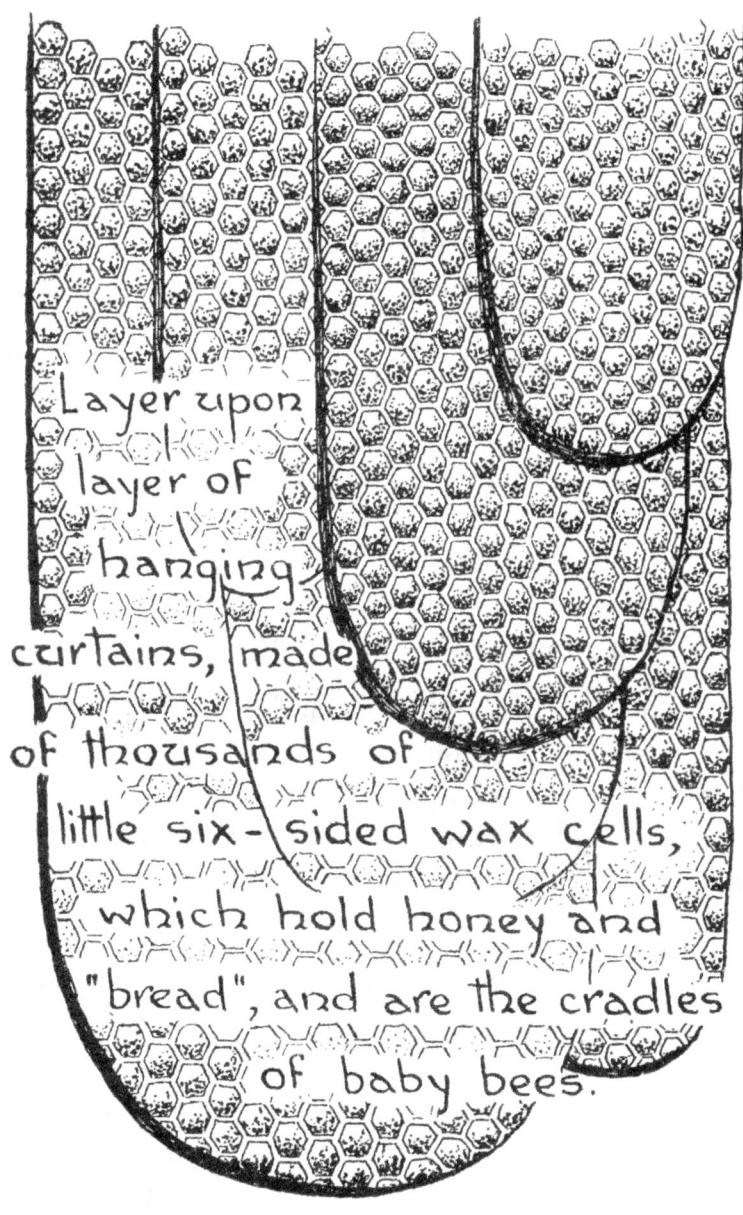

Layer upon layer of hanging curtains, made of thousands of little six-sided wax cells, which hold honey and "bread", and are the cradles of baby bees.

finished writing whole books before they could come to the end of the amazing things that bees can do.

A bee starts its life as a tiny egg which its mother—the queen of the hive—lays in a six-sided cell specially made for this purpose. The workers make these cells out of wax that they manufacture in their own bodies.

The queen works very hard at her job, laying about 3000 eggs a day, yet she carefully inspects each cell before placing an egg in it, and if she finds it the least bit dirty or imperfect, she passes it by without using it.

Three days after the egg has been laid, it hatches out into a tiny grub or larva. Nurse bees come along and feed it, first on royal jelly—a very precious food—and then on honey and pollen. They do this for five days, and the little larva grows and grows, shedding one skin after another. Then, when it is quite big, one of the nurses covers its cell with wax. This is the sign that it must now stop eating and become a pupa. And, of course, while it is a pupa, all of those marvellous things happen that are necessary when an insect changes from one form into another quite different one.

Goodness knows how long we would take to produce these same changes in a laboratory—but in a mere 13 days, when the top of that wax cell is pushed off, out comes a perfect bee. Certainly it looks a little tired and limp to begin with, but in no time it has straightened and combed itself out, and is ready to get on with its life's work.

And, in most cases, a life's work it is. A full hive contains about 50,000 or 60,000 bees, and by far the most of these are workers, who just keep on working without a stop until they die—usually after a few weeks—ragged and worn-out. All of these worker bees are the queen's daughters—some of the most talented and versatile little creatures in Nature.

They make wax, as well as building it into great hanging curtain-like walls, containing thousands of perfect little six-sided cells. For a while, they make royal jelly in their heads. They keep every tiniest part of the hive perfectly clean. They also control the temperature of the hive most cleverly. When it is too hot, they stand together at its entrance and fan currents of air through it with their wings. When it is too cold, they gather together in a large crowd, so that the air around them becomes warm from the heat of their bodies packed together. Although there is a special police force to protect the hive from enemies, there are times when extra help is needed. Then the workers come forward as warriors and thrust their stings into the hostile strangers, even though this means their own almost certain death, for their stings have barbs, which stick so fast into the enemy that they cannot be pulled out quickly without tearing the bees in two.

The workers also travel backwards and forwards endlessly, carrying pollen and nectar to their hive from wherever the best flowers are growing. These may be near at hand, or they may be many kilometres away, but whatever the distance, the workers carry great loads on each return journey, with their wings joined together by a row of hooks to give them greater strength. They carry the pollen in special little baskets on their hind legs, and they carry nectar inside their bodies in what is called the honey-stomach.

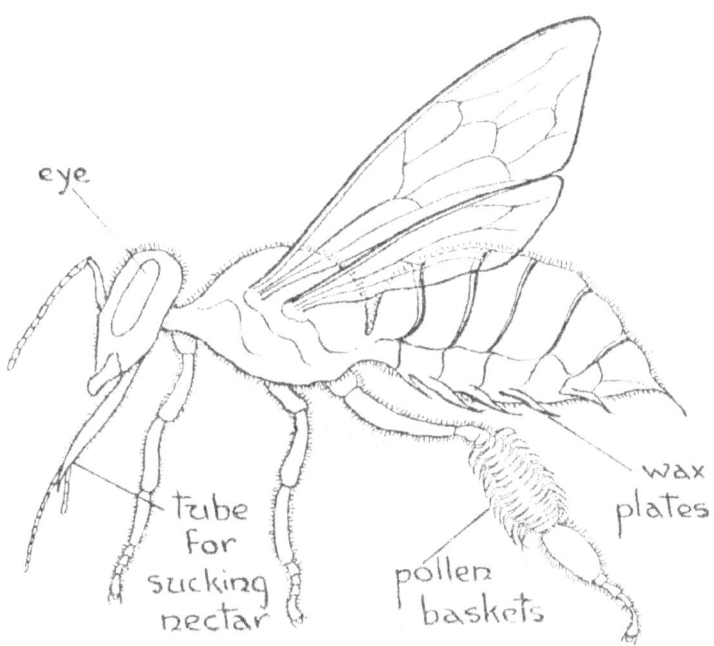

While they are carrying the nectar, chemicals in their honey-stomachs get busy on it, changing it into honey. Back in the hive, they hand it over to other workers, who pack it into the large group of cells known as the honeycomb—but only after they have worked it around in their mouths to get as much moisture out of it as possible. When a cell is quite full, one of the workers closes it up with a little wax lid that is perfectly airtight.

The pollen is packed into other cells, and mixed with a little honey to make a special kind of bread for the use of the colony.

If we were doing all this manufacturing and building, nursing, cleaning, carrying, air-conditioning, processing and storing of food, just think of all the things we would need—building materials, tools, trucks, waxes, varnishes, chemicals, and of course, all kinds of machinery, a few factories, and a laboratory. Yet the worker bees carry in their own tiny bodies all the equipment that is needed for the health, strength, comfort and cleanliness of their whole vast community. Whatever they are called upon to do, they can do it with their own natural resources. Isn't that wonderful!

In a community of bees, everything runs in perfect order. Left to themselves, they never make a mess of things. Yet they have no leader to tell them what to do. Each of them knows what to do, by the amazing instinct with which it is born, and which guides its

When the queen rests from egg-laying, all the bees near at hand hurry forward to do her some service

every action through life. They honour the queen and give her every attention, even combing her little fur coat and feeding her on nothing less than royal jelly as long as she lives, but she does not rule the hive—and nobody else does, either.

It is interesting to realise that the eggs laid by the queen bee are almost all exactly the same. There are no "queen" eggs, or "worker" eggs The little creatures that hatch out of them grow into different classes of bees because of the kind of food that is fed to them. (There is another kind of bee that we haven't talked of yet, the "drone" whose eggs have just the queen's bloodline in them, without her husband's.)

Larvae which are fed entirely on royal jelly become queens instead of workers. It seems to be as simple as that. Or at least, they become queens if they are lucky enough not to be killed by the other newly-born queens. For this is what so often happens.

When the existing queen is slowing off in her egg-laying job, the workers wisely produce a group of new ones—and these, as soon as they are born, fight one another fiercely until only one is left. They jostle, pull at and sting one another—and as their stings are made differently from those of the workers, they can use them again and again without hurting themselves. Finally, only one is left, and she, of course, becomes the new queen.

There are times, though, when two queens survive. This happens when the hive has become over-crowded, and a large number of its inhabitants are preparing to leave it, and set up another colony somewhere else. Naturally, they too must have their queen—so a crowd of workers quickly hurries along to protect one of the rivals—and when the victorious queen finds that she cannot get to this last remaining one, she forgets all her other victories and yells with rage. But the little worker bees stand firm and are not afraid, for they know that they are safe from the queen's sting. She uses this only on royalty.

When the time comes, they themselves perhaps, among many of their fellow bees, pour out of the hive with one of the queens they have raised so carefully. This is called "swarming", and is something that no other insects are known to do. When they find a good place for a new home, they settle down, and another colony of bees begins.

In each colony, there is a third group of bees apart from the workers and the queen. It is made up of a few hundred male bees or drones—and you cannot help feeling sorry for them. They are built in such a way that they can do nothing whatever to help with the constant work in the hive except to help with air-conditioning the hive when the temperature is wrong, and they have to depend on the "good nature" of the workers for their food, since they are also unable to feed themselves. They flit from hive to hive, since they don't really fit in with all of the busy hive activities. Their whole job in life is—if needed—to become one of the queen's husbands when she leaves the hive on a high, swift marriage flight. Many drones follow her, but usually only one can keep pace with her. High up in the air, they marry, then immediately the drone falls to the ground, dead. So the queen of the bees is always a widow—but she is now able to lay eggs which will grow into new bees.

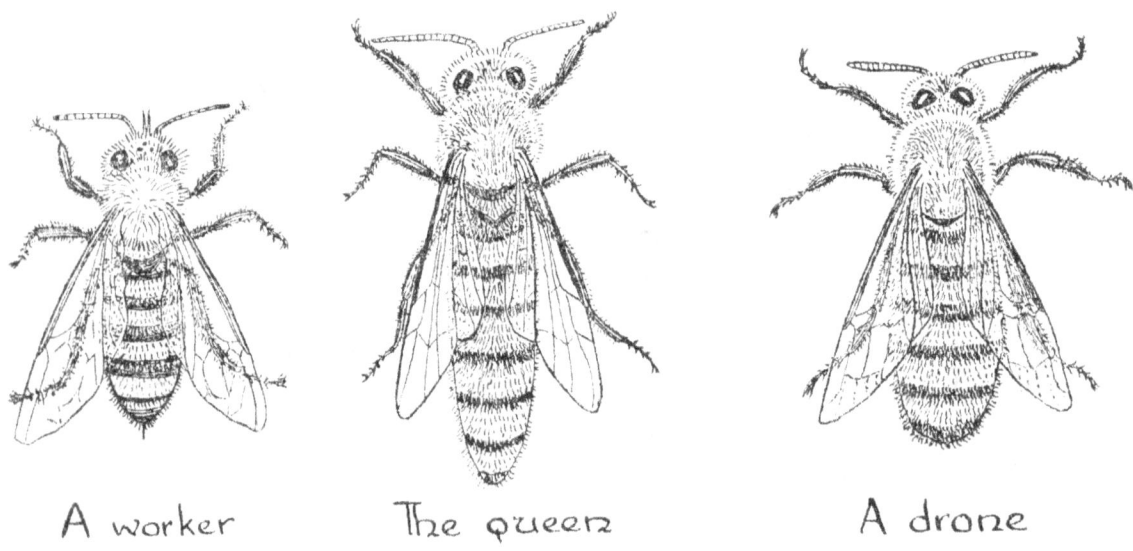

A worker   The queen   A drone

Usually, the drones are allowed to stay around until winter. But then, life in the hive becomes more difficult, and "useless" members can no longer be supported. So the workers throw the poor old drones out, to die of starvation and cold.

Of course, everybody knows that bees make honey from nectar—and while they are taking this nectar from flowers, the bees' little furry coats get a good dusting of pollen, which then brushes off on the next flowers they visit. This is called pollination, and it is very important to the flowers, as it enables them to produce seeds.

But what everybody has *not* understood for a long time is how the bees tell one another where the best flowers are.

A scout bee goes out to explore. She finds a good patch of flowers, returns to the hive, and in a few minutes other bees come pouring out, and go straight to where the scout has just come from. How is it done?

We do know now that the returning bee "speaks" to the others in the form of a dance, but we do not yet understand the meanings of all the variations in this dance. Sometimes the movements go round in circles, sometimes in straight or wavy lines, up and down, the different movements are repeated many or few times, and in these various ways the "scout" bee tells the others exactly where the flowers are—their exact distance and direction from the hive.

Following her instructions, the next bees that go out never make a mistake. When *they* return to the hive with their pollen baskets full of pollen and their nectar sacks full of nectar, they also do a little dance, and more bees go right straight out to the same patch of flowers. Then, at last, one group of bees comes back without dancing. This means that there is no more nectar left in that particular flower patch—and no more bees will be found going there after that.

Don't you agree now that, in the whole great world of insects, bees are some of the cleverest and most wonderful? Without them, so many things in our own world would be different, that it would scarcely seem like the same place. And what would flowers do without them, I wonder?

So, always be kind to them, won't you? And try to learn more about them, for the more you learn, the more delighted you will be.

Galls—and Other Oddities

QUITE often you must have noticed odd shapes and swellings on the leaves and stems of plants—even on their flowers and roots—and wondered what they were. Well they are known as galls, and one of these days, when plants know better, they will stop making them, for they do the plants a great deal of harm. They come about like this:

A fly, beetle, wasp, thrip, or some other small insect pierces the outer skin of the plant and lays an egg, or perhaps several eggs just underneath it. If the plant knew how to look after itself, it would produce some sort of chemical which would stop the eggs from hatching. But instead of this, it actually builds up around them a warm, comfortable shelter of plant cells. This shelter is a gall—and the strange thing is that the plant produces a specially shaped gall for each different kind of insect.

Sometimes it is round like a ball, other times like a bundle of tiny twigs. It can look very much like the cup moth's cocoon, or a ninepin, or some other curious shape. But whatever it looks like, the eggs inside it do very well indeed.

When the time comes, they hatch out into tiny larvae, which eat away until they are ready to become pupae. Still inside their comfortable shelter, they go into their pupal "sleep", and after a while they work their way out as adult insects ready to lay more eggs around which plants will build more galls.

Some of the strangest looking galls, like heads with spreading horns, or collections of curved tubes, are caused not by the eggs, but by the larvae of some kinds of scale insects. These tiny larvae fasten on to leaves or stems—and the plant immediately builds galls around

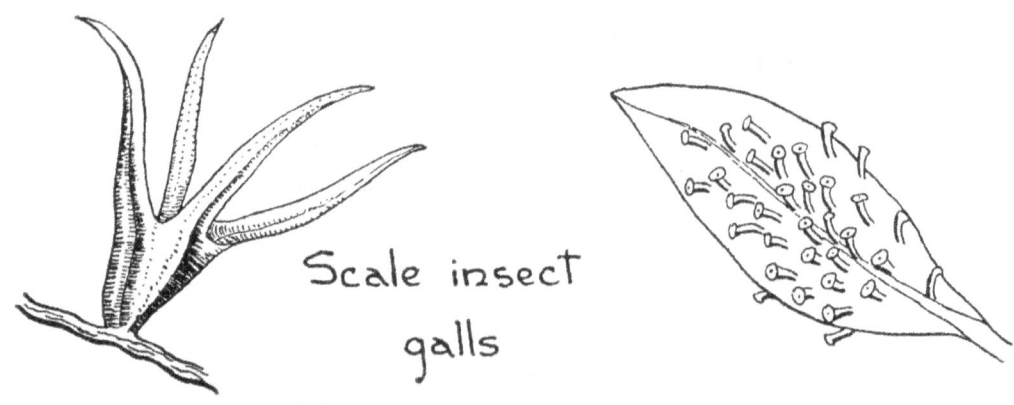

Scale insect galls

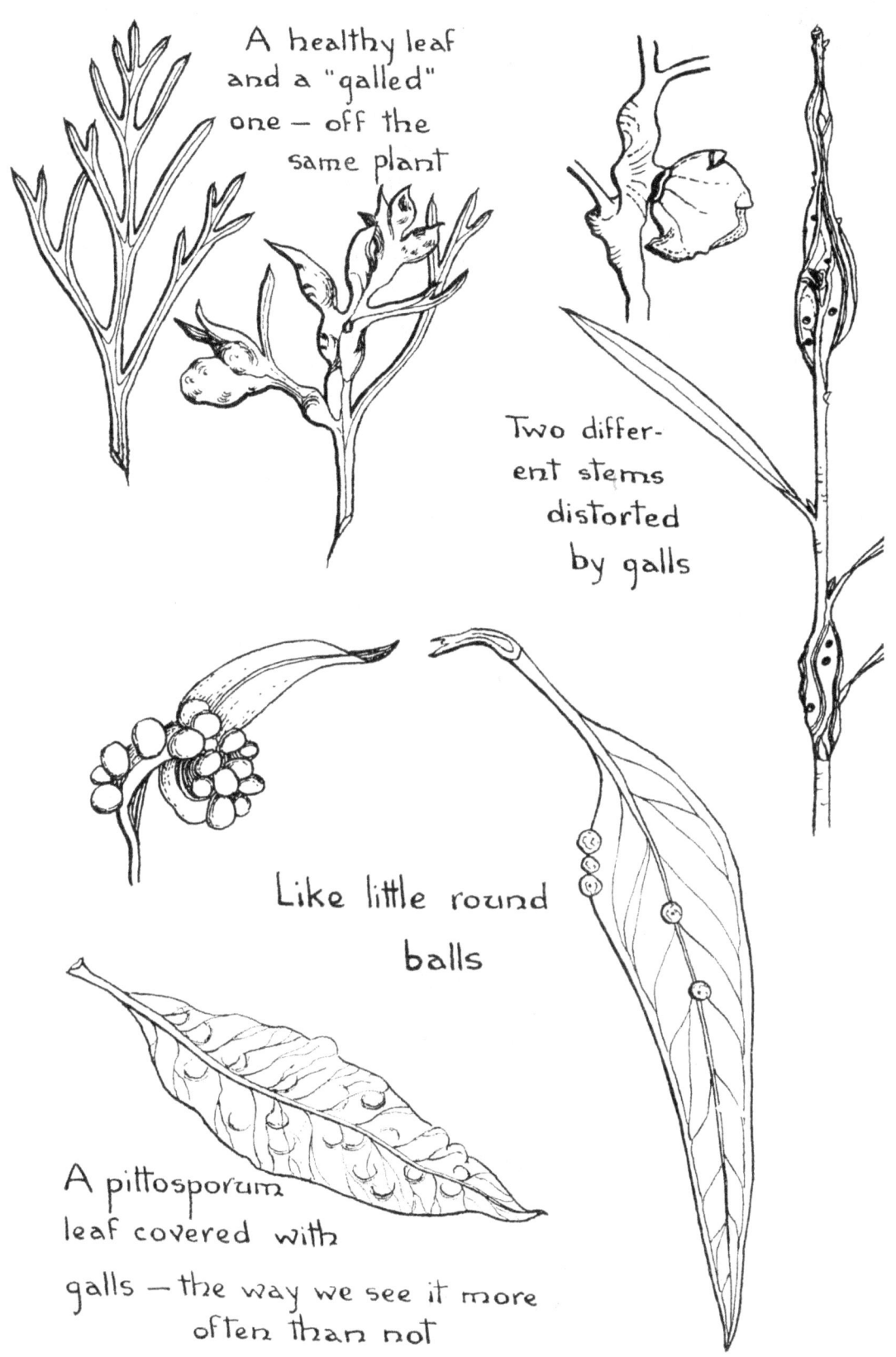

them, as it does around the eggs of other insects. And the little soft woolly patches that you sometimes find on gum-leaves are caused by one of the mites—a tiny animal with eight legs, like a spider.

The leaves and stems of the wild daphne (or pittosporum) are so often covered with galls, that a tree without them is almost abnormal. They are caused by two of the tiniest flies you could imagine—just like specks. One kind attacks the leaves, the other kind, the stems—and the strange thing is that they don't seem to do the tree too much harm. In this case, plant and gall-making insect have reached a kind of balance. But even so, the tree would be a lot better off and better-looking without its invading armies of tiny flies.

Altogether, as our drawings show, plants are distorted horribly by these galls. Also, their food supplies and their very tissues are steadily eaten by the tiny creatures sheltering inside them. So there isn't a good word to be said for them, as far as plants are concerned.

Another thing you might have wondered about is the "scribbled" look that you often see on the leaves of nasturtiums and other plants. These marks are actually the homes of certain little grubs or larvae.

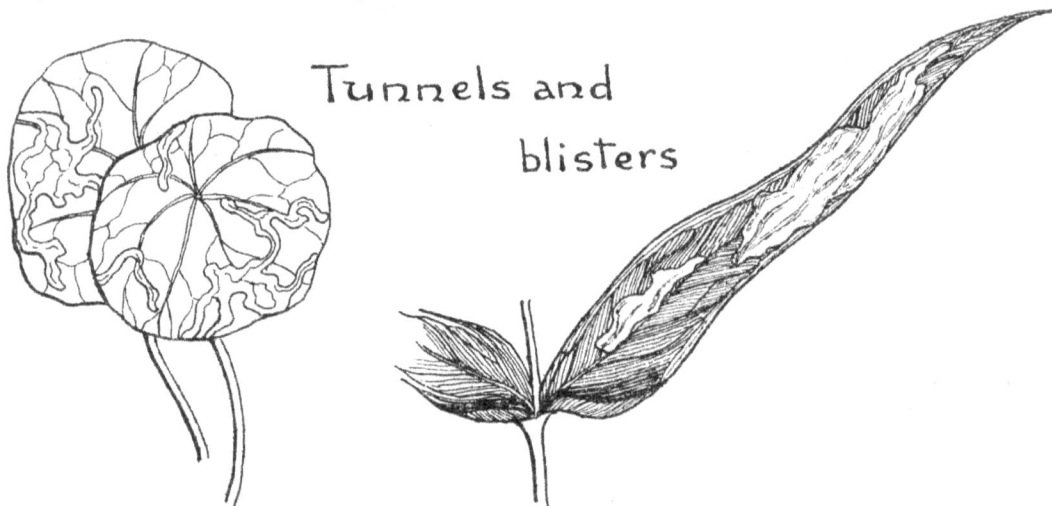
Tunnels and blisters

They are tunnels that the larvae have bored out just underneath the surface of the leaves, and safe inside these, they can feed on the cells of the leaves to their hearts' content. Then, still safe and sound inside their tunnels, they settle down into pupae—and at last, when the time comes, they work their way out into the open air as fully grown insects—perhaps as some kind of weevil or fly.

Of course you know that when leaves fall to the ground, they gradually rot away. The fleshy parts of them decay first, and you will often find a "skeleton" leaf on the ground with nothing but veins—a close network of them. Sometimes, though, you may find one of these skeleton leaves still on the tree. As it hasn't just rotted there, what has happened to it? Most likely it has had all its fleshy parts eaten by masses of little grubs—the larvae of one of our saw-flies. When the leaves of fruit-trees are attacked in this same way, it's probably because a black-coloured cherry and pear slug has been having a feed, on its way to becoming another kind of sawfly.

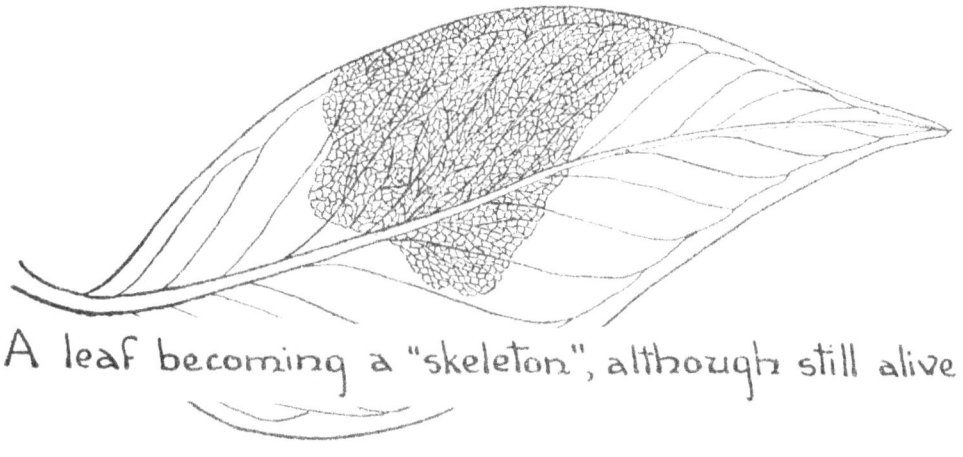

A leaf becoming a "skeleton", although still alive

Then, there are those big blisters that you often see on leaves. These are mostly caused by yet another kind of sawfly, whose larvae live safely underneath the blister, and eat the soft parts of the leaf.

It is a great pity that all of these insects do so much damage to plants, for plants are some of the more beautiful things on Earth, as well as some of the most important.

It Eats Everything—and is Paper-thin

THE two insects on these pages do not look very much alike, yet both of them are cockroaches. This first one, you will often see running around where it shouldn't—in your sheds or garage, or even right inside your home. It used not to live in Australia at all, but came here from Europe—and others have come from Asia and America.

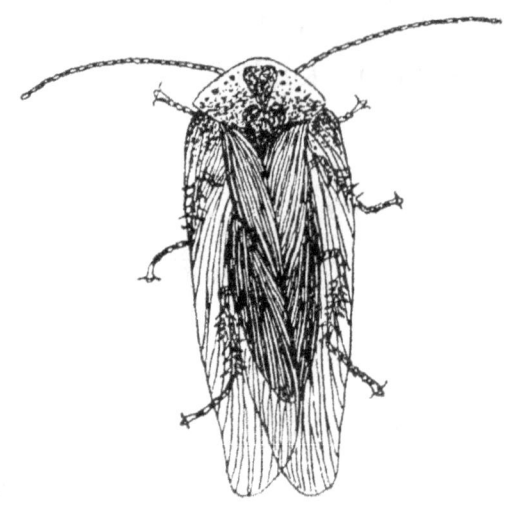

They are a terrible nuisance to us in large numbers, for they eat almost everything—shoes, books, wallpaper, fur, and so on. But they also eat the dead bodies of their own kind and of other insects, so they do quite an important cleaning-up job as well. We can usually find a good point to balance a bad one, can't we?

Lady cockroaches seem at first to be good, careful mothers, for they lay their eggs side by side in a little bag, and carry this around with them constantly until the eggs are ready to hatch. But then, they just attach the bag to anything that happens to be lying around, and forget all about it. So they are not really very thoughtful after all.

The baby cockroaches, or nymphs, come out of their eggs without anyone to watch over them, and without the slightest idea that they ever had a mother. At first they are very small and pale, and they have no wings, but as they grow bigger and moult one skin after another, they gradually become darker—and when they are quite grown-up, they have four wings, the same as most other insects.

The two on top are tough, and fold over each other, protecting the two frailer ones underneath. But some Australian bush cockroaches have only tiny wings, or none at all—and others who do grow them, find them such a nuisance as they rummage about among fallen leaves, bark and other bush litter, that they get their fellows to pull them off.

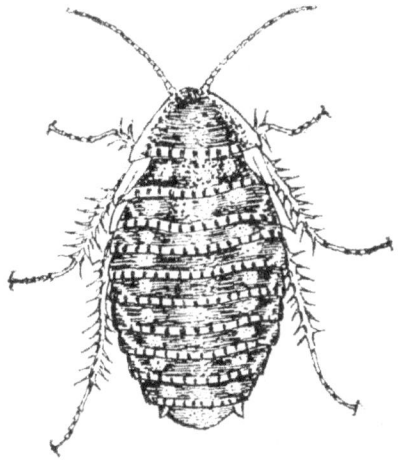

Here is one of our bush cockroaches, its dark brown skin prettily marked with lighter patches. It doesn't run around in city homes, making itself unwelcome. It just lives happily underneath rocks and leaves and bits of bark—and, as you see, it is wingless. It might look fat in our drawing, but that's just because it is wide. Actually it is so thin that it is hard to imagine where it keeps its insides. Resting on a piece of paper while we drew it, it seemed scarcely to rise above the paper.

Nearly all cockroaches are thin like this—which is one reason why there are so many of them on Earth. And another reason is that they run like lightning. If an enemy approaches, all they have to do is to disappear like a flash into some tiny crevice where the enemy cannot possibly follow them—and so they escape unharmed while slower or fatter insects get killed.

You will, of course, find cockroaches in the daytime, but when you do, it is mostly because they have been disturbed, and they are rushing away under cover again, for they feel most uncomfortable out in the open or in the light. They are creatures of darkness who mostly rest during the day and go out eating at night. And judging by the number of things they enjoy, one could scarcely imagine that a cockroach would ever go hungry.

Those "Waspish" Fellows!

DID you know that paper is made out of wood? It's hard to imagine, isn't it? Yet it's the truth. And when people discovered how to do this, they took another great step forward in civilisation. Yet a group of tiny, fragile insects had already been making paper out of wood countless centuries before people even dreamt of it.

The insects didn't, of course, make it to write on, or to wrap parcels in, but to use as the building material for their nests.

You would have to be a very light, dainty little creature indeed to be able to move around a paper house, and work in it, without breaking it, and these insects—the paper wasps—are just that. They have delicate wings that fold alongside their bodies like fans. Even the largest of them wouldn't be more than 12mm long, they have the tiniest waists, and they are prettily coloured in brown and yellow.

Wasps do not always live in groups—many of them prefer to stay alone, or in pairs—but the paper wasps form communities.

Do you remember some other insects that form communities? Ants, bees, and termites. But paper wasps are very different from these others. They are not so highly developed—not by a long way—and their "city" does not go on living and growing year after year. They do not make honey as the bees do, or store food as the ants do, or cultivate gardens as the ants and termites do.

The queen paper wasp begins the nest by attaching a "paper-pulp" stalk to anything handy, like a fence, a tree, or the underside of eaves. (At home, we once found a dozen or more nests in a mass of Virginia creeper.) Next, the queen builds a little six-sided cell on to the stalk, very much like the cells that bees make. Around this first cell, she builds a few more—and in each of them she lays an egg, fixing it firmly to the bottom of the cell.

After a while the larva hatches out of this. It's a small, helpless creature, like a grub, with no legs, and it too stays fixed to the bottom of the cell. If the queen did not feed this first batch of larvae, they would surely die of starvation, but instead they grow bigger and

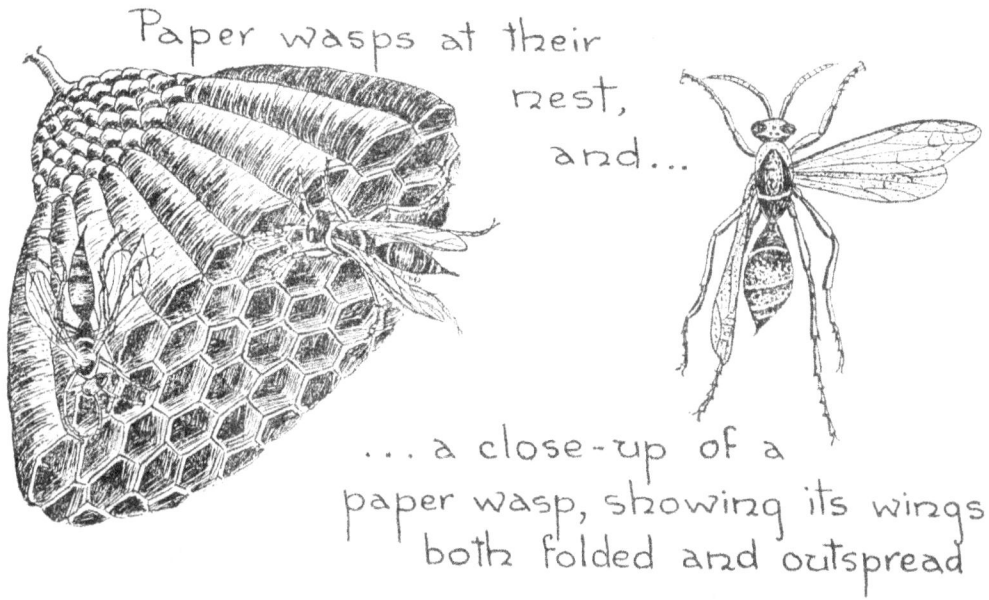

Paper wasps at their nest, and... ...a close-up of a paper wasp, showing its wings both folded and outspread

bigger until they are ready to become pupae. Now, for the first time, they do something useful. They spin a silky covering for their cells before settling down in readiness for their great change.

When this change is complete, out they come from their cells—full-grown worker wasps ready to help their queen. And, the same as in other insect colonies, these workers are female.

They immediately set to work building more cells for the queen to lay eggs in, and gradually the nest grows bigger. When the new larvae hatch out, the workers feed them as carefully as bees, ants and termites feed *their* young—only on a different diet. Paper-wasp larvae are reared on delicious, chewed-up caterpillars and spiders. And in return, the workers take small amounts of liquid from the mouths of the larvae. They seem to enjoy this as much as ants, which enjoy the oiliness that they lick off the skins of their larvae.

As well as being good builders and nurses, these workers are also fierce guardians of their nest, and, even if they only imagine that someone is going to interfere with it, they rush out angrily with a very painful sting. So do be careful if ever you find a wasp's nest.

Well, all of this activity goes on for several months—the queen laying eggs, the workers chewing up spiders and caterpillars, and feeding them to the larvae, and moulding new nest cells, and fighting off intruders. But, clever though they are, they never think of storing food away in any of those cells. So, when winter comes and there aren't many insects or other small creatures around, the colony dies of starvation.

Just before this, however, a few male wasps emerge—for the first time in the colony's history. They marry a few of the female wasps, then die with all the rest, and only those few newly-married females—or young queens—are left to carry on the paper-wasp story.

But now, they are all alone. They have no company of busy workers flitting around them, and none of the summer warmth that made their lives so pleasant and gay. Their pretty little paper nest is abandoned, with no tiny white babies—or larvae—in its cells, so they just creep away into some sheltered spot and stay there, under cover, right through the winter.

If they did not do this, there would never have been any paper wasp colonies after the first one. But as soon as warmer weather starts, the young queens creep out again and choose a good place to begin a new nest. They scrape little shavings of wood off trees or fences, mix these with saliva, then mould them into the stalk and those first cells that we spoke of at the beginning.

There are many other kinds of wasps, some of which build homes of clay. You may find a group of little clay tunnels hidden away somewhere, or a pretty little clay "vase" made by potter or mason wasps attached to a stem. You may find a big ungainly-looking mass of clay tubes made by mud-dauber wasps, perhaps with a number of holes in it where the adult wasps have come out.

These mason and mud-dauber wasps feed their young in a way that seems most unpleasant, even though it is clever.

Inside each clay nest there are separate cells—sometimes many, sometimes only a few. As soon as she has built one of these cells, the wasp goes out on a hunting trip for spiders or caterpillars, and, if

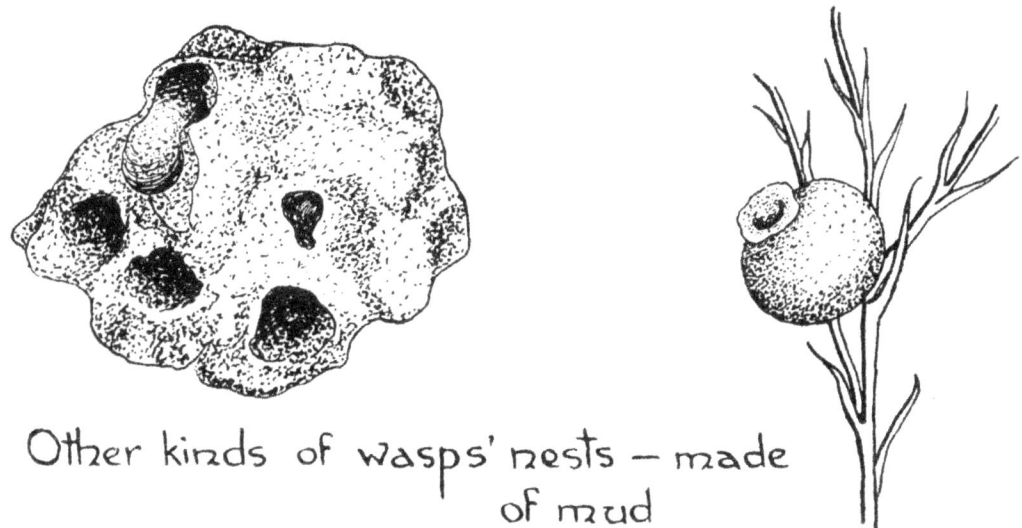

Other kinds of wasps' nests – made of mud

her victims are slow-moving caterpillars, they give her no fight. She quickly stings one, and immediately the spider or caterpillar is—not killed, but paralysed. In this state, she drags it to the nest, pushes it down into the cell, then seals the cell up with a covering of clay.

In due time, a larva hatches out of the egg—and ready to hand is food enough for its whole larval life. It will eat fresh spider or caterpillar meat—which, of course, remains fresh because the animal is still alive. Then, when it has eaten enough, the larva will spin a cocoon around itself and become a pupa. And at last it will come out in the form of a wasp which will build more clay cells and paralyse more creatures.

Other wasps build underground tunnels in sandy soil, with "cell" tunnels branching out from them, just a little bit like the tunnels that ants build. Only into each of the cells they drag a paralysed spider or cicada, then deposit an egg which in a short time will feed on the poor, living, though helpless creature.

So, we cannot feel happy about the behaviour of wasps toward their fellow beings, but also we should remember that they do not think out these cruel ways for themselves. It's just Nature's arrangement to make sure that the baby wasps will have plenty of fresh meat to eat, even after weeks, in hot weather, without the help of a refrigerator. And we can at least be glad that, most likely, in its paralysed state, the insect or spider being eaten feels no pain.

> Your stings are most unfriendly, and
> Your temper, wasp, is frightful.
> If one just goes up *near* your nest,
> You feel annoyed and spiteful.
>
> But what I'm really grateful for,
> You vicious little raider,
> Is that *I* am not a caterpillar,
> Spider, or cicada.

A Moth Without Wings

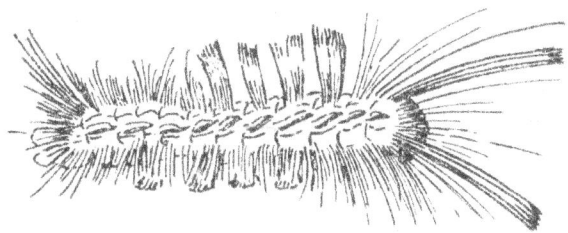

ONE day, at home, we found a small fluffy caterpillar that rather puzzled me, for it was nibbling happily at a gum-leaf, and I knew that it was supposed to eat wattle-leaves—and a gumtree is not a wattle.

It was such a beautiful little thing, with soft silvery-grey "fur" and four white "plumes", that Tess immediately called it Prince, and we brought it inside, with a branch of gum-leaves, to watch.

As the days passed and it ate more and more, it kept growing bigger and more handsome. Those four plumes seemed to grow thicker and silkier, and it had two lovely black-tipped "horns" on the head, which also seemed to grow longer and thicker.

Then one evening Tess announced excitedly, "Mummie, what do you think? Prince is making a cocoon!" And sure enough, there it was underneath a couple of gum-leaves which it had already fastened together, spinning away with fine, pale-yellow silk. Backwards and

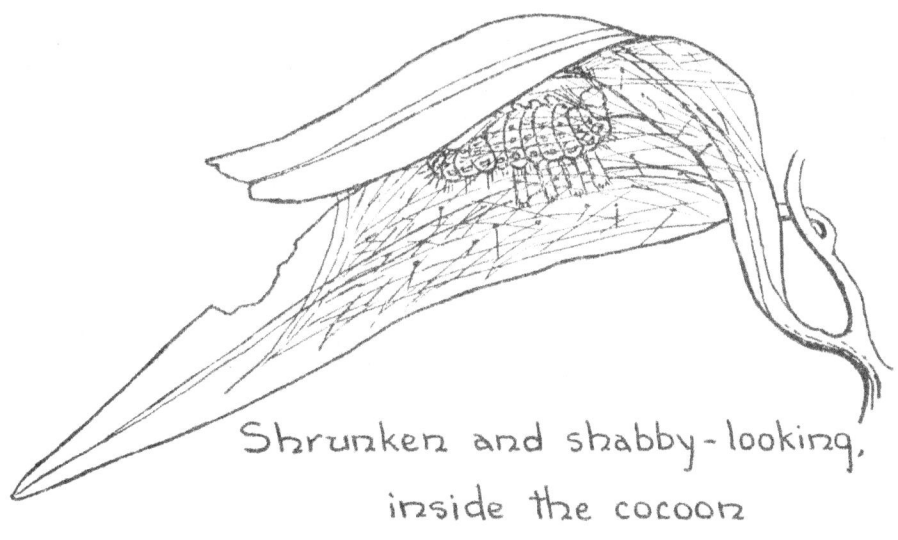

Shrunken and shabby-looking, inside the cocoon

forwards went its little head, upwards and sideways, carrying the silk in all directions, making a soft, delicate mesh.

By the end of the next day it was lying very quietly in that silk cradle, but looking a great deal thinner and sort of ragged. Those plumes were quite small, and the "horns" seemed to have disappeared altogether. Then we realised that it had woven the threads from these into the cocoon.

We had read about this type of caterpillar, and we knew that when it became a moth it would be either a gentleman with prettily patterned wings, or a lady without wings at all, and with a round, dumpy little body. Tess said, "I do hope Prince isn't a lady." But as the days passed, and we kept watching through the thin, silky cocoon, it became obvious that it was a lady after all. So now we had to start calling it Princess instead of Prince.

But she didn't look the least bit like a princess, and for a while we were *all* disappointed. It does seem so odd for a moth not to have pretty feelers and wings.

Then one morning—11 days after the cocoon had been made, two tiny white eggs appeared inside it—and by the end of that same day, there were dozens of them, and by the next morning there were more

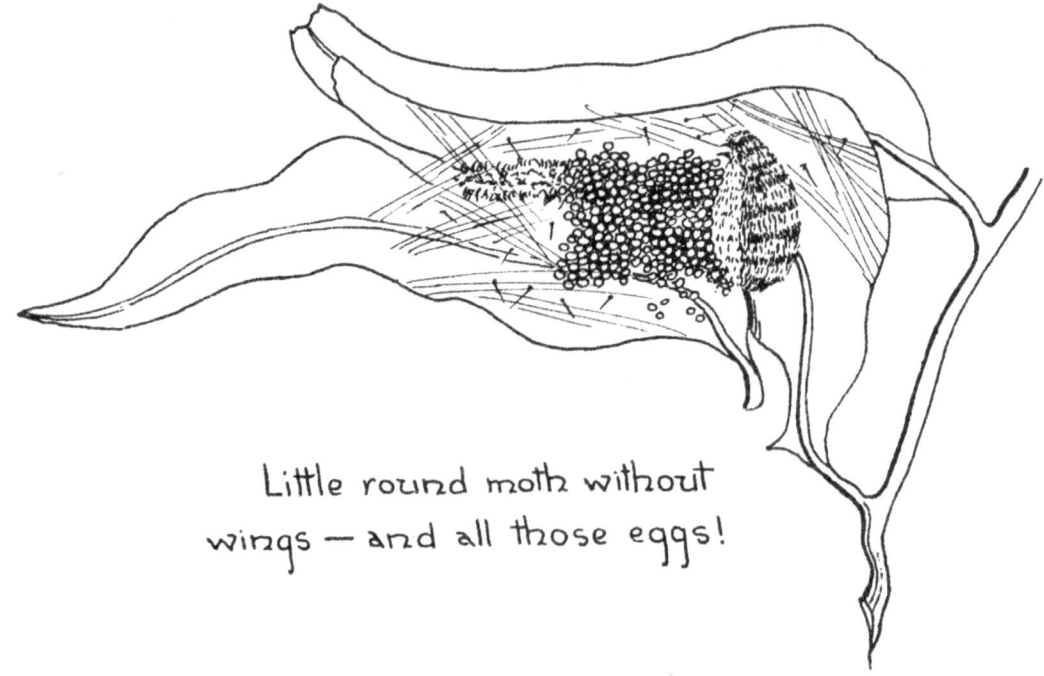

Little round moth without wings — and all those eggs!

again. It was a whole mound of eggs, and still the little round moth was there, inside the cocoon, eating nothing, seeing nothing of the beautiful world into which she had been born—just laying all those eggs, and then waiting to die.

By this time we were no longer disappointed. We loved the little soft round thing even more than we would have loved a showy gentleman moth with wings, and we felt rather sad for her. But after all, for her, that was as long and as full a life as any of us live in our different ways.

In time, each of the eggs that she had laid could hatch out into another handsome silvery-grey caterpillar with four white plumes and two little brush-like horns with black tips—just like Prince—and the whole story would begin all over again.

What our moth would have looked like if it had been "Prince"

Caterpillars That Decorate Their Homes

INSIDE each of the little cases drawn for this story, lives a caterpillar—and it has just about the oddest habits that any caterpillar could have.

It hatches out of its egg inside one of these cases, and immediately works its way out and drops on to a leaf, swinging down on a long silky thread. It must be great fun. At this stage, the baby caterpillar is very tiny, and has a long life ahead of it—fully a year—so it sets to work right away building itself a little shelter. It weaves this cleverly with the silky thread that comes from its own body.

At first the shelter looks like a tiny ice-cream cone upside-down, or a party cap, and underneath it the baby caterpillar feels quite safe. It eats away and keeps growing bigger and bigger, and gradually enlarges its shelter until, instead of being a mere covering, it now has a real little home. And, as well as adding to its home's size, it actually begins to decorate that home.

It breaks off bits of leaves and twigs, and fastens them on to the outside of the home in numbers of different arrangements. Sometimes such homes (or cases, as they are called) are really beautiful.

This funny little caterpillar stays indoors for the whole of its life. Only the top part of its body ever comes out, to move around or to eat. But if anything frightens it, it quickly slips right back in again, out of sight, and holds the top of its case tightly closed.

It moves about quite rapidly when it wants to, clinging, walking and climbing with its tiny front legs, its home swinging along below it.

Then one day, it fastens this home on to something extra tightly, closes the top of it for the last time, and settles down to become a pupa—still inside it. If it is going to be a gentleman moth when it wakens, it turns around head-downwards; if a lady, it stays upright. So it's a queer little creature in every possible way, isn't it?

The gentleman moth, when he is ready, pushes out of his case and flies for all he is worth, looking for a mate. He dashes around so

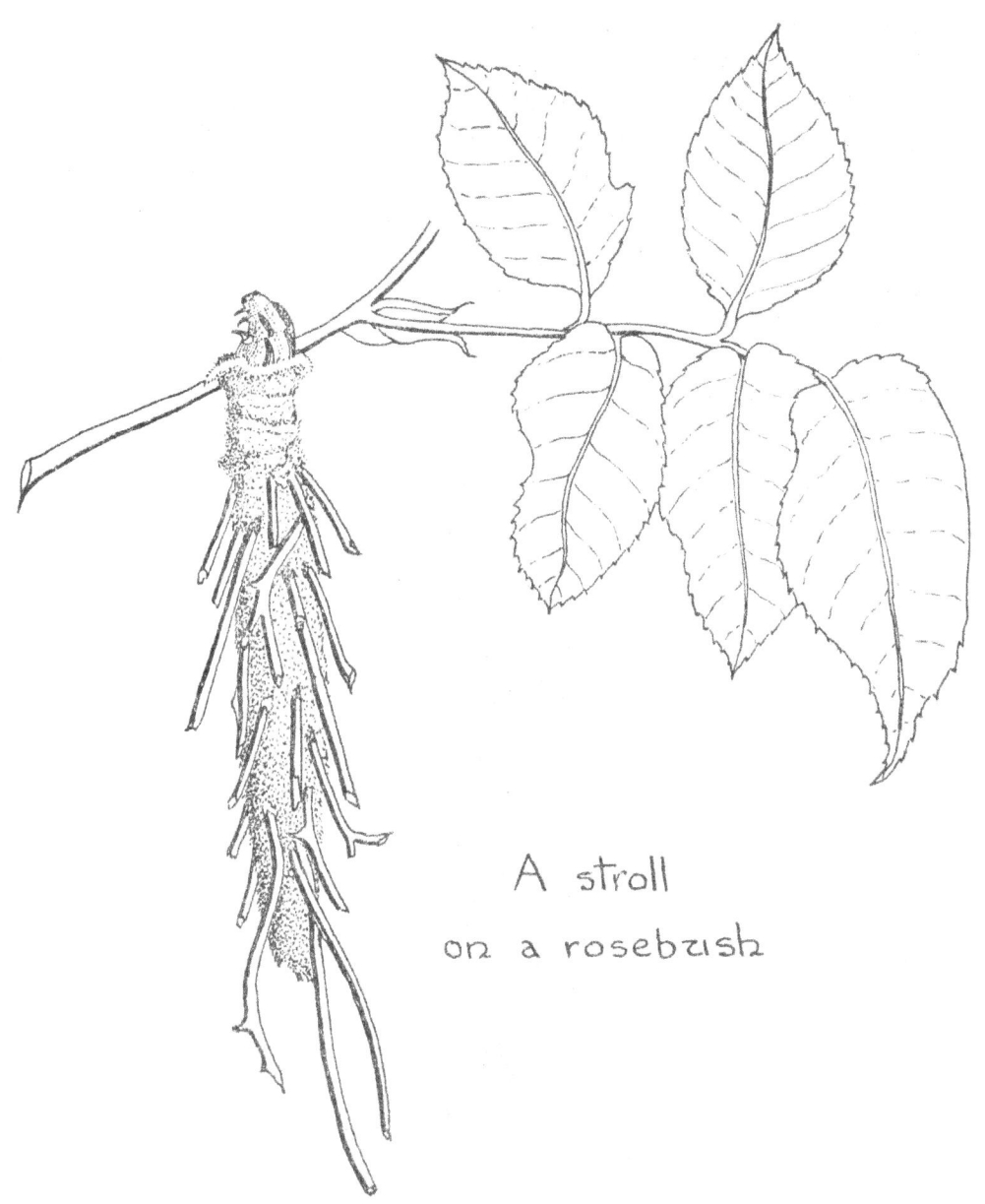

A stroll on a rosebush

recklessly that he soon breaks his wings and looks very ragged indeed. But the lady moth is quite different.

She has no wings, no real legs, mouth, or eyes, and never knows anything about the outside world. Right there, inside her little decorated case, she lays her eggs and dies.

Then, of course, in time, tiny new caterpillars hatch out of the eggs, and swing down on fine silken threads until they find some nice leaves to eat. Quickly they start building their little cone-like shelters—and there we are back at the beginning of our story.

When you next see one of these little cases hanging on a tree, a wooden fence—even on a brick wall or a window-sill—stop and have a good look at it, and you will find yourself marvelling at the caterpillar that made it with such patience and skill—and with such an "eye for beauty".

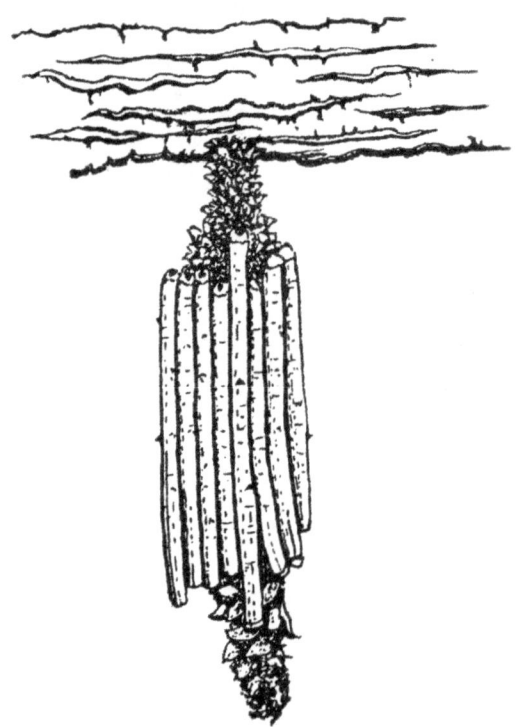

Casemoth at rest

The Caterpillar That Became a "Hawk"

HERE is a real giant of a caterpillar, with a fierce-looking spine at its tail. But the spine isn't fierce at all in reality, and we very nearly passed by without even noticing him on our privet hedge, for its colours are green, grey and white, and with these it can hide perfectly among the privet leaves and branches, in spite of its large size.

When we did see it, we brought it inside with a few branches, and set it up comfortably to watch. Tess said, "It can't grow any bigger, anyway." But it did. And it had an enormous appetite. We always seemed to be getting fresh branches to eat.

Chris said, "If we had a few more like this, we wouldn't have a hedge."

Tess told him not to be impolite, because a giant caterpillar had to have a giant appetite, and that this one had a very nice gentle nature, besides. As she said this, she went to stroke it—and just as if to show how ungentle it could be, it reared up suddenly like this

and seemed quite annoyed at having been disturbed. Tess sprang away with shock. She had never seen a caterpillar behave like this before.

Well, one day it stopped eating and just kept wandering around restlessly, this way and that, as though it had no idea of what it wanted. And at last, a few hours later, it burrowed down under the earth and disappeared from view. Now, we knew, it had finished with life as a larva, and was going to become a pupa.

We had heard that these larvae took a long time to pupate, so we were careful about disturbing it. Then, after about a week and a half, we gently pushed the earth aside to have a look—and to our surprise, there it was, still a caterpillar, moving its head around—only instead of having a nice "privet" colouring, it was now a dirty grey.

We quickly put the soil back over, and didn't look again for more than two weeks. Now, it was a very odd-looking creature indeed—a large, hard pupa, dark brown and shiny, with a funny little hook bending backwards from the head. Well, we had a good look, and sketched it, then put it back into the earth—and nothing else happened for a few weeks.

Then, one evening, we heard a sound, and when we looked, there—just about to try its beautiful wings—was a large, furry moth, mostly grey in colour, and very lovely indeed. It had a longer body than moths usually have—fattish at the top, and narrow at the end—and underneath its face was a long coiled tube. This was what had been inside the pupa's hook, and when we set it free, our moth would use it as a straw, for sucking nectar from deep down in flowers.

The next day we did set it free. For a while, it tumbled about very clumsily on the ground, but when it took flight, it shot off so quickly that it was hard to believe it was a moth. Now we knew why these are called hawk moths—for hawks are the swiftest of birds.

We hurried after it, and there, at the other end of the garden, it was hovering over a flower, sipping nectar from it while resting in mid-air with its wings fluttering. So now we knew why these are sometimes also called humming-bird moths—for humming-birds do exactly the same.

The next moment it had shot away again—this time out of sight—and we went inside marvelling at this strange and beautiful moth, nicknamed after two very special kinds of birds. Certainly we could never have imagined this moth coming from that large green caterpillar on our privet hedge with its up-rearing front, and a spine at the tail.

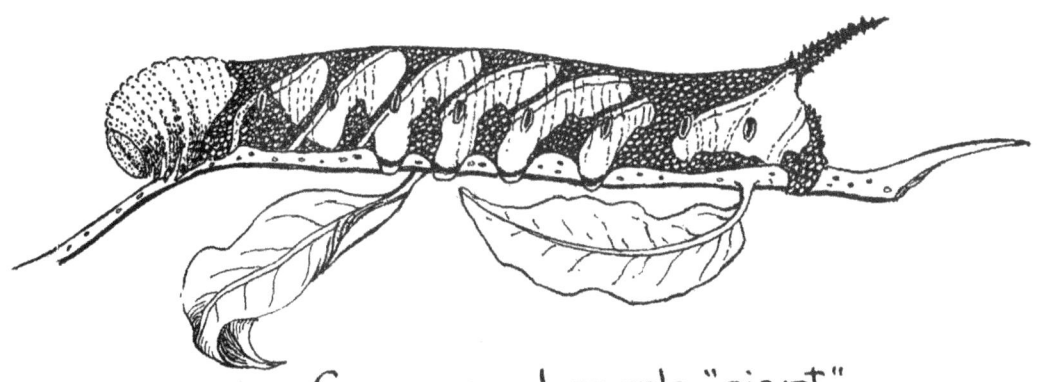

Green and purple "giant"

The pupa — like polished wood

Grey-brown "hawk"

Caterpillar With a Sting

MOST insects and caterpillars are really beautiful when you look into them—and this one is no exception. It has a lovely pattern of yellow, white, black and grey—and its eight little tufts of spines (four at the front and four at the back) are red.

But you have to be very careful not to pick this caterpillar up with your fingers or brush against it, because those pretty little spines will give you the most awful sting, which you will keep on feeling for hours.

Chris knows. He touched this particular one without noticing, as he brushed past one of our young gumtrees—and he said he had never felt such a painful sting.

You can see how different this is from most caterpillars. It's more like a slug, and the whole of its underneath is smooth and pale yellow, with great suction strength. You simply cannot shake it off anything that it wants to stay on.

When it is resting undisturbed, its eight groups of spines sink down and fold inwards so that you'd never know they were there. But if you jerk the leaf it is resting on, or touch it lightly with a twig, it suddenly raises its body at both ends, and all its spines shoot out, looking pretty, but also rather fierce.

This caterpillar's cocoon is almost as odd as it is, looking very much like a gumnut or an oval cup. When the caterpillar—now changed into a moth—is ready to come out, a neat little round lid at the top of the "cup" lifts off. Through this tiny door, the soft brown moth wedges its way out into the open air—and the empty shell that it wore while it was a pupa comes out too. But it comes out only a little way—just enough to show itself in the opening of the cocoon.

And now, can you guess what this moth is called? Think hard, and you might easily find the right answer—cup moth.

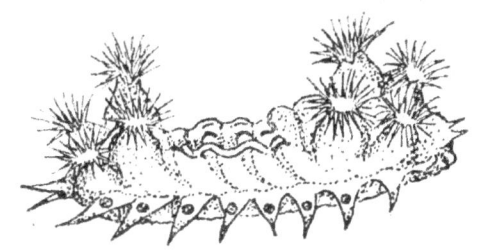

With all bristles spread

Cocoon — like a little wooden cup

When this moth came out of the cocoon, fragments of its pupal case came out, too

A "Twig" That Loops

CHRIS found this quaint little creature making its way up one of our gumtrees, and excitedly called Tess to come and look. If she hadn't hurried, it would have gone out of reach, for it was travelling really fast in its funny "looping" style.

It moves quite differently from ordinary caterpillars, which have little foot-like "grippers" along their bodies. This one has six tiny feet way up at the front, two larger grippers at the back, and none at all in between. When it "walks", it draws those back grippers right up close to its front feet, so that the centre part of its body has to go up into a loop. Quickly it stretches out to the full length, and repeats the whole thing over and over—and in no time at all, travels quite long distances.

Being careful not to hurt it, we brought it down to a lower branch, and then it was really funny. This was something that it hadn't chosen, and it wasn't at all sure that it would accept it. It looped its way excitedly along the edge of a leaf to the very leaf tip, then held on to it with its rear grippers and swayed its whole body out into mid-air, trying to feel what was there, twisting in all directions, throwing itself around like a circus acrobat.

When it didn't touch on to anything, it surprised us by lying straight out in the air—and stayed like this, completely still, for so long that it seemed to have gone to sleep. Fancy feeling comfortable in that position!

Of course, when it does stay quite still in this way, it looks exactly like a twig, so birds pass by without noticing, instead of snapping it up and making a meal of it.

Try to find one of these quaint little "loopers" for yourselves, and see how their colouring also is exactly like bark-dark brown, with lighter patches here and there.

We found a tiny baby one soon afterwards. Every now and then it playfully dropped over the edge of a leaf, and dangled from it on the end of a silky thread so fine that you could scarcely see it.

The same as other caterpillars, "looper" will go to sleep inside a cocoon one day, and when at last it comes out again, it will have pretty little wings with scalloped edges, and a new name—a geometer moth.

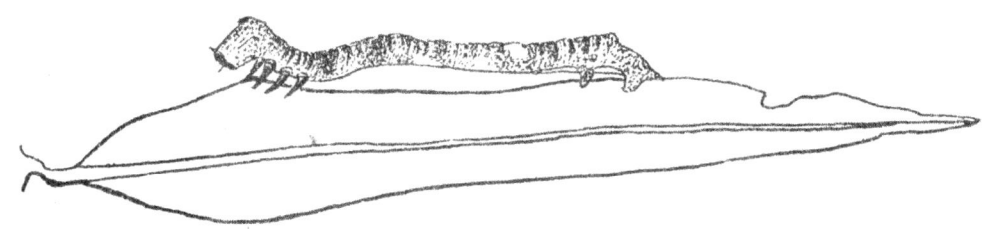

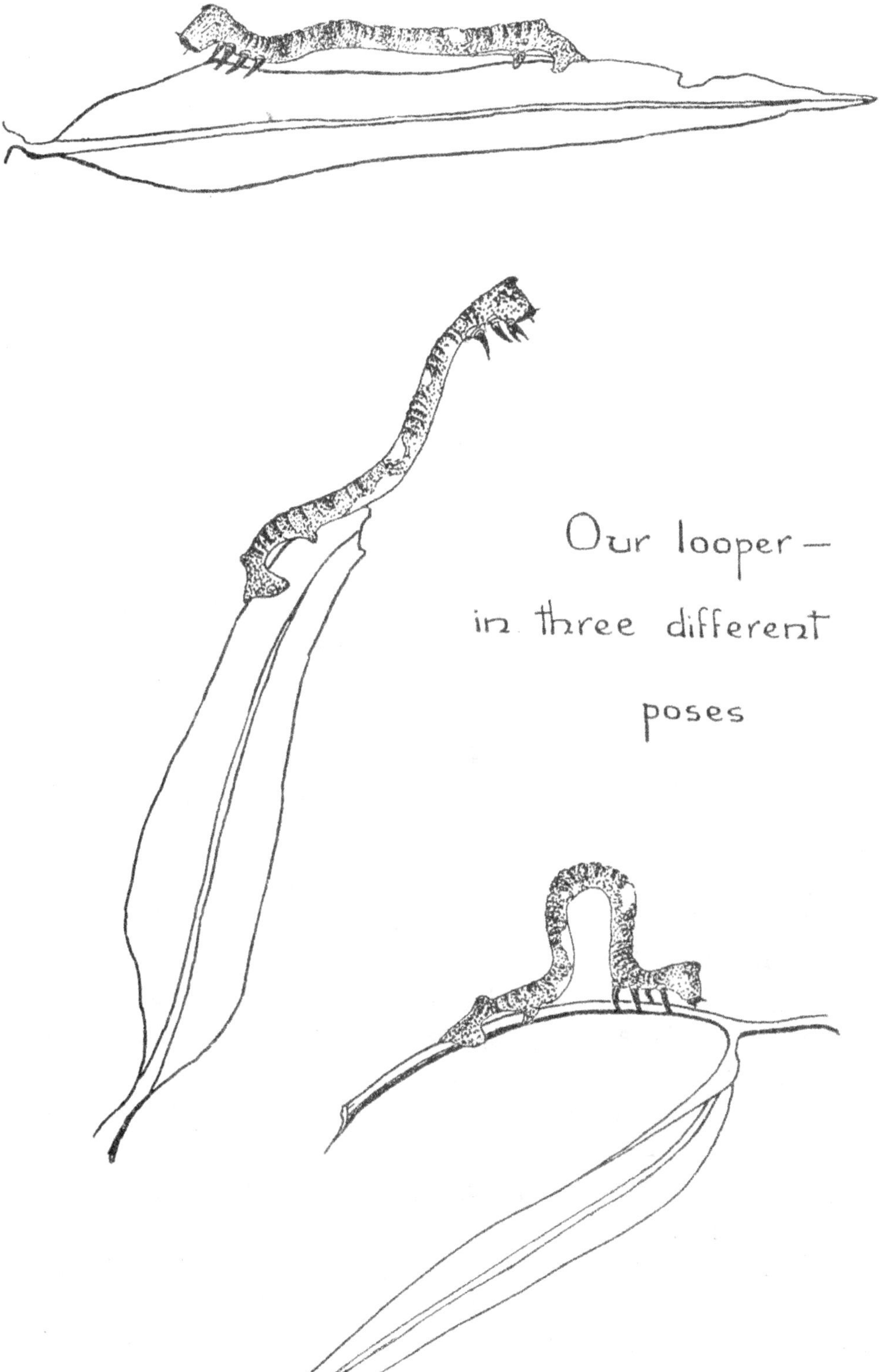

Our looper — in three different poses

Caterpillars That Eat Their Home

WHEN we found any amount of the young tender leaves of our kurrajong-tree chewed and matted together with webbing, we were not at all pleased. Whatever it was that was doing this, we didn't want it to go any further, so we picked off all the webbed-up leaf bundles that we could find.

We broke one of them apart to see what was inside—and what a mess it was! The leaves on the inside were nothing but skeletons, with all their flesh eaten away. And here, too, in amongst a confusion of webbing and dirt, were the villains who had done the damage—dozens of little golden-brown pupae.

They were pretty little things, and harmless enough now, all bundled up and asleep. But a short while back, in the form of caterpillars, they had made this awful-looking mess.

They live and eat together in groups, these kurrajong leaf-rollers. At first, they pull a few leaves together and fasten them with webbing. While sheltering inside these, they eat them threadbare. Then they fasten down a few more leaves and eat them, too, then more and more, until the bundles are quite big.

When they have eaten enough, they simply curl up, go to sleep, and become pupae—still there inside the shelter which has also been their food.

It's just as if we were to spend our lives eating the homes we live in—a strip of wall for breakfast, a bit of the floor for lunch, and the roof for dinner.

It doesn't seem to make sense, but the arrangement suits these little animals very well—and there they stay as pupae until they're ready to come out as something else.

We still felt rather upset about what they had done to our kurrajong-tree, but we took a few of the little pupae inside to see what would come out of them. Their golden-brown colour was lovely, and they were as smooth and shiny as satin.

Well, after a few days their thin outer skin cracked open, and out wedged the prettiest little moths you could imagine—bright yellow, decorated with black, only about 25mm across, and ever so soft.

Certainly we didn't approve of their caterpillar mischief, but now there was a difference. We couldn't help loving them, also.

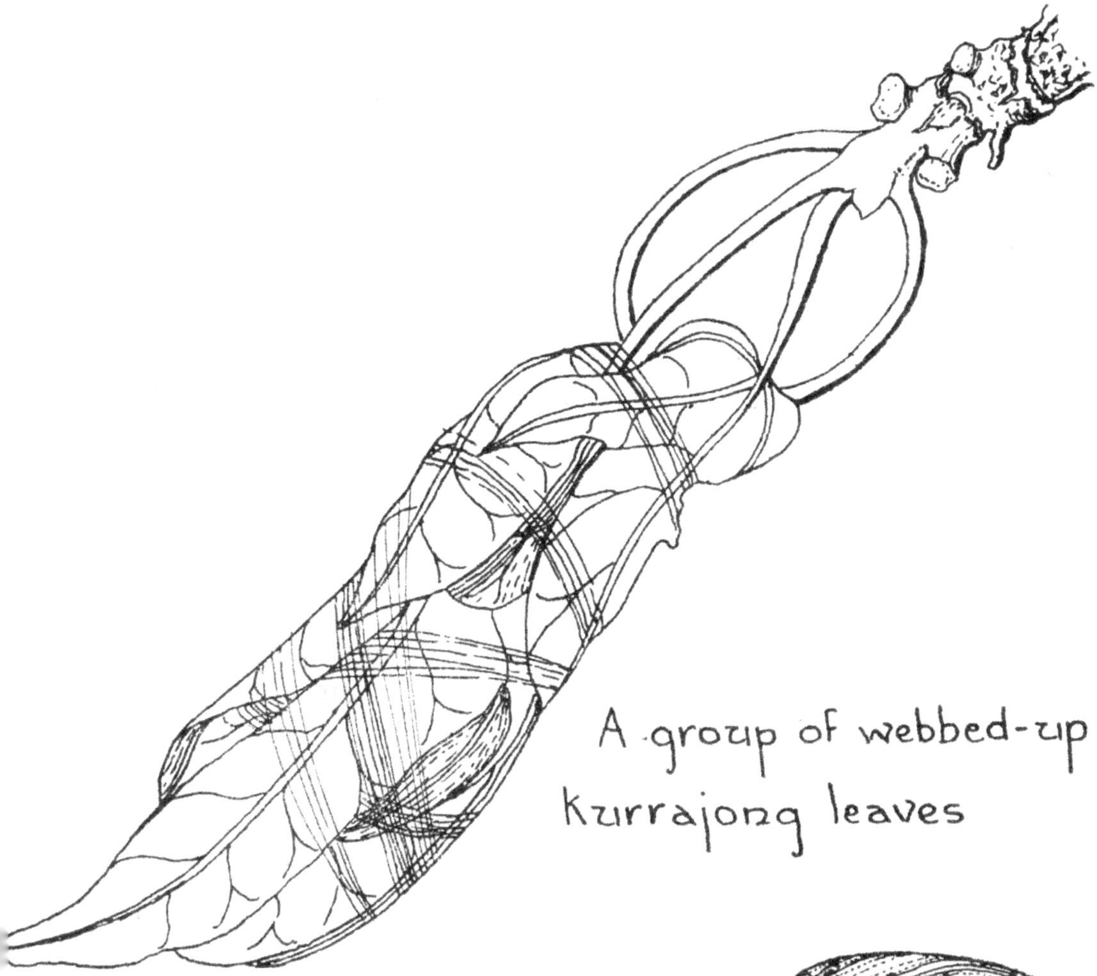

A group of webbed-up kurrajong leaves

One of the "villains" inside

Pretty little bright-yellow moth

A Moth Emperor

THE handsome moth of this story is called the Gum Emperor, because at first this caterpillar ate only gum-leaves. But now, this same caterpillar eats so many different kinds of leaves that it might just as easily be called Pepper-tree, Apricot, Silver Birch, or even Rose Emperor. And it seems to be adding new ideas to its diet all the time.

Anyway, whatever its name, this is one of the most beautiful moths you will find anywhere. It is very large and furry, its main colours are brown and fawn, and it has a circle on each wing, like a large round eye of blue, black and reddish brown.

The lady moth has straight, undecorated feelers, while those of the gentleman are beautiful things, like feathers. But this is starting at the end of the story instead of the beginning.

At the beginning, there is a row of little oval eggs, placed side by side on a leaf. Then, out of each egg comes a tiny caterpillar—black, hairy, and quite different from what it will be when it is bigger.

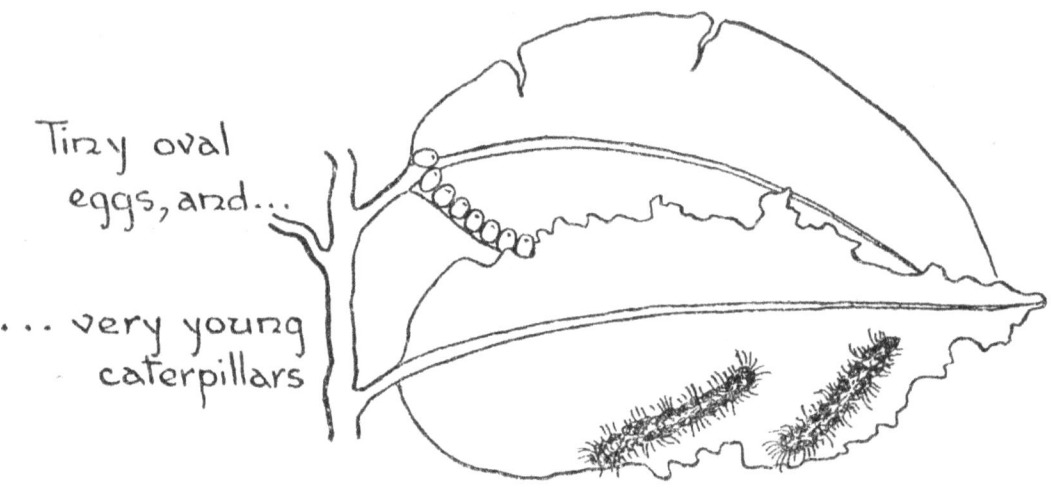

It eats and eats. It has a never-ending appetite—and no wonder, when you realise how big it is going to grow. It sheds one skin after another, and gradually its colour changes, until it is a lovely clear shade of green. By this time it is a huge caterpillar, 100mm long and very stout, but what you notice most of all are its many spines, each with a little blue or flame-coloured tuft of hairs at the top.

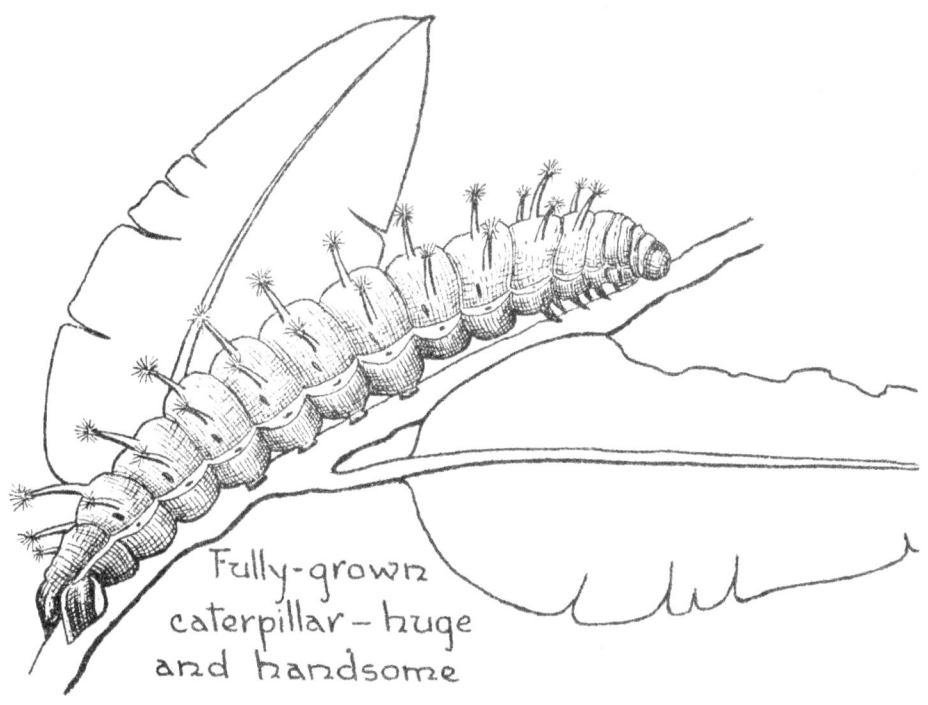

Fully-grown caterpillar — huge and handsome

Now that it is fully grown, of course, it must become a pupa, but first it turns a strange purplish colour and, instead of eating any more, looks around for a good place to spin a cocoon.

At last it curls up and starts work on the cocoon which will become home until it has changed into a moth. And it is because of this cocoon that it is often called the Australian silkworm, it spins with a beautiful silken thread. But then, the cocoon hardens into a woody substance, so that the thread cannot be unwound, as it can be from the cocoon of the true silkworm. By now, also, the cocoon is very dark brown in colour—and, inside, the pupa awaits its great, exciting change.

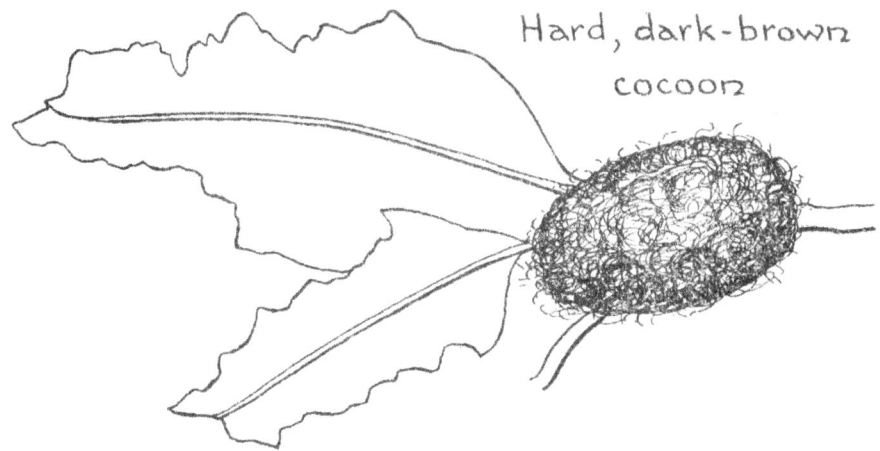

Hard, dark-brown cocoon

Sometimes it has to wait only about a month. Then again, it has been known to wait more than two years. But when at last there is a perfect moth inside the cocoon instead of a curled-up pupa, you may be surprised, one day, to hear a scraping noise. This is the moth, busily sawing its way out of the hard, woody case. For this purpose, Nature has supplied it with two sharp teeth on its shoulders, which it sheds as soon as they have done their one important job.

At first, when the moth emerges, it looks far from beautiful. It is soft, crumpled, and rather messy, but it breathes in deeply, its wings unfold and stiffen, and only an hour or so later it is—as we said at the beginning—one of the most beautiful moths you will find anywhere... a real emperor among its fellow moths.

The glorious Gum Emperor moth

A Blue Triangle from a Green Caterpillar

HERE is a beautiful green caterpillar with tiny black-and-white horns, and a fat face. Tess found it resting on the bark of a camphor-laurel tree, and brought it home with the exciting news, "Mummie, look! I've got a bull-dog caterpillar!" And it really did have a bull-dog look about it.

We decided that its life-story would have to go into this book, but it wouldn't stay still for a moment to have its picture drawn. It kept twisting around this way and that, and walking all over the place, quite uninterested in all the lovely camphor-laurel leaves we kept offering.

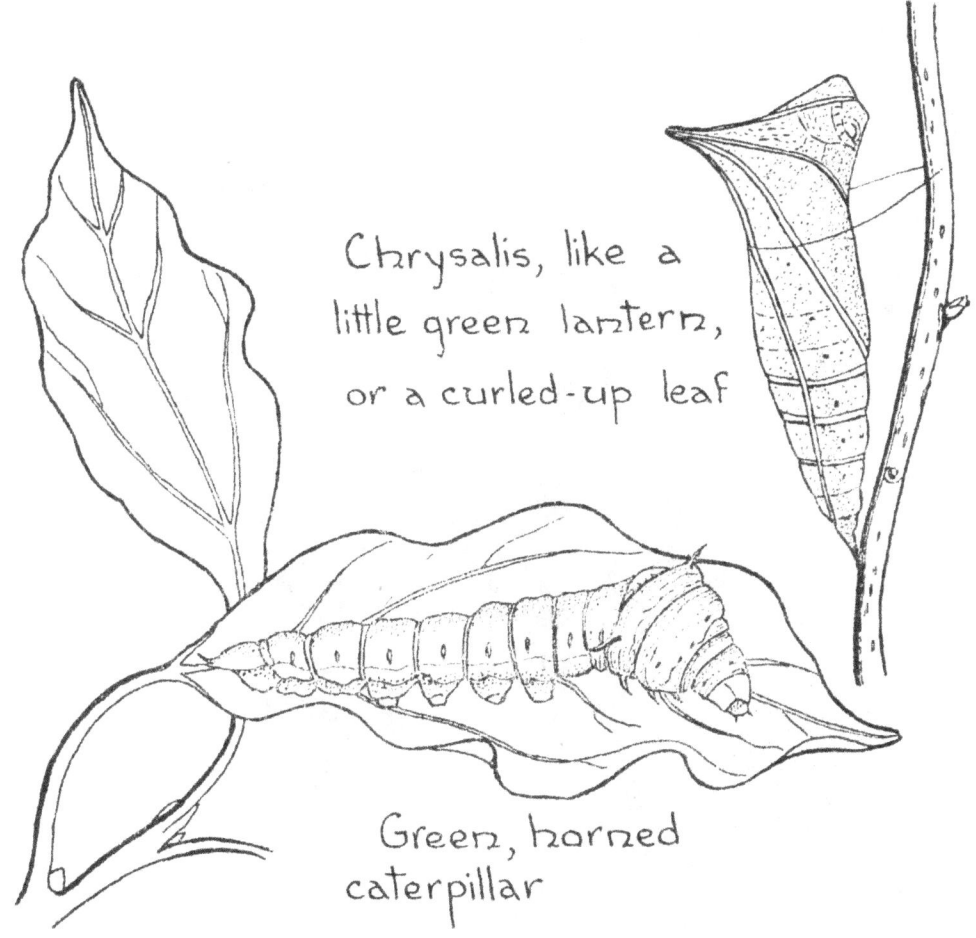

Chrysalis, like a little green lantern, or a curled-up leaf

Green, horned caterpillar

Of course, this meant that it had finished with being a caterpillar (or larva) and was feeling the need to become a pupa. So we hurried to make a sketch—and this was just as well, because the next morning it was already very still, and a lot smaller, and was suspended by a fine silken thread to the inside of the large box we had put it into. This thread went round its middle , and was so thin that we could see it only in certain lights.

By the end of the day it was still smaller, and looked like a little green lantern, or a rolled-up leaf with five straight veins running down the length of it. Very occasionally it gave a sudden jerk from side to side, but otherwise it was quite still, and the only thing about it that reminded us of Tess's "bull-dog" caterpillar was its colour. Strange to say, this hadn't changed at all.

Well, now we could only wait—and as it was already autumn, we knew that we would have to keep on waiting until after winter.

Beautiful blue-and-black swallowtail

(More than double life size)

If the "lantern" (or chrysalis) had formed in summer, its butterfly would have taken only a few weeks to come out. But when at last the great day arrived and the little green chrysalis shell cracked open, we felt that it had been well worth waiting for.

Out of it—slowly and with great effort—came something that looked like a damp; crumpled piece of silk. With its tiny feet it clung to the frail, broken shell which had sheltered it for so long, quivering in the strange atmosphere of the outside world. Then, very slowly, its wings unfolded, straightened out, and lost their first limp, helpless look. It was almost as if someone were very gently blowing them up. And at last, the most beautiful butterfly rested there before us, with small patches of red underneath its wings, and the tops of them prettily marked with black and bright blue,

Its name was Blue Triangle—one of the large family of Swallowtail butterflies—and you should have seen how joyously it fluttered off into the sunshine as soon as we set it free.

The "Twig" with a Butterfly Inside

FANCY calling this butterfly, with all its lovely markings, the Dingy Swallowtail! It is velvety black, patterned with white, and on its underwing there are a few red spots. It is anything but dingy. And its larva (or caterpillar) is quite beautiful, too—black, with rows of yellow and white spots, and of little black spines.

The first one we met was eating away at an orange-leaf—for the leaves of oranges, lemons and limes are their favourite foods. It wasn't very big, but when Chris touched it, he got quite a surprise. Immediately a little flame-coloured Y-shaped object rose up just behind its head, and a strong citrusy smell came out. All of this made it seem rather angry, but really, it was only Nature's way of scaring off those enemies—the ichneumon wasps—which become parasites on so many defenceless caterpillars.

Of course we decided to watch this caterpillar, so we shifted it to our "observation centre" and gave it plenty to eat. It seemed very happy indeed, and then, when it was a little more than 40mm long, it grew restless one day, and we knew that it was looking for a good place in which to become a pupa.

Sure enough, in a few hours' time, it had settled on a nice big stem. It attached itself to this stem by a fine silky thread, then hunched itself up a bit, with its head tucked under. Already it was looking quite different from the caterpillar we had known. But by the next morning, it was much more different again. Now it was woody-looking, with rather a dull colour like putty, and with little horns at the top. From time to time it jerked suddenly from side to side, as it settled into this queer new arrangement—and then, by the end of the day, it was quite still, and so exactly like the stem it was attached to that you simply couldn't tell them apart.

Nothing ever looked more like a broken twig than did that strange little chrysalis. We just kept marvelling at it. Tess said, "But Mummie, it's *exactly* like a bit of branch—and it got like that in less than two days. How can it do such a thing?"

Well, the only answer to that is that it is one of Nature's countless miracles. And the next miracle was the changing of our black-and-yellow caterpillar into a butterfly.

Out with the horns!

Just like a broken twig

Inside that woody covering, something happened which people could not do, no matter how much they tried. The caterpillar dissolved completely—every bit of it—and then, gradually, the stuff it had been made of formed up again into a new creature altogether—into the beautiful Swallowtail butterfly that came out of our "broken twig" a few weeks later.

You yourself simply must try to see this wonderful happening some day—a moth or a butterfly coming out into the open from its cocoon or chrysalis, after it has been so completely remade. It is one of the loveliest and most wonderful "small" things to be seen on this Earth.

World Travellers on Fragile Wings

ONE day, Tess came in from the garden and said, "Look, Mummie, what do you think this is?"

She showed me a little, but long and narrow leaf with three eggs on it—and when I realised that it had come off one of our wild-cotton or milkweed bushes, I said, "Well, don't get too excited, dear, but I wouldn't be very surprised if they're the eggs of a Wanderer butterfly."

It was all very well saying not to get excited, but how could we help it? We were both excited, just at the thought of it—and when Chris heard about it, he was, too, for the Wanderer is one of the most enchanting butterflies in the world.

A few days went past—and then suddenly, there were three of the tiniest caterpillars moving around on the milkweed leaf. We examined them through a magnifying glass, and even then, while they were still so small, there could be no doubt about it—they were Wanderers.

They had little round, black heads and greenish bodies. One of them was busily nibbling at the frail, transparent shell of the egg it had just come out of—and as there weren't any other shells on the leaf, we realised that the other two caterpillars must already have eaten them. That's a strange thing to have as one's first meal on Earth.

Well, we brought in a branch of milkweed for them, knowing that—oddly enough—this was the only thing they would eat. And in no time at all they changed their first baby skin for one with pretty little stripes. They grew two long delicate horns behind their heads, two shorter ones near their tails, and they looked just what they were—very special little caterpillars indeed. We felt really honoured that they had come to us.

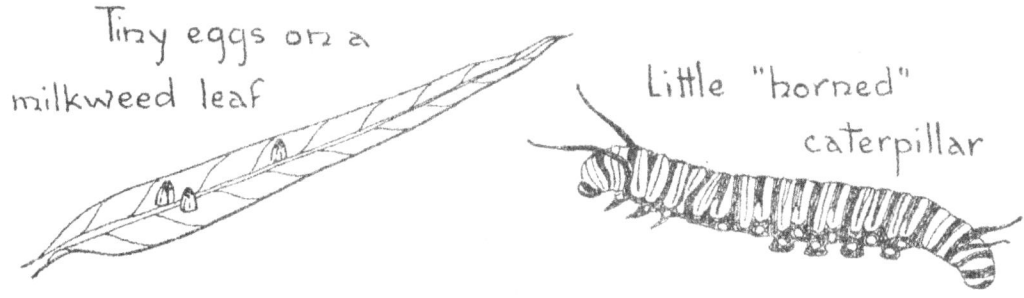

Then, about a fortnight after they had hatched out of their eggs, they began to change. They hunted around for a nice strong branch, and when they found one, they attached themselves to it by their tails, with fine silky threads.

They had been busy enough all their lives—eating, growing, and moulting—but now, hanging head-down, their plump little bodies exercised as never before. They twisted and squirmed, they turned themselves up and then swung down again, they sent little waves of movement along their whole 50mm of length.

Soon, a split appeared in their familiar striped skins, and as this grew it revealed something different altogether inside. Instead of being prettily marked with black, white and yellow, our caterpillars were now becoming pale green—and instead of being a caterpillar, each was becoming a chrysalis. A mere few hours later the change was complete, and we wondered if anything could be more miraculous than what we had just seen.

Chris said, "Of course we *know* how wonderful it is for a pupa to become a moth or a butterfly—but heavens! Just look at that chrysalis! And only a few hours ago it was a striped caterpillar with horns!"

Tess and I felt the same about it, and we all agreed that this was also the most *beautiful* chrysalis we had ever seen—pale green decorated with tiny gold "beads"—a very special chrysalis for a very special caterpillar and butterfly.

Gradually as the days passed the chrysalis grew darker. Soon, through its fine, transparent skin, we could see the lovely markings of butterfly wings appearing—and about two weeks after our caterpillars had attached themselves to a branch by a collection of silky threads, three little chrysalis skins split open one after the other, and out of each came a precious Wanderer butterfly.

At first, of course, it was very limp, moist and crumpled. But as it dried and strengthened, it was a real glory in form and colour, its large beautiful wings bright orange on top, with black veins and masses of white spots.

We would have liked to keep these lovely things as pets, but we knew how impossible and unkind this would be, and—as soon as they were strong enough—we set them free to flutter about sipping water and nectar, and to fulfil the rest of their marvellous destiny.

Always, when we set our moths and butterflies free, we wonder rather sadly what might happen to them—if they will be able to live their short lives unharmed, or if some bird or other enemy will pounce upon them and finish them off in a gulp. But we had no fears for our three Wanderers, because we knew that, for some strange reason, no bird or other enemy would attack them. Their bright colours are there for all to see, but maybe they give off an odour which warns other animals that they would be nasty to taste, for they certainly lead a charmed, undisturbed life.

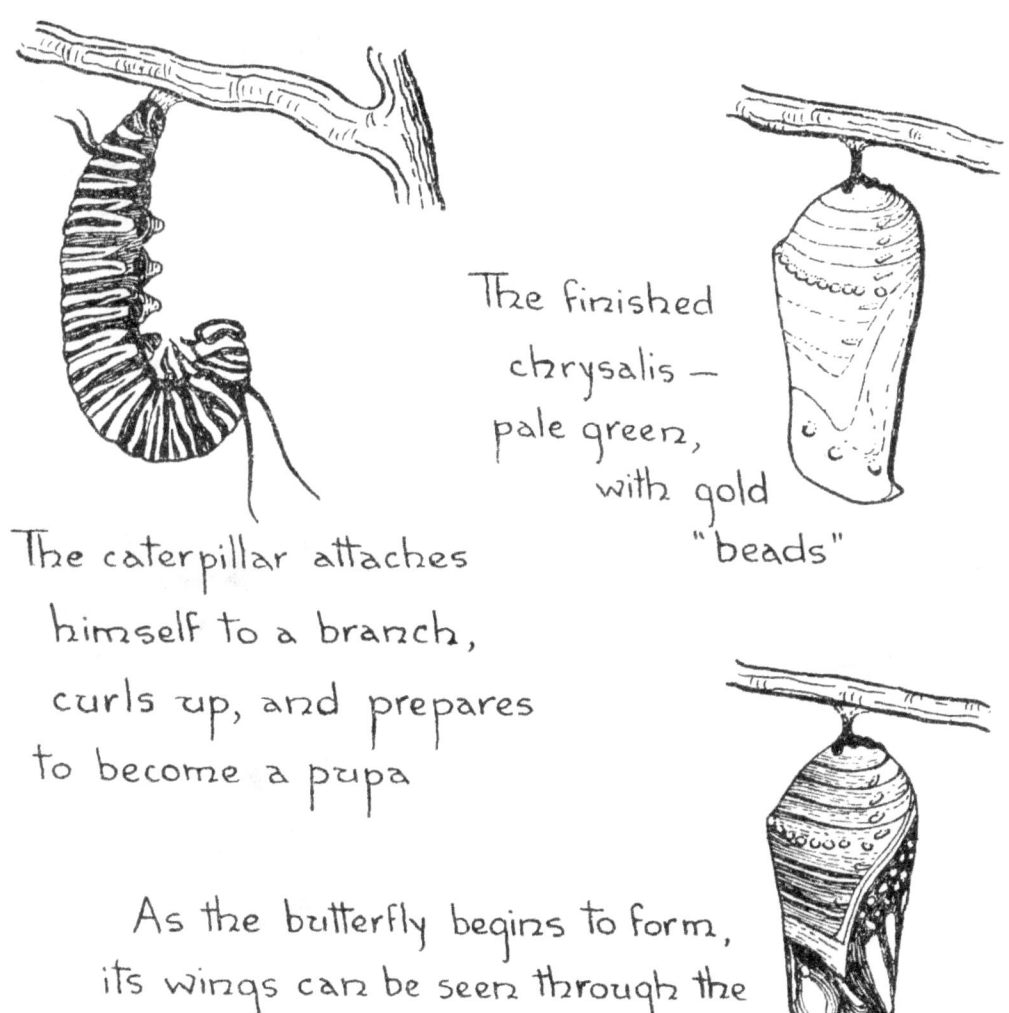

The caterpillar attaches himself to a branch, curls up, and prepares to become a pupa

The finished chrysalis — pale green, with gold "beads"

As the butterfly begins to form, its wings can be seen through the transparent chrysalis skin

This in itself is remarkable enough, but more remarkable still is the fact that Wanderer butterflies migrate the way some birds and other animals do. It does not seem possible that a frail, fluttery, short-lived thing like a butterfly could travel any real distance at all, yet Wanderers live for nearly a year, and can travel more than 2000km in their search for a warm place to roost for the next generation of eggs to be laid.

As summer draws to a close in the part where they were born, they lift their beautiful wings and begin their great journey—either north or south, as the case may be—to where warmer weather is coming in. They do not rise up and depart in a great mass of thousands, the way birds do. They slip away so quietly—one or a few at a time—that nobody quite realises what is happening. And when they reach their destination, they do so in the same quiet way.

Then, in their new home, they lay eggs which at last develop into new Wanderers. And—here is another very remarkable thing—at the end of summer, this new generation of butterflies returns to exactly the same spot that their parents came from, even though they themselves have never been there at any stage of their lives. Sometimes they even return to the same bushes—and the cleverest scientists still do not know how they do it.

The first home of Wanderer butterflies was North America, but

The beautiful Monarch – or Wanderer

gradually they have spread around to most parts of the world, which means that they have actually crossed oceans on their fragile wings.

How right it is to call them Wanderers! And how right, also, for them to be called Monarch Butterflies, as they are in America! For they have proved themselves monarchs indeed—triumphant over their enemies, over great distances, and over the shortness of a butterfly's normal life. They do no harm to anything, either as caterpillars that eat only milkweed, or as butterflies that sip only nectar and water—and in return, it seems, nothing does harm to them.

No wonder we felt so delighted and honoured when those three tiny eggs appeared on one of our milkweeds!

A Few Other Small Animals

The Changeable Frog

AT some time or other, every boy and girl catches tadpoles, and hopes to be able to keep them until they turn into frogs. Have you? If not, you should try to, because a frog is one of the most interesting things in Nature, and the way it changes from a tadpole is really wonderful.

But when you do catch one, be very careful not to hurt it, and make sure that you keep it in conditions where it can feel happy and "at home".

You may even be lucky enough to find a group of eggs, floating near the top of a pond in a little mass of jelly. This jelly is very important, for it protects the eggs perfectly.

Chris and Tess were quite excited when they found a group in a pool of water near Berowra, one day. They scooped them up in one of the jars that we always carry around with us "just in case", and we set them up at home in a little garden pond. Then, several times a day, we looked at them through magnifying glasses, and at last we saw that the small dark round patch in the centre of each egg was changing its shape. It was beginning to look like the two little ones in our drawing down here—and also, it was wriggling a bit.

Soon afterwards, the baby tadpoles pushed out of their eggs, and attached themselves, under water, to a leaf of water weed. They were

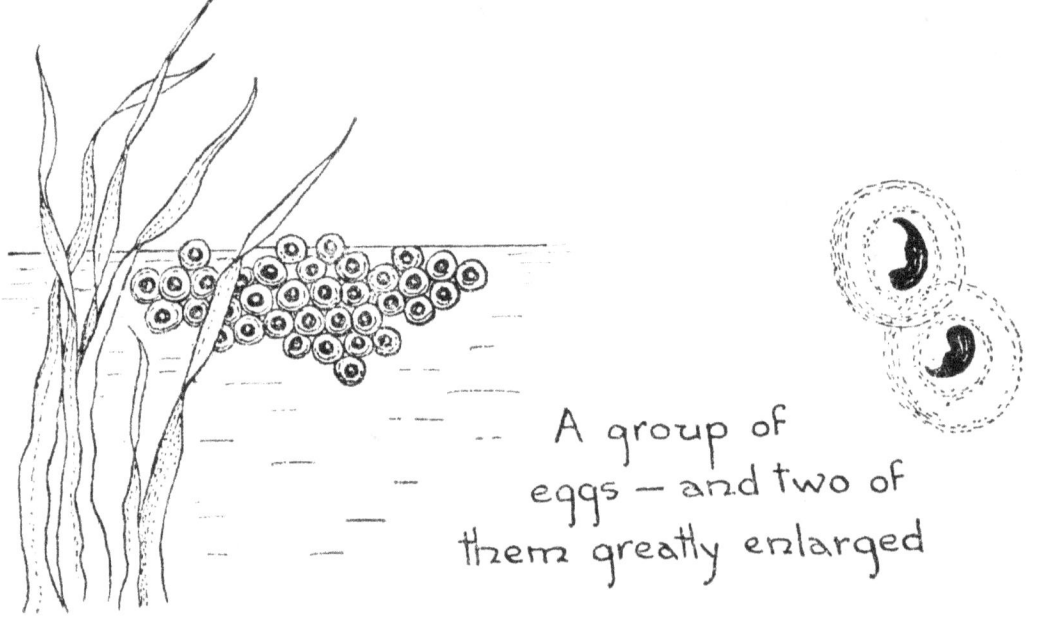

A group of eggs — and two of them greatly enlarged

quiet little things at this stage, with their eyes closed, taking no notice of anything. But when at last they let go, and went wriggling out across the pond, they were very quick and lively indeed. For a while they didn't bother about food, but when they did, there was plenty of green alga for them—and that was a good thing, because otherwise they would have set to work and eaten one another. So, if you want to keep your tadpoles, be sure that you give them plenty of this tiny water plant to eat.

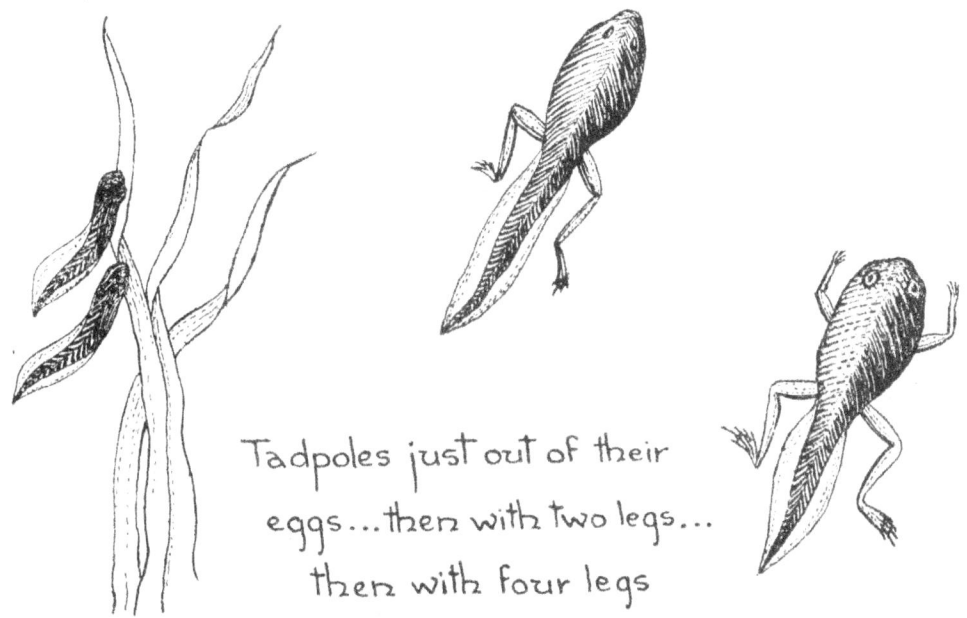

Tadpoles just out of their eggs...then with two legs... then with four legs

Well, for the next few weeks, our little tadpoles went steadily on, growing bigger and fatter, and then an important thing happened to them. They each grew a pair of hind legs, and perfect little feet. Next, tiny front legs and "hands" appeared. So now, although they were still swimming around, living as fish, their legs were making them look rather like land creatures.

Now came the most important changes of all—changes which were going to make it possible for our water-living tadpoles to become land-living frogs. Most of these changes went on inside them, so we couldn't see them, but while they were taking place, the tadpoles couldn't eat, and were able to go on living only because of their large tails, in which a good supply of food was stored.

Just think—they had to give up breathing with gills the way fish do, and start breathing with lungs the way *we* do. But of course, before they could do this, they had to *get* lungs. Then, the channel through which their food passed had to become shorter, because when they started eating again, they would be eating quite different things—not tiny green plants any longer, but flies, mosquitoes and other insects. Their bodies had to flatten, and grow lighter in colour. Their heads had to change completely, too, before they could become real frogs—those quaint little wide-mouthed, goggle-eyed creatures that look so pretty sitting at the water's edge.

A frog — with a tadpole's tail

It would be funny to have a tongue like a frog's, which folds back toward its throat while its mouth is closed. But when a tasty morsel like a mosquito happens along, the tongue shoots out as if on a spring. The mosquito sticks to it, and the tongue snaps back in again, carrying the unfortunate insect with it.

Then, what about the frog's goggle-eyes? It would be rather good fun to have some like *those*. Scientists say that a frog's eye is one of the most marvellous things in Nature. Not only does it see very sharply and with great accuracy, but also, it decides what is worth observing and what is not. If it chances upon something stationary which is neither useful nor a danger to the frog, it simply doesn't see it. But if there is something useful or dangerous which is moving, that frog's eye sees it more clearly than our eyes possibly could. Scientists are so impressed by this, that they are trying hard to copy it in their laboratories, but so far they haven't come anywhere near it.

Another thing that frogs can do is change their colour to match their surroundings—and it would certainly be fun if we could do that.

Just imagine if we ourselves turned green when we walked among masses of ferns or shrubs, then gold among autumn leaves, and crimson if we were holding a bunch of waratahs! Suppose we were out in the garden picking blue hydrangeas, and changed to the same colour ourselves! Some of these colours mightn't suit us, but when Nature gave the frog this ability to change she wasn't thinking of making frogs look beautiful. Her whole idea was to protect them from enemies by becoming as invisible as possible. When you come to think of it, we don't very often find frogs, do we? Yet we can hear them quite often.

And if you do hear them at home, please don't do anything to frighten them away, for they eat a lot of flies and mosquitoes which would otherwise make a great nuisance of themselves.

So you see, a frog is not only interesting and wonderful, but also very useful—and a most charming little creature as well.

Fully-grown frog

Forty-six Legs

HOW would you like to have as many legs to manage as *this* invertebrate has?

It's a centipede, of course, and you probably have quite a number of them in your garden, only you don't very often see them, because they hide away in the daytime and come out at night.

Perhaps when you are helping with the gardening you might turn over some dead leaves or a stone, and find one sheltering underneath. Then what a squirming and wriggling there will be, as this long dark creature with all of those legs tries to get away under cover again!

Most likely you won't care for the look of this creature very much, and will leave it well alone. But if you should want to keep it for an hour or so to examine it, pick it up in a trowel and place him in a glass jar. Be careful not to touch it with your bare hands, as it can give you a very painful bite. But please don't kill it, either. When you have had a good look, put it back in the garden, and let it creep away into some dark shelter—because, during the night, it does a useful job for you, eating many harmful insects, and is a special enemy of the poisonous trap-door spider.

If you count those legs, you will think that there are 21 pairs of them, but actually there are 23 pairs. What looks like a forked tail is another pair, and—most surprising of all—it's yet another pair of legs that it bites with. These curved, sharp nippers fit closely around its head, and you would never guess that they were legs.

There's another kind of centipede that you might often find in your garden—very thin, much shorter than the one drawn here, and orangey-red in colour.

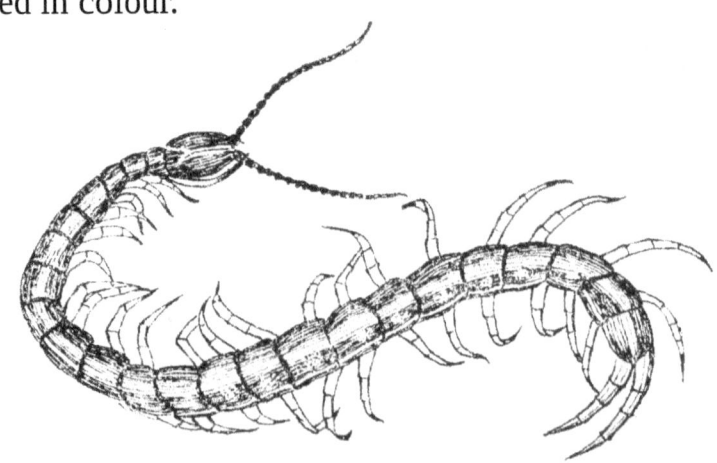

Slugs and Snails...

WE are so used to thinking of shells as pretty little objects to be found on the beach, that we do not realise how often we find them in our gardens. Yet every snail that makes a hobby of eating our choicest plants has a shell, and belongs to the enormous family of molluscs that we shall soon be talking about, and whose shells we so much enjoy finding at the seashore.

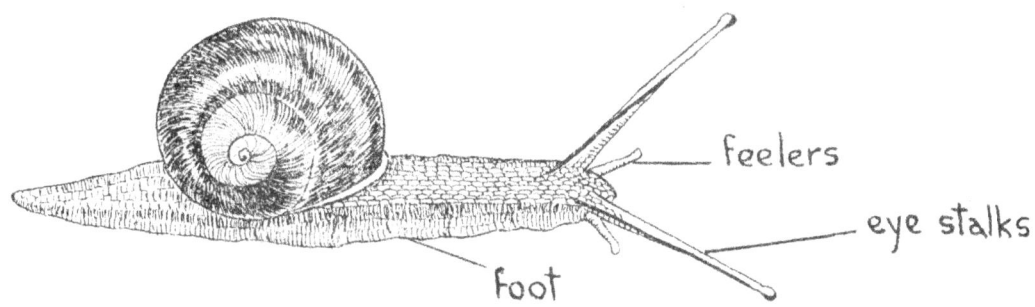

Unless you live near the sea it isn't easy to study salt-water molluscs, for they would soon die if you took them away from their natural surroundings, and you couldn't very well build a make-believe beach so realistically that your molluscs would be fooled. But snails are right there, in your garden, almost asking to be studied.

Many kinds of snails have moved away from the sea, and can be found living happily in fresh-water ponds, but our garden snail has moved still farther away, for it doesn't even need a pond to live in. It is satisfied with nice damp ground.

There is nothing it loves more than strolling around a garden in the rain, nibbling at all the titbits he can find. And, of course, there is nothing that a gardener enjoys *less* than this sort of nibbling.

Apart from all the eaten plants it leaves behind, a snail also leaves a silvery track, so you can see exactly where it has been. But it doesn't have this in mind when it leaves this trail. It's just that it can't get along very well without some sort of moisture, so its body produces a sliminess which makes it able to move easily, even in dry places. Then, when the sliminess dries, it has a silvery look.

Chris thinks it would be great fun to have *our* eyes perched on the ends of stalks the way snails have, but surely it would be an awful nuisance! They would always be getting in the way—and jostled and bumped. Then, if we drew them in quickly, the way snails do, we wouldn't be able to see anything until we put them out again. We would have to stop whatever we were doing—and say to anyone with us, "Please excuse me a minute, until I get my eyes unrolled."

Of course, the snail has no clocks to worry about, no buses to catch, and is never in a hurry, so the business of getting those eyes in and out isn't a bother in the least.

Then, it has another pair of stalks on its head—shorter ones. These are feelers. And there is a mouth, with an enormous number of tiny teeth—not around its jaws, but on its tongue. This tongue is rough like a file, and every piece of roughness is a tooth. It has about 20,000 of them. If we had 20,000 teeth, I wonder what we would do with them?

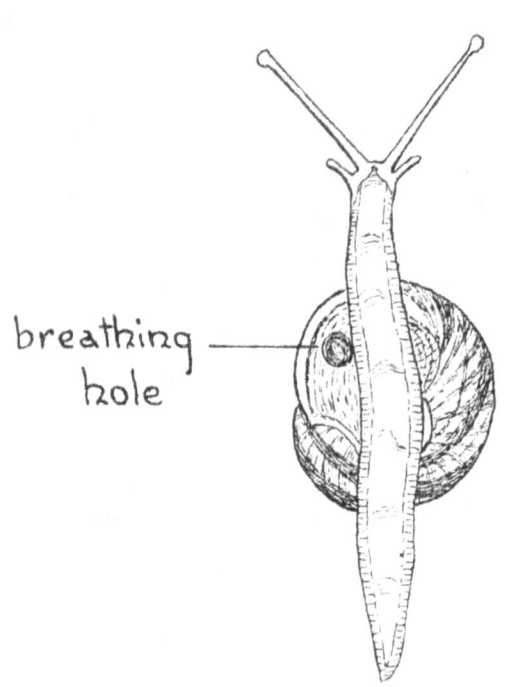

When you bring a snail in from the garden to have a closer look, you should put it at the bottom of a glass jar and watch how it almost "ripples" its way up to the top, with wavy movements of the long underneath part of its body, called the foot. Also, while moving up the jar, you will notice a fairly large round hole just underneath the shell on the right-hand side—although, seeing it like this, it will look as if it is on the left. It is through this that the snail breathes. So, in spite of its funny position—beside its foot—that hole is actually its nose.

Now, we all know how happy snails are when it is wet and warm. But what about those long dry spells, or when it is very cold? They don't come around anything like so much at those times, so where do they go, and what do they do?

They find a nice sheltered spot and go to sleep in it. They curl themselves right away inside their shells, seal up the openings with a layer of slime, and rest comfortably where the dryness or the cold cannot get to them. Then, when the weather is more to their liking, they wake up, stretch themselves, and once again stroll around the garden, nibbling as though nothing had happened.

Have you ever heard people speak of a slug as a snail without its shell? This is not quite true, because it *has* got a shell, even though you cannot see it. It's a very small shell, inside its body just behind its head, and doesn't seem to have any purpose at all. Perhaps it is slowly disappearing. Perhaps, in a million years or so, slugs won't have it at all. But while they do have it, they remind us of a few other molluscs that we shall soon be meeting, like the cuttlefish, squid, and spirula.

Of course, the slug doesn't belong to their group, for they all have lots of tentacles and it hasn't—but our slug *has* got a shell inside, and so have they.

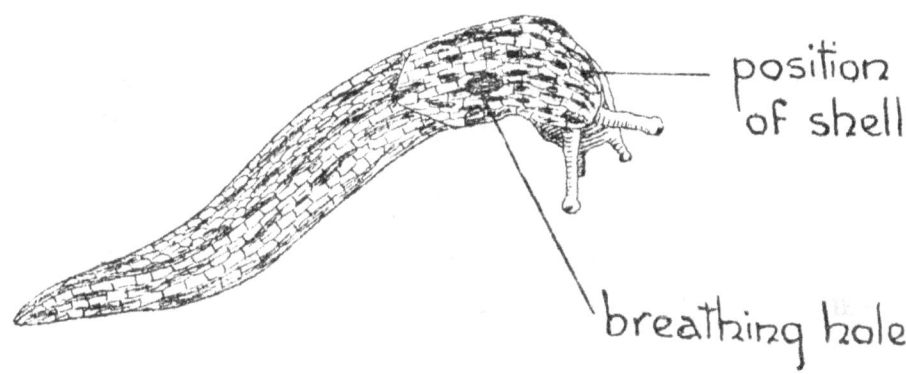

Spiders, and Their Webs

OPPOSITE is a spider you will often come across in the bush. We met hundreds of them around Oxford Falls one day—and Tess started off badly by running into one of their webs. That wasn't a bit nice, because—as you know—spider web clings and drags in your hair, and you wonder if the spider itself is there, too.

Of course, spider web is sticky, and it's even stronger than if a thread of steel were pulled out to the same thinness, so no wonder it makes a nuisance of itself when you run into it.

It's a great nuisance to insects that fly against it, too. Some of them are big and strong enough to struggle free, but others get hopelessly caught, and it's these that the spider eats.

Quite often, in Nature, you will find that the building is done by the ladies—and it's like this with spiders, too. The lady spider builds the web. The material for it comes from her own body, through a group of little openings underneath her.

Have you ever watched a web actually being built? Do try to. It's so interesting. First, the spider chooses a good spot, and here she attaches the beginning of her web. Dangling on the end of the first thread, she now drops to the ground, or a grass blade, or a branch, or any other suitable thing. Then she climbs back again, and waits for the wind to blow her across to something else; from here, to something else again—and so on, until she has an outline for her web.

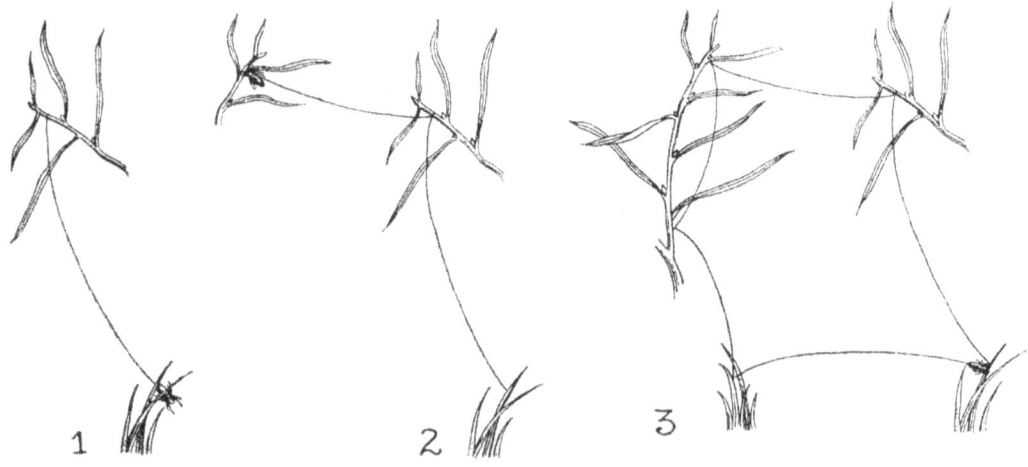

Her next job is to fill in this outline with threads running up and down, across, slant-wise—in every direction, all of them crossing one another in the centre, like spokes of a wheel.

Then she goes to the centre, and from there carries her thread round and round in an ever-widening spiral, attaching it firmly to each of the

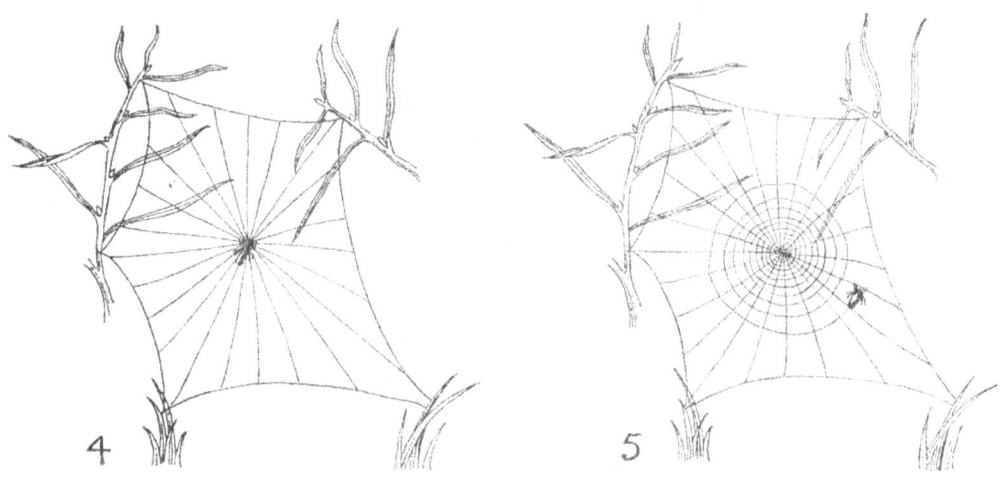

spokes as she passes, until she has finished one of the lovely delicate webs that we all know so well.

Lastly, she goes over it all again, with a new sticky thread which most small insects would be quite unable to get away from once they were caught on it.

In spite of their cleverness, spiders are disliked and feared by many people. Perhaps it's because of their unpleasant habit of trapping insects, then killing and eating them. Lady spiders even eat their own husbands, quite often. Also, they are "creepy crawly" things with their eight legs—and often they are hairy, too, which seems to make matters worse.

Many of them are quite harmless to humans, in spite of all this, but a few of them—like funnel-webs, trapdoors and redbacks—are extremely dangerous, and have been known to kill people. So you always want to be careful about touching spiders, just in case.

But look at them closely, and you'll see how beautiful many of them are. The bush spider on the previous page, for instance, is covered with the loveliest markings on both sides of her body and on her legs. Her legs are brown, with yellow joints. The underneath of her body is covered with a small pattern in brown, yellow and orange, like mosaic. (Do you know what mosaic is?) On top, it is a paler colour—yellowish-grey—and very daintily marked.

Well, whether we approve of them or not, we must admit that most spiders are clever home-builders. But there's one funny little one who is just a scallawag without a serious thought in his—or her—head. The lady doesn't bother to make a proper web—just a shapeless little scrap of a one now and then—for she isn't interested in any settled home. She just goes from place to place willy-nilly—jumping at the slightest thing. And the little gentleman jumps around, too.

You might come across these small, grey, jumping spiders almost anywhere. They can bite but it's harmless and painless unless you're an insect—and they're amusing—and seldom more than 12mm long. But you can't help wondering what they are doing among the large, serious family of spiders when they don't even build a web.

Of all the spiders I have met,
    My favourite one is very small,
And plays around in such a way,
    It isn't spider-like at all.

A proper spider builds a web,
    But this wee fellow never
Does anything that even *looks*
    Important, wise, or clever.

While other spiders stay at home
    And trap their meals with sticky thread,
My tiny friend just practises
    High jumping, like a frog, instead.

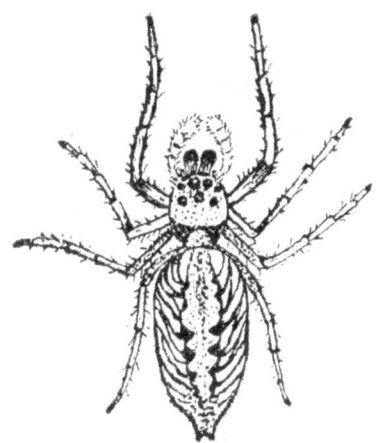

Tiny jumping spider

Spider With a Cross

IT is easy to see why this is called the St. Andrew's Cross spider. She spins a cross in the centre of her web with strand after strand of her silky threads, until it looks pure white and is ever so strong. No doubt it's to make her web stronger that she builds it—and then, she does a curious thing. She herself rests in the very centre of it, places her legs together into four pairs, and lays them against the four sides of the cross.

She's a harmless spider—except to the insects that get caught in her web—and her markings and colouring are really beautiful. I wonder if any of us could think out a prettier way to arrange tiny patches of white, yellow and brown.

From the time we first noticed this particular one, suspended against the cross on her web, in one of our own shrubs, we went out to have a look at her every day.

A spider's life is a queer thing. There she hangs, sometimes doing nothing at all for hours. Then, if a large insect gets caught in her web, she hurries along to bind him up with strong silky threads so that he won't be able to break her web with his frantic struggles.

There she leaves it, completely bandaged, while she eats her smaller catches. Then after a while, at her leisure, she goes back and sucks its juices out until only a tiny skeleton and a bit of dry skin are left.

If her web gets broken, she mends it with great care—and then, once more, has nothing else to do.

How would *you* like to be a spider?

Spider in a Leaf

AT first, when we kept coming across ragged masses of spider web with leaves in them, we thought that the leaves had just blown against the webs and got caught.

Then, when we looked more closely, we found that each leaf was curled around into a sort of funnel, and held like that by hundreds of white silky web strands. More surprising still, we found that the spiders were using these curled-up leaves as homes. And usually they stay inside all day, coming out only at night, to dine on any insects unlucky enough to have got entangled in their webs.

One of those that we came across, however, was either very inquisitive or very brave. Without meaning to, we had disturbed its web, and after a while, out crept the spider from its leaf shelter in a slow, doubtful way, to inspect the damage.

Before we left, we made a sketch of it—as you can see—and also had a good look at it through a magnifying glass. The pattern on its body was so beautiful that we all marvelled at it. It was like the finest black lace spread over creamy white. And all this on a little spider hidden away inside a leaf for most of its life.

When we make anything, we put a lot of work into the parts that other people will see, but very often make rather a mess of the inside or the underneath, which won't be seen.

But when something is made by Nature, you can be sure that it is absolutely perfect, no matter how small it may be, or how short a time it may live—or even if nobody will ever see it at all.

Our Friend the Worm

THE more you learn about Nature, the more you realise that it is wrong to despise anything in it, no matter how lowly. What, for instance, could be more lowly than a worm? Yet worms that live in the ground are some of our most useful helpers.

You know how important it is to loosen-up the soil before planting in it? Well, this loosening-up is exactly what worms do—and if they didn't do their job so well, our job would be a great deal harder, and the soil wouldn't be so healthy.

Now, how does a worm loosen soil? First, it burrows down into it—and next, it eats large quantities of it. In these large quantities are small pieces of decaying leaves, flower petals and so on, which are nice useful food. The soil itself is not needed as food, so it passes right through its body, but on its way through, it is crumbled up into fine pieces. The worm then comes up and casts it out on the surface of the ground—and this little mound of digested earth is known as "worm castings". In the early morning, if you look, you will probably find many of these castings in your lawn and garden.

So you can see what a lucky person you are if your soil has plenty of worms in it. And you don't even have to worry about their eating your plants, for they never eat any living ones—only tiny pieces of dead ones.

Now take a closer look at this small creature who does such an important job, and what do you find? A moist slippery tube, without legs or feet, eyes, ears, feelers or wings. Yet it can sense vibrations in the earth. At night, when it comes out looking for food, it will quickly disappear into its burrow again at the feeling of an approaching footstep. And it does have a type of eye, with several special cells along its body that are sensitive to light, helping it to escape if it senses a sudden change in light which may indicate a predator nearby.

The wetness of its skin moistens the earth and makes it easier to work through. And it also has rows of tiny bristles all the way up its length, which can draw in and out at will. When they are out, they grip the soil quite firmly, and when they are drawn in, they allow our worm to slide forward easily with nothing to hold it back. Its whole body is made up of ever so many rings—sometimes hundreds of them—which stretch and contract as a means of moving around.

Gently—but mind, very gently—take one of your garden worms out and watch the way it moves forward by stretching itself out long and thin, and then drawing itself up short and fat. But don't handle the worm too much because the salt on our skin is poisonous, and makes our worm wriggle around violently in a reflex action against that poison.

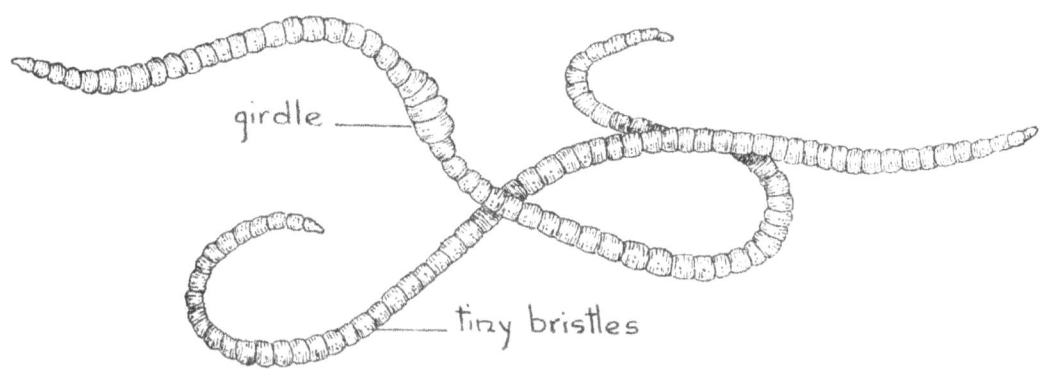

Perhaps you are wondering about the girdle that you will sometimes see on a worm. This is used to lay eggs in. Then the worm casts it off and leaves it in the earth, sealed up at both ends so that the eggs are perfectly sheltered. It is now called an egg cocoon. Usually only one of the eggs hatches out into a baby worm, and this baby stays inside its cocoon for a while before wriggling out into the open soil. All earthworms can have this girdle, and that's because earthworms are both male and female in the one body. When two worms join to make eggs, both worms end up with a batch of eggs to lay, increasing the chances that the new generation will survive.

Considering how helpful worms are, it is good to know that if they should break in half, the top half—and sometimes even each half—will grow into a whole worm again. But please be careful *not* to break any of them, won't you? Because one of the happiest things we can do on this Earth is to act kindly towards all our fellow creatures.

Plants

The Story of Plants

LONG ago, when the Earth was young, plants lived only in the sea. The very first of these was a little alga, with only one cell.

As time went on, bigger and more complicated plants began to appear. Animals also developed in the sea, to eat the plants (and then to eat each other as well).

Then plants, followed by animals, started to live on land. The first plants to do this were algae and fungi, which joined together to survive in the new, more dry land environment as lichens. Without the fungi in lichens to break down rocks and make soil, plants would have had a much harder time moving onto land. Then about 500 million years ago, liverworts came up out of the sea to live in this newly made soil—and you can still find more than 8,000 types of these today, looking very much the same as they did all those ages ago. Liverworts don't have different types of cells for stems or leaves, or special tubes for moving water and food around, but do have things that look like leaves; and they love to live in wet places.

We will be visiting these amazing lichen, fungi, and liverworts later on.

Mosses began to appear, following upon those liverworts. Then, 360 million years ago came ferns—and then 300 million years ago came plants with cones on them, like pine-trees.

Things went on like this for another 100 million years or so before the first flowers appeared on Earth. That's hard to believe, isn't it? It's hard to imagine a world without flowers.

Well, when they did begin at last, there gradually became more and more of them. New kinds of them kept coming along as the hundreds of millions of years passed by, until today it would be almost impossible to count the numbers of different flowers all over the world.

Just as people are the most developed of the animals, so flowering plants are the highest among plants. But everything is still growing and changing, and perhaps you are asking the question that I often ask myself, too....

What will come next? What wonderful new thing will follow after flowers in the next few million years?

Well, none of us knows—but it's fun thinking, isn't it? Try to imagine what it might be like!

Plants That Are Never Green

WHENEVER we go bush wandering—as we often do—Tess has the keenest eyes for those odd little plants called fungi. She loves them.

Do you know what a fungus is? It is one of the thousands of plants in this world which are not green. We are so used to thinking of plants as green that we don't realise how many are not. Yet you can find fungi in every imaginable colour *except* green, and some of these are really glorious. In our first drawing here, there are four different fungi, one white with pale-yellow tips, another flame-coloured, another buttercup-yellow, and the fourth a very bright blue—so bright that Tess thought it would surely shine in the dark. It didn't of course, although there are fungi that even do that.

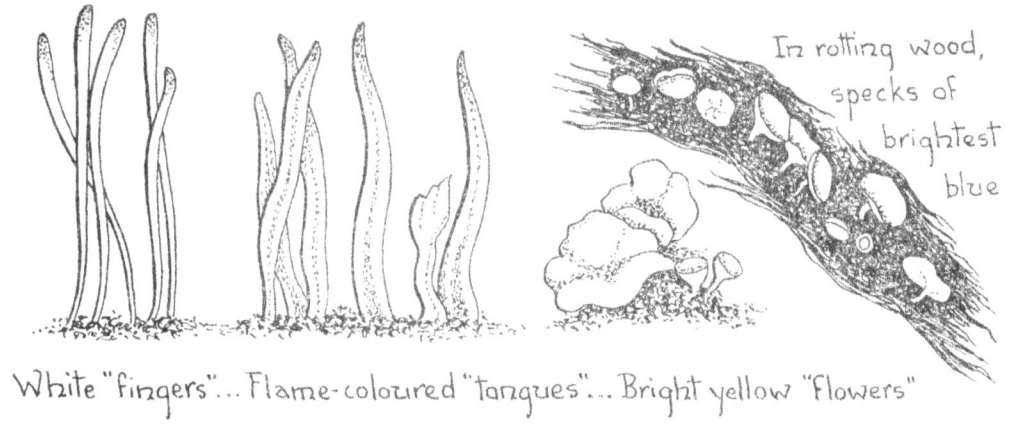

White "fingers"... Flame-coloured "tongues"... Bright yellow "flowers"

In rotting wood, specks of brightest blue

But looking pretty isn't the only thing in the lives of fungi. They also have quite serious problems.

Green plants are very clever. With nothing but their own greenness, sunlight, water and air, they can actually make food for themselves—mostly sugars and starches. Plants that are not green cannot do this, so they have to do something else.

Some fungi are quite nice about it, and live on things that have once been alive but are now decaying. Others, though, are not quite nice about it. They attach themselves to things that are still alive, and steal food from them.

Plants and animals that do this sort of thing are called parasites. Here is one of those parasitic fungi.

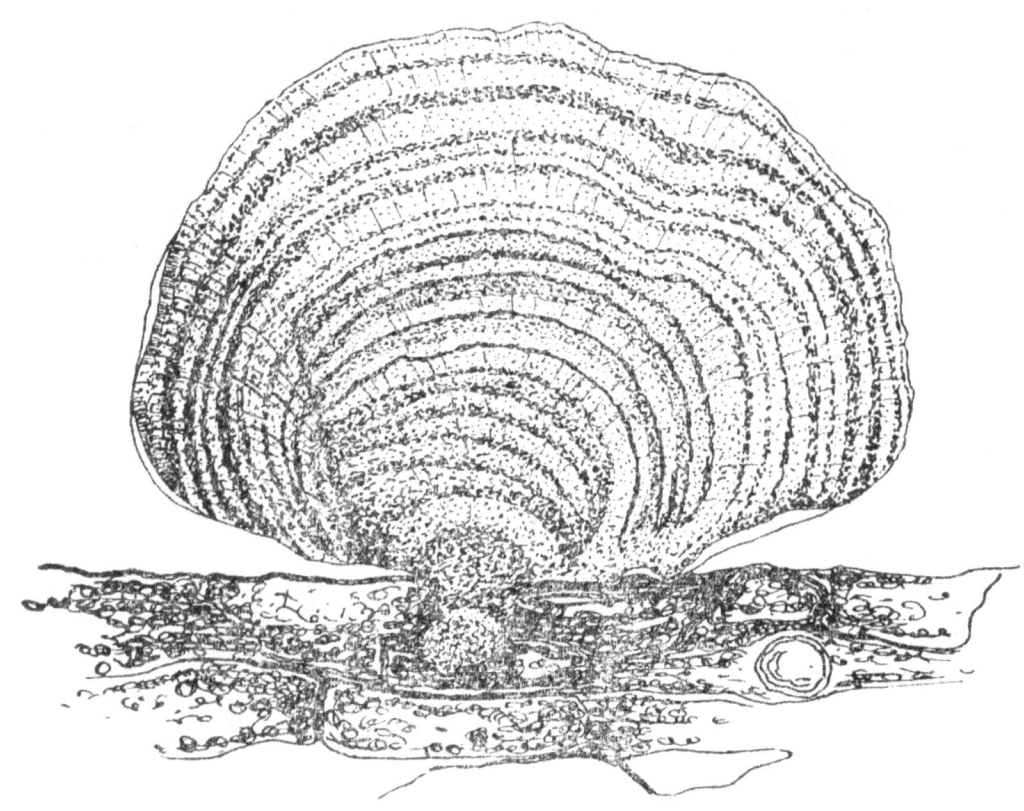

Plants that look like this are called bracket fungi. Sometimes they are very big and thick, other times thin, and yet other times quite small. They may be striped or plain, and their colours are mostly beautiful, but they are villains just the same. You will sometimes see a tree with great numbers of them sprouting from its trunk, looking gay and pretty. But they are taking so much nourishment from the tree that they will end up killing it.

When you next find a bracket fungus, look underneath it, and you will most likely see hundreds of little holes there. Inside the holes is a sort of powder, and if you could look at this powder under a microscope, you would see that it was actually thousands of tiny specks called spores. Each spore is a kind of seed, and could grow into a new fungus plant. So just think of how many new plants could come from one bracket fungus if all of its spores grew!

As well as coming in every colour of the rainbow, except green, fungi also come in almost every shape—round and squat, long and narrow, flat, thick, branched, frilled, like fans, like cups, like nests, like flowers. And they grow in some of the most surprising places. Tess found these two at home.

The pretty little fan-like one was sprouting happily from the top of a palm-seed, and the quaint little "dishes" were dotted around between the bricks in one of our walls. Then later we found more of these "dishes"—jet-black, this time—in Megalong Valley, on a piece of rotting wood.

Coral is, of course, something that belongs in the sea—but sometimes, in the bush, you wonder if it mightn't belong there, too, for some kinds of fungi are so much like coral that you almost have to touch them to make sure that they are not. The one we sketched was a delicate pinkish colour—and beside it are a couple of "puffballs". Could any two plants look less alike?

You will find puff-balls very often, in the bush or in your own gardens. They are pretty little things, mostly white, yellowish or brown, and when they mature they are filled with spores. When ripe, you only have to touch the balls for thousands of spores to come out, like puffs of smoke, leaving the balls empty and crumpled.

Now here's a fungus that you'll love to find—so watch for it particularly in damp spots where wood and leaves are rotting. It looks

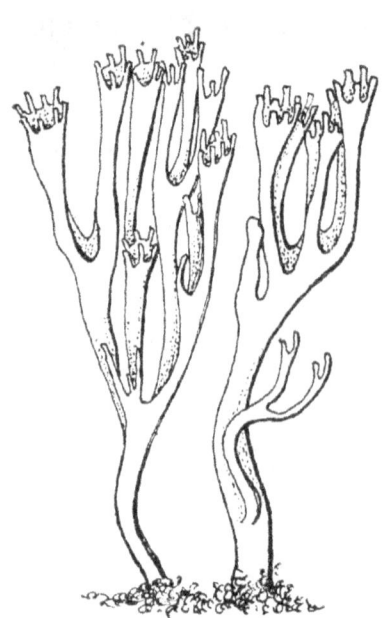
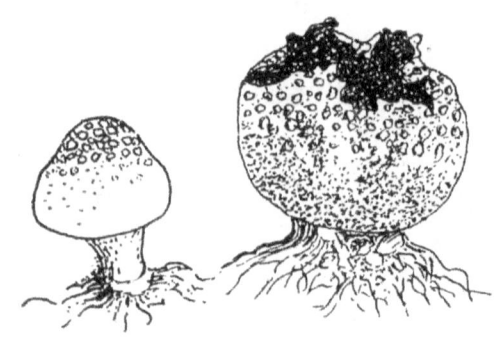

Like pale-pink coral... and round, fat puff-balls

very much like a tiny nest with eggs in it. There are two kinds sketched here, which we found in the bush around Yarrangobilly Caves. The smaller ones were yellow, and easy to see, growing in the cracks of a rotting log, but it's a wonder that we saw the larger ones at all. There they were, growing on a few dead rose twigs, in mud along the side of the road—and they were very much the colour of mud themselves.

Each of the tiny "eggs" in these nests is filled with spores. It drops to the ground when rain splashes into the "nest", and eventually its walls rot away. Only then are the spores inside it set free.

Well, you may or may not have seen this kind of fungus, but you have certainly seen any amount of another kind—toadstools. These have a lovely little goblin look about them, and their different sizes, colours and styles seem almost endless. But they all have a stalk with a cap on the top, and on the underside of the cap they all have masses of thin little shelves hanging side by side. These are called "gills", and if you looked at one of them under a powerful microscope, you would see that it was made up of tiny intertwined threads, with thousands of spores along its outside edge.

The mushrooms that we eat often also have stalk, cap and gills, so they belong to this same group of fungi—and what a large group it is! The sketches here show only a very few of them. See how many different kinds you can find.

People don't normally call fungi plants, since they don't make their own food from sunlight. They completely rely on food that has already been made by another plant or bacterium. Like plants though, they have a type of root that goes through the earth searching for food, in tiny filaments called 'hyphae'. All of those hyphae make a meshlike root structure, called a 'mycelium', that can be truly enormous. Some mycelia are the largest living organisms on earth, as large as a square which is 3km on each side.

Mycelia are often vital for plant growth … they hold the earth together, stopping rain from washing soil away. They exchange chemical messages from one plant to another, and also collect nutrients and water for the plants. For example, many plants such as corn, apples, pine, oranges, and peas use the phosphorus and nitrogen fertiliser collected by mycelia from the soil to grow, and in return they give those mycelia some of the food the plants make with the help of sunlight. (You may be interested to know that some plants also use bacteria to bring in nitrogen from the air. Examples are peas, beans, soybeans, and alfalfa.)

But the most important function that mycelia perform is recycling. Mycelia are the main workers that break down dead plants and animals into soil, and maintain the cycle of life on our planet Earth.

When we see a fungus' mushroom popping out of the ground, or from a tree trunk making spores, that is just the fruiting body of the mycelium. When you pluck that mushroom you are not killing the fungus inside. So these fungi sometimes not only share with the plants

they live with, but also with us when we enjoy a meal of mushrooms. Make sure that if you *do* go "mushrooming", you go with someone who can identify the safe ones to eat, as there are some of the gilled mushrooms that are very poisonous!

There is certainly no shortage of mushrooms and toadstools in the fields and forests of this Earth, but if every spore that they produced were to grow, there would scarcely be room in the world for any other kind of plant. Just think of a million. That's a big enough number for anyone, isn't it? Now think of a trillion, or a million millions. That's a number almost too big to imagine. Yet one single large puffball mushroom produces about seven trillion spores, and a large bracket fungus can put out 30,000 million spores every day for 5 months. As it happens, very few of these spores ever grow, and that is why the world is not overrun by mushrooms and toadstools. But doesn't it seem strange that Nature produces so much merely to go to waste?

There's another type of fungus which does not grow hyphae to make those long mycelia, and which you may have already heard about. This is yeast, which we use in many of our foods and drinks. Yeast cells are good at eating sugar and making alcohol, and all the while they give off lots of carbon dioxide gas, which makes the bubbles in bread and beer and wine. Yeasts have been used to not just make alcohol, but also to generate electricity, so they can have many uses. Not all yeasts are helpful; some of them will spoil our food if we leave it out in the air for yeast cells to settle on.

The soft woolly stuff that grows on stale cake or bread is another fungus, and still another one is the "rust" that sometimes covers the leaves of plants, and finishes up by killing the plants if you don't do something about it. But when we talk about fungi, we usually think of something nicer than these kinds. We think of those quaint fruiting bodies that crop up in all manner of damp places, with their pretty colours and odd shapes, like gay little surprises.

Four Plants That Look Like One

THERE are quite a number of different plants in the pictures here, but all of them are lichens—and we think they're some of the prettiest things we ever see in the bush.

Lichens grow almost everywhere on the face of this Earth—on mountains and in valleys, in hot countries and in cold ones. Also, they grow on all sorts of different things—on rocks, on the ground, on fallen logs, and on trees.

When lichens grow on rocks, they help to break these down into soil. Rocks can also be broken down by water and wind erosion, so lichens accelerate this process. Of course, without soil most plants could not grow, and we ourselves wouldn't be here. So you can see how important lichens are, and what a good thing it is that they do grow everywhere. They likely were the pioneers for plants on earth, making soil for all of the other plants and animals to live in.

One of the reasons why you find them everywhere is that they spread so easily. You see those little cup-like things on some of our sketches? Well, inside them there are hundreds of spores. They're so tiny that you cannot see them without a microscope, yet each of them could become a new lichen plant under the right conditions.

Then also, you will often notice a powderiness over a group of lichens. With a magnifying glass, you would see that this is actually tiny pieces of lichen ready to separate off and become whole new plants.

And now, here is perhaps the most interesting thing of all, about lichens. They are not one kind of plant, but often three or four organisms, all growing together. One of them is a fungus, which takes up water the way roots do and provides a stable home with its nets of hyphae. Others may be a green-coloured alga and even a special 'cyano-bacterium', either of which has the green or red colouring needed to make sugar with the help of energy from sunlight the way green leaves do.

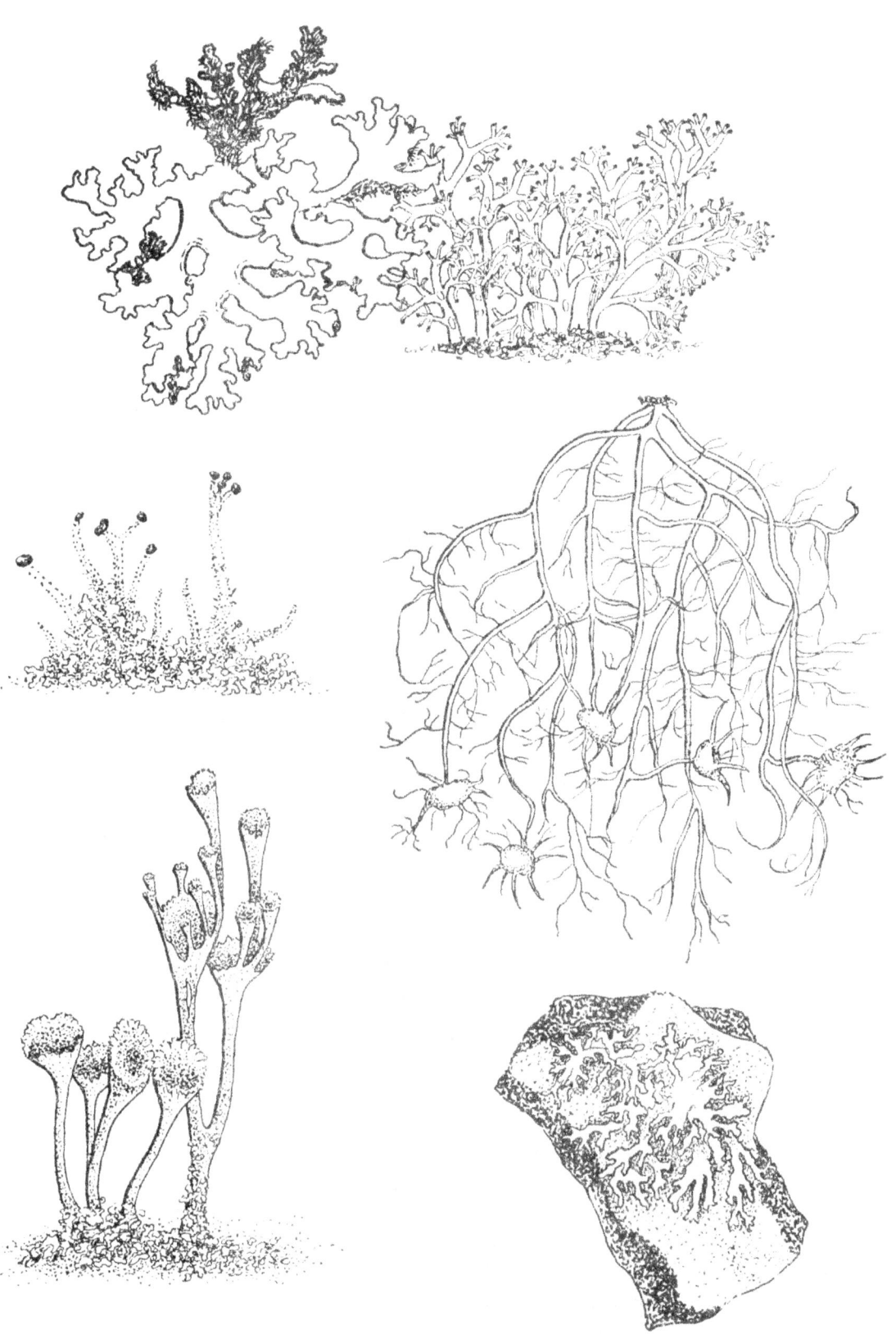

But added to this partnership is also most often a yeast, which is a special type of fungus that does not form threads of hyphae. This yeast seems to help form a hard top layer that protects the delicate hyphae underneath, and without this yeast the lichen cannot survive.

If our lichen is the type that contains 'cyano-bacteria', these also make their own nitrogen fertiliser from the air. So these combinations do very well together. Do you remember that beans and peas have their bacterial and fungus partners? It's amazing how Nature has developed these tiny little self-sufficient partnerships.

The fungus in lichens does another amazing trick with its fine threads of hyphae. It pokes into tiny imperfections and narrow crevices in the rock it is growing on. These hyphae exert enormous pressure as they grow into the rock, and help to split it apart, piece by piece. And when those rock pieces come away they could even move inside the hyphae, where oxalic acid dissolves the rock minerals to make a very nutritious soil for plants to grow in. If fungi and bacteria and algae did not work so beautifully together, we would not have so much nutritious soil for plants to grow in.

Of course, you couldn't tell that a lichen was made up of two or three or even four organisms just by glancing at it. But under a microscope you would see their separate cells closely twined together.

> Oh, lichen, what would teacher say
> If I should do my sums, one day,
> In your peculiar, lichen way?
>
> For one and one do *not* make two
> When added up the way you do.
> Two plants make only *one* of you!
>
> And two and two, when they are adding
> Should make four, but you're amazing;
> There's *still* just you remaining!

A Plant Pioneer

WE were pottering about in National Park one day, taking special notice of all the ferns and mosses growing in a very damp, lush part. We had been talking about the differences between ferns and mosses when suddenly Chris called out, "Well, then, what's *this* one?"

He had wandered down to his favourite spot—to the creek with all its rocks, and its masses of trees all leaning over in the one direction—the way the water was flowing.

We scrambled down over the rich dark earth covered with fallen leaves, and with logs and branches decorated by pretty little fungi. And there, on a rock being constantly splashed with water from the rushing creek, was a beautiful carpet of green. This was the plant he was asking about, and it was neither moss nor fern, but a liverwort—one of the first plants to come up on land out of the sea, after the lichens made soil for it.

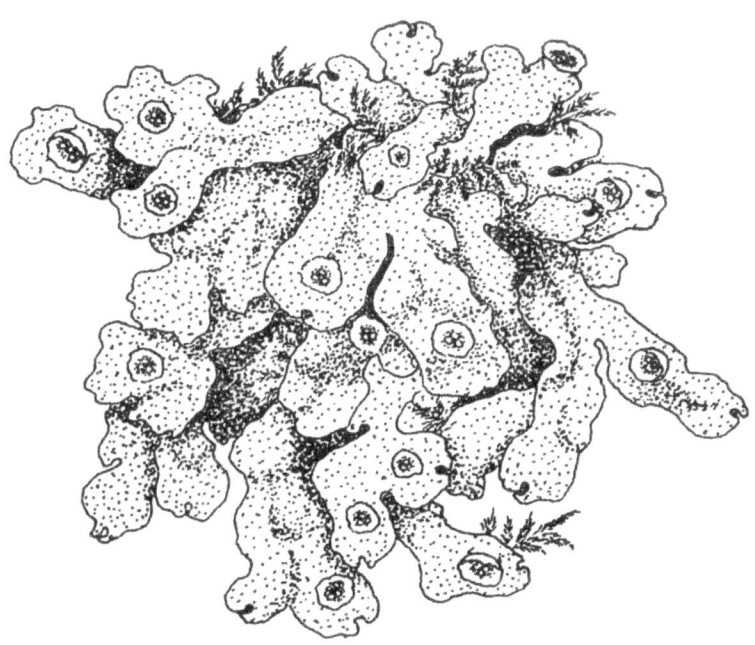

When it did this, it was a real pioneer—just as algae and fungi were, in those lichens. And now, here we were looking at one of its descendants, unchanged for 400 million years.

It clung to the rock closely, getting all the food it needed from the little bit of earth that happened to be there—and of course, plenty to drink from the creek.

In fact, most of the liverworts haven't altogether learnt how to live on dry land even yet—so you very seldom find them in dry spots. But around creeks and waterfalls, they are really happy.

See those little cups all over them? In each one there are several tiny spores—and of course, a spore is a kind of seed.

When you find liverworts in your own bush wanderings, remember about their being some of the most ancient of land plants, and take a really good look at them. Look at them through a magnifying glass if you can, and you'll see tiny whitish spots all over them. These are very pretty, but they have a serious job to do as well. They are the liverwort's breathing holes.

Those Lovely Carpets of Moss

NO matter how often we see moss, in the bush or in our own garden, Tess never grows tired of it. A tree-trunk or a rock covered with moss is always one of her most exciting finds—and if ever Chris should trample on any, she scolds him severely.

Usually, we think of moss as something soft and green and ever so small—and so it mostly is. But the tall moss drawn here was 75mm high, and we have found it even as high as 330mm. And recently, in New Zealand, we saw mosses hanging from the branches of trees in great strands, looking for all the world like ferns.

Now, look at our sketches again, and you will see that nearly all of them show little cases held up on the ends of long thin stems. These are called capsules, and they have hundreds of spores in them, which makes them very much like the seed-boxes of flowers. All mosses, at some time or another, grow capsules.

When the spores are ripe—and usually when the weather is warm and dry—these capsules open up and the spores are set free, to grow into new moss plants if they find a place that suits them.

At the top of each capsule is a pretty little tuft of hairs, soft and silky. (Can you see them in some of our sketches?) When the weather is damp, these hairs fold inward, so that the spores can't get out. But when it is dry, they spring open suddenly—and then, the spores can't stay *in*. This is Nature's clever way of seeing to it that the spores are not washed away and lost in heavy rains.

Notice the little shallow cup on top of one of the plants? If you could look at this under a microscope, you would see lots of tiny curled-up things in it which are as important to moss plants as pollen is to flowers. When you read about flowers, you will understand this better.

Among all the plants on Earth, mosses are some of the most primitive, and in the early days of plant life on land, they did a very important job. With algae, fungi and liverworts, they kept growing and dying and decaying, century after century—and as they did this, they helped to build up soil. When there was enough soil, larger plants were able to grow on Earth—ferns, shrubs, and trees. So that, if it hadn't been for the work of these tiny, humble plants, hundreds of millions of years ago, we wouldn't have our lovely bushlands and forests today.

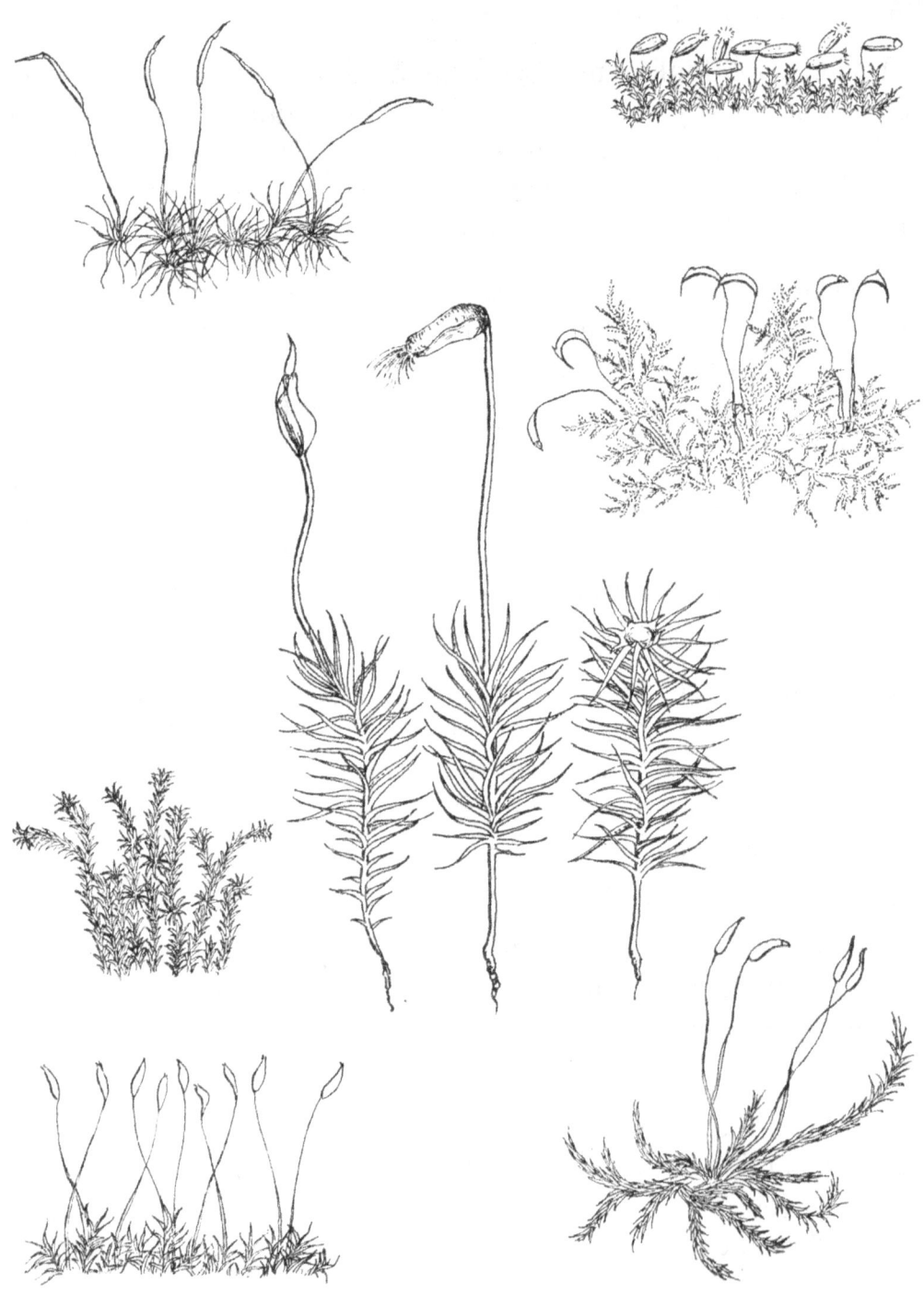

The Magic of Ferns

HAVE you ever imagined what our bushlands and gullies would look like without ferns? Of course, if there were no ferns, there would be something else instead, but surely nothing could be quite so lovely.

In almost every kind of bush or forest you will find some type of fern. Mostly they prefer gullies and other damp, shady places. But some of them, like wire-fern and bracken, also grow out in the open where it is sunny and often dry.

One of the most beautiful sights in the bush is maidenhair—that lover of creeks and gullies with its showers of dainty leaves. And another of the most beautiful sights is the greenness around waterfalls—thousands of soft, green ferns draped over the rocks, wedging out of even the tiniest crevices, sparkling and quivering in the constant spray.

Ferns can be as small as mosses, and as big as trees, and there are countless different sizes in between. Sometimes their leaves are simple—almost like grass. Other times they look like the teeth of a saw, or they may be divided up into dozens of little pieces, as in maidenhair. They seem to be just endlessly varied. But this is not the only interesting thing about fern-leaves.

Have you noticed the little dark patches that often come underneath them? Look at these with a magnifying glass, and you will see that each patch is made up of many powdery specks. These specks are fern "seeds" or spores. Some ferns can have spores on any of their leaves, but others have to grow special leaves for them, and these always look different from the ordinary ones. Sometimes they are thinner to look at but thicker to touch, as their edges are rolled back around the spores. Other times they are long instead of short, but always they have *some* sort of difference.

See how many ferns *you* can find that grow special leaves for spores.

By the way, you know the thin black stems of maidenhair, the long tough ones of bracken, and so on? Well, these are not real stems at all. They are just leaf stalks. The real stems run along under the ground, sprouting roots that grow downwards, and tiny rolled-up "fronds" that push up above the earth and then slowly uncurl into full-sized leaves.

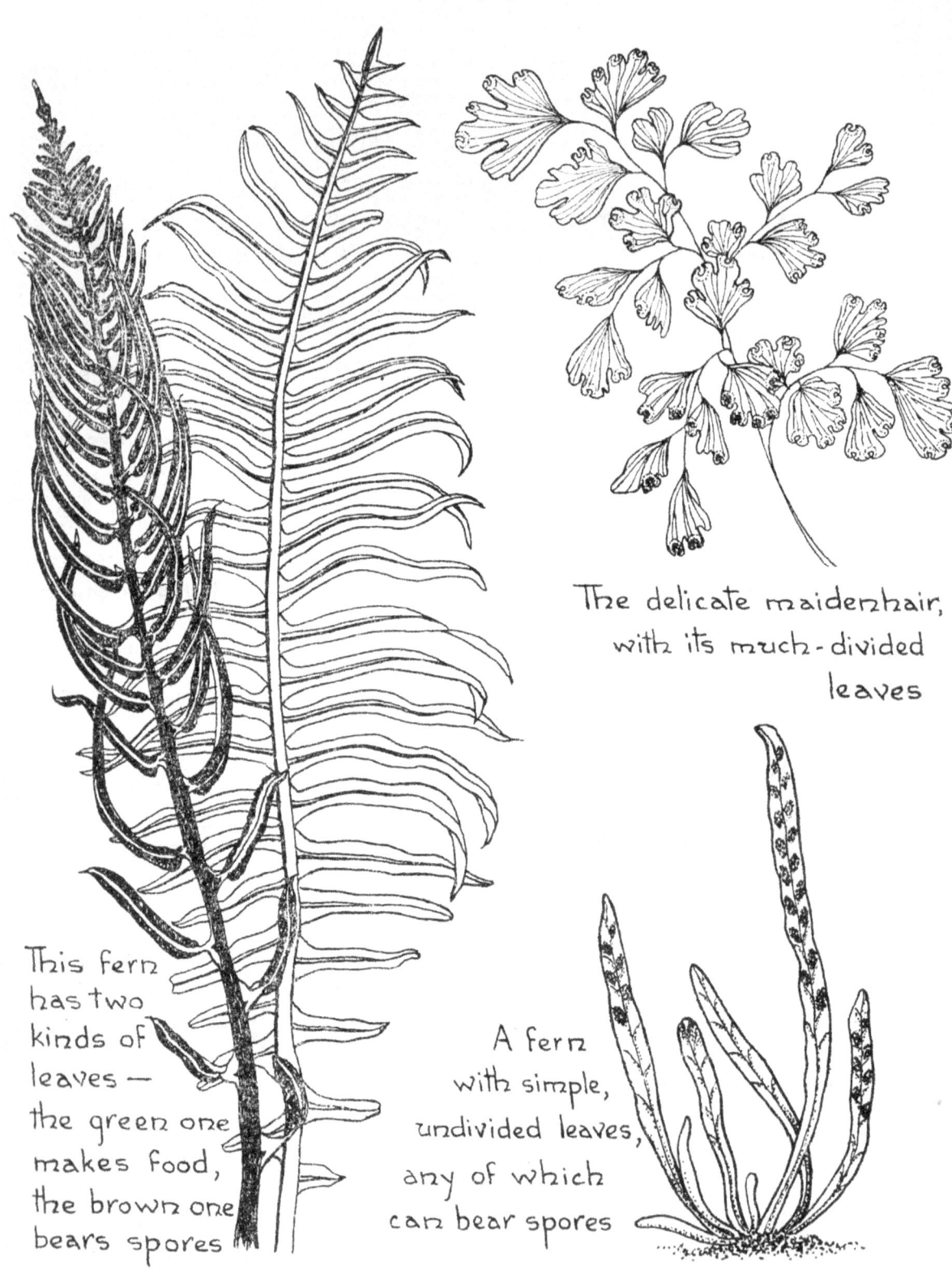

The delicate maidenhair, with its much-divided leaves

This fern has two kinds of leaves — the green one makes food, the brown one bears spores

A fern with simple, undivided leaves, any of which can bear spores

Mostly, the whole separate fern plants that you see are not really separate, but just clusters of shoots from the one trailing, underground stem. As you can imagine, ferns travel quite long distances in this way. And wherever they travel, they carry their magical beauty.

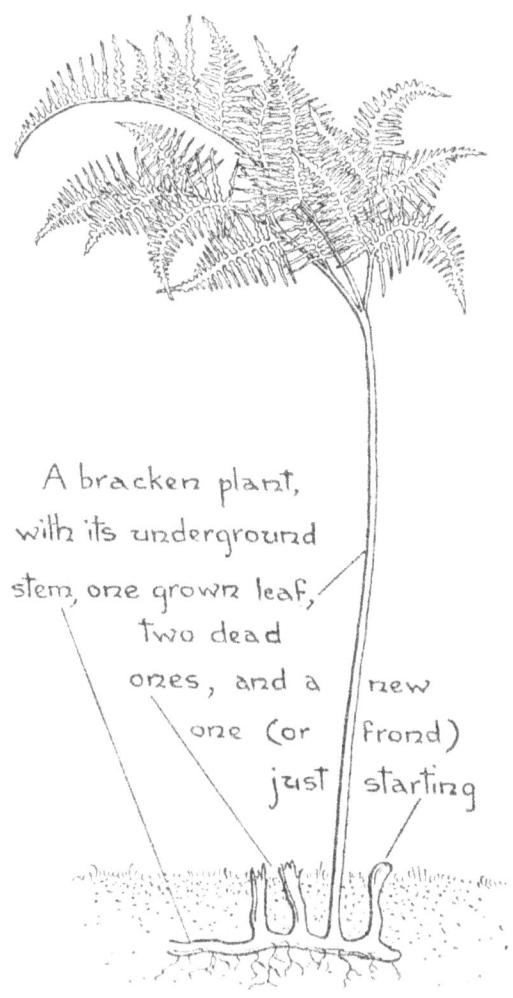

A bracken plant, with its underground stem, one grown leaf, two dead ones, and a new one (or frond) just starting

Next time you have a chance, stoop down and examine one of those tiny moss-like ferns with leaves that look almost transparent... very gently touch some of the soft little curled-up fronds of bigger ones... then stand under the great spreading leaf-umbrella of a giant tree-fern... and you will realise that ferns are not only lovely to look at. They are also real, living friends.

Plants That Have Cones

A CONE is the nearest thing to a flower that any non-flowering plant produces. In a way you could almost call it a brown flower—and some cones are nearly as pretty. There is one kind which looks exactly like a brown rose when it loosens out. Then there are the famous pine cones that everyone knows. They are not like flowers, but they're quite as beautiful in their own way, and—with a little white paint dotted over them to look like snow—they're one of our prettiest decorations at Christmas time.

Unlike mosses, liverworts, ferns, lichens and fungi which produce spores, cone-bearing plants produce true seeds. A spore is a fairly simple thing, often with only one cell and a hard wall, but a seed has a great deal in it. It has the tiny baby plant (or embryo), and seed leaves (or cotyledons) in which plenty of food is stored for that important time when the embryo is about to grow bigger and emerge into the outside world. When the seed is about to sprout like this, we say that the seed is germinating.

Although cones produce seeds, they do not produce them in the same way as flowers do. Flowers keep theirs tucked up inside special little boxes, but cones keep theirs down at the bottom of woody leaves or scales. While the seeds are still not ripe, the scales are pressed together closely, but when the seeds *are* ripe, the scales open out and separate. Now the seeds—each with a delicate little wing—can escape.

They flutter to the ground prettily—or sometimes, if there is a wind, they go whirling off ever so far before settling down to grow into new trees. These are real travellers, and, of course, they spread their kind far and wide.

Even though you must all know pine-trees quite well, perhaps you have never noticed that they have two different types of cones—male and female. The large cones that everybody knows are the females. These are the ones that hold the seeds. The males come in clusters on other branches, and are so small that you might not even see them unless you were specially looking.

Although they are so much smaller, these male cones have the same

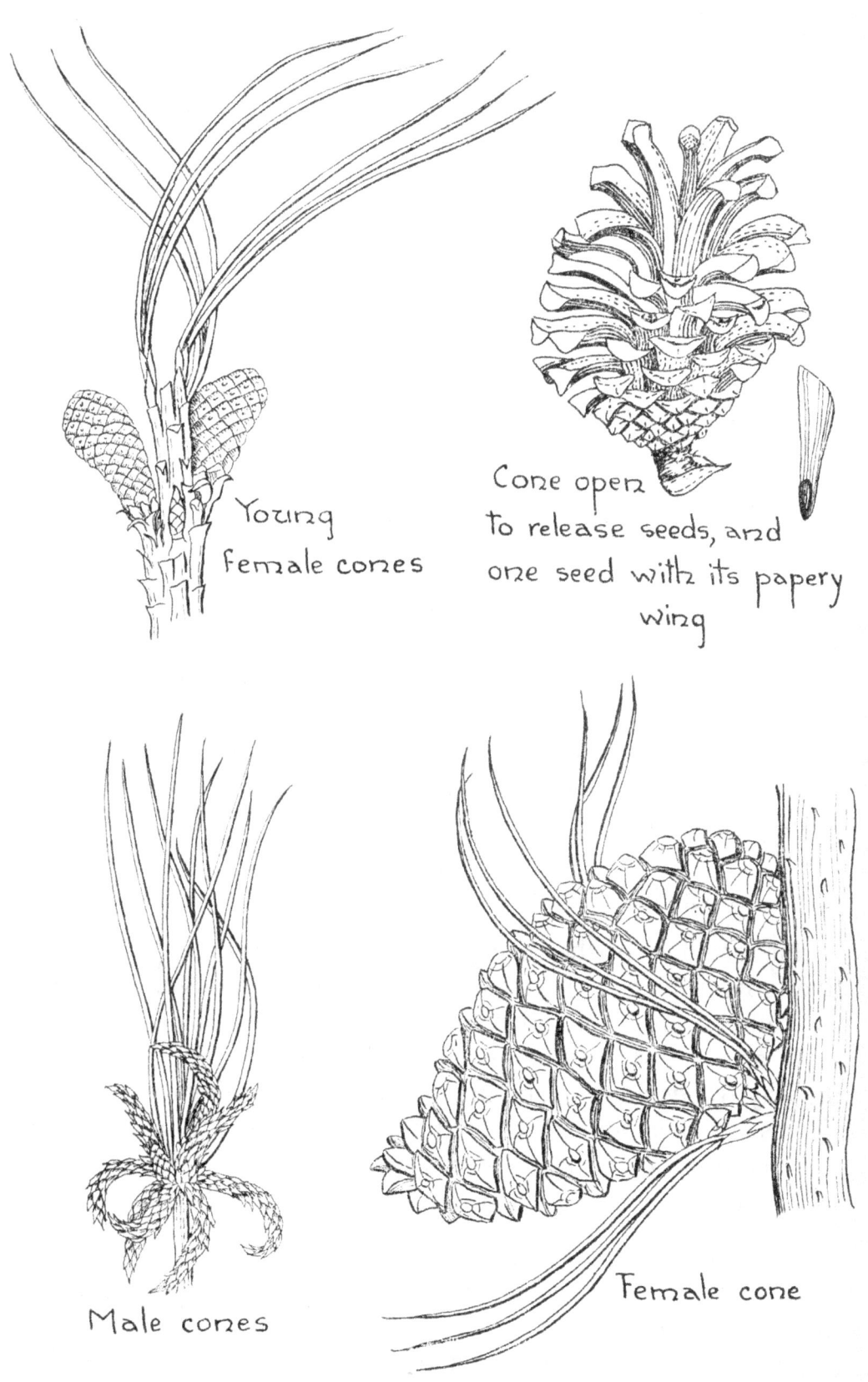

arrangement as the females, with many little leafy scales pressed closely together. Only instead of young seeds at the bottom of each scale, there are pollen grains—like the pollen in flowers. When this pollen is ripe, the scales open apart and set it free. It comes out in a powdery shower, like a yellow cloud, with thousands—perhaps millions—of grains in each cloud. Nature has to produce enormous numbers of pollen grains, for—as they are blown about by the wind—so many of them get lost. But some of them arrive where they are meant to, on the young female cones.

At this stage, the female cones are quite small, and their leafy scales are well separated, so that the pollen grains can get in between them and find their way to the young seeds. After this happens, the seed goes on developing until it can grow into a new plant. But if no pollen grain comes along, the tiny undeveloped seed just shrivels away and dies.

Plants with cones belong to two big families. Pines, cypresses and many others that grow in cool climates are called conifers—and you may have noticed that these have special kinds of leaves. You never see a conifer with large flat leaves like those of the oak, plane, or kurrajong, or oval ones like those of the Moreton Bay fig. They are often thin and needle-like. That's why pine leaves are called "needles". Or they may be small, and closely packed together up their stems. And when conifers grow into big trees, they are some of the most beautiful and handsome in the world.

But members of the other cone family—the cycads—look more like ferns or palms, and these seldom grow very high. Their leaves are called a crown, for they grow in circles around the top of the stem, and spread out like great, deeply divided fronds. They unroll the way fronds do, too, and in the very centre of them is a single tall impressive cone pointing right up to the sky. Their trunk looks rather like that of a tree-fern, since the lower-down fronds die and fall off, leaving a pattern of dry frond residues all around the trunk.

Some plants have a large female cone, and others a smaller male cone—and it's the same story of pollen grains and young seeds all over again. Some cycads have developed interesting helpers; for example, some use beetles to spread their pollen, instead of hoping

A cycad, with its crown of leaves and one central cone

that the wind will blow it into a neighbouring female cone, and some use light-sensitive cyanobacteria to help them make food with energy from the sun, and nitrogen from the air.

When you go motoring around, you should look for these beautiful plants, which grow mostly in warm or hot climates. And when you find them, you can feel that you are looking at some of the world's earliest history. Way back in prehistoric times between 100 million and 300 million years ago, cycads abounded on Earth, looking the same as they do today. We know this because of fossils.

But up in Queensland, near Mount Tamborine, there's one of them, still alive, that is almost old enough to be a fossil. It is actually 10,000 years old. That's hard to believe, isn't it? Yet there it is—very famous, with a brass plate telling all about it, and its photograph on many postcards. Just think... 10,000 years ago, people were just beginning to learn how to grow crops, which made it possible for them to live in a settled home, instead of having to spend their lives wandering from place to place in search of food. And right back then, at the very dawn of civilisation as we know it, that ancient cycad in Queensland was sprouting its first leaves.

You can imagine how quiet and thoughtful Tess felt, standing beside it while I took her photograph with it.

Scale from a male cone, with dozens of little boxes filled with pollen

Scale from a female cone, with two seeds

Flowers—and the Clever Things They Do

ONE day when we were out bush wandering, I asked Tess what she thought were the most exciting of all plants. That seemed impossible to answer for a few minutes, then she said, "Well, perhaps mosses and ferns."

Then I asked Chris, and he said, "Oh, I don't know. It would depend on what kind of flowers they had."

"But in any case, they'd be plants with flowers?" I asked. He agreed—and that, I think, is how most people would feel.

There's a very special excitement about flowers—mainly because of their colour, of course. Then, there's the lovely perfume that some of them have, and many of them have strange and beautiful shapes.

All of this is why, as we said before, it is difficult to imagine a world without flowers. Yet for many, hundreds of millions of years, that is exactly what our Earth was. And the first flowers to appear were probably not very different from cones. Then, gradually, all kinds of changes took place.

Wonderful as it may be to look at, the one serious purpose in a flower's life is to produce seeds. Its colour, its perfume, and its form have all been planned for this one important reason. Now, let us look more closely, and see what a flower is made of.

First, there is a ring of little leaf-like things called sepals, and the whole group of them together is called the calyx. These protect the flower when it is a bud, and help to hold it firmly together afterwards.

Just inside these, there are the petals, which, as a group, are called the corolla. Inside these again there are the stamens in which pollen is formed, and in the very centre is the pistil.

Well, we have had a lot of new words already, and now we are going to have some more, because the pistil is made up of three sections. At the top is the stigma—often like a little button. Attached to this is the style, which is a stalk that dips right down deep into the flower and connects with the ovary or seed-box. Inside the ovary are the ovules or baby seeds, but—the same as with the baby seeds in cones—these would never be able to grow into new plants without the help of pollen grains. A pollen grain must find its way to each tiny ovule, and unite with it, before a true seed can form. So, in the making of seeds, the pollen grains and ovules are equally important, and all the interesting things that a flower has—its shape, colour, and perfume—are to make it easier for the pollen to reach the ovule.

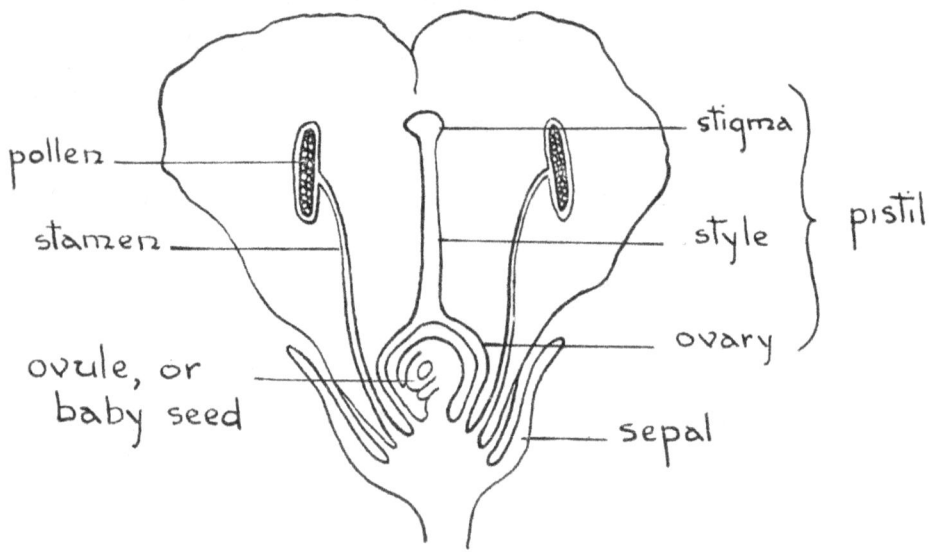

Diagram of a Flower (cut down in half)

You may remember how the pollen from cones is carried by the wind—which means that a great deal of it must be lost and wasted. But if, in some way, it can be carried straight from one flower to another, it isn't wasted nearly so much. And this is exactly what happens with many flowers. Their pollen is carried from one to another by insects.

Of course, the insects do not know that they are doing this. They visit the flowers because they are attracted by their colours and the delicious smell of their nectar. (So now we can understand why flowers have grown to look and smell the way they do.) Let us pause for a moment and see what happens.

Along comes a bee, intent upon gathering pollen and nectar to take back to her hive. She burrows deep into a flower to sip its nectar. At the same time—as she brushes past its stamens—pollen collects in the special little baskets on her back legs, and much of it dusts off on to her pretty fur coat. Then, following up this particular taste of nectar, she visits another flower of the same kind. She burrows down into it again, and as she does so, she cannot help brushing against the flower's stigma.

When the flower's ovules are fully grown, its stigma is so sticky that some of the pollen on the bee's fur coat catches on to it. This is called pollination, and it is exactly what was meant to happen. From the stigma, the pollen grains grow down the style, and their tips find the ovules, and then at last true seeds can form.

Many flowers are satisfied that when an insect visits them, it will pollinate them in return for the nectar meal that they provide for it. But others, it seems, are not so sure, and—through thousands of centuries—these have become very clever and cunning. To make doubly certain, they have grown into special shapes, and mastered some really clever tricks.

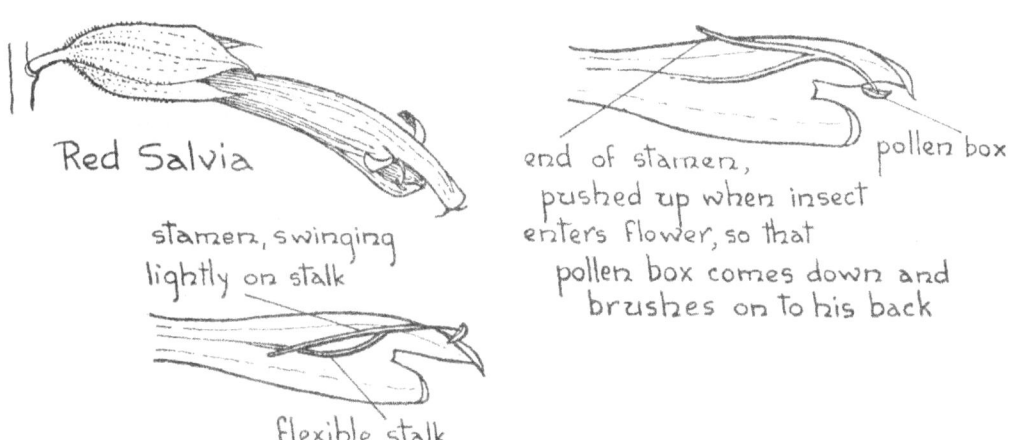

Look at the salvia, for instance. Its petals are joined into a short or long tube—short in the purple salvia, long in the red one. Its two stamens are attached to this tube in a special way. Sometimes they form a kind of lever, other times they swing lightly on the top of a delicate stalk. A bee calls on the flower for nectar. She lands on the lower rim of the petal tube, burrows down into it, and—without realising it—touches the stamen in such a way that the top of it, where the pollen is kept, swings down and taps her lightly on the back, powdering her

with pollen. Then she goes to another salvia flower, whose stigma, if it is ripe, is hanging down from the top of the flower, sticky enough to collect some of the pollen off her back.

In the bush you must often have come across the bright-pink flowers of trigger plants. Next time you do, stop and have a closer look at them. They each have four little petals, arranged like the wings of butterflies. Rising up from the centre of the flower is a column, which is a combination of stamens and pistil—but the pollen and stigma ripen at different times. As soon as an insect alights on the flower, the column snaps down on to its back, either giving it a good dusting with its pollen if its pollen is ripe, or collecting some of it off its coat if its stigma is ripe.

Then, there's a clever little greenhood orchid—also very common in some parts of the bush. The same as all other orchids, it has a special petal called the labellum—only, when an insect lands on this particular one, its labellum snaps up hard so that exit is impossible without a certain amount of pushing and squeezing. And of course, with those pushes and squeezes, it has to brush up against the orchid's column, which carries its pollen and stigma.

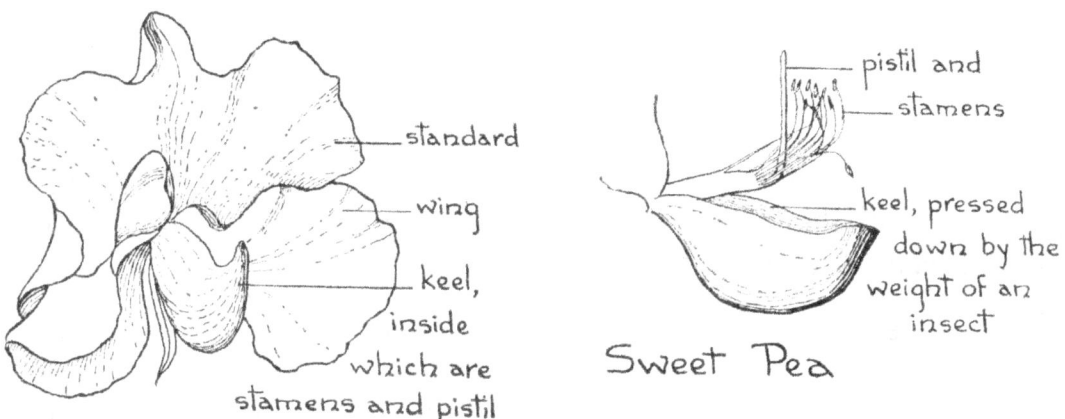

Sweet Pea

The sweet pea is another interesting flower when it comes to pollination. We all know how light and flouncy it is, like a fairy in a party-frock. But look closely and you will see that it has three different kinds of petals—a large spreading one at the back called the standard, two fluttery ones at the sides called the wings, and two joined together in the front, something like a boat. These are called the keel. Lying snugly inside the keel are the stamens and pistil. Along comes a bee, and lands on the keel. This immediately sinks down under her weight, bringing her up against either powdery pollen or sticky stigma, as the case may be. There are ever so many members of the sweet pea family—both in gardens and in the bush—and you can get a lot of fun studying the way they behave when insects are around.

Tess had been pottering in her little garden patch one day when she came in and asked me suddenly, "Mummie, why do some flowers grow separately, and others all together in bunches?"

"Well," I said, "what do you mean by a flower that grows separately?"

"Oh, dandelions and sunflowers, you know."

"But that's just what dandelions and sunflowers *don't* do," I told her. "One dandelion 'flower', as you call it, is made up of dozens of tiny flowers all massed together. And a sunflower is too. Only with a sunflower, the flowers are all in the centre. You actually *call* them the 'centre', in fact. And the big yellow things that we call petals are also flowers – only those are just pretending flowers."

"*How* just pretending ones?" she asked.

"You see, long ago they *used* to be real flowers, but gradually, during thousands of years, they changed. They lost their ability to make seeds, and became just big showy things instead. Of course, this doesn't mean that they're not important. They *are*. They attract plenty of insects with their bright colour, and they also help to hold that very special 'centre' together, where all the real flowers are."

So we went outside to have a look, and Tess was delighted with this new discovery about dozens of tiny flowers that looked like only one. Then we talked a little about all the other ways in which flowers can arrange themselves.

Each of these arrangements is called an inflorescence, and there are many different kinds of inflorescences. Sometimes flowers will grow all the way up a stem with the oldest at the bottom and the youngest at the top. This is called a raceme inflorescence, and it is the one you find most often. But look at all the other kinds in our diagrams. Did you realise that flowers arranged themselves in so many different ways?

The next time you find a number of flowers grouped together on a stem, see if you can tell what their kind of inflorescence is. At first you might hesitate quite a bit, but after a while you will become really clever at it.

Have you ever looked carefully at the leaves of flowering plants? If so, you may have noticed that some of them have networks of veins while others have parallel ones—that is, long, straight lines of them, running in the same direction. If you *have* noticed this, you may also have looked to see if their flowers were different in any special way. Actually, plants with parallel veins in their leaves often have the parts of their flowers in threes, or in numbers multiplied by three. For instance, they may have three sepals and petals, six stamens, and a pistil made up of three parts joined together. But the plants with networks of veins in their leaves mostly have the parts of their flowers in fours or fives.

If you have noticed these things already, you must be a very keen observer. If not, they will give you some idea of the many interesting and surprising facts that are all around you, waiting for you to discover them as your eyes grow sharper, and as you train your mind to work *together* with your eyes, thinking out possible connections between different things.

There's another little secret about plants with parallel veins or with network ones. When we were talking about cone plants, we mentioned that their seeds have special leaves. Do you remember their name? Cotyledons. Well, the seeds of flowering plants have cotyledons too, packed full of food for the baby plants to use when they start to grow. But plants with parallel veins in their leaves usually have only one cotyledon in their seeds, while those with network veins usually have two.

If you think of how a pea, bean, cashew or almond nut is made, with two halves of the seed able to be easily separated, you clearly have two cotyledons. On the other hand, a maize (corn) or wheat seed has only one fleshy part that does not split easily into two similar halves, so these are called mono-cotyledon plants.

However, whether there are one or two halves to a seed, all seeds

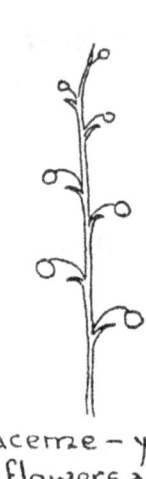
Raceme — youngest flowers at top

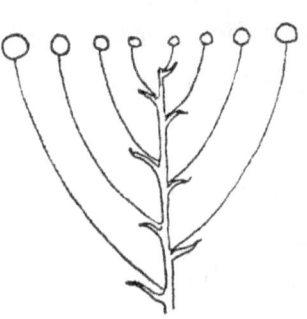
Corym — like raceme except that older flowers have longer stems

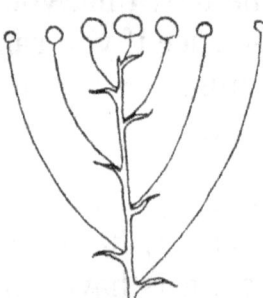
Cyme — like corym except that younger flowers have longer stems

Panicle — branching racemes

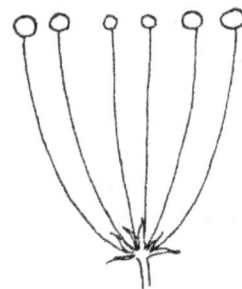
Umbel — all flowers coming from same point

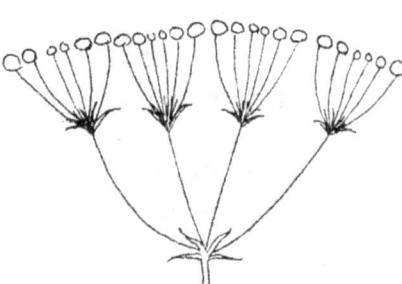
Compound Umbel — branching umbels

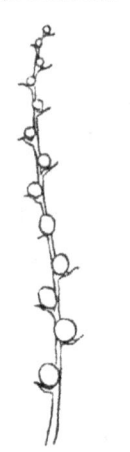
Spike — flowers very close to stem, and to one another

Catkin — like a spike, except that each flower has a protective scale

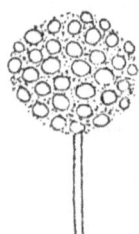
Head, or Capitulum — Top of stem has broadened and flattened. Flowers, massed together over it, look like a button

Types of Inflorescence

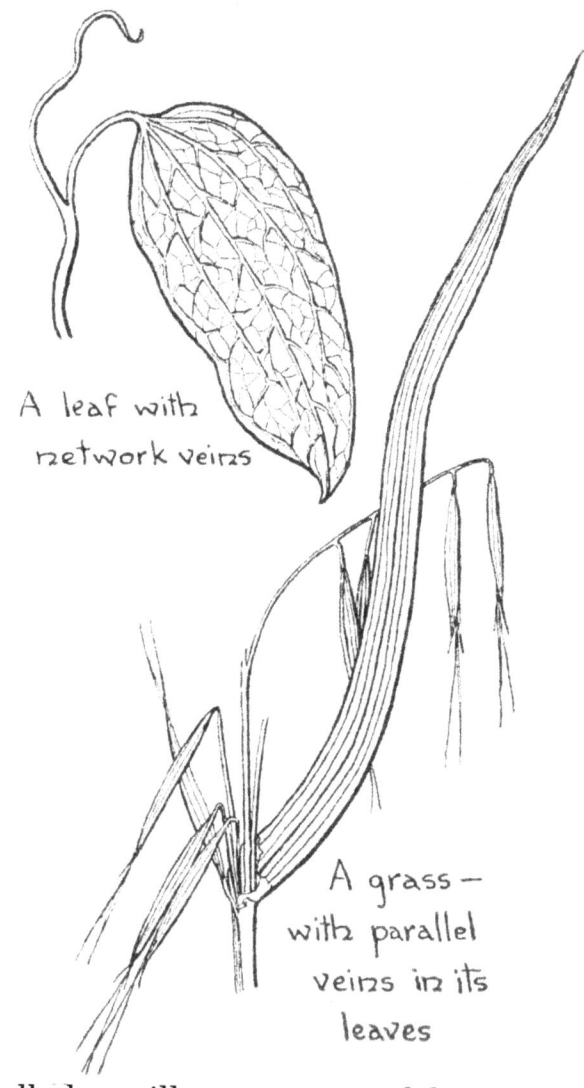

A leaf with network veins

A grass — with parallel veins in its leaves

have one little stalk that will grow up out of the earth, using the food from those cotyledons to make the trip to sunlight.

Chris said, "I know about parallel veins. Grasses have them, don't they?"

When I said yes, Tess exclaimed, "Heavens! Then there must be more plants with parallel veins than any others."

But there aren't. Only about a quarter of the world's plants have parallel veins—and one cotyledon. The rest have mostly network-veined leaves, and have two cotyledons.

Now just think for a moment. Could you pick out any one flower as more beautiful than all the others? Most likely not, because they're all so lovely. Well then, is there one that you would pick as the highest among flowers, just as people are the highest of the animals? There *is* one, I think—a very advanced flower indeed. It's the orchid. And it doesn't have to be large and showy and colourful, like the orchids that you see in florists' and glasshouses. It can be one of the shyest flowers in the bush, swaying almost invisibly among tall grasses, or scarcely raising its little brown head above the earth. And I always think that there's something rather elfish about orchids in the bush, because it really does seem, at times, as if you have to have special eyes to find them.

> I try, in thought, to see that way-back hour
> When, shy and rather plain, maybe,
> With no one there to know or see,
> There bloomed the Earth's first flower.
>
> It may have lived one single day, no more—
> Yet Earth awoke, that day, to find,
> Deep in her forests green, a kind
> Of magic never known before.
>
> And ever since, with petals softly curled,
> The blossoms of a million springs—
> Like fairies borne on rainbow wings—
> Have spread their bright enchantment through the world.

How Seeds Travel

HAVE you ever thought of what would happen if seeds never travelled? Suppose they just dropped to the ground immediately below the plant that produced them! There would be so many of them, all in a bunch, that in dark and dry areas there wouldn't be enough light, water, or soil to go round, so the plants would be stunted and sickly.

Also, there would be a huge group of waratahs in just one part of the bush—of wattles in another—of boronias in another—and we would never have the thrill of coming across an odd plant of this or that where we least expected it. So there wouldn't be anything like so much fun in bush-wandering, and the world itself wouldn't be nearly so beautiful.

But Nature, in her wisdom, has looked after this problem by seeing to it that when they need to move, those seeds can travel far and wide.

Now, when we want to travel, we go by train, bus, ship, aeroplane, or some other thing that moves—and some day, we might even go from country to country by rocket. But what do seeds do? Certainly they don't book flights on aeroplanes—they have wings of their own. Or, if not wings, bits of fluff or hairy parachutes.

They don't step on to trains and buses, but they catch on to animals and people, and get carried around like that. Some of them have little bristles and hooks to catch on with, others have such a gluey coat that they stick on.

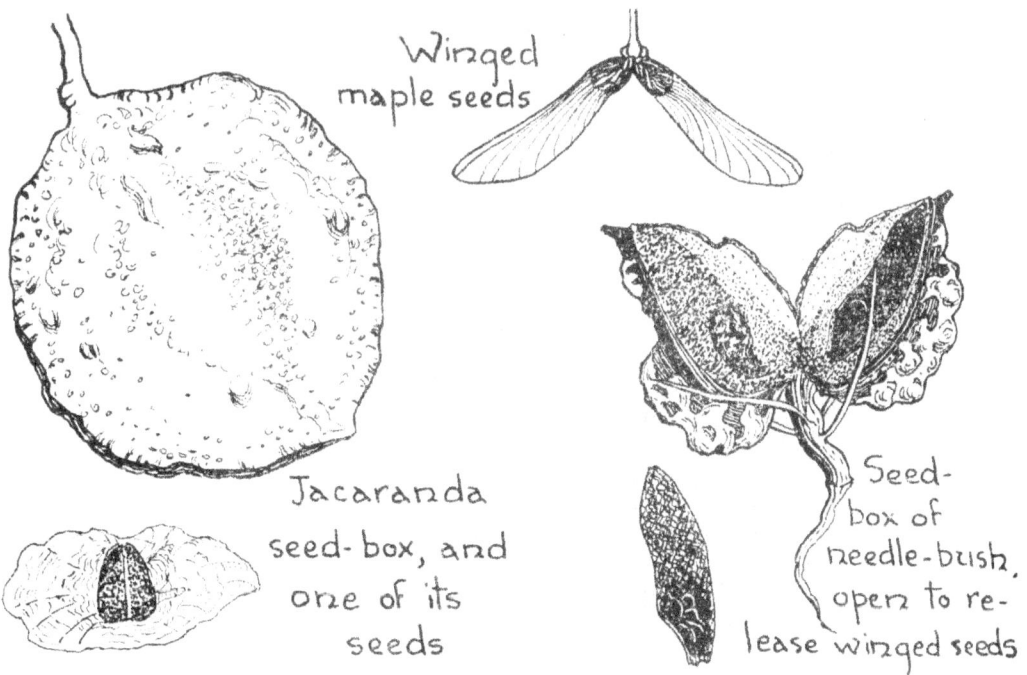

Winged maple seeds

Jacaranda seed-box, and one of its seeds

Seed-box of needle-bush, open to release winged seeds

Two common wayside plants—with their barbed seeds

Seeds do not cruise the oceans in ships, but then, they don't need to, for any amount of them can float—or at least the fruits that enclose them can. Off they go riding on currents and bobbing about on waves, from island to island, or country to country. Coconuts float like this, and the fruits of she-oaks and mangroves, and those of some grasses, rolled up inside a dry-grass "roly-poly".

No one, as yet, has built a rocket for seeds—but that's all right, because some of them can act like rockets themselves. As soon as they are ripe, the little cases enclosing them become dry and brittle, and snap open. Sometimes they even twist like a spring as they open, but in any case, the seeds shoot out in all directions, and land quite a distance away.

So you see, one of the most interesting things you can do is to watch how seeds behave and what they sometimes "wear" when they set out for their new homes—for those places where they will settle down and try to grow into new plants. You will find any amount of them with wings, like those that we have already met on many of the cone plants. Needle-bushes have seeds with wings, and also mountain-devils, waratahs, jacarandas, maples, sycamores, and many others.

Usually the seed is attached to just one end of its wing, but sometimes—as in the elm, and jacaranda—it perches fair-and-square in the middle of it.

With a fair breeze blowing, these little flying seeds can travel quite surprising distances. So can the ones with fluffs (like the milkweed and clematis), and hairy parachutes (like the dandelion). These fluffs and parachutes are extremely frail, but they are blown about all the easier for this—and besides, with their seeds so light, they don't need to be any stronger. Studies done as recently as 2017 have shown that dandelion seeds, with their flat and airy parachutes, move through the air with just enough friction against the air flowing through them to form smooth circles of twisting air currents (called 'vortices') in their wake. This helps them to move the furthest possible distance in the

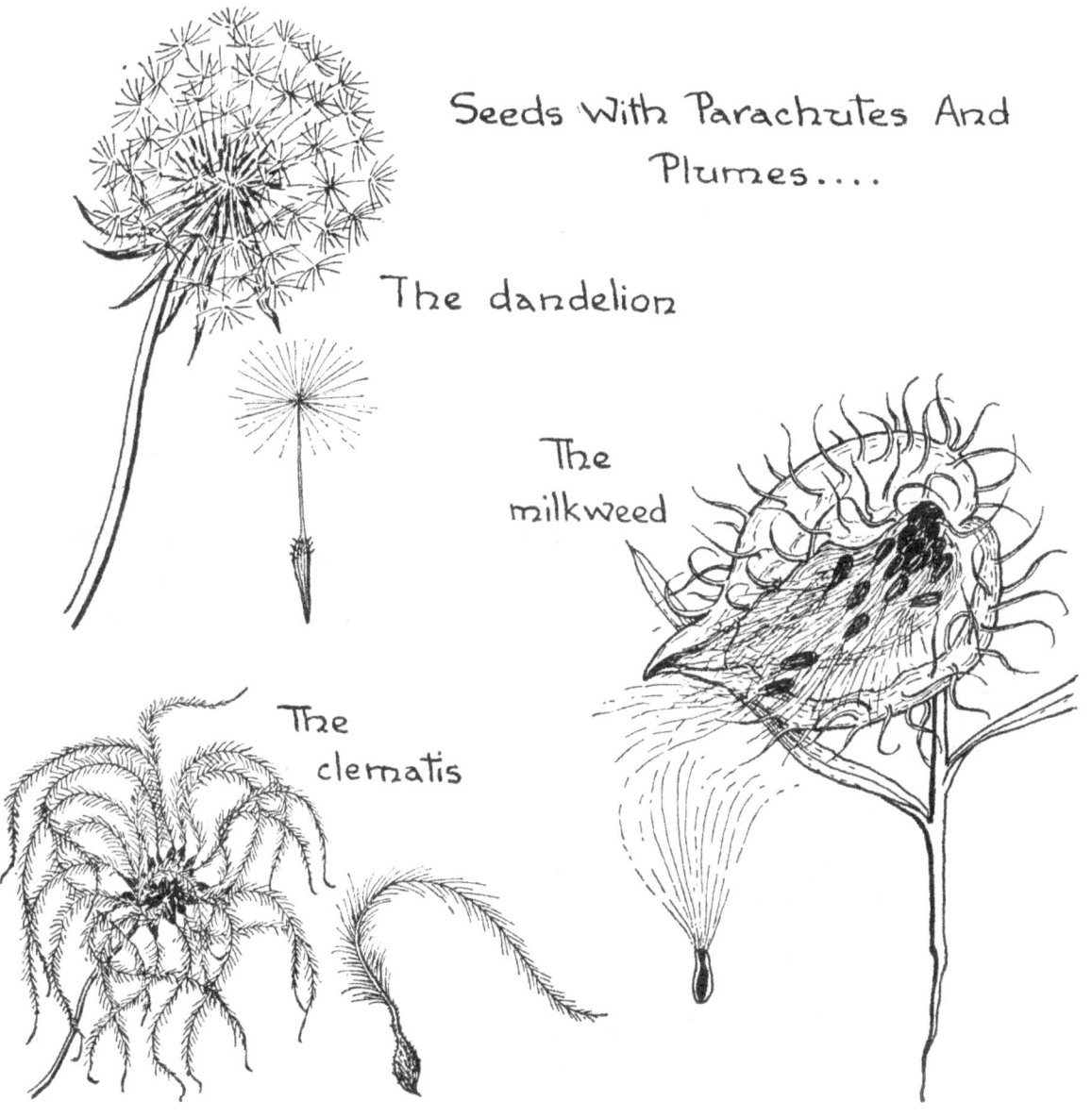

Seeds With Parachutes And Plumes....

The dandelion

The milkweed

The clematis

gentlest of winds. Even now, after we have been making rockets and airplanes and seem to have conquered movement through air, these ancient seed designs are still able to teach us how we could do it better.

All of these seeds are pretty little things, too, which we often find ourselves stopping to touch and admire. But seeds with hooks and barbs (like burrs, and bidgee-widgees) are a different story altogether. They prick us and plague us, and all we want to do is to pull them off and throw them away. But by the time we do this, we have walked some distance from where we collected them—and this is exactly what their plants have wished for.

The mistletoe and wild daphne (pittosporum) have sticky seeds which some birds eat—but many of these seeds also rub off onto the sides of their beaks. Sometimes, too, the seeds cling to the legs and feathers of birds, and so get carried around from tree to tree. And of course, there are hundreds of plants whose fruits are eaten by animals and people, while the seeds are thrown out onto the ground—as Nature intended. Every time you eat an apple or an orange and throw the seeds away, you are doing exactly what those fruit-trees need for the spreading of their kind. Seeds are *such* a successful method for spreading plants, that you have to be careful what seeds you throw out, so you are not spreading invasive weeds through the bush.

Many of the seeds that are shot through the air, by a sudden opening and twisting of their cases, belong to the pea family and the wattles. Try it for yourselves. Touch one of these seed boxes when it is dry and brittle, and see how it snaps open with a twist, sending the seeds flying out. Even when a seed-box doesn't twist, the suddenness of its opening is usually enough to jerk the seeds out, and spread them around.

Then, there are seed-boxes that behave like little salt and pepper shakers. Holes appear over the tops of them, as soon as the seeds inside them are ripe—and as these shakers bob about in breezes, the seeds are shaken out. Poppy seed-boxes have very tiny holes, but those of gumtrees are usually quite large.

In the North of Australia, all around our hot, wet, and muddy coast, an amazing network of roots form into a dense forest at the water's edge. This 'root forest' is only around 1m high, but it's really hard to walk and slosh through. Roots emerge high in the air from the trunks of mangrove trees, then poke down into the salty water and mud. Unlike most other plants, mangroves can drink salt water so they never get too thirsty. Another mangrove advantage is the plentiful sunlight in our hot tropics.

This special mangrove also has special seeds, as you may have already guessed. The seeds start growing into a little plant while they are still attached to their parent. Their roots grow downward, ending in a sharp pointed spear at their tip. If they drop and do not float away, they could be immediately planted and start happily growing, making that dense mangrove swamp even denser. So maybe a trip to a mangrove "beach" may not be so much fun for us! But many creatures enjoy the rich muddy food that these "forests" harbour, and mangroves do help to stop powerful waves from washing away our coastline.

You could make a really interesting hobby of studying the many clever ways in which plants get their seeds to grow in the best possible ways. You could even have a little notebook set aside for sketching them, and writing down all the wonderful things you find out about them.

> If I could be a tiny seed,
> I wonder what I'd wear—
> A wing, a hook, a parachute,
> Or just a tuft of hair?
>
> I'd have to choose most carefully,
> For that would then decide
> If, travelling round, I'd fly, or swim,
> Or merely "hook" a ride.

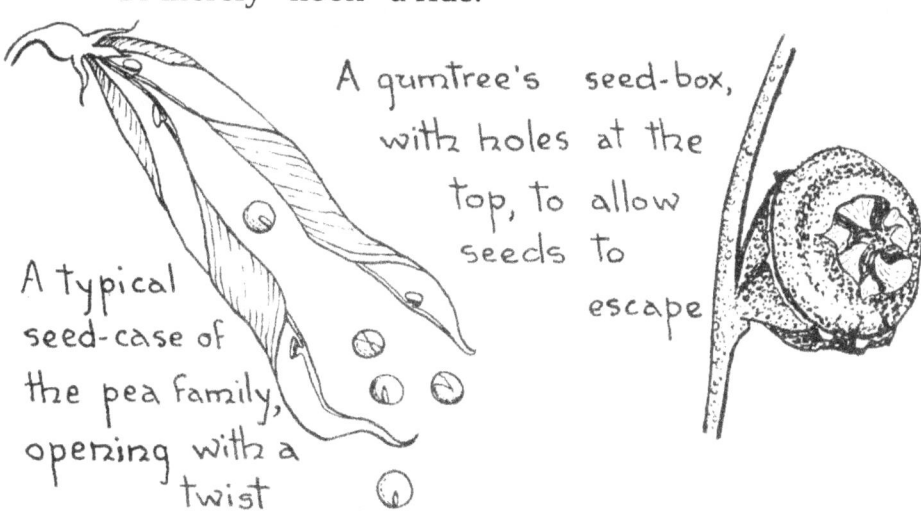

A typical seed-case of the pea family, opening with a twist

A gumtree's seed-box, with holes at the top, to allow seeds to escape

Plants That Pretend

TESS and Chris always take special delight in the way some animals hide to protect themselves from danger.

The stick insect hangs quite still among tree branches, and often you cannot see it even if you are looking for it. The colours of many caterpillars and moths blend perfectly with their surroundings. The frog changes colour as it moves from one place to another. The polar bear is as white as the icy world it lives in. Some crabs cover themselves so completely with seaweed that you wouldn't suspect they were there. Starfish on the bottom of a rock pool look just like the mottled surface of the rock itself. The Wanderer butterfly has a nasty taste which protects it from birds.

There are so many clever and interesting things that animals do, just to pretend that they are not what they really are, or even that they are not there at all. But when I mentioned to the children one day that many plants also pretend—as much as animals do—they looked very surprised indeed.

"I've never seen a plant that looks like an elephant or a kangaroo—or like anything else that isn't a plant," said Tess. So I reminded her that looking like an elephant or a kangaroo wouldn't help with a plant's problems, which are so different from those of animals.

For the most part, plants do not have to protect themselves from the viciousness of other plants, but they do need protection against dry weather. Of all things, this is perhaps their chief enemy. Leave a flower out of water, and you know how quickly it dies. Unless you keep your garden well watered during the hot summer months, many of your plants will wither away. Plants simply cannot live without water, any more than animals can. But animals can move around looking for it here, there and everywhere, and this is something that plants *cannot* do. Mostly they are anchored for their whole lives in the one spot—so, if they are going to make sure of their water supply, they have to be very clever indeed.

Now, the leaves of a plant are very special and important. They are its greenest parts—and because of this, they make most of the plant's food. You will remember that fungi cannot make food for themselves because they are never green. A plant's greenness is called chlorophyll. With chlorophyll, sunlight, air and water, a plant can manufacture sugar and starch. So naturally, as the leaves are the greenest parts, they do most of the manufacturing. For this reason they are often spoken of as a plant's factories.

But they also have a lot of tiny openings on their undersides called stomates—and in hot dry weather, water passes out of the plant through these stomates, leaving it limp and thirsty.

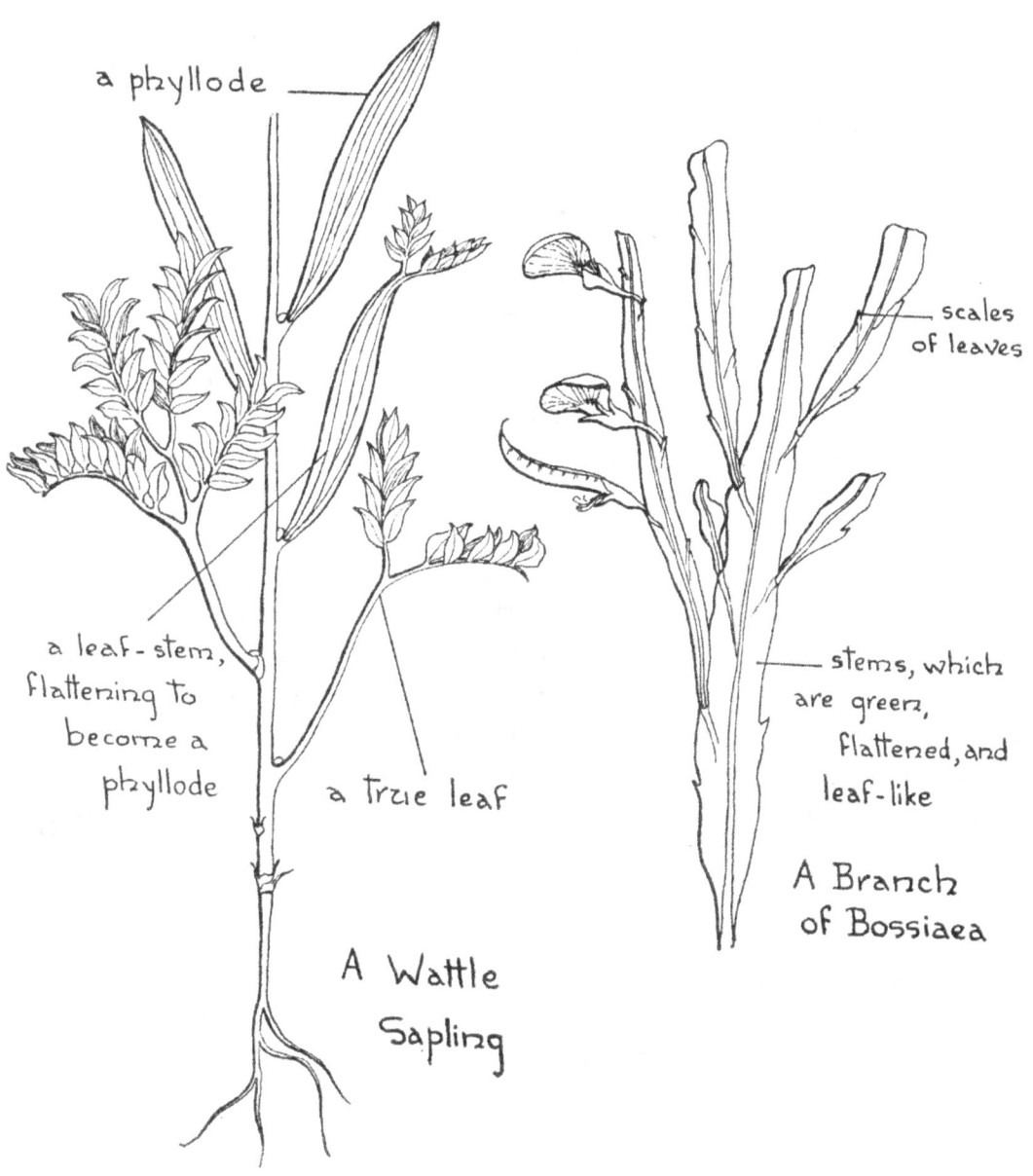

However, plants go on living all over the world in spite of this because, when they grow in difficult parts, they do all manner of ingenious things to protect themselves against the awful business of losing water.

Our own country is a very dry one, with vast deserts in its centre, and with very few parts that get too much rain. There are deserts in many other countries too, yet Australia has been called "the most arid continent on Earth." So let us see what a few of our plants do about this.

First, there are gumtrees—so many of them that you cannot think of Australia without them. As you know, they are not very shady trees—because their long, slender leaves hang down instead of spreading outwards. If they spread outwards, they would catch the direct rays of the sun, and would quickly have the moisture dried out of them, but in their downward position, they are protected.

Chris said, "But gumtrees aren't pretending anything by doing that—and you said that plants often pretend, the same as animals."

So I told him about a few of the ways in which they do pretend, and the next time we were in the bush we looked around for examples of them. We were looking for a certain kind of wattle to begin with, and Tess was the first to find it.

There are some wattles with leaves so long and thin that you could easily mistake them for gumtrees. But in reality, these are not leaves at all. They are stems which have flattened out so that they look like leaves, and when they do this, they are called phyllodes. As phyllodes are green, they can manufacture food just as well as leaves can. But they are, after all, stems—and stems haven't as many pores as leaves have, so the plant doesn't lose anything like so much water through them.

When these trees are very young, they do grow a few true leaves—ferny, feathery little things—and you often see a few on the trees' new shoots as well, but soon the stems begin to grow broader and more leaf-like, and the true leaves grow smaller, until finally they disappear altogether.

The pretty little bossiaea, with its red and yellow "pea" flowers, is another of our plants with stems instead of leaves. The whole plant is made up of them, and the tiny notches that you see here and there along their edges are the last remaining traces of whatever so many centuries ago were the bossiaea's leaves.

But perhaps the greatest of all our plant "pretenders" is the she-oak, or bull-oak. Most of these trees have the female flowers on one bush and the male flowers on another. (The female flowers have pistils but no stamens, and the male flowers have stamens but no pistils.) The strange thing, however, is that people mostly call the female trees bull-oaks, and the male ones she-oaks. And why they should be called oaks at all, is another puzzle. Just compare one of them with an oak-tree, and see if you can find any likeness between them!

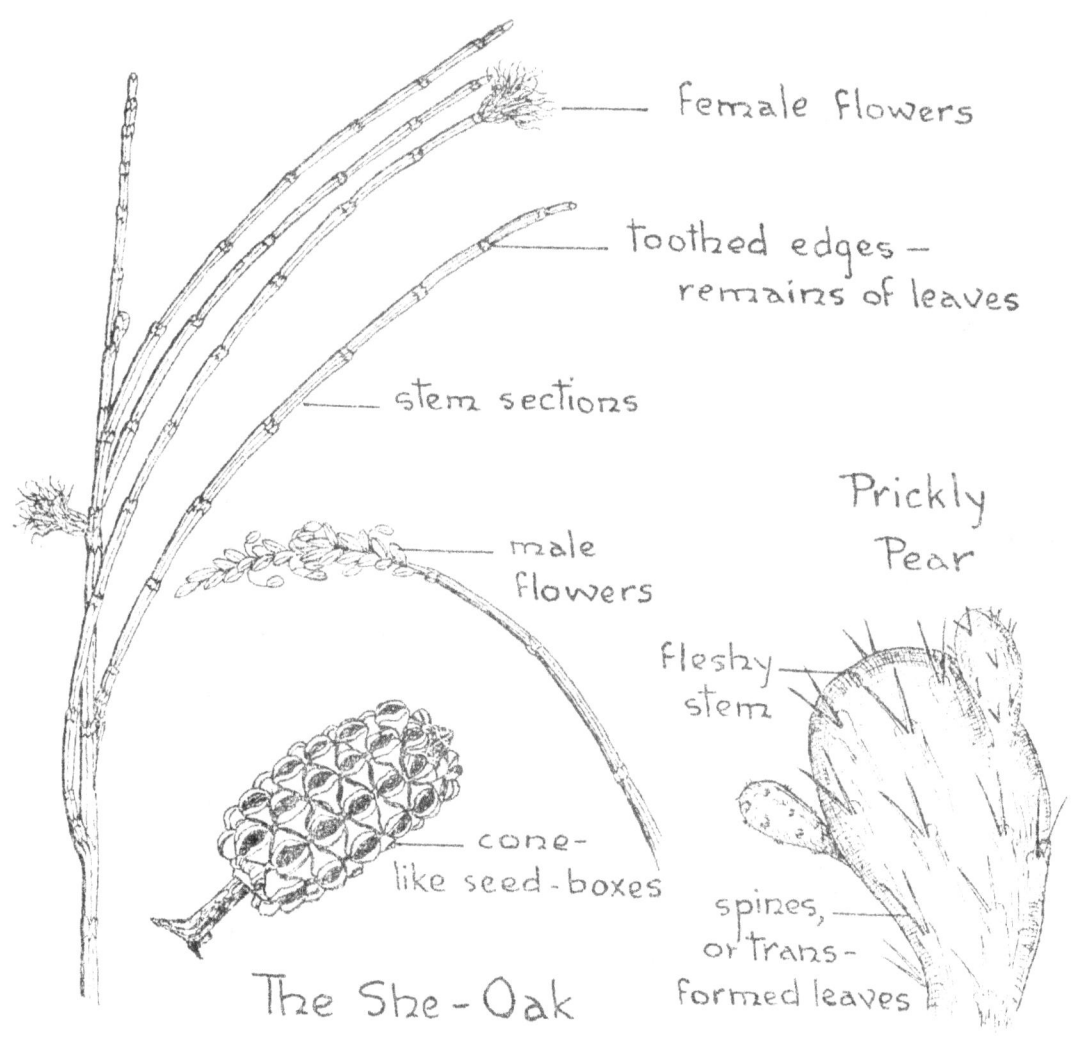

Another of the she-oak's make-believes is its "cone"—which isn't a cone at all, but a collection of tiny seed-boxes. And do you know *why* it isn't a cone? Think carefully, now, and you will have the answer—

Because, as we said a moment ago, the she-oak has flowers—true flowers—so it is not a cone plant.

Then finally, this remarkable tree has no leaves. Its long, drooping "foliage" is made up of stems. If you pull the stem, it comes apart in sections, and the top of each section has a little toothed edge. These "teeth" are all that is left of the plant's original leaves. I wonder what *kind* of leaves they were—long, long ago.

Soft and delicate as it looks, you often find the flannel flower growing in hot, dry places, and living there quite happily, because it too has found a way to stop itself from losing too much water. It wears a thick fur coat—not to keep it warm, but to keep it cool and moist. Under the protection of those soft hairs, the water that is so important to the plant is able to stay in it rather than passing immediately out into the dry atmosphere.

Then, of course, there is the prickly pear, which has found another way to prevent itself from losing water—a way common among cactus plants. When you touch a prickly pear and get badly "stung", you would never think that you had been pricked by a leaf, yet that is actually what has happened, for the spines of the prickly pear are what used to be its leaves—and so as to stop them from losing water, Nature gradually transformed them. Also, of course, the stems of cactus plants are mostly thick and swollen, filling up with water during rainfalls and keeping it stored for the plant's use during the long, dry spells that always follow. And the spines on cactus plants are important for another reason, too. They discourage desert animals from biting off the juicy stems, and eating them because of the water stored in them.

Pig's-face, (or "Koch's pigface"), is a plant that you often find in rockeries, or on slopes which do not hold water as well as flat ground does. This plant has kept its leaves, but has turned them into little water-storage tanks.

Needle-bushes—those rather untidy shrubs covered with prickly leaves and, in season, with lovely little delicate white flowers—have also been clever about water-saving. They have rolled their leaves into tiny long cylinders ending with a sharp point—and these are so thin that only a tiny section of leaf is ever presented to the sun. Then, our pretty little native heath curves the edges of its leaves under, so as to cover their stomates.

Getting enough water is an important problem altogether, in Australia, and the people are finding many wonderful ways to solve it—but the ways of plants are also very wonderful, don't you think?

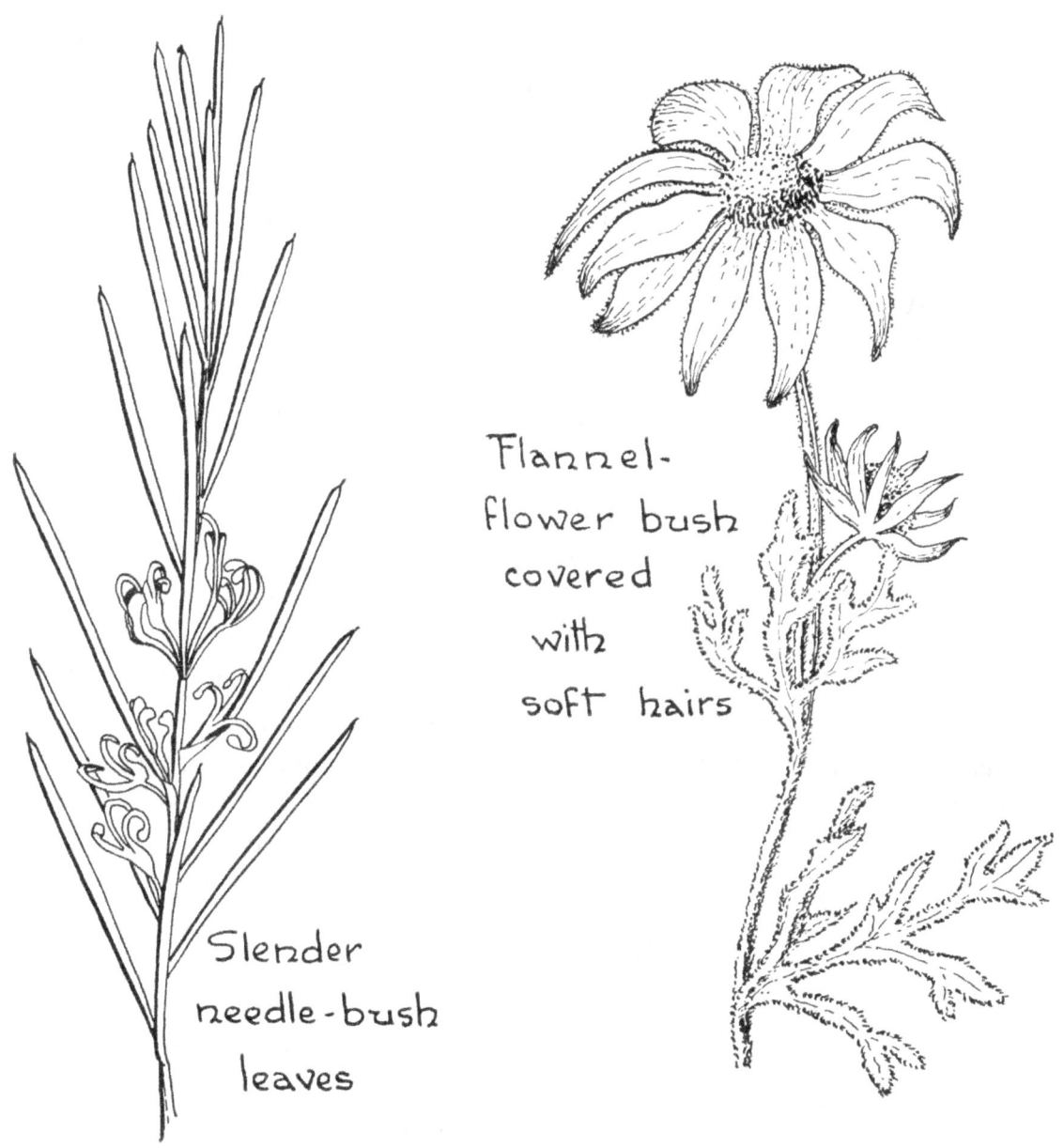

Slender needle-bush leaves

Flannel-flower bush covered with soft hairs

That "Taker", the Mistletoe

ONE of the commonest sights in the Australian bush is a tree with clumps of mistletoe hanging from it. Sometimes there will be only one or two clumps, but other times there are so many that the whole tree seems to be made up of them. And, with their long narrow leaves—green, tinged with red—these clumps can look really beautiful. But their habits are far from beautiful, for they are parasites, draining nourishment from the trees on which they are growing.

Usually you will find them on wattles and gumtrees, but the other day, at home, we were most upset to find several outcrops on our lovely pin-oak tree. We immediately cut off the branches where they were growing and—before burning them—made a few sketches. Have a good look at these sketches, and you will see for yourself what mistletoe does.

Its seeds are so sticky that they cling fast to any branch where they happen to be deposited. Each one, as soon as it starts to grow, sends out a little sucker which works its way into the branch and drinks up water and food from the soil from that branch. From now on, the plant on which the mistletoe is growing is called the "host", for it provides the parasite with food. But, if it could stop to think, what an unwilling host it would be!

After all, its roots are taking water and certain foods from the soil for its own needs—and now a stranger has come and sat down at its table, and starts grabbing everything that the branches are trying to pass around equally and fairly.

As you can imagine, a small piece of mistletoe would not do much damage to a large tree, but the mistletoe doesn't stay small. Its creeping stems twine around branch after branch, sending endless suckers into them. Then it produces flowers, and the flowers produce seeds, which invade other parts of the tree with new plants—and if all of this goes on unchecked, even the largest tree can be killed by mistletoe.

Then, of course, the mistletoe itself has to die, for its host cannot go on providing good things after it has been killed. So you see, a parasite doesn't have everything its own way after all. Not in the long run. By always depending on others rather than itself, it could thus get into serious trouble.

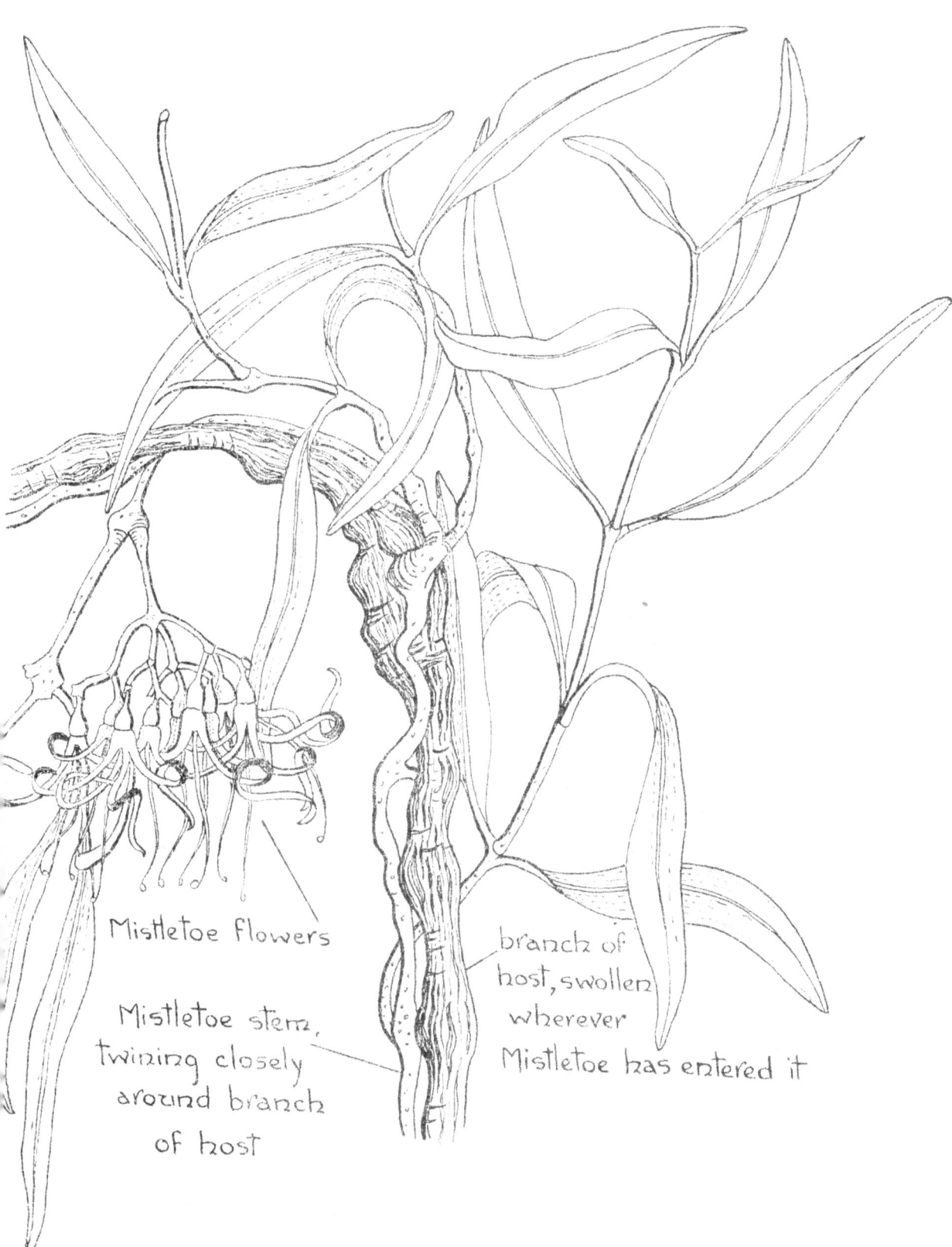

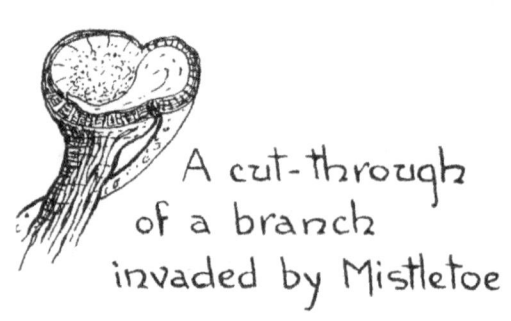

A cut-through of a branch invaded by Mistletoe

Sticky seeds of Mistletoe

But mistletoe isn't a complete parasite, the way some fungi or insects are, but only a half-parasite; it does not take all of its supplies from its host. Do you know why? Try to think.

Do you remember our saying that its leaves are green? Well, there is your answer.

A plant with this greenness can make its own sugars and starches, as long as it also has sunlight, air and water. With the mistletoe, sunlight and air are no problem, but water is—unless it can get it from another plant. Mistletoe has no proper roots or root hairs of its own with which to take it straight from the soil. So, what it takes from its host is called "raw materials". But this doesn't make it any better, because the host cannot make its precious sugars and starches without raw materials any more than the mistletoe can, so it gradually dies—of thirst and hunger.

There's another of these half-parasites that you often see in the bush. It is called cassytha, it looks like a great entangled mass of green strings, twining all over the host plant and sending suckers into it the way the mistletoe does.

There is research being done today to find out more about the damage caused by mistletoe, and some believe that mistletoe has spread enormously in Australia because of land clearing and uncontrolled burning of forests. Though it is a half-parasite, it is also a rich food source for many birds and animals like possums, which also act to contain it. So, perhaps in the future, we may have to re-think our dislike of the dreaded mistletoe.

I wouldn't like to be a parasite though, would you? A whole one or a half one. If I were, I would feel I was doing harm to others, and—because of this doing harm to myself.

Plants That Eat Animals

IT'S such a commonplace thing for animals to eat plants that we don't think twice about it—but when plants eat animals, that's quite a different story. In fact, it's a story that seems too odd to believe. Yet it is true, and it happens more often than you think.

Out in the bush, in any moist or swampy part, you will most likely find many little plants whose leaves look as if they are covered with

Two different kinds of sundew. The one on the left has greenish hairs on its leaves. The one on the right has bright red ones.

remains of insects

glistening dewdrops. But look more closely, and you will see that in reality these dewdrops are sticky globules on the tips of hairs. They spread out from the leaf in all directions, and are held right up so that they sparkle prettily in every glint of sunlight. So, naturally, these plants are called sundews.

You don't even have to be in a moist or swampy part to see sundews if there has been a bushfire. One time we were in the Blue Mountains outside Sydney after a bushfire. The blackened earth was covered with red-greenish sundews, while other plants had not yet been able to regrow. Maybe the sundews were making the most of the insects that survived the fires, by hiding in their tunnels beneath the ground. Sundews are also able to tolerate poor ashy soil and take advantage of the destruction of other competitive plants.

When an insect sees our pretty sundews, and goes to have a closer look, it goes to its death. It probably thinks that the shining little globules are something good to eat—too good to resist—and the next moment it finds that it is something good to eat, instead. The globules are so sticky that there's no escape from them. It twists and struggles, but seems only to get worse stuck all the time. Then the hairs start to close in and over—first the nearest ones, then those farther away, until every one of them is bent over and around, making a complete prison cell.

This in itself would be bad enough—but now, to make things worse, the plant begins to eat its prisoner.

As you know, we have digestive juices that work on the food we eat, breaking it down into a form that our bodies can absorb—and the hairs of the sundew act in the same way. They pour digestive juices all over their captive insect. Gradually the softened body parts are dissolved, and the prison hairs stay firm until nothing is left but a few small, hard pieces and the wings. Then the hairs slowly unfold, ready to catch another inquisitive insect, while the wind blows away what is left of the last one—and you can almost imagine that the sundew has a satisfied, well-fed look about it.

But these are not the only animal-eating plants. There are some which climb around trees in tropical forests, and then hang down from them looking very much like graceful vases—or else they send their "vases" straight up from the ground. These are called pitcher plants—and again, no insect should go anywhere near them if it values its

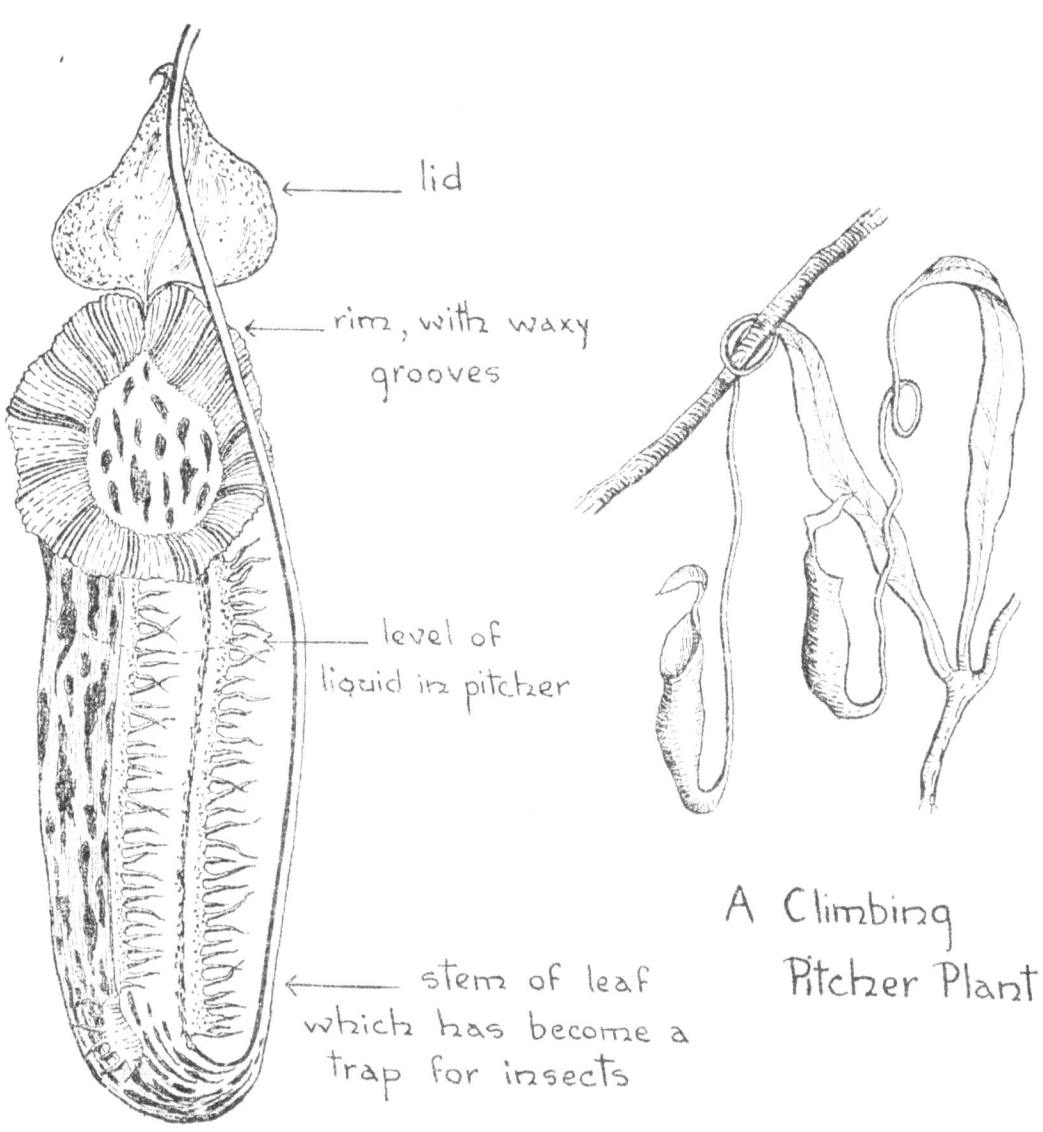

life. If it does go near, to find out more about the lovely sweet smell coming from the hanging "vase", it will land on the wide pitcher rim, which is extremely slippery, with fine little grooves leading inwards. The insect obediently follows the grooves, then loses a firm footing, and goes tumbling down—legs over feelers, landing in a large pool of digestive juices. These get busy right away, and soon there is nothing left except a few hard little scraps.

Then there are the bladderworts, that float around in watery places, and these also eat insects. They have no roots—just a few feathery leaves and a lot of little round bladders with a trap-door at one end. Around the trap-door there are many long bristles. Tiny water creatures, rushing away from their enemies, take shelter among these bristles, and feel quite safe for a moment—until they push against the trap-door. This immediately opens inward, and the insect goes through into what it perhaps feels will be greater shelter. But now, the door closes behind, and when it tries to get out again, there isn't a chance. The door opens inwards only, and all the pushing under the sun will not make it open outwards. The tiny prisoner can do nothing now except swim around inside the bladder until it dies through lack of food and air. Then the plant digests it.

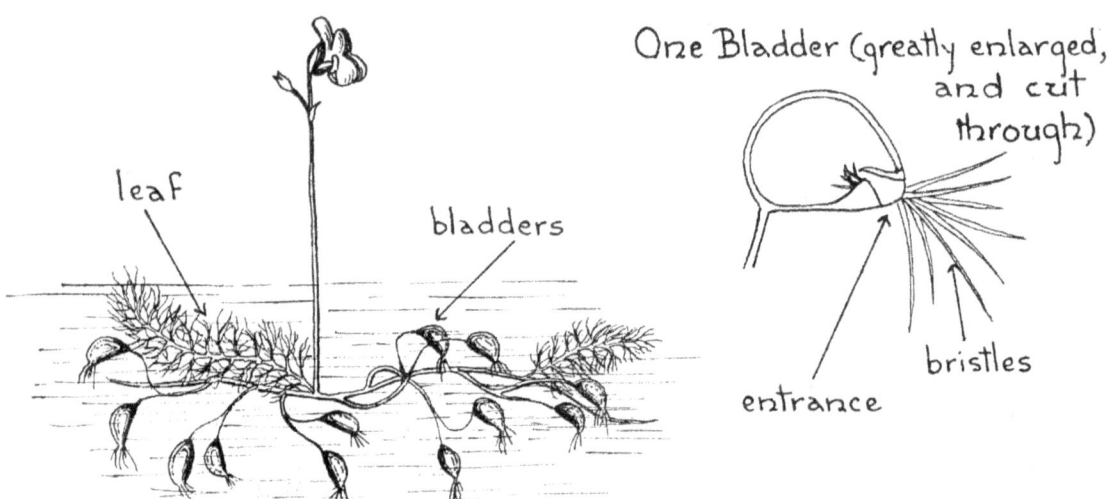

If you are wondering why certain plants trap insects in these various ways, and eat them, the answer is that they cannot get all the nourishment they need from the swampy ground in which they live. They need a lot more nitrogen—and they can get this only from the bodies of insects. So you see, they are not just being cruel and blood-thirsty. They are only doing what they *have* to do, to live.

> If we were insects, oh how careful
> We would have to be
> If any plant invited us for
> Breakfast, lunch or tea!
> It isn't nice to see a host,
> With luscious banquet spread,
> Turn up his nose at it and start
> To eat his guests, instead.

The Seashore

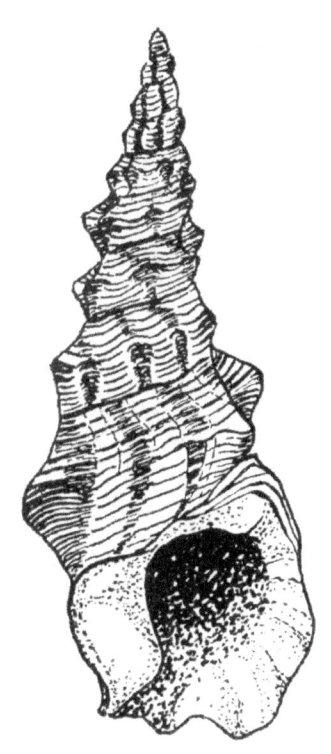

What ARE Shells?

SHELLS—what would we do without them? Just imagine if there were none of these beautiful little creations dotted about over our beaches or decorating our rock pools! How lonely we would feel! But as it is, there are such countless thousands of shells that there is no fear of the world ever going short of them.

Do you know what shells really are? Long before Chris and Tess were born, I lived for a while on an oasis in Argentina, where its people, descended from the ancient South American Inca population, had no idea that the sea existed. There were quite a lot of shell fossils over the surrounding desert, and the people called them "curly stones". You all know better than that, of course, but perhaps you do not realise that they are an actual part of the bodies of certain animals, just as legs and arms are parts of our bodies.

Animals with shells are called molluscs, and, apart from their shells, they are soft, "squashy" sorts of creatures. The drawings on these pages are diagrams, giving a general idea of what goes on inside the different kinds of molluscs. From the outside, of course, you don't very often see much of the animal apart from its shell.

In toward their centres they have organs for digestion, breathing, and so on. Then they have a "foot", which they use either for clinging to things, or digging, or "walking". And the part just inside the shell is called the mantle. It is called a mantle because it enfolds the animal's

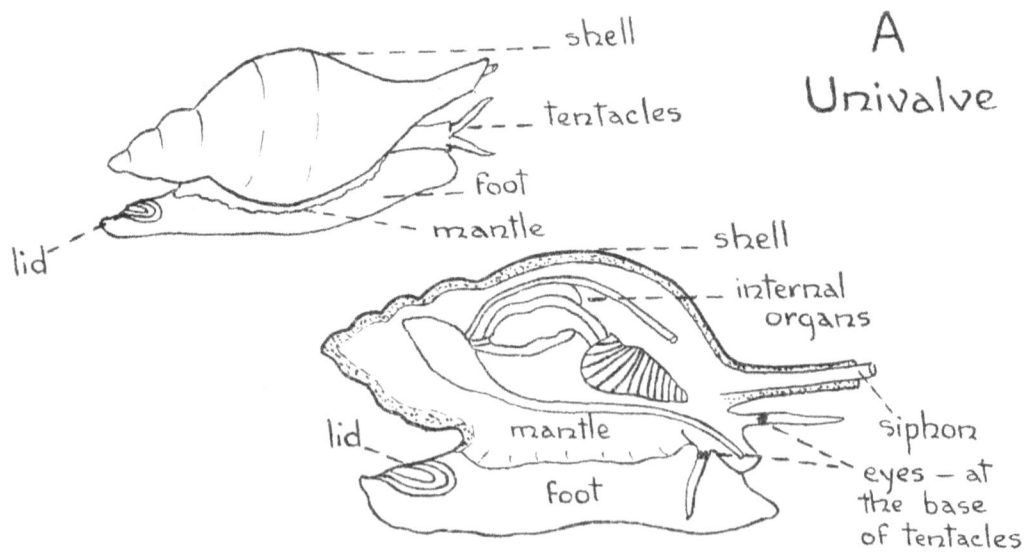

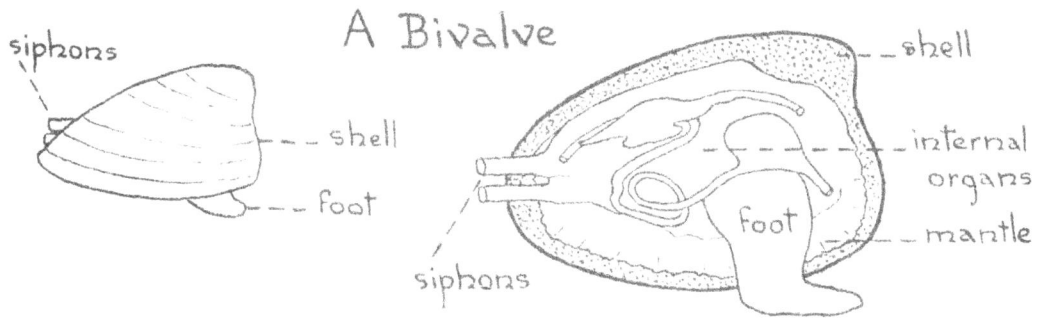

inner parts like a cloak. It is sometimes beautiful, with frills and bright colours, and it does a very wonderful and clever thing. From the food that the mollusc eats, it separates and puts aside the calcium, which is what shells are made of—so we can really think of it as the shell-maker.

Of course, molluscs do not all look alike—and neither do their shells. A great many of them have their shell all in one piece—like snails and periwinkles. These are called Univalves.

Then, another very large group have their shells in two parts, like the oysters and fan shells. These are called Bivalves.

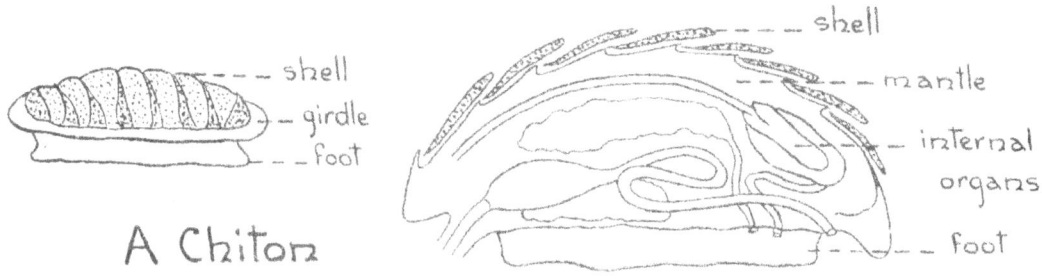

There's another strange group with eight parts to their shells, overlapping one another like a coat of armour, and held together by a "girdle". These are called Chitons.

A few molluscs have queer-looking shells like tusks, so—naturally—they are called Tusk shells. And, although you do not see their shells, the octopus and cuttlefish are molluscs, too.

Mostly, in this group—the Cephalopods—shells grow either inside the animal or not at all, and the foot is divided up into many arms or tentacles.

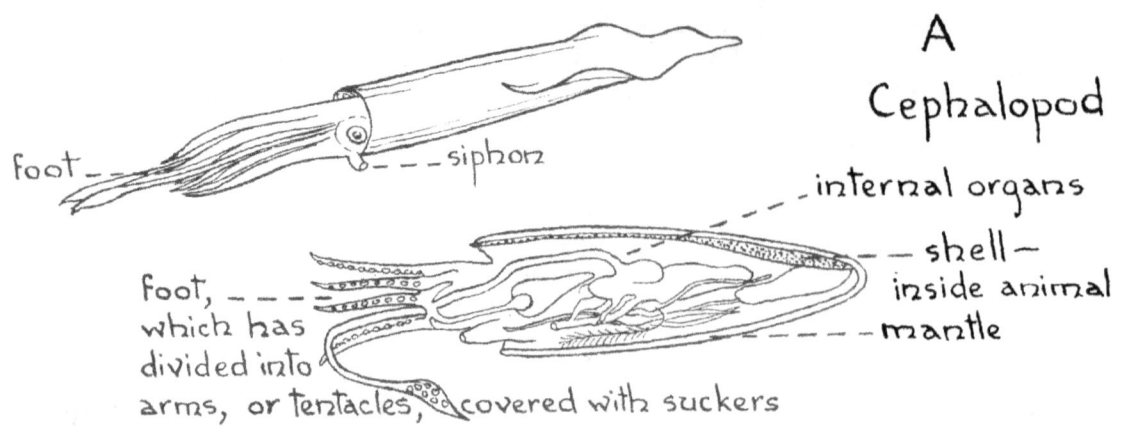

So there you are—with five groups of molluscs, and goodness knows how many different kinds in some of those groups. So many different kinds that they truly seem endless. See how many you can find in one quiet little section of a good shelly beach—and try to imagine how many you would find if you were able to roam over all the beaches in the world, and explore all of the oceans!

Up around the Barrier Reef, there are many large, colourful shells, but these are not always the most beautiful. Sometimes the smaller a thing is, the lovelier it seems, for it is more delicate and fragile. Sometimes a large grain of sand will turn out to be a tiny shell of the most wonderful perfection.

If you carry a magnifying glass about with you in your beach, bush and garden wanderings, you will be astonished at the marvels all around you. After a while you will feel like Alice—only instead of finding your Wonderland through a looking-glass, you will find it through a magnifying glass.

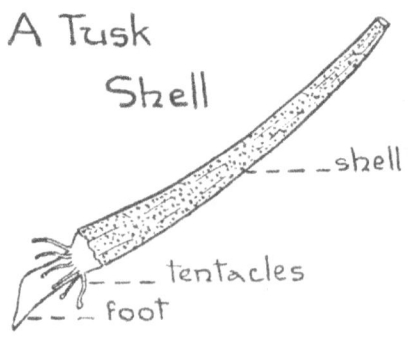

Shells Made of One Piece

WHEN you go exploring around beaches and rock pools, many of the shells that you find are univalves, or single shells complete in themselves. These are very tiny when their molluscs are babies, but as the animals grow, they have to have larger living quarters, so they keep adding to the size of their shells.

Often univalves look like little towers, or turbans, but some of the commonest are like tents—and this is what they actually are, with the animals sheltering inside them. These are limpets—and my, how they cling to whatever they are attached to—mostly rocks! With all of your strength you cannot dislodge them. It's a real marvel how such tiny creatures can grip so tightly. Of course, it isn't the shell that grips—it's the soft, jelly-like foot.

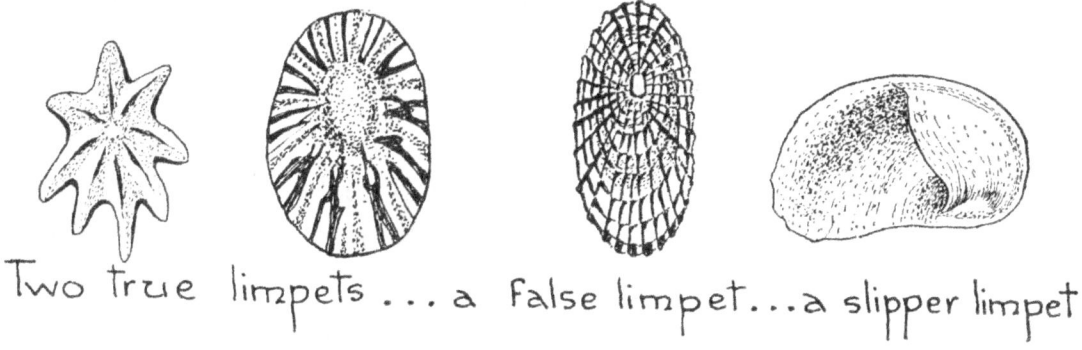

Two true limpets ... a False limpet ... a slipper limpet

There are some true limpets that look more like stars than tents, but there's another group of shells which only pretend to be limpets. You have to look at them very carefully to tell the difference. Perhaps it's a hole at the top, or a tiny slot at the edge. But whatever it is, it makes false limpets of them.

Then, there are those odd little shells sometimes called slipper limpets. Underneath, they have a pocket that makes them look rather like scuffs, and they don't very much care what they attach themselves to—rocks, other shells, or even other slipper limpets.

Some of the shells that Chris and Tess most enjoy finding are the beautiful ear shells. Whether they are tiny baby ones, or huge roughened ones, they are always exciting. You can tell them by the row of holes that they have, following the rolled-over edge of the "ear", and by the glorious shiny colours inside them—colours so much like opals that a lot of pretty jewellery is made out of them. The molluscs of these shells have feelers that slide through the row of holes.

Ear shell, and... Stomatella

There's another little shell, rather like the ear shells, only it is rounder, and it has no holes, and its shiny colours are much paler and more delicate. It is called stomatella, but Tess always thinks of it as a little fair, plump baby.

Although it doesn't look like it, stomatella belongs among the top shells, which have a conical shape that could perhaps spin like a top. The most famous of these top shells is the big trochus from which pearl buttons are made. But the family is a large and beautiful one, with some of its members striped like zebras, and others mottled. Some of them are sandy-rough to the touch, but this "roughness" is the most perfect, beaded moulding. And others are satiny smooth, with opal colours inside.

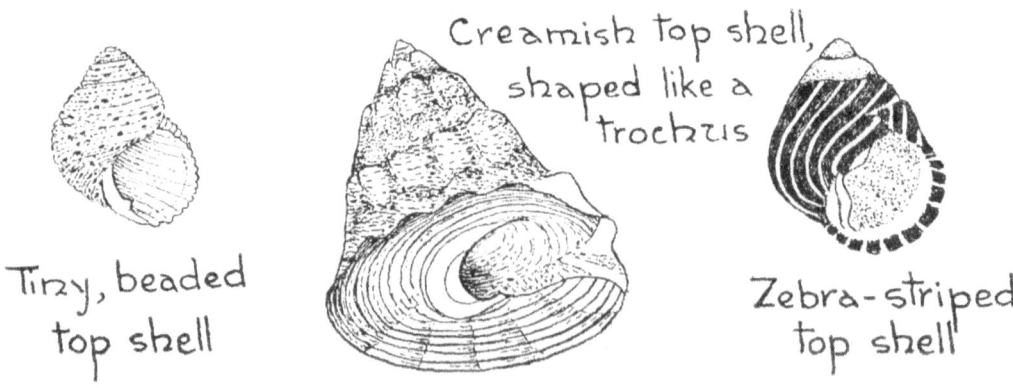

Tiny, beaded top shell

Creamish top shell, shaped like a trochus

Zebra-striped top shell

Kelp shell, and... pheasant shell

These are some of the kelp shells. You often see them threaded into necklaces, with their outside brownish coats cleaned off so that the whole shells look like opal. Other kelp shells have bright-pink stripes, or brown zigzags. And they get their name from the fact that they live on kelp, or brown seaweed.

I think we all love finding those prettily marked and coloured shells known as pheasant shells, and the big rounded turban shells with their green zigzags outside and their pearly colours inside. Univalve molluscs often have a hard little disc which fits tightly into the opening of their shells like a closed lid. This is a great protection for them while they are alive, but of course, when they die, the little "lids" drop away, and you often find them on the beach among shells. They are what you call cat's-eyes—very tiny sometimes, but those that belong to turban shells can be quite large.

Green-striped turban shell, and... Two different kinds of cat's-eyes

Then, there's that other large family of medium-sized shells, the periwinkles. There are knobbly and ridgy ones—but those that you find most often around our beaches are tiny blue ones that cluster over the rocks in simply thousands. They're *such* pretty little things.

Among all of the other periwinkles and top shells that crowd over seashore rocks, there are the strange little dome-shaped neritas—some of them jet-black, with white markings underneath, and perhaps

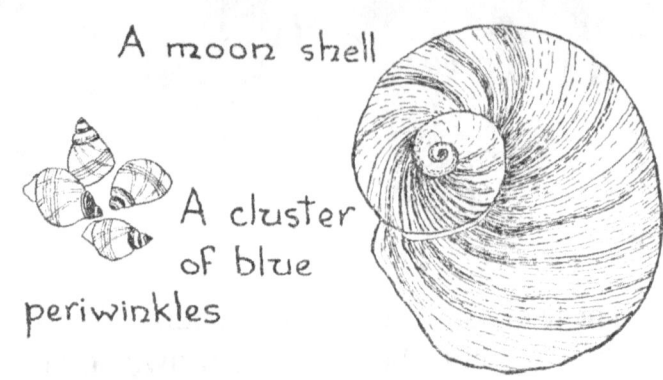

a tiny white "button" on top. And along some beaches you will find any amount of round moon shells, or sand snails.

These are usually fawn, yellowish or white, and their molluscs have the strange habit of laying eggs in a round sandy collar. But Tess doesn't like them, because they eat the animals that live in bivalves. How often do we see bivalves lying around the beach with little holes in them! Most likely these holes were the work of moonshell molluscs drilling their way to a meal.

For this same reason Tess dislikes the pretty little dog whelks, in spite of their lovely shapes and markings. "I suppose they don't know any better," she says, "but just the same, I think it's awful of them to eat other animals."

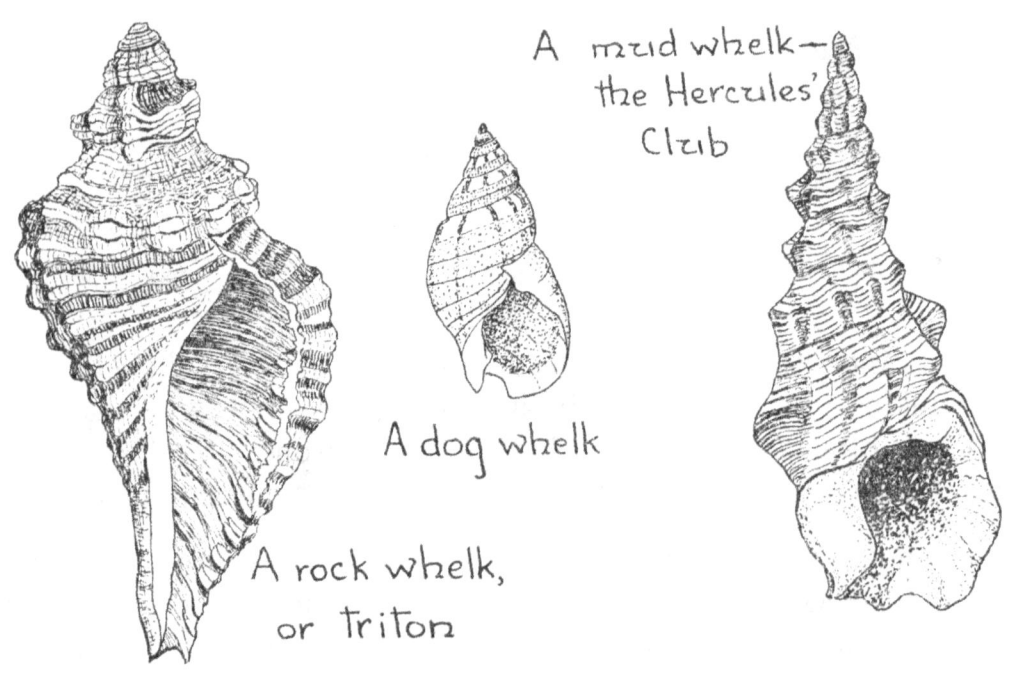

Mud whelks are different. They live on decaying matter in muddy places, and the Hercules' Club whelk is quite famous. It was the first Australian shell to be described by the early explorers. Captain Cook's scientists were amazed by it. They had never seen another shell like it. It lives in mud and mangroves instead of salt water and seaweed, and some of its relatives even climb trees. It is quite a large shell, too, growing about 100mm long.

The shells around the southern parts of Australia are not usually very large, but some of the exceptions are the rock whelks, or tritons. The one in our drawing is a big rugged shell with heavy ridges and knobs like knuckles running around it, and occasional ridges running downwards. It is yellowish-brown outside and white inside, and it can grow up to 150mm long.

Another shell with heavy ridges running around it is called the cart-rut shell, but this belongs to a different group. It is fatter and squatter, with a much wider mouth, and for some reason or other you often find this shell covered with worm tubes. Although it doesn't look like it in the least, it belongs to the same family as the mulberry shell, whose mollusc has as keen a taste for oysters as some people have. So it, too, is a cannibal. But its shell is certainly pretty—dark purple inside and covered with little dark knobs outside—quite like a mulberry.

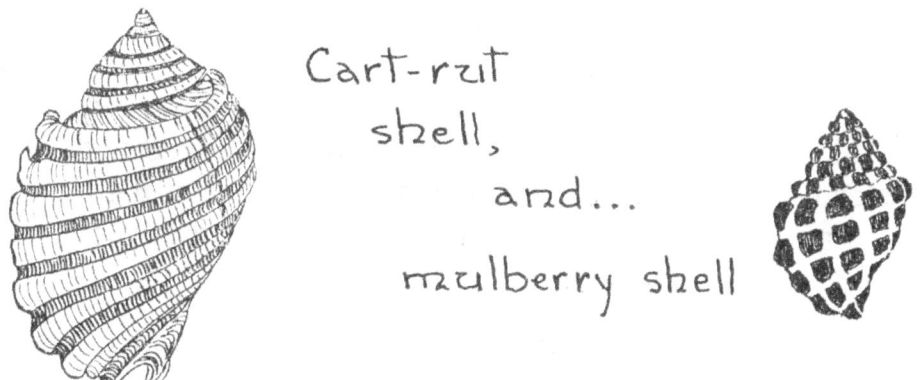

Cart-rut shell, and... mulberry shell

There are some shells that Tess and Chris always particularly enjoy finding, whether they are large or small. It's something to do with their shapes, and also perhaps with the fact that you do not come across them quite so often as many others. Some of these are the cones, cowries, wentletraps, helmets, and bubble shells.

Usually the cones around our more southern beaches are dainty little things—pink, heliotrope, fawn, or splashed with strange brown markings. Up north, they are often large, with the most wonderful patterns and colours, but the molluscs belonging to some of these shells are very dangerous. Their bite is so poisonous that it can kill. So, if you are ever lucky enough to visit the Barrier Reef, and you feel tempted to pick up any of the beautiful cone shells nestling among the corals, it would be wiser not to, in case the animal were still alive—unless, of course, you were wearing thick rubber gloves.

A cone shell... bubble shells... a wentletrap

Bubble shells *can* be quite solid and sturdy, but many of them are very much like their name—frail, bubbly little things, like bits of coloured foam. Some are mottled with brown, others are white with two red lines running around them, and other white ones have lots of dark brown or black lines. Bubble-shell molluscs are sometimes extremely beautiful. (One of them has a body that flows out around its shell like a pink flower whose frilly petals are edged with blue.) And instead of being either male or female, each one of them is both together—a real he-she. Do you remember that earthworms are like that too?

Wentletraps are very special shells—beautiful little white, tapering spires with upward-running ridges. Our Australian wentletraps are mostly rather small and thin, but the Precious wentletrap of Queensland and China is much rounder, and more delicately lovely, and people used to pay large sums of money for it.

Those big, glorious shells that you often see with carvings on them, like cameos, are called helmet shells. But of course, there are many other kinds of them, too, and the ones you find around Australian beaches are much smaller. You couldn't very well carve on them, but it is always wonderful to find one, and hold its smooth roundness in the palm of your hand, and enjoy the little dark and light bands around its lip.

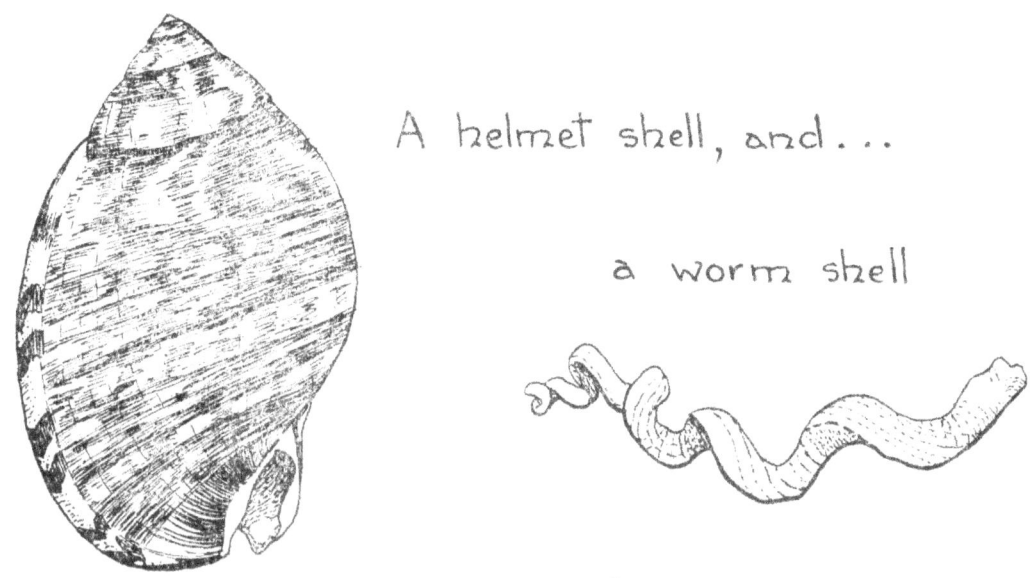

A helmet shell, and...

a worm shell

Mostly, when a mollusc builds a shell in some kind of a spiral, it goes about it very neatly: It might build it long and narrow like a spire, or short and fat like a button, or somehow in between. Of course, each time the larger shell segment is formed, it makes room for the growing mollusc inside. But the worm-shell mollusc is different. It starts with a loose little coil which looks a bit like the beginning of a spire, then loses interest and goes on building an untidy tube that might turn as easily in one direction as in another—and the first little coiled piece is so frail that it has mostly broken off by the time you find the shell.

Cowries, on the other hand, are just about the neatest of all shells, and some of the loveliest. Most of them are oval in shape, beautifully marked, and highly polished, and they have a row of little "teeth" all the way down both sides of their opening. Everyone loves cowries. The natives of some countries wear them as their favourite jewellery, and in Africa, India and some of the South Pacific Islands, they have been used as money. Wouldn't it be fun to have a purse full of shells instead of coins?

The reason why cowries are highly polished outside as well as inside is that their molluscs completely cover the outsides of their shells with their soft mantles, protecting them from the rasping sands and corals which would otherwise scratch them. Some—like the tiger cowries—are very large, and others are quite tiny. Cowries like the warm waters of the tropics more than any others, and it's ever so exciting finding them among the corals in our own Barrier Reef, but a few smaller ones do live in cooler waters, like the lovely little white one that we find on beaches around the south of Australia. This is not as shiny as the tropical ones, but it has lots of little ridges running around it, and a few pink patches on its back—and it has the look of a treasure about it.

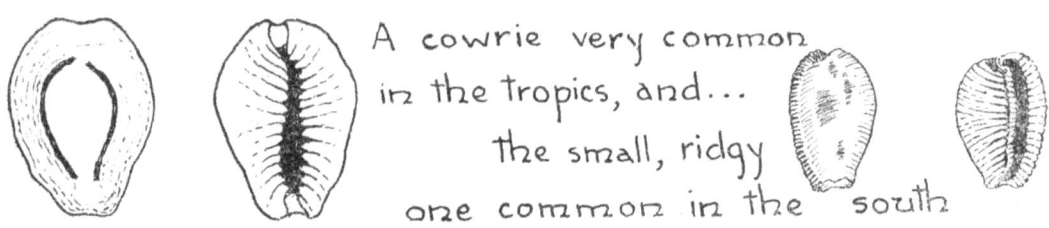

A cowrie very common in the tropics, and... the small, ridgy one common in the south

But then, in reality, *every* shell is a treasure, no matter how common it may be, for a thing does not have to be rare to be precious. It has only to be beautiful.

Shells Like Butterflies, and Fans

MANY of the shells that you find on beaches look something like fans, triangles, spoons, or butterfly wings—but unless you find two of them joined together, they are only half shells, for these are called bivalves, and it takes two of them to make a whole shell.

As they are joined together by a hinge at only one point, you do not often find a complete pair unless the animal is alive inside them, holding them together. But there *are* some that do not fall apart so easily. When their mollusc dies, the two halves of the shell merely spread out, and lie around on the beach, looking like pretty little butterflies—bluish, pink, orange, or cream. So of course, they are often called butterfly shells. Actually they are a small kind of wedge shell—and you see more wedge shells on our beaches than almost any other kind of bivalve. The larger creamish ones, with purple inside them, are often called pipis—but please do not confuse these with the trough shells, which are often purple inside too, but which tend to be deeply scooped, and which have grooves running around them as though they were gramophone records.

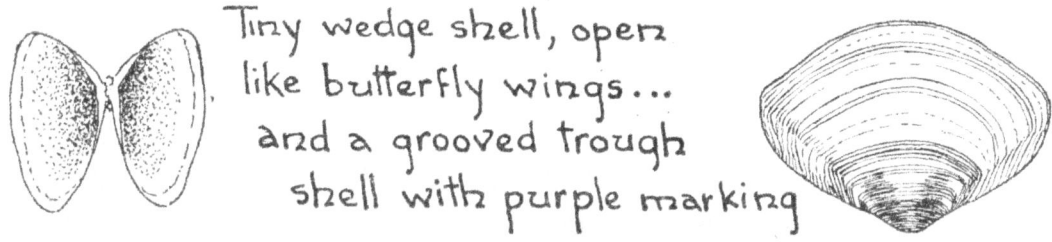

Tiny wedge shell, open like butterfly wings... and a grooved trough shell with purple marking

Other very common shells along our beaches are the arks. These are easy to recognise by their rows of tiny, even "teeth", and by their hinge, which is long and straight. Sometimes an ark shell itself is also long, and rather narrow. Other times it is more like a triangle, with heavy grooves running downwards. But it always has that long, straight hinge, and those tiny "teeth".

Many bivalves look so much alike that it isn't always easy to tell the difference between them, but you could never mistake a scallop shell for any other kind, any more than you could mistake a fingernail shell. The fingernails are long, narrow, and fairly sharp, and would be terribly awkward to manage if they really were fingernails. But their mollusc finds them quite comfortable, and even helpful, no doubt. If an enemy should appear it quickly digs itself down into the sand with its strong foot, and its long narrow shell slips down much easier than a bulky one could. Usually it is cream in colour, marked with fawn, or a pretty shade of pink.

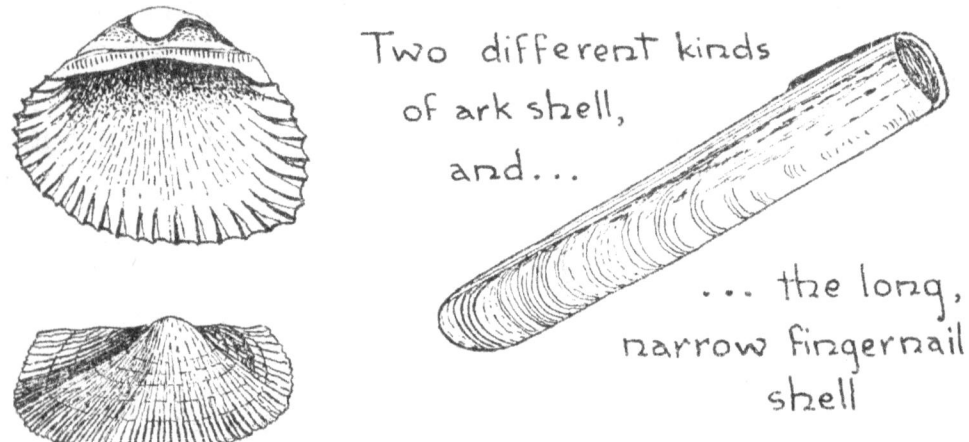

Two different kinds of ark shell, and...

... the long, narrow fingernail shell

The molluscs of scallop shells are also fast movers. In a way, they jet-propel themselves through the water, opening and closing the two halves of their shells, and showing their pretty mantle as they do this. The king scallop has a very lovely shell, with two little wings, and with grooves spreading out like the rays of the sun—mostly pink, orange, purple and white—and around the edge of its mantle it has a row of wide-open blue eyes only about 1mm across. Yes—these are real eyes, but different from our own. They have a lens, like our eyes, and

Scallop shells, with even and... uneven wings

two retinas on top of each other to sense light and send nerve signals to the brain, the way our single retina does; but behind the scallop retinas there is a curved mirror of transparent crystals which reflect the light back through the retinas so that they get another chance at seeing even in very dim light.

"Scallop shells can grow to 100mm across, but their close relative—which you will find more often on our southern beaches—grows to only half that size. This is the little fan scallop, with one wing larger than the other. You find it in all sorts of colours—yellow, orange, brown, purple—and sometimes it has spines raying out over it to make it even prettier.

Cockles are often called heart shells because, with their valves together, many of them look very much like hearts. They are not as common in the south of Australia as they are in the north—which is a pity, for you could scarcely find anything more beautiful than the curves of the shells themselves and of the many deep grooves that spread out over them. In the south they are mostly white, whilst northern cockles show almost every colour in the rainbow.

A cockle, and... a jingle shell

But some of the brightest of all are the jingle shells. These may be white, yellow or flame-coloured, and they shine like crumpled cellophane. One of their valves is straighter than the other, and usually has a hole in it. Through this hole the animal is able to cling on to things. And there it stays, holding on—sometimes to rocks, sometimes to other shells—using them as its home.

Platter shells are pretty little things—round, white, flat, and very much like plates. Sometimes they are decorated all over with fine ridges.

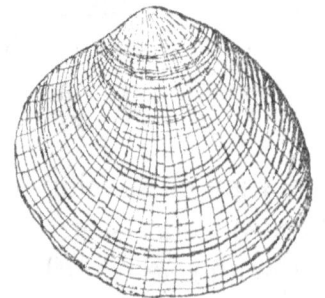
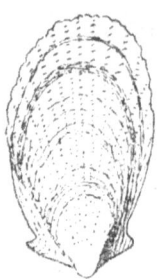
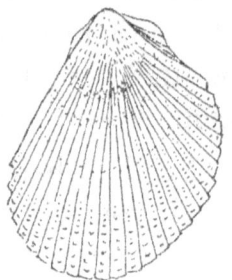

A platter shell, and... two different kinds of file shell

Then, there are those other finely grooved white shells, some of them like scoops, and others like wings. Tess and Chris have always called them spoon shells, and used to have great fun, when they were little, actually using them as spoons to sprinkle salt and sugar. But they are mostly called file shells because of their sharp, raspy edges.

A very common bivalve around our beaches is a cream one covered with zigzags and "flames" of a darker colour—orange or even brown. This is the flame dog cockle, and you want to be careful not to mix it up with the lovely tapestry shells which sometimes have the same kind of marking. But a tapestry shell is always covered with fine grooves as well. Since these grooves run around lengthwise, and the patterns cross them by running downwards, you would really think that the whole shell had been beautifully woven. So its name is easy to remember.

Tapestry shells belong to the Venus shell group, and they always have a rare, precious look about them, but perhaps the most precious of this group is the frilled Venus shell. It lives in mud flats, yet its colour is creamy or a soft shade of pink, and it has rows of little frills all around it. It's so pretty.

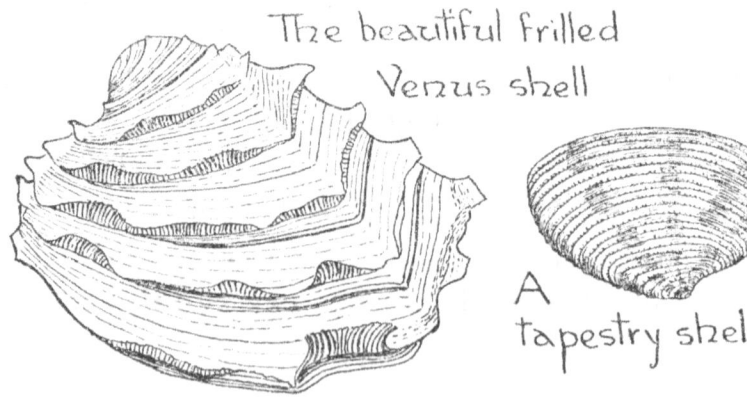

Flame dog cockle

The beautiful frilled Venus shell

A tapestry shell

Whatever you do, when you are shell hunting, look out for the beautiful pure-white angel's wing. This is a really remarkable shell, for—thin, narrow and frail-looking as it is, it actually bores its way into rock. Now, how ever does it manage to do this? Wouldn't you think that, instead of scraping the rock away, it would scrape its own little spines off? But it doesn't, of course, and it lives comfortably protected inside its rock shelter while so many other shells, living on *top* of rocks, get roughened and battered.

The mussels are rather a rough lot, although some of them have quite a graceful shape, and very lovely, shining colours inside their shells, almost like the colours in black opals. Outside, they are usually dull brown, or black, and you will often find them with a "beard" of coarse hairs over them. Many people enjoy eating them—as they do oysters—but one of the most interesting things about them is the way many of them attach themselves to rocks or wooden pilings.

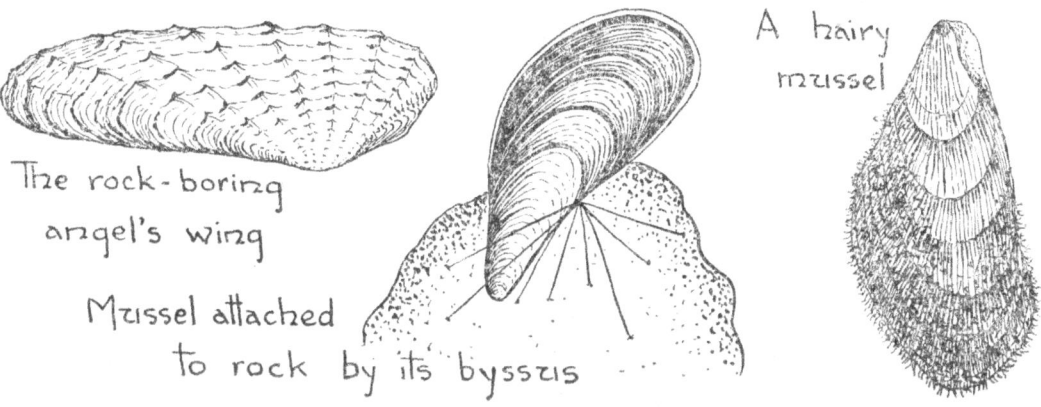

The rock-boring angel's wing

Mussel attached to rock by its byssus

A hairy mussel

Almost like spiders, they spin threads, only they thicken and harden these so much that it is really difficult to cut through them, and all the fierce battering of waves does not break them. The whole group of threads is called a byssus—and next time you come across one, if you test it, you will be surprised at how strong it is.

The poor old oyster has a terrible time, considering how many people like to eat him. And his shell is rugged and untidy, as though he knew that his main purpose in life was not to be admired—just eaten.

When the tiny oyster mollusc first hatches out of his egg, it swims around happily for a few days without a care in the world, and it is hard to think that this frisky little creature will later become such a sleepy stay-at-home. But indeed, after those first few days, it attaches its shell to something—mostly a rock—and there it remains for the rest of its life. The shell gradually grows to its full size, with one valve hollowed out to make room for our oyster, and the other one almost flat. The edges of the two valves are often frilled, but they have none of the delicate moulding that we find in most other shells, and they do not fit together neatly. Often one is bigger than the other, and—as time goes on—they tend to get a rough, dirty look.

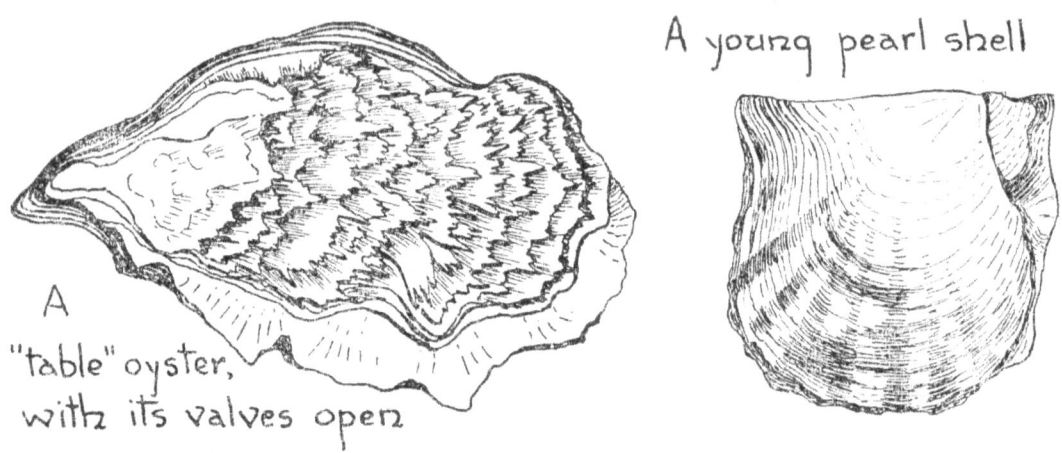

A "table" oyster, with its valves open

A young pearl shell

Of course, there *are* times when an oyster is admired as a thing of beauty—when it produces pearls. These are some of the most precious gems on Earth—and it's interesting to realise that the oyster makes them when it is feeling irritated by something. If we turned every little irritation into something beautiful, the world would be a much better place, wouldn't it?

Even a tiny grain of sand, caught in the oyster's sensitive mantle, will be enough to start a pearl. To stop this grain from hurting, the oyster surrounds it with a layer of lovely, smooth mother-of-pearl. Then another layer is added—and another—more and more of them until a perfect pearl is formed.

Almost any oyster can produce pearls—some mussels can, too— but the pearl-shell molluscs of Western Australia, Iran and Sri Lanka are particularly clever at it. Around our southern beaches you may find a few small pearl shells, fairly thin, with bluish mother-of-pearl inside, but those of northern Australia are huge; about 300mm across, with thick mother-of-pearl, like rich cream satin.

You will not find clams around our southern beaches, but we must say a few words about them as they are such a famous bivalve. Some of them, up around the tropics, grow very large, and there is one kind so strong and huge that if a you were caught in it, you would need a lot of help to get free again. But at least the clam wouldn't eat you, whereas people eat plenty of clams. And in spite of the way a clam will grab and hang on, its mantle is one of the real beauties of the sea.

Tess, Chris and I wandered among any amount of them on the Barrier Reef recently—very carefully, of course—and their colours were almost too vivid to believe, especially when we swam right over one. We could look right down on the richly coloured mussel living in its open clamshell, just waiting for a tasty meal to come along and get snapped up. Then, here and there we would come across a black mantle—and this was just as beautiful as the others, like soft black velvet.

When you go gathering sea shells, don't be satisfied with scratched and broken ones. Go on looking until you find nice new ones that haven't as yet had time to get rubbed and battered against rocks and sand. Then examine them closely—all their lovely ridges and markings—and you will be amazed at what treasures you have found.

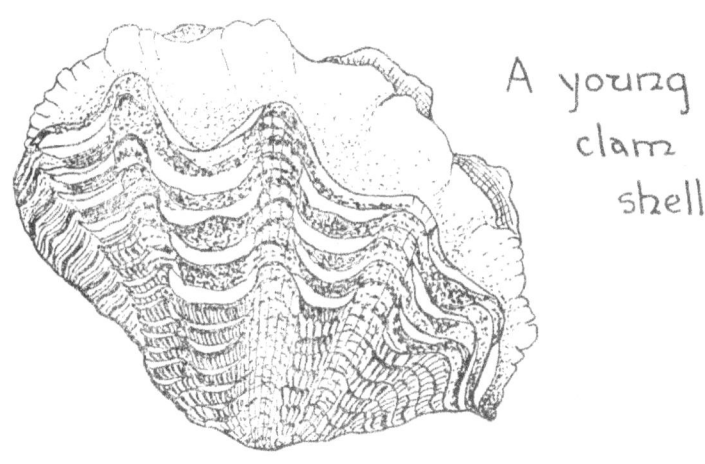

A young clam shell

Roly-Poly Molluscs—and Inside-Out Ones

JUST as if it isn't enough to have a shell made of two parts instead of one, there are some funny little molluscs that go to extremes and have their shells in *eight* parts. These are the chitons, and you will find them all around our coasts, hiding under rocky ledges and clinging to the sides of rock pools. Most of all, they seem to like shady places. And they cling to their bit of rock as tightly as limpets do.

They also remind us of limpets in another way, for their shells are also rather like tents, with the mollusc sheltering underneath it. But chitons are cleverer than limpets. Can you guess why?

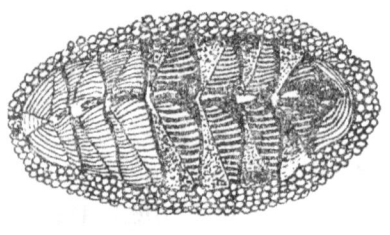

A chiton

One of the middle plates of its shell, and...

an end plate

If you *should* ever manage to get a limpet off its rock, there it is entirely at your mercy, with no protection for its soft flesh. But if you get a chiton off its rock, it slowly curls up into a roly-poly—flesh inside, shell outside—and, as its shell is in eight small separate parts, it can do this quite easily.

While the chiton lives, its shell is held together with tough bonds called ligaments, but of course, when it dies they all fall apart, and you will find any amount of them on our beaches among the other shells—pretty little things, like small butterflies with wings outspread. On the outside, they are a dull brownish-green, but on the inside they are delicately coloured with blue, green and white—which makes them look all the more like butterflies.

Another strange little shell that you find quite often is called the ram's horn, because, curled round the way it is, that is what it looks like. It is pure white, with a pearliness inside, and it's quite a mystery to many people, for they never find one with the animal alive in it—and in any case, it is divided up into lots of tiny sections, each one sealed off, and none of them big enough for an animal to live in.

Well, the explanation is that the mollusc belonging to this shell doesn't live *in* it, but around it. It belongs to that strange group of inside-out animals who not only live outside their shells, but whose feet have become their heads—and very queer heads, at that. As well as having what we would *expect* a head to have—two eyes and a mouth—they branch out into eight or ten long, waving arms, or tentacles.

These are the cephalopods, and they are the latest to develop of the molluscs, just as flowers are the latest to develop of all of the types of plants. But cephalopods can be most unpleasant, too, for the squid and octopus belong among them, and we all know how wickedly these most intelligent of the invertebrates can behave, if they are given half a chance.

Our little ram's-horn mollusc isn't particularly wicked, and is only very seldom found. This is strange, because there must be ever so many of them in the sea, judging by all the thousands of ram's horns on our beaches. But the secret is that this mollusc swims in fairly deep waters way out in the Atlantic and Indian Oceans, and it's only when it dies that this light little shell rises, bobs about on the surface of the water, and is finally washed up on to our beaches.

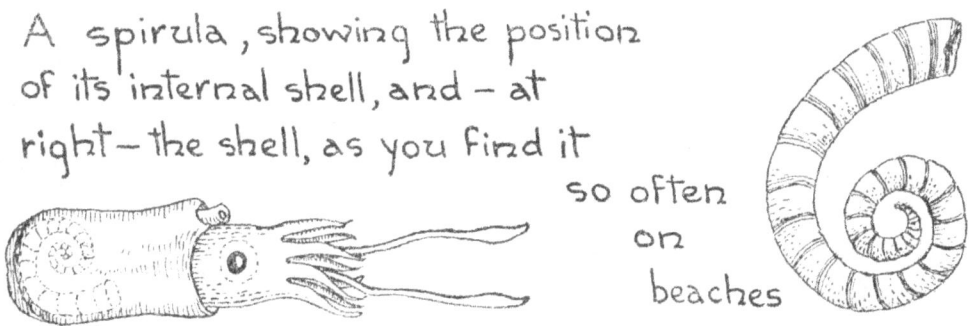

A spirula, showing the position of its internal shell, and – at right – the shell, as you find it so often on beaches

Its real name is not ram's horn, but spirula, and looks rather like a small squid, with ten arms or tentacles, two of them longer than the others. Also, like a squid, it can suddenly swim backwards if it senses danger, so is quite an agile little fellow.

The cuttlefish is another of these head-footed creatures, or cephalopods, whose shell finds its way on to our beaches in great numbers. You know those rather soft, oval-shaped things, pink and white in colour, with a spike at one end? People often put them in bird cages, and the birds love pecking at them. Well, each of these is the shell that a cuttlefish has carried around inside it, and that drifts up to shore after it has died.

Squids have a long, narrow inside shell called a pen, because it looks so much like one. But the most beautiful of all cephalopod shells is the nautilus, and this is to be found only in warm, tropical waters. The nautilus is a real oddity among cephalopods, for its shell is worn outside instead of inside—but that doesn't make it a univalve mollusc, for, like spirula, it has ten arms instead of a foot. Its shell is one of the most graceful in all the oceans, smoothly rounded, with a soft pearliness inside, and many separate little rooms.

When very young and small, the first tiny room is built, but then it grows too big to fit inside. Then that first room is sealed off and another room gets built next to it, a little larger, and so on and so on, until it and its shell are both full-size—and although, in the end, it has

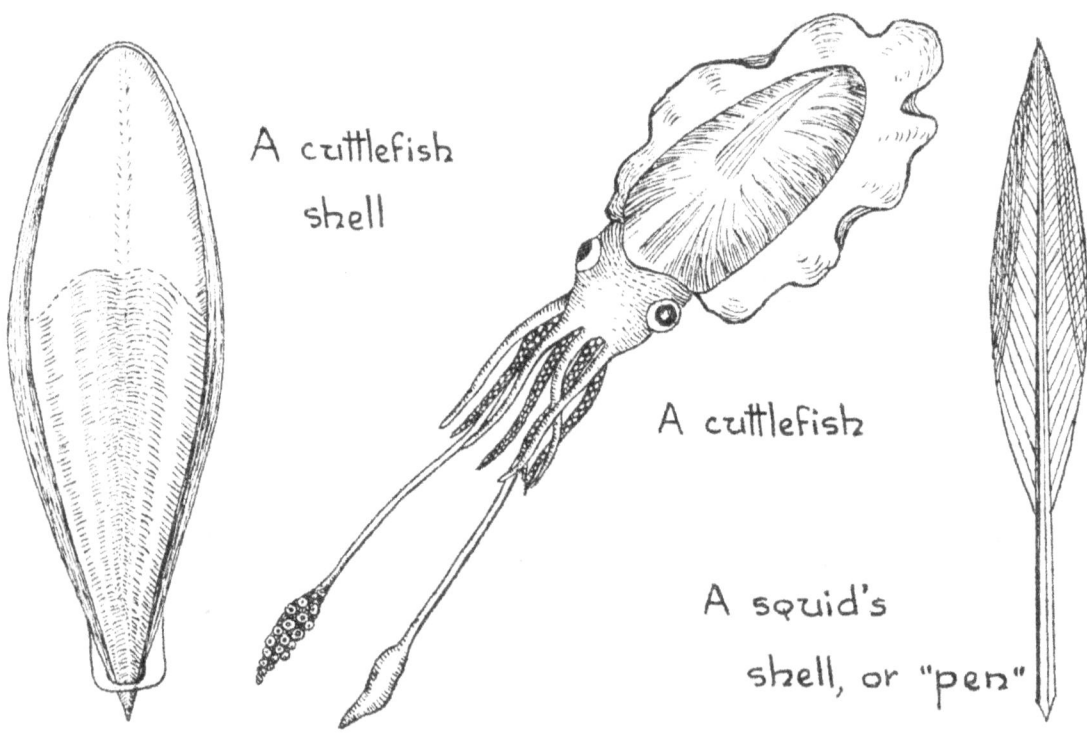

A cuttlefish shell

A cuttlefish

A squid's shell, or "pen"

a wonderful pearly palace with many rooms, but only ever lives in one of them.

A strange character indeed—yet no more strange than any of the others in its family, with shells inside them, and with their arms, head and foot all in one!

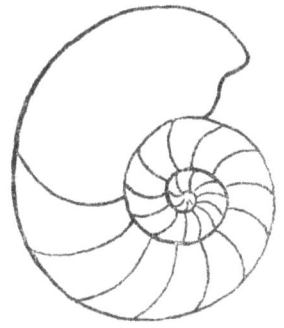

A nautilus cut through, to show the separate "rooms"

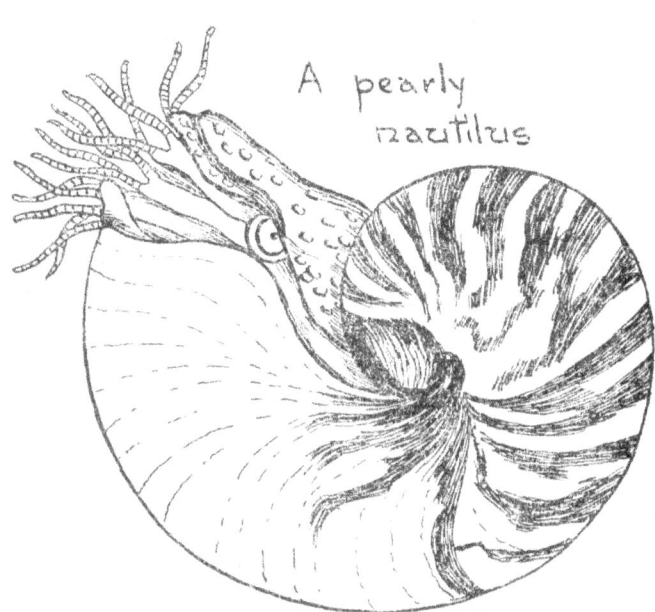

A pearly nautilus

One Rock Pool

THE rock pools around Cape Solander are really beautiful. Of course, there are beautiful ones in many other parts too, but we enjoy Cape Solander at the southern side of Botany Bay particularly. The glorious colours and patterns in all the rocks around there, and the way many of them have been weathered away into a sort of honeycomb pattern, really feel special for us.

One day when we were browsing around there, Chris called out, "You ought to see *this* pool. It's got *everything* in it."

Well, we were busy with our own discoveries for a while, but when we did get round to his, we were delighted with it. It had all sorts of things in it.

Tess said, "You know, Mummie, I'd be happy if I knew about all the things in just this one pool."

So we started talking about them right away—and these are the things we found to talk about:

First of all, around the edges of it, there were crowds of barnacles. Now, you all know that a barnacle lives inside a shell, so you might begin by thinking of it as a mollusc. But it is very different from a mollusc, for it has legs with joints—and molluscs have no joints. Even the arms of cephalopods are jointless—just long, waving ribbons of flesh. So you see, the barnacle belongs to that enormous group of jointed animals that insects belong to, and spiders and centipedes, as well as crabs, shrimps, crayfish, and so very many more.

When it is a baby, it enjoys itself swimming around with three pairs of legs, but as time goes on, it grows three more pairs of legs and a shell. Then it settles down on something and refuses to budge for the rest of its life. With that shell remaining firmly fixed to that something, our barnacle happily stays inside, comfortably standing on its head.

During low tide its shell stays tightly closed. But when the tide rises, and water starts washing over, it opens the two little "doors" at the top of its shell, and puts those six legs out to gather food. This works very well indeed, for its legs are covered with hairs which catch tiny particles of animal life as they wash past. Then it swishes that tasty

Two barnacles at rest, and one feeding

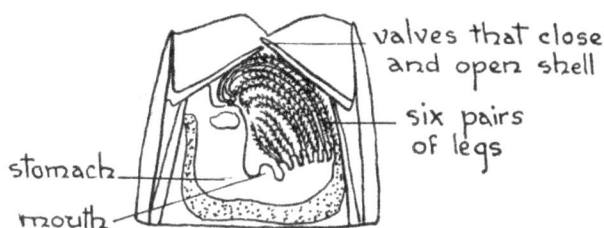

A barnacle cut through, showing the animal curled up inside — head down

valves that close and open shell
six pairs of legs
stomach
mouth

catch down into its mouth—again with those legs. Just imagine if we were to use *our* legs like this! There seems to be no end to the funny things that animals do.

Also nearby, around this same pool, there was even a cluster of tiny pink barnacles that people sometimes mistake for coral.

In one part of our pool there was a little overhanging ledge of rock, and hiding away underneath this were several chitons—those queer little molluscs with eight separate parts to their shells. Very carefully, so as not to hurt it, Chris loosened one of them off with a knife blade, and it immediately started to curl itself up, as we were expecting it to. Chitons are amusing little things, so sure that—rolled up like this—they are safe from any danger. And it is our special delight to know that, as far as we are concerned, they *are*.

In a way, this pool looked rather like a float-bowl with flowers in it, for it was the home of ever so many sea anemones—and no animal looks more like a flower than they do. Some of them were emerald green, others bright red, and they made a most beautiful sight.

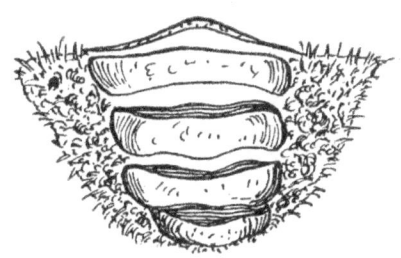

One of our rock-pool chitons — girdle covered with soft bristles — doubled over for protection when lifted off his bit of rock

The children were both sure, at first, that they were some kind of plant—and they took a lot of convincing otherwise. Tess said, "But Mummie, they just *can't* be animals!"

So then we talked a bit about how hard it is, sometimes, to tell the difference between primitive plants and primitive animals, especially when the animals have "branches" and "petals" that look very much like those of plants, and when they also "take root" the way plants do.

Sea anemones do sometimes move around a little, but their real nature is to stay put, and capture their food as it washes past them in currents of water. Their "petals" are actually tentacles which sting and paralyse small fish, molluscs, and other sea creatures that come their way, then carry them down into the anemone's mouth—the round hole around which the tentacles grow. The food then passes down a sort of throat into a "stomach", where it is digested.

When sea anemones are quite contented and covered with water, their tentacles all spread out and wave around very prettily. But when they are alarmed, or exposed out of water, they fold their tentacles in tightly, and look merely like blobs of jelly. Some particularly timid ones cover themselves with sand and pieces of shell grit so that, when they fold their tentacles away, you would scarcely know that they

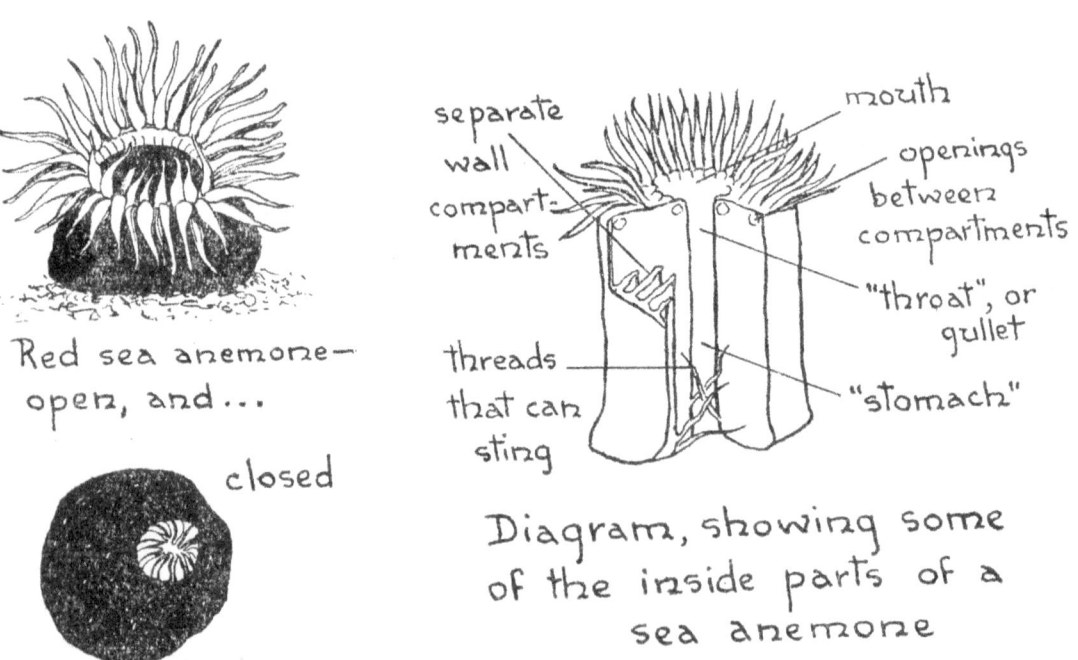

Red sea anemone—
open, and...
closed

separate wall compartments
threads that can sting

mouth
openings between compartments
"throat", or gullet
"stomach"

Diagram, showing some of the inside parts of a sea anemone

were there at all. We happened to see a group of them in a rock crevice alongside our pool just because Tess noticed a slight movement in one of them. There must have been dozens of them in that crevice, yet we would never have known, had it not been for that slight movement.

Strange as it may seem, these soft little sea anemones are very closely related to the small animals (or polyps) which make coral.

The next thing to take our attention in that pool was a number of little bristly brownish balls or sea urchins. You often find the empty "shells" of these on the beach—green, heliotrope, or pink in colour—and you call them sea eggs. They have ten bands of little knobs running from the hole at the top to the hole at the bottom, and between these, many very tiny holes. But when they are alive, they have a movable spine attached to each of the knobs, and thread-like tube feet coming out of the little holes. These tube feet can hold on to things with a very strong suction when they want to, and then let go again quite easily. They do this by having sea water pumped into and out of them.

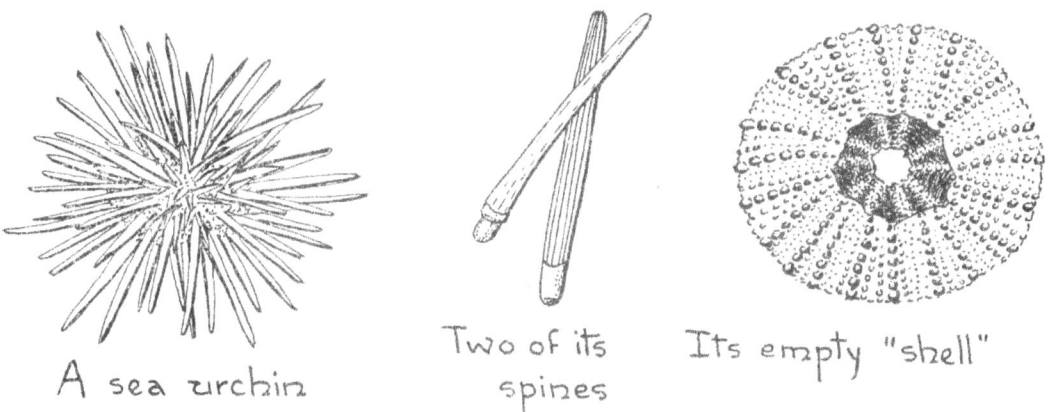

A sea urchin   Two of its spines   Its empty "shell"

Sea urchins look rather fierce with all their spines, and some of them are so poisonous that you should never touch them. These live in deeper pools. They have long purple spines, and they destroy molluscs. But most of the others are quite good-natured, seldom eating anything except seaweed—and perhaps a little decaying animal matter now and then.

Also, in our special pool, there were several pretty little starfish, mostly bluish and yellowish in colour. Starfish can sometimes have very long thin arms, and also more than five arms. But these little ones were squat, with five short arms.

We lifted one of them off the rock and out of the pool—and its dozens of tiny tube feet waved around trying to find something to hold on to. Before we let it go, we had a look at the hole in the very middle of it. This was its mouth, and the children were quite amused, once again, at the upside-downedness of so many sea creatures. Fancy having a mouth underneath you!

Upper side of starfish

Under side, showing central mouth, and a few tube-feet outspread

There is something else about a starfish that seems altogether the wrong way around. The usual thing to do, when eating, is to take something into your mouth, chew it up, and then swallow it down into your stomach. But when the starfish is about to eat something, it brings its stomach right out through its mouth, surrounds its meal with it, and digests it there and then, out in the open. Only after it has finished eating does its stomach slide back into position again, through the starfish's mouth.

Tess looked quite disgusted when she heard about this, and Chris said, "That's even queerer than the barnacle's way of eating."

"Do starfish eat seaweed?" Tess wanted to know. But of course, they don't. They eat the living flesh of molluscs, fish, and other sea animals, and their tiny tube feet are so strong that they can force open a valve shell and hold it open while they digest the animal inside it. You can imagine what a lot of damage starfish do in oyster beds. You probably know that the Crown of Thorn starfish have done enormous damage to the corals in the Barrier Reef, already under stress due to agricultural run-off and the warming of the oceans. Yet in spite of all the harm they do to other creatures, starfish themselves seem particularly hardy. Even if one of their arms breaks off, they can set to work and grow another one.

Perhaps most remarkable of all was that here, in this one pool, were three colours of seaweed, yet it is more usual for the colour of seaweed to change in different depths of water. Up at the surface you will mostly find the green ones, down a little deeper the brown ones, and deepest of all the pinks and reds. But occasionally you will find some pink ones up near the surface of a seashore, stiffened with little crusts of lime—and here we were lucky. Such dainty little feathery plants they were!

The covering of lime on these seaweeds is so thick that it remains even after the plant itself has died. Those little white, brittle, fernylooking things that you often find on beaches are the outside "skeletons" of red seaweeds—and they are so much like certain kinds of coral that they are actually called corallines.

Quite different were the brown seaweeds in our pool—like strings of knobbly beads. And the greens were soft delicate things, moving gracefully in the water.

Just as sea animals are usually quite different from land animals, so also are sea plants. Most land plants have roots, stems and leaves, but seaweeds have no real stems or leaves, and their "roots" are called holdfasts, because their whole purpose is to anchor the plant down firmly—not to take in water and foods, the way the roots of land plants do.

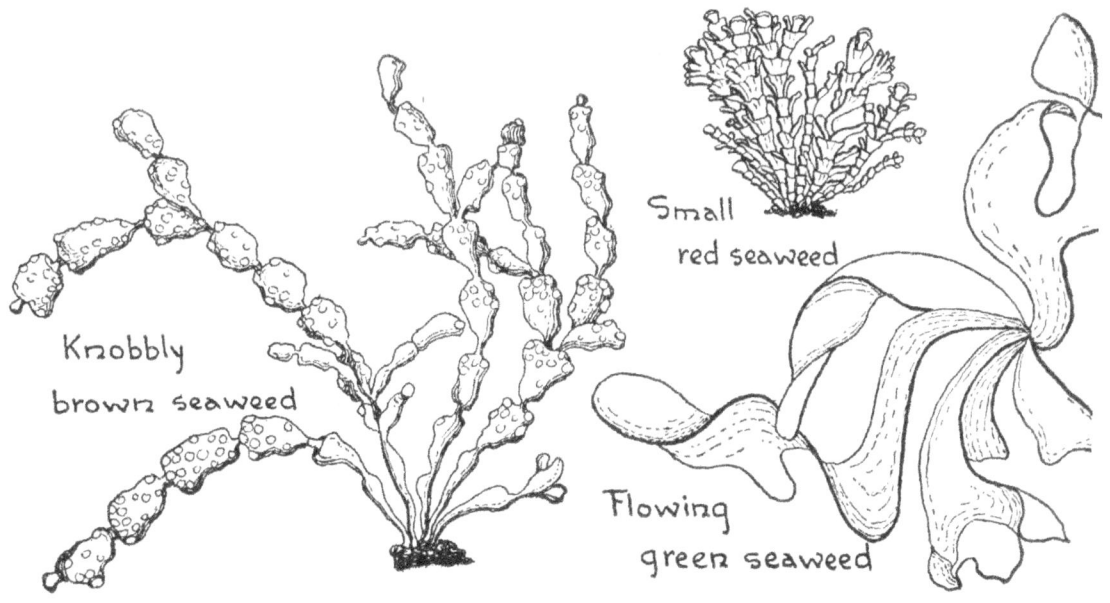

Sometimes a seaweed might seem to have leaves and stems, but there is no real difference between them except in shape, and the "leafy" part is called a frond.

There is another strange thing about seaweeds. You might remember that some of the earliest plants to appear in the waters of the Earth were algae—and very small, timid-looking plants they were, too. Then some of them began to find their way up on to dry land. They were still very tiny at this stage, and many of them still are. Yet all seaweeds are also algae, and some of them can be monsters over 30m long, even while others are so small that they form the slithery "slime" you so often find on rocks around the seashore.

We talked about seaweeds a bit more, then Chris asked, "What about sponges? Are they a kind of seaweed, too?" And he was most surprised to hear that they were not plants at all, but groups of tiny animals, living together in communities.

"Animals again!" he said. "Heavens, these sea things are queer, all right! You could *never* be sure of what they were just by looking at them, could you?"

We quite agreed with him, but by then it was late, and we had to go home.

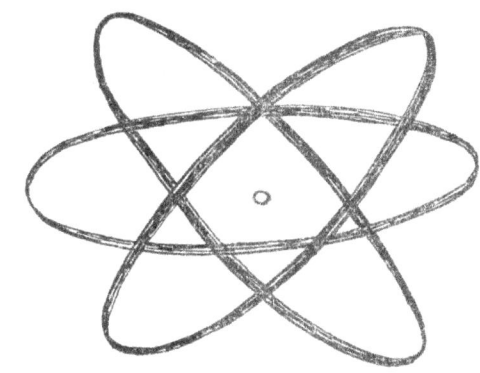

Remarkable Everyday Things— and Rocks

Light—The Fastest Thing There Is

HAVE you ever stopped to wonder how we would get along without light? We use it in almost everything we do. The most important of all our five senses is Seeing—and of course we cannot see anything without light.

In the beginning of our history on Earth, our days would have begun and ended with the sun, for this was the only light. But when we discovered fire, and then—much later—gas and electricity, we became able to bring light into the hours of darkness. So we got much more time in which to do interesting things.

When we talk about getting light on a subject, what we really mean is that we are understanding it. The Middle Ages in European history—when most people there were ignorant and filled with foolish superstitions—are known as the *Dark* Ages. So light is important to us not only as a fact in our everyday lives, but also as an idea. Yet when you ask yourself what light actually is, it takes quite a lot of explaining.

I was talking about it with the children one day, and mentioned that it was really a continual series of waves and vibrations. Chris already knew this, but Tess—two years younger—looked puzzled.

"Waves and vibrations? But those move," she said, "yet light is often quite still."

So I explained to her that nothing is actually quite still, because everything in our world is made up of atoms—and atoms are always on the move. They have a nucleus in the centre, with tiny electrons moving around it, just as Earth, Mars, Venus and the other planets move around our sun. That is why it is often said that an atom is a little solar system all to itself. What could seem stiller than a rock? Yet the atoms that make up a rock are constantly moving, as all other atoms are.

But there is something peculiar about the electrons in atoms that give out and receive light. Instead of moving around their nucleus in one fixed orbit, they jump in and out between two orbits—and it is this jumping in and out of the electrons that gives us light, or absorbs light.

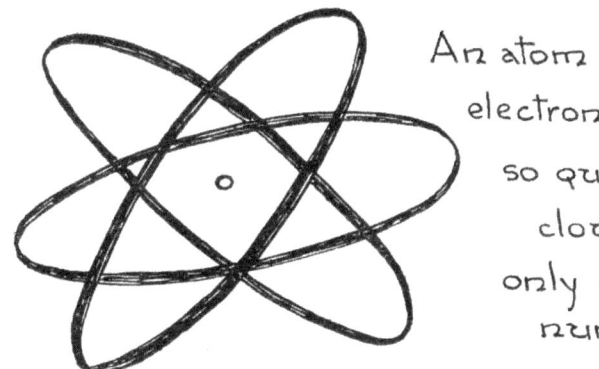

An atom has a nucleus, with electrons whirling around it so quickly that they look like clouds. There may be only one electron, or any number up to 92.

Also, of course, light travels from one place to another—and there isn't anything in our universe that travels faster. It goes at almost 300,000 kilometres a second. That is difficult to imagine, isn't it? When we travel fast in an aeroplane, the fastest we go is about 300 metres per second, so that's a million times slower than light. If we tried to go even two or three times faster, our plane would melt from having to push the air away, so how does light move so fast and easily? You could imagine particles of light being so small that atoms of air do not need to get pushed away to let the light through. You could also imagine that these light particles are vibrating, and atoms of air nearby vibrate together with the light as it passes through, in a collaborative motion. It turns out that both of these ideas are close to what happens. We call these particles of light 'photons', after the Greek word 'photos' for light, from which we also get the word 'photograph'.

Considering that the sun is 150 million kilometres away from us, can you work out how long its light takes to reach us? Yes, about eight minutes. But the sun is merely a next-door neighbour. The whole universe is so vast that the light from some of its stars takes thousands and millions and thousands of millions of years to reach us. In fact by the time their light does reach us, many of those stars no longer exist.

THE COLOURS IN LIGHT

Now, let us come back to Earth for a moment. Did you know that light is made up of colours? Yes, all the colours of the rainbow. But as you do not usually see them, you mostly think of light as white. Let it strike against a drop of water, though, or a prism, or the slanted edge

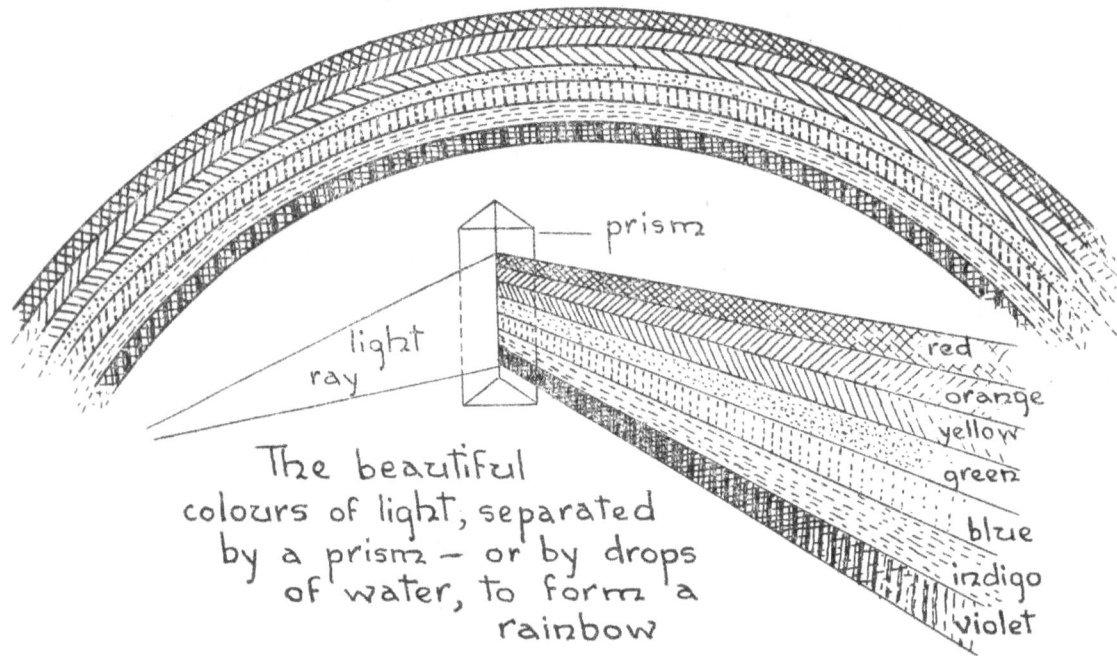

The beautiful colours of light, separated by a prism — or by drops of water, to form a rainbow

of a mirror, and you will immediately see a tiny set of rainbow colours, just like those that cross the sky in a glorious span when sunlight shines through rain. This happens because the glass or water has the effect of separating the colours in light, and then often reflecting them back to us, so that the colours become separately visible to us.

And what *are* these colours? We say that there are seven of them—red, orange, yellow, green, blue, indigo and violet, in that order.

Tess looked very puzzled indeed when I told her this. She said, "It's rather hard to understand. What makes the different colours?"

"Oh, different wave lengths," Chris answered. And that was right.

You see, light travels in waves, the same as sound does, only the waves of light are much shorter than those of sound. Red has long waves and the slowest vibrations, violet has the short ones with the fastest and most energetic vibrations, and the other colours have wave lengths in between.

When you waken in the morning, your room fills with daylight. But there are lots of colours in your room, too—perhaps a green cushion, a red dressing-gown, and all sorts of colours in the covers of books. This means that each of those separate things is treating the white daylight differently, because it has a different chemical arrangement. The green cushion is reflecting back into the room the green part of the daylight, much as a mirror reflects your face when you look into it. But the other six colours are of no interest to it, so it absorbs them away into itself and you do not see them.

The red dressing-gown, on the other hand, reflects the red part of the daylight and absorbs the green, together with all the other colours, stowing them away out of sight.

Now take these things and put them in a dark cupboard. What has happened to their colours? Unless some kind of light shines on them, colours just do not exist, because colour is actually an ingredient of light. All they have, inside that dark cupboard, is the *ability* to be certain colours as soon as a glimmering of light touches them.

As you might have guessed already, white reflects all seven colours at once, so that you do not see them separately any more than you do in light itself—and black soaks them all away without reflecting any of them.

Some animals can see more colours than we can; for example, bees and other insects can see light which is more violet than the blue or violet that we can see. That's called "Ultra-Violet" or "UV" light, and flowers have learnt that bees can see this light, so they make their petals reflect it so that insects will be strongly attracted. But that ultra-violet light has so much energy in it that it can also hurt us, even though we can't see it. When we go to the beach and get a sunburn, or when we go into bright sunlight without sunglasses, the atoms in our skin and eyes should stay attached to each other in their normal ways, but they get broken apart from each other by UV, so that's not a good thing.

There's another 'colour' that we experience every day. Just as we can't see the very energetic UV light rays, we also can't see the light rays that vibrate slower, and have longer wavelengths, than red light. This is called "infra-red" or "IR" light and we can feel it on our skin, since it warms us up. We also give off that IR light ourselves, since our warm bodies have jiggling atoms which radiate this gentle type of light all around us, When we go past a "PIR" or "Passive Infra Red" detector and an electric light turns on for us, our body's IR radiation is the cause.

Amazingly, there are animals that can see this IR light also. Can you imagine what kind of home would have animals which can see in the dark? Caves are a great place to find 'pit vipers', which are snakes that have regular eyes, rather like our own, but behind those eyes they have another pair of 'eyes' which are very sensitive to heat, inside deep pits in their skin. At the top of those pits there are small holes which act like a simple lens for the IR, allowing the IR's direction to be known. When a mouse goes past the viper's face, the IR radiated from that mouse's body tells the viper where the mouse is moving; and a quick strike makes that mouse into a meal.

If we allow our "light" photons to have even slower vibrations and even less energy, they become something that we use in our microwave ovens, in our mobile phones, and radios and televisions; these radio waves heat food and allow us to communicate over large distances. So light is an amazing thing, even when we can't see it. It's around us in some of its forms and "colours", all of the time.

MIRRORS AND LENSES

Of course, you know what mirrors are, but do you understand how they work? They are made of glass, and light passes through glass, yet it doesn't pass through mirrors. Why? Because on the back of the mirror glass there is a thin coating of silver or aluminium, and light cannot pass through these metals. Instead, it bounces off, carrying with it the image of anything that happens to be in front of the mirror—only, of course, the image is reversed.

A secret message, which can be read by looking at it in a mirror

That is why, if you put writing in front of a mirror, you see it back-to-front. Then, on the other hand, you can give a secret message to a friend in back-to-front writing, and your friend will be able to read it quite clearly by holding it in front of a mirror. The famous artist-

scientist-engineer Leonardo da Vinci (who painted the Mona Lisa) wrote his 13,000 pages of notes in mirror writing. Do you think he did that to keep them secret, or was it because he was left-handed and found it easier?

One of the most interesting things that you can make with mirrors is a periscope. With this, you can see over fences, or other people's heads in a crowd, or even around corners, without any craning or standing on tiptoes. Chris has often made periscopes, and he and Tess have always had a lot of fun with them.

Just a box with two mirrors fitted into it, and two holes cut in it, and this little boy has a fine, working periscope

All you need, to make one, is a long narrow box and two mirrors. You place the mirrors slantwise in the box, as shown in our drawing—the lower one facing up, and the upper one facing down. You can hold them in place by fitting them through slits in the box, and securing them with "sticky tape". You also have to cut two holes in the box—one in front of each mirror. Then, of course, whatever the top mirror reflects, is reflected again by the lower mirror, which is facing it—and when you look through your peephole, in front of this lower mirror, you can see many "out of reach" things quite clearly.

Another way in which you can see "out of reach" things is with the help of lenses. A lens is a piece of glass shaped in such a way that when we look through it, we see things that we cannot see clearly—or at all—with our own unaided eyes.

It is the lenses in telescopes which make us able to see amazing numbers of details among the stars and planets. Owing to the lenses

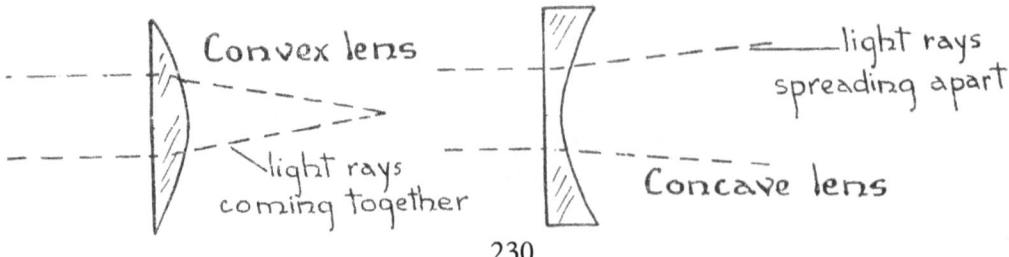

in microscopes, we can see the smallest details in the tiniest things. Near-sighted people (who cannot focus well on distant things) and far-sighted people (who cannot focus well on close objects) will be able to see everything quite normally if they wear the right kind of glasses—and these, again, are lenses.

Now, these wonderful lenses are pieces of glass that are made either concave (thin in the centre) or convex (thick in the centre). Light rays passing through a concave lens spread outwards, but rays passing through a convex lens come together—and this can make all the difference to the way we see things.

You know how you have to move your hand lens or magnifying glass up and down until you get a perfect focus. This is because of its special curve. If it were curved less or more sharply, your perfect focus would come at a different point.

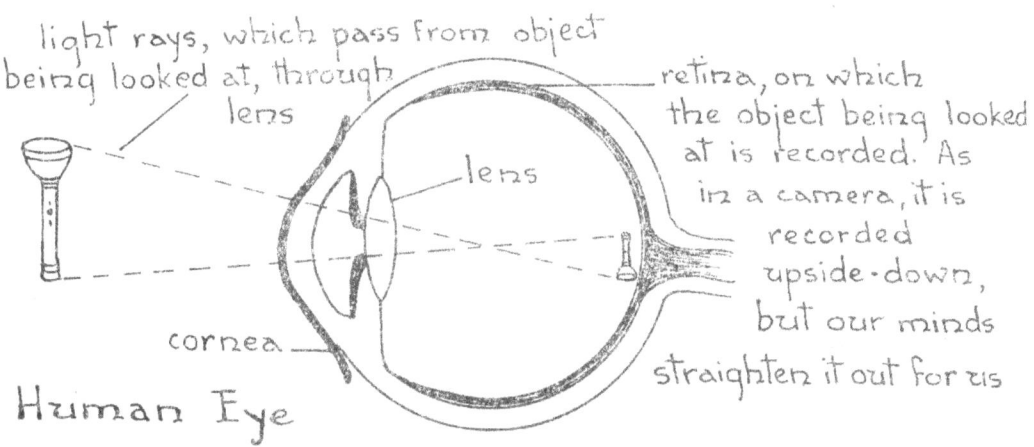

As you may know, we have lenses of our own—one in each eye—and there are muscles controlling these, which normally make each lens thinner in the centre when things are far away, and thicker in the centre as they come closer. But if the muscles are lazy, they do not do this sufficiently, and our near or far sight becomes blurred. The specialist who studies our eyes finds out exactly what curve of lens we need to correct the mistakes of our own lenses—and when we wear a pair of glasses made of these, we have much better vision.

THE PATH OF LIGHT

If light is not interfered with, it always travels in a straight line. You can see this if you shine a torch on to a mirror and watch what happens. The torch-light bounces off the mirror and strikes upon some other object—perhaps a wall, a ceiling, or a piece of furniture—and the path it takes is a perfectly straight line.

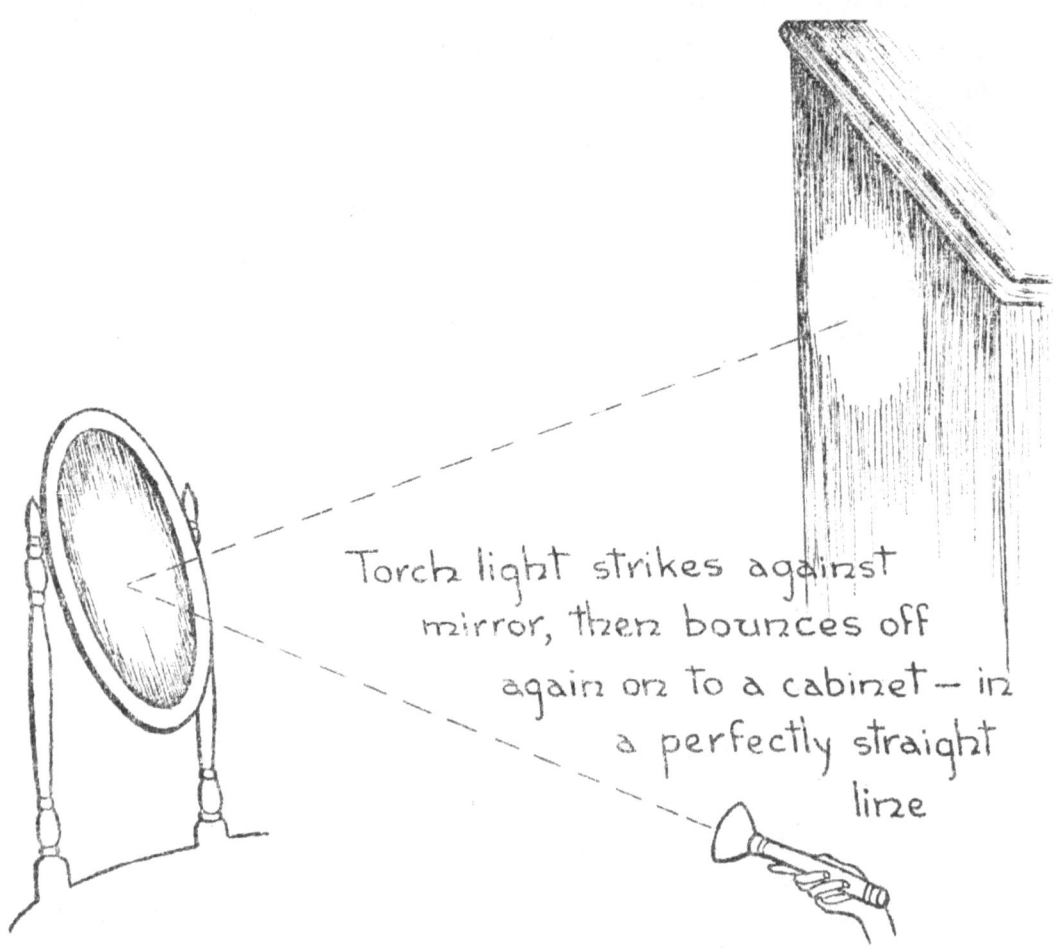

Torch light strikes against mirror, then bounces off again on to a cabinet — in a perfectly straight line

But we have seen how a lens can make the rays of light spread apart or come together. Lenses work they way they do because light sometimes "side-steps" a bit before continuing on its course. This is when light has to pass through something more solid than a vacuum or air. In a vacuum there is nothing—not even air—to hold light back, and in air there is very little. But water and glass are more solid than air, and they do hold it back a little since light has to make the atoms around it vibrate with it as it passes through. When light strikes upon glass or water, its speed is lessened, and its direct course is bent to another angle. We then say that the light is refracted. That is why people's legs look so funny when they step into a swimming pool, and why a straw in a glass of water looks as if it is broken. Refraction is just how a lens works; the light gets refracted across the lens surface into the correct angles, focusing a wide beam of light into a point.

So you see, light—this commonplace everyday thing which we just take for granted—is very special indeed, and when we try to understand it, we learn all kinds of surprising and exciting things. Also, as well as needing it in almost everything we do, we wouldn't even be here without it. Without light there could be no green plants—and no human beings or other animals. I suppose that is why, long ago, people used to worship the sun as a god.

But Tess now thinks of light in another way altogether. As she said to me one day, walking through the city, "Mummie, just think! Isn't it wonderful! Even though we can't see them, we're right in the midst of rainbows all the time!" And we all know what a happy thing a rainbow is.

Sound Is Never Still

TESS said to me one day, "Mummie, you couldn't possibly make a sound without some kind of movement, could you?" And of course, that is right. A world of complete stillness would also be one of complete silence. No matter how tiny the sound is, *something* has to move in order to make it.

But that isn't all. There is a lot more movement, even though we cannot see it. When a sound is made, it pushes the tiny particles of air around and causes quite a disturbance among them. If the sound is a pleasant, musical one, this disturbance is quite rhythmic and orderly, but if there are many sounds together—the screeching of car brakes, the roar of an aeroplane, a dog's bark, a postman's whistle—you can just imagine what a shoving and jostling goes on among the air particles.

When your parrot decides to say something, he sets sound waves in motion. These circle out like the waves around a stone dropped in a pool. They have a backwards-and-forwards movement, which makes the air particles crowd up together, then fall apart... crowd up together, then fall apart... over and over again.

Now, the same as light, sound moves from one place to another in "waves". But the waves of light are different from those of sound. Light waves vibrate in an up-and-down way, something like the waves of the sea which move up and down while travelling along, while sound waves move backwards and forwards, in the direction that they travel. They strike against certain air molecules and give *them* a push. These in turn bump into those next to them and give them a push—and so it goes on, until the waves reach your ear.

Inside your ear there is a piece of stretched skin called the eardrum. When the waves strike against this, it vibrates, and sends messages to your brain. Then your brain tells you many things about the sound—where it came from, what it is, and if it is high, low, soft or loud.

Sound waves are different from light waves in another way, too. They have longer wavelengths than than the light waves that we can see with our eyes, and they do not travel anything like so quickly. Whereas light travels at almost 300,000 kilometres a second, sound travels at only about 346 metres a second through air. That is why you always see lightning much sooner than you hear the thunder that goes with it in an electric thunderstorm.

But like light, sound doesn't always travel at the same speed. Sometimes it goes faster than this, and other times even slower. It depends on what it is moving through. Since sound needs one set of atoms to push up against the next set of atoms to make the wave move forward, if those atoms are close together in a solid, rather than in a gas like air, sound moves quickly. So this is the opposite of light, which moves slowly when it has to vibrate the large numbers of atoms in a solid. Sound moves faster through things like water, wood and

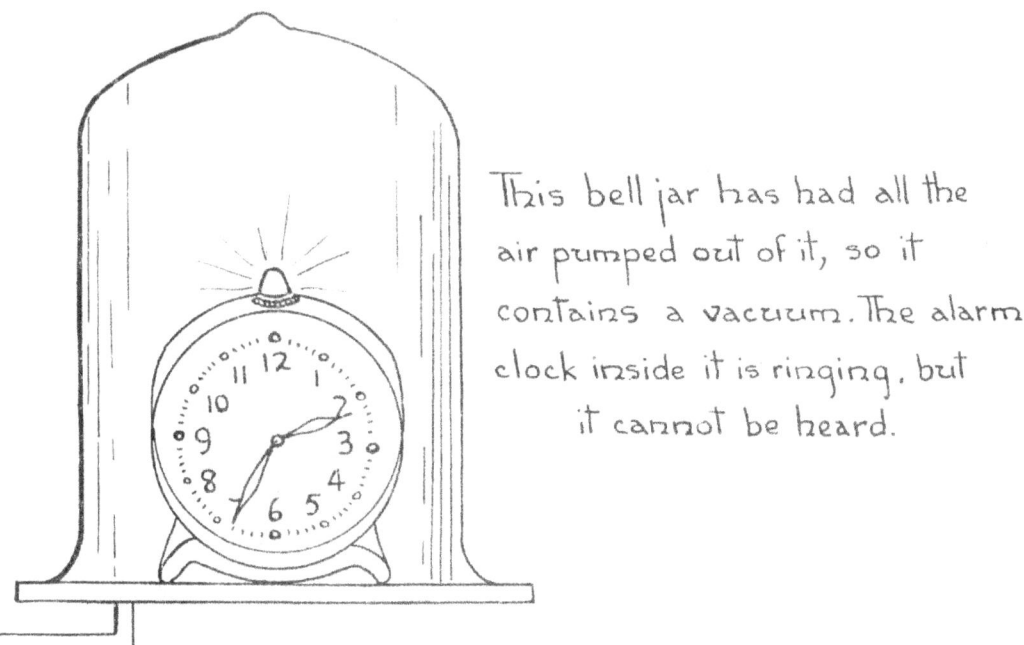

This bell jar has had all the air pumped out of it, so it contains a vacuum. The alarm clock inside it is ringing, but it cannot be heard.

Speaking into one tin

iron than it does through air. And in a vacuum sound doesn't move at all. As you know, light travels quite freely through the "airlessness" of outer space—but this is something that sound cannot do. If you had an alarm clock ringing inside a container, and gradually pumped air out of the container, the ringing would gradually grow fainter. If you managed to pump *all* of the air out, there would be no ringing at all. But you would hear it again immediately you allowed air to flow back into the container.

So, as sound cannot travel through vacuums, it has greater difficulty getting through air than through water or earth or iron. That seems *very* back-to-front, doesn't it? But it explains why it was said that Native Americans would put their ears to the ground when they wanted to find out as soon as possible if anyone were approaching them on horseback. It also explains how a string-and-tin telephone works.

Listening in the other tin

You can make one of these for yourself quite easily. All you need is two empty tins, a length of string pulled out tightly with each end attached to one of the tins, and two people to talk and listen. While one person talks through one of the tins, the other person listens through the other tin—and, thanks to the string stretched tightly between the two tins, the speaker's voice can be heard quite clearly at the other end. The sound waves have travelled along the string much easier than they would have through air. But you must be careful that the string doesn't touch anything whatever except the two tins.

Tess and Chris have often made one of these telephones, and had great fun talking to each other in mere whispers, from one end of the garden to the other.

Another thing that they particularly enjoy is calling out in some parts of the mountains, and having the mountains call back to them. This, of course, is an echo. Just as we saw that a torch-light bounced off a mirror on to something else, so does sound bounce off things and come back to you, if there isn't too much in between to interfere. Call

It's fun when the sound waves from your voice bounce off a cliff-face and come back to you in the form of echoes

out toward a smooth-faced cliff or mountain-side across a clear space, and you will quite possibly hear a good strong echo. But the smooth surface and clear space are important.

You know how our voices and footsteps echo in an empty room? Yet we hear no echoes in a room filled with furniture and heavily carpeted. This is because the sound waves cannot travel any distance without bumping into something which absorbs them.

We had been talking about sound one day when Tess asked, "What makes some sounds different from others? You know, pretty or ugly, I mean—and high or low."

"High or low is called pitch," Chris told her. "And pretty or ugly could be called quality," I added. Then we talked about how these differences come about. They are all, of course, a matter of vibrations. When sound waves vibrate only a few times a second, the sound you hear is a low one, but if they vibrate a great many times a second, the sound is a high one. If the vibrations are smooth and rhythmic, the sound is enjoyable, but if they come joltingly, in fits and starts, the sound can seem more ugly, or at least to have a lot of 'character' or 'timbre'.

An example of smooth sounds is that of a flute, which can give out one almost-pure note of a single vibration speed when it is used to play a high and steady note. However a drum, when it is hit, produces a whole range of vibration speeds, starting at the moment it is hit with a 'bang'. These notes can be high and low tones, all mixed together. The note never sounds as pure as that of a flute, but if the drum has a big metal 'kettle' under its top drum-skin which can resonate, you will be able to hear a single tone coming from the drum, after the initial 'bang' noise has died down.

Here is another interesting thing about sound: As you know, there are things too small for us to see without using special equipment—like atoms. And there are certain colours which we cannot see—like infra-red and ultra-violet. So, also, there are very high-pitched sounds which we cannot hear. Yet dogs can hear them, for their ear-drums can respond to much faster vibrations than ours can.

Think of this carefully for a minute, and you will realise how foolish it is to believe only in what we ourselves can see, hear, taste, touch and smell. Clever as we are in many ways, our senses are by no means as sharp as they might be. So there may be wonderful things around us right now, that we aren't as yet aware of. That's rather exciting, isn't it?

Mysterious Magnetism

HUMAN beings have learnt a great deal about many things, yet they still know very little indeed about some of the things that are most commonplace.

Think of magnets, for instance. We all know the ones that we can easily buy in shops—the straight or bar magnets, and the curved or horseshoe ones. Yet actually our whole world is filled with magnets, for it is made up of atoms... and each atom is a nucleus surrounded by moving electrons... and each electron creates magnetism as it moves—so, in a way, we can think of it as a tiny magnet. Most amazing of all, the Earth itself is one huge magnet. Yet magnetism itself is still rather mysterious to us, with many discoveries being made even today, especially with the very tiny magnets that are used to store computer information on our hard drive memories.

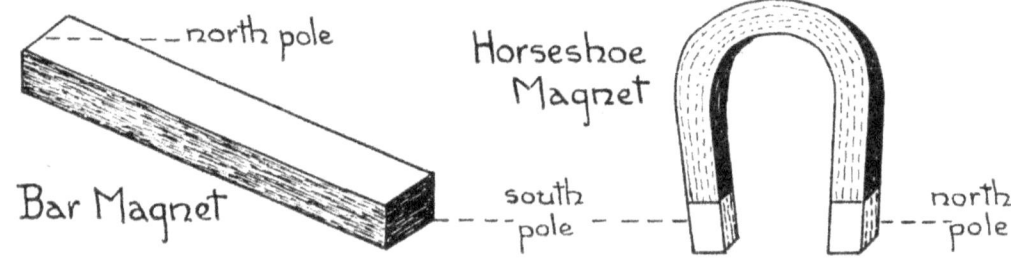

We know what magnetism does, and much about how it comes to exist—but on the other hand, we cannot weigh it or measure it, nor can we detect it with any of our five senses. You have never heard of anybody smelling or tasting magnetism, have you? Or touching, or hearing, or seeing it? So all that we can do as yet is to study its laws, and to use it and be very grateful for it, because without it we would live in a strange world indeed. Certainly we would have very few of the things that make up our modern civilisation. We would have no telephones, radios or televisions, which use magnets to make the sounds we hear from them, and also to receive the signals that come from radio waves; and no refrigerators, trains, buses, or any of the other things that are run by electric motors—for all motors also have magnets in them somewhere.

WHAT IS A MAGNET?

First, let's look at the many materials that could make a magnet which we can use to attract iron or steel. These materials are called, naturally enough I suppose, 'ferromagnetic materials', since the Latin name for iron is 'ferrum'. There are metallic minerals such as magnetite, which is a mixture of iron and oxygen; and pure metals such as iron, cobalt and nickel; and combinations of various metals, often including iron, with oxygen to make magnetic 'ferrites';—and we also can combine metals together to make magnets which are the strongest magnets we know of today. These metal mixtures are called alloys.

Now, how would we make ourselves a magnet? First, take a ferromagnetic material, and then magnetise it by rubbing it with another magnet in one direction, or putting an electric coil around it to make it an 'electromagnet'. If we have a true 'hard' ferromagnetic material in our hands, even after we stop magnetising it, it will retain a good portion of the magnetising power that we started it out with. We could also simply find an already-magnetised piece of magnetite in the ground (which is then called a 'lodestone').

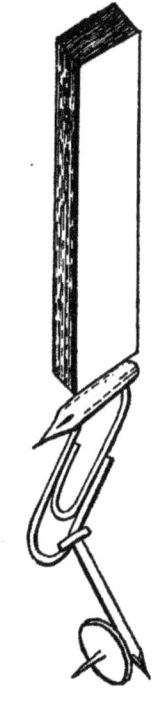
Objects clinging together, though magnet touches only one of them...

Take a small magnet around with you and touch all kinds of different things with it—a glass, a pair of scissors, a wooden ruler, your shoes and socks, pins, paper clips, a book, nails and screws. In this way you will soon find out which materials are affected by magnetism and which are not. You will find that when they are, your magnet does not even have to touch them. From a short distance they actually jump towards it, and the magnet holds them firmly.

You will also find that your magnet can *hold* things without touching them. Give it a nail to hold. Place a paper clip on the end of this nail, and they will cling together. Place a needle on the paper clip and it, too, will cling. These different things would not have clung together by themselves. It is the magnet which is making them do it, even though it is touching only one of them.

.... then still clinging together, without magnet

Now take the nail away from the magnet and you will see that the other things still hold on for a while. Separate them, then bring them together again, and—sure enough—they stick to one another. This shows that a certain amount of magnetism has passed into them from the magnet. So these also would be made of ferromagnetic material.

What actually has happened to change these things into magnets—even weak ones?

To understand this, take two magnets—either bar or horseshoe ones, or one of each. Put them together, and you will see that in certain positions they pull towards each other while in other positions they push apart. This is because the two ends of a magnet are always opposite in nature. One is called the north pole, and the other the south pole. If you bring the north pole of one magnet near to the south pole of another, the magnets approve of this arrangement and pull strongly towards each other. But if you try to bring two north poles or two south poles together, you will not succeed. The magnets fight against this with all their strength, and unless you really force them, they will never even touch.

Now, you remember how every electron moving around the nucleus of an atom creates magnetism? This means that every electron creates a north and a south pole. In most atoms the poles face around in all directions, making the overall magnetism a jumble. But in some materials—like magnetite—the electrons can be made to all face in the same direction, and we say that they are "lined up". It is this lining-up of its atoms that makes magnetite magnetic.

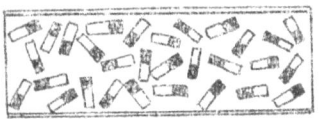

Atoms arranged haphazardly in non-magnetic material

black stands for north pole—white for south pole

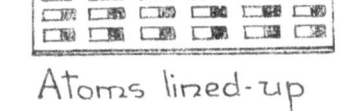

Atoms lined-up in magnetic material

The atoms in your bar and horseshoe magnets are thus lined up, but those in nails, safety-pins, spoons, nail-files, and so on, they are not. However, they do quite readily line up if a magnet comes near them, and they can keep a memory of that even after the big magnet has been pulled away.

Perhaps you would like to know exactly where the north pole of a magnet finishes, and where its south pole begins. Your guess is that this would be in the very middle, so that if you cut your magnet exactly in half, you would have something with a strong north or south pole at one end and a weak north or south pole at the other end. But it doesn't turn out like this. Cut your magnet in half, and you have two perfect magnets, each with a north and a south pole. Cut one of these in half again, and the same thing happens—and if you went on cutting right down to the merest scrap, you would find that this scrap was also a perfect magnet with its north and south poles. And of course, it *has* to be like this, since every electron is a magnet in itself.

MAGNETIC FIELDS

Do you know what a magnetic field is? It is the area over which a magnet makes its power felt. You can find this out for yourself in an interesting way. All you need is a magnet, a piece of firm paper, and some iron filings. You can get the iron filings from a machine shop, or out of a small chemistry set, or you can make them yourself by sawing or filing through a few thick nails and gathering the metal powder, but this is hard work, and you have to be very careful not to hurt yourself.

Now place your magnet on a table, with the piece of paper over it. Sprinkle the iron filings evenly over the paper, covering as large an area as possible, gently tap the paper with a little stick, and see what happens. The tiny filings move around as though they were alive, forming themselves into patterns of smoothly curving lines. They do this because of the magnet underneath them. The lines that they form into are called lines of force, because they show the directions

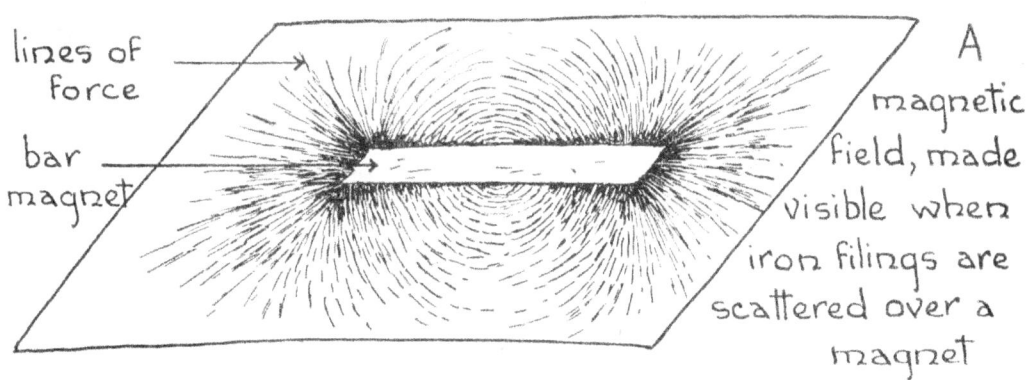

in which the magnetism is flowing. And the whole area over which the iron filings move shows the general shape of the overall magnetic field.

Now get two magnets and place them (under the paper and the iron filings) in different positions—with their north and south poles facing, or with their two north or two south poles facing—and watch the lines of force appearing again. This is one of the most interesting things you can do with magnets—making their invisible power show itself in these curving line pictures.

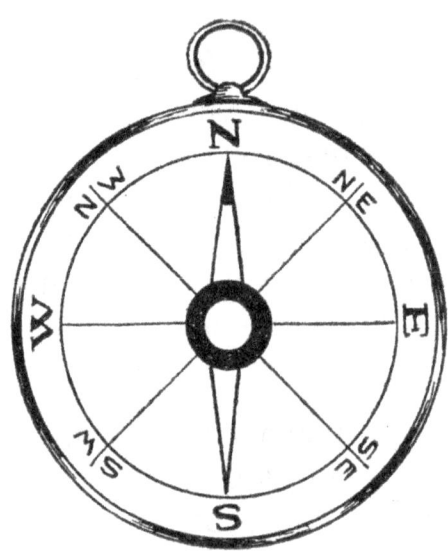

COMPASSES

Have you ever wondered about compasses, and how a person can use one of them to find the right way around? You know that in the centre of every compass there is a little needle that moves around. This is a piece of magnetised metal, and because it is magnetised, it has two poles. Now, you will remember how the whole of our Earth itself is one great magnet, so it also must have two poles. But these are different from the north and south poles that we hear about so much. They are the *magnetic* poles, a short distance from the official pole positions—and it is to these that the needle of a compass will always point, unless there is some other magnet near at hand, attracting it in another direction. Left alone, the needle's north pole points northward.

So a person with a compass can always tell where north, south, east and west are—and need never be lost. There is a convention in labelling magnets; we put an N symbol on the part that is North-seeking, and an S symbol on the opposite part that is South-seeking. So all bar magnets, if suspended in their middles, will rotate until the N points North and the S points South.

But perhaps you are puzzled by our compass needle's north end pointing north instead of south, since it is the *opposite* poles of magnets that attract each other. Well, you are right to be puzzled—and the fact is that if we regard the Earth as a gigantic bar magnet, then we would label it with an N in southerly Antarctica, and with an S at the north pole region between Canada and Russia.

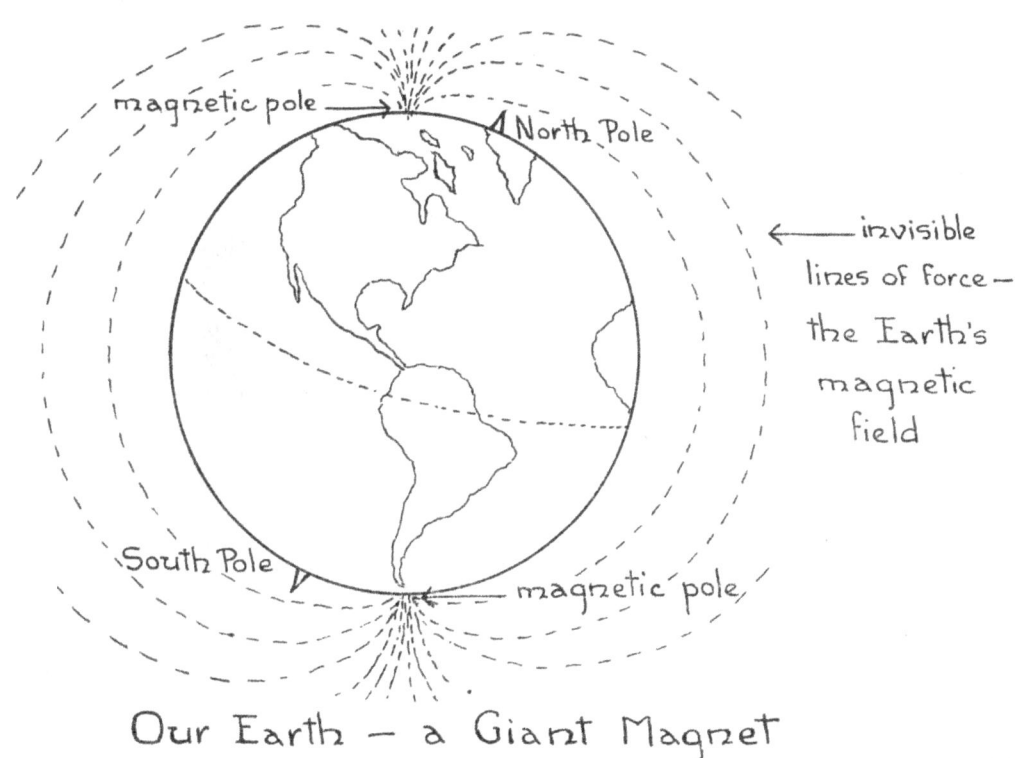

Our Earth — a Giant Magnet

ELECTROMAGNETS

We have seen that new magnets can be made by bringing certain metals into contact with an already-existing magnet. They can also be made by stroking a piece of metal across one of the poles of a magnet—*always in the same direction*, not backwards and forwards. But a magnet can also be made with electricity.

Suppose you had a piece of steel which you wanted to change into a magnet. All you would need, apart from the steel, would be a dry-cell battery, and a piece of 'insulated' or 'magnet' wire covered with something that does not conduct electricity - such as plastic - so that when the wire is wound around the steel it will not conduct electricity in a 'short circuit' to the iron, but make the electricity go through the entire long wire circuit. First, you would wind the wire around the steel, leaving both of its ends free. Then, you would cut the insulation off these ends, and place each of them on to one of the battery's terminals. Your piece of steel would now be an electromagnet—and its magnetism would probably last for quite a while even with the electric current removed, if the steel is a good 'hard ferromagnet' that holds its remanent magnetism.

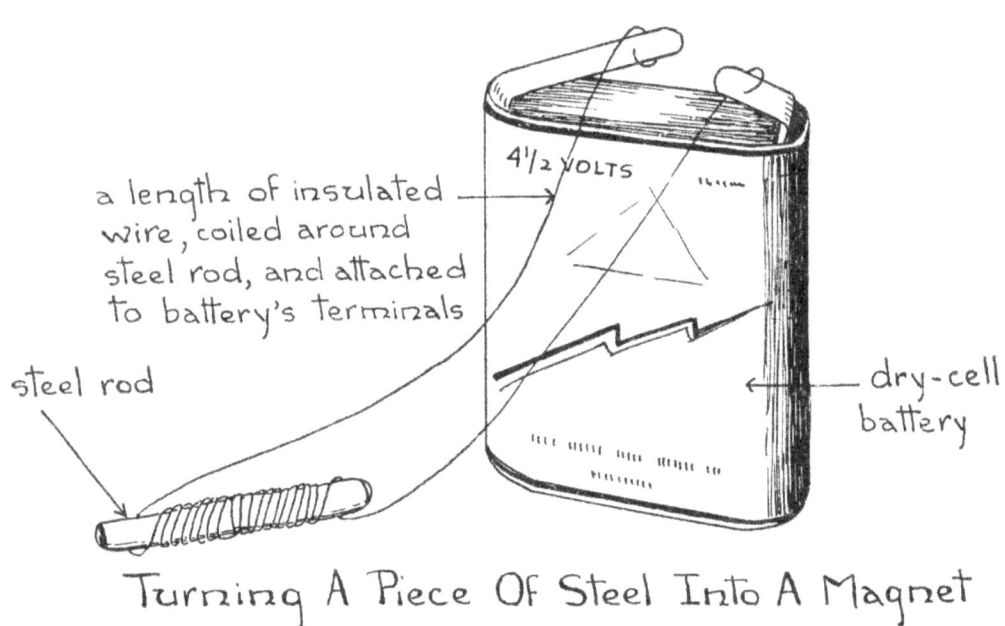

Turning A Piece Of Steel Into A Magnet

If you did the same thing to a piece of soft iron with a low remanent magnetic field it, too, would become a magnet—but only while the electric current was flowing through the wire. As soon as the current stopped, the iron would lose its magnetism, and anything clinging to it would drop. Mankind uses electromagnets in all sorts of ways, big and small. They play a most important part in many of his "gadgets", as well as in heavy industries. You can see them at work in an electric bell or magnetic door locks, for instance—as well as in those huge cranes which pick up large masses of scrap iron from one place and deposit them in another. They pick them up with soft iron which becomes magnetic when an electric current flows through it. But then, as soon as the current is switched off, the iron loses its magnetism, and drops whatever it has picked up.

Another important use for electromagnets is in electric motors. When magnets are placed in a circle around a shaft that also has magnets attached to it, we can turn the outer electromagnets on and off in a circular pattern. This makes making the inner shaft magnets move around in a circle, following the rotation of the outer magnetic field. In this way we can make big motors turn for us, doing far more work than we could manage on our own.

And now, of course, you are wondering exactly what soft iron is. It is iron which has been heated to a very high degree so that the directions of its atoms are thoroughly jumbled, and they are not locked in any one direction by hard crystal or 'grain' edges. An electric current passing through it will bring all of its atoms around in the same direction, changing it into a magnet. But when the current is switched off, the atoms immediately go back to their jumbled positions, and the magnetism disappears. Iron which behaves in this way is called soft iron.

Even the smallest child loves a magnet to play with. It's such fun picking things up with it and feeling its "pull". But as you grow a little older and understand what magnetism really is, that's where the real fun begins, don't you think?

Where and What Is Electricity?

MAGNETISM and electricity are so alike that we can think of them as two members of the same family. Run a plastic comb briskly through your hair, then put it near a scrap of tissue paper, and the paper will lift up and cling to it, just as a pin will cling to a magnet. Rub a glass rod or a blown-up balloon with a piece of material like silk, wool or nylon, and the rod or balloon will "lift" any small, light object—like bits of thread, fluff, or paper.

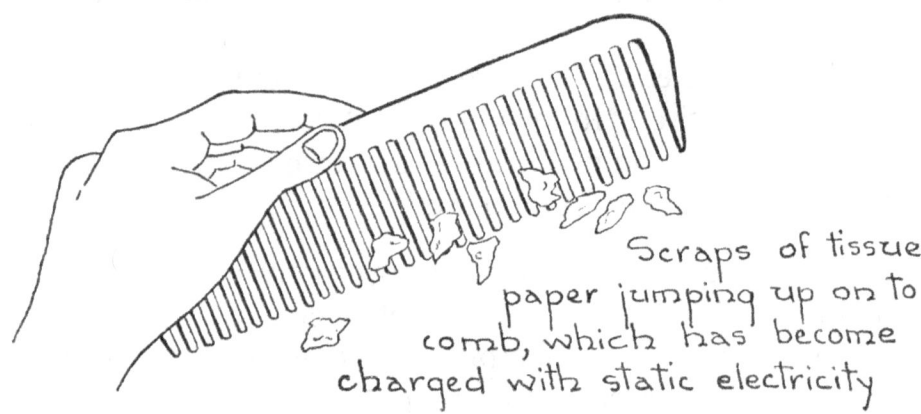

Scraps of tissue paper jumping up on to comb, which has become charged with static electricity

It seems at first that the only difference between this and magnetism is that a magnet will attract only metals, whereas this other kind of thing will attract almost anything else. Its name is electricity, and when it occurs like this—remaining in something instead of running through a wire to something else—it is called static electricity.

The ancient Greeks made an important discovery about two and a half thousand years ago. They noticed that after a piece of amber had been rubbed, it attracted all kinds of little things toward itself—and as the Greek word for amber is *elektron*, it is easy to understand how electricity got its name.

You will remember that one of the most important laws of magnetism is to do with its poles—opposite poles attract each other, whilst like poles repel each other. And we find this same pulling together and pushing apart in electricity. Only we don't talk about north and south poles with electricity. Instead, we talk about positive and negative.

Try to bring two negative or two positive electric charges together, and you will not succeed, for they push strongly apart. But try the same thing with a negative and a positive, and you will find that they naturally draw together.

You can rub two glass rods with a piece of cloth, then quickly bring them close to each other, and see how they move apart. This proves that they are both charged with the same kind of electricity—positive or negative. But rub a glass rod and a plastic one with a piece of cloth, and they move towards each other with quite a strong pull. This, of course, proves that one of them has become charged with positive, and the other with negative electricity. They are different kinds of materials, and they respond differently to the rubbing. We shall see *how* differently a little later on.

Now, what is electricity? And how do things become charged with it?

It is a movement of electrons. And things become charged with it when electrons move either on to them or away from them.

To understand this more clearly, think back for a moment about atoms—those infinitely tiny things of which everything in this world is made. You will remember how an atom has a nucleus and any number of electrons, and how the electrons revolve around the nucleus the way planets revolve around the sun. The planets are held in their orbits by gravity's attraction to the sun—otherwise they would just fly off anywhere into space. And electrons are held in *their* orbits by attraction to the nucleus—electrical attraction.

The nucleus is charged with positive electricity and the electrons with negative electricity. So they all hold together, in the form of the

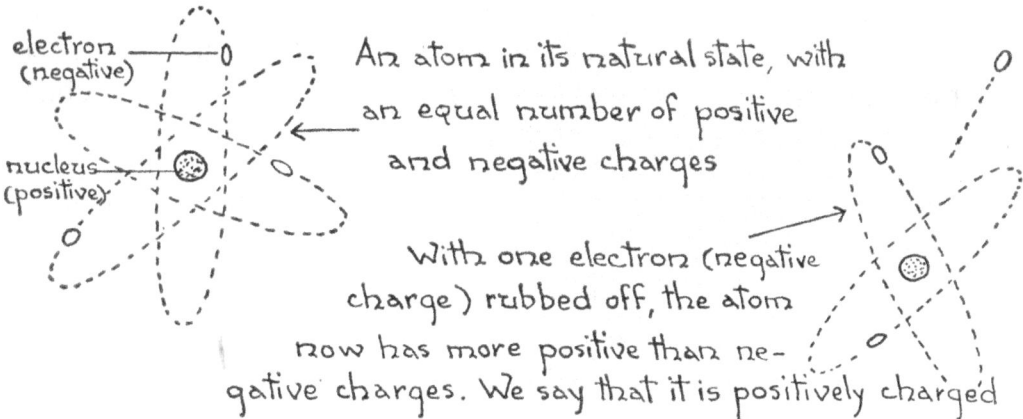

atom. But as the positive exactly balances the negative, this balanced atom itself does not exert an electrical force on other things. That is, not unless something unusual happens to that atom.

You can *make* something unusual happen to it when you rub it—as when you rub a plastic pen on a piece of cloth, for instance. When you do this, you actually rub some of the electrons off the cloth's atoms on to the pen. And the electrons, you remember, have negative electricity. So the pen is getting a lot more negative charges than it had before, and the cloth is being left with less. The pen is now negatively charged, and the cloth is positively charged.

When you rub a glass rod with cloth, the electrons flow the other way—towards the cloth—so that the rod becomes positively charged and the cloth negatively charged.

But whichever way it goes, this state of affairs—this movement of electrons—creates static electricity.

Tremendously high positive and negative charges, up in the clouds, produce the electricity that we call lightning. Sometimes, when you take a nylon shirt or blouse off in dry weather, you will hear a crackling sound and maybe see some sparking. This is electricity that has come about by the nylon's rubbing against your skin. So you see, electricity isn't something that we can take from mines, like coal or silver. It is something that we have to produce, by moving electrons away from their regular atoms. And we do this in a number of different ways, but mostly with the help of magnets.

ELECTRICITY FROM MAGNETS

You have learnt about electromagnets—how an electric current flowing around a piece of iron will change the iron into a magnet. And the opposite also happens—as a great scientist called Michael Faraday discovered more than 100 years ago.

He connected the two ends of a coil of wire to a meter for measuring small amounts of electricity. Then he twisted the coil between the two arms of a magnet, and the needle of his meter moved slightly—which meant that he had created a small electric current. Had he done it the other way—turning the magnet inside a coil of wire—the result would have been the same.

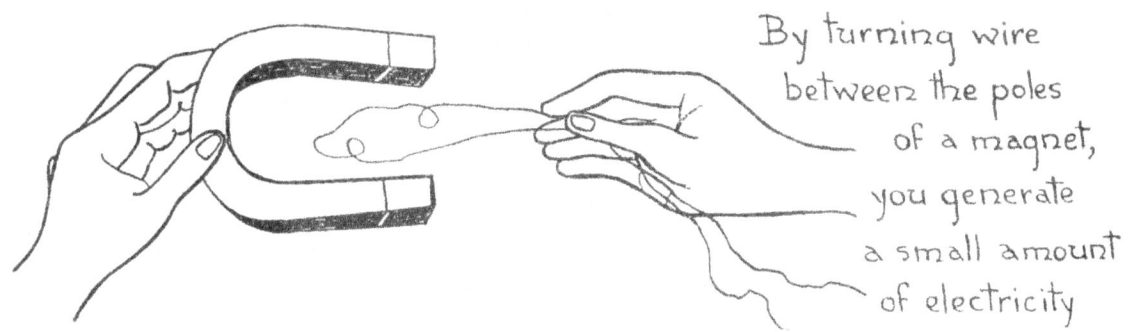

This simple arrangement, on a very large scale, is what we call a dynamo or generator. Sometimes the magnet or electromagnet in a dynamo is like a great tunnel, with the coil turning inside it. Other times it is the moving core of the dynamo, with the coil arching around it.

Of course, some kind of power is needed to make the huge core whirl round, inside the tunnel—and this is where water or steam comes in.

If you were to run a tap on the blades of an old toy windmill, the force of the water would send the blades spinning. The same thing would happen if you held the blades edgewise to a volume of steam coming from a boiling kettle.

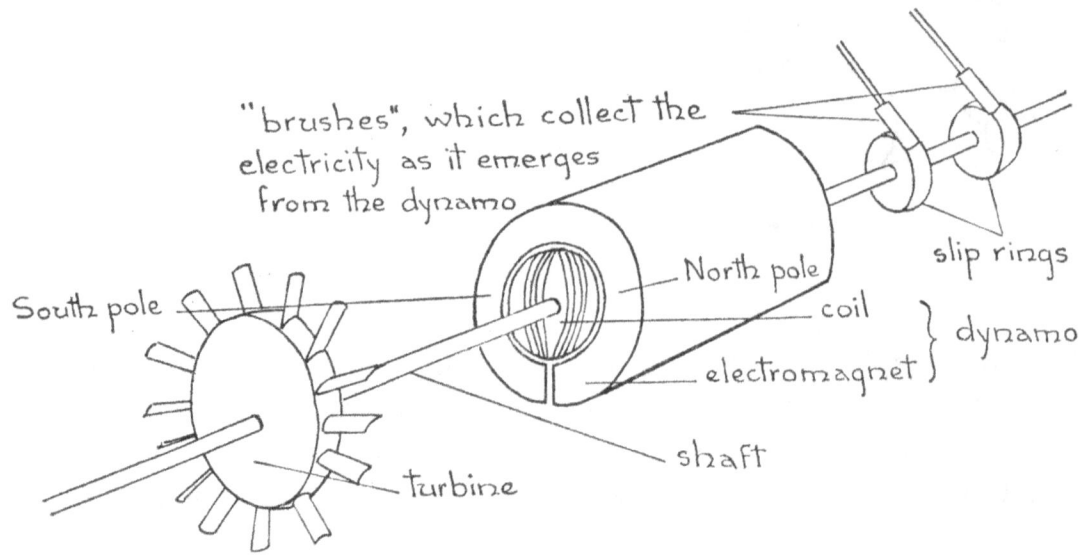

In great schemes for making—or generating—electricity, the blades would be called turbines. They would be attached to shafts connected with the giant coils or magnets inside the tunnels—and they would be made to turn by the power of water in dams, or at other times by the power of steam that comes from burning fuel. The water or steam is made to rush through pipes which lead directly to the turbines.

Of course, some of the earliest 'turbines' were windmills, which were used to power mills to grind flour, or to pump water, or to drive mechanical looms. But those were small affairs, only perhaps 10m tall. We now are using enormous windmills to make electricity, more than 200m high, as tall as a skyscraper. Instead of burning fuel to make steam to turn turbine blades, we use the wind all around us, turning magnets inside coils of wire to get our electricity in a modern, yet really old-fashioned way.

MAKING ELECTRICITY FROM SUNLIGHT

We have all seen solar cells on rooftops, making electricity in a very modern way without any moving magnets, or coils of wire. Most of the panels we see are coloured a deep blue, and sometimes look quite black. The darker the panels, the more light from the sun is absorbed and so the more electricity we can hope to get from each panel. But how does a dark panel make electricity from sunlight? There are clues that we have seen from plants and from the colours of light we get from the sun.

One clue is from plants, which make food from sunlight with their green leaves. The other clue is that Ultra-Violet light can change chemicals in our skin and make for real trouble such as sunburn or eye damage. Surprisingly, our solar cell panels use those pieces of knowledge about light to do their job.

When UV light hits our skin, it makes electrons jump from one atom to another and causes chemical bonds to break, changing the chemistry of our skin. The energy of that UV light is so high that it is able to move most electron bonds pretty easily and so cause a lot of damage.

In a green leaf, the blue and red light photons have lower energy than UV photons, but they hit atoms in the very special 'chlorophyll' molecules which is sensitive to that lower energy, moving electrons from one atom to another, and those moved electrons then provide just enough energy to combine carbon dioxide from the air with water from the soil, making sugars that the plant can use.

Solar cells use a special type of material that is neither an insulator nor a conducting electric wire, but is rather what is called a 'semi-conductor'. 'Semi' means 'half', and so these only conduct electricity when they are treated just right. Some of these semiconductors are selenium, germanium, gallium arsenide, lead sulphide, copper oxide, and many other compounds. Even carbon is a semiconductor in its crystalline form of diamond, so is precious for more than one reason.

The most common semiconductor however is silicon, and you will likely have already heard about this famous material, since it is used in most of our electronics, like phones and computers and radios and TVs. Most solar cells use silicon, also.

We get silicon by removing oxygen from sand, which is fine grains of quartz. When you think of how much sand we have on beaches you can see that there is plenty of silicon available.

What makes semiconductors so special? Remember that UV can move electrons around in nearly all materials and that blue, and even red light, could move electrons in a very sensitive molecule in green leaves. So now I think you can guess the special thing about semiconductors; it's really easy to move electrons from their resting places in semiconductors. In silicon, even the sun's Infra-Red light can do the job.

And then, since semiconductors are not like a conducting wire, once we have moved the electrons, they can be held away from their original location for long enough that we can grab them with a wire connection and take them to where we want to use them.

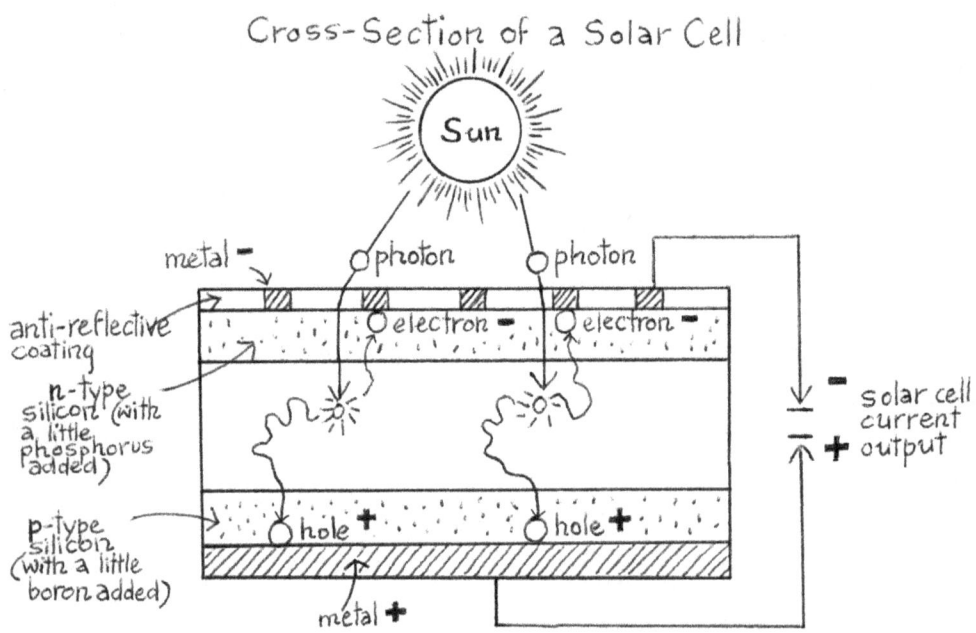

You will see in the picture one idea for how to make a solar cell. We have a photon coming in that hits an electron out of its resting place. This electron then bounces around rather randomly but will tend to move upwards, into a region of the silicon that has a little phosphorus added to it. This makes it attractive to electrons, so it becomes the negative terminal. The metal lines on the top of this terminal are narrow, to let the sunlight come in while taking the electrons out for us to use.

The other part of the silicon has a little boron added, to make it less favourable to electrons, and so electrons move from there to fill the "hole" left by the electron that just moved away. This leaves a hole at the bottom positive terminal, which causes the electric current to flow. That's how we can make a little battery that runs on sunlight.

HOW ELECTRICITY TRAVELS

After electricity has been made by the turning of the coil inside the magnet, or turning the magnet inside the coil, or by moving electrons in silicon with light, the next problem is to get it to where it is needed—to our homes and businesses and factories. Countless millions of electrons cannot find their own way to the right places. They must have some kind of path to follow—and the paths provided for them are those wires that you see, suspended between telegraph poles, throughout the length and breadth of the Earth's countries.

There are certain things—like glass, rubber or plastic—through which the electrons will not travel. These are called insulators. But anything through which they travel easily—like certain metals—are called conductors. The wires between telegraph poles are excellent conductors—usually made of aluminium or copper.

Electricity is sent through these wires with tremendous pressure at first. This pressure, in electricity, is called voltage. It enables the countless millions of electrons to travel through the wires with little waste.

Some very early power stations used less pressure, at only 100 volts or so. While folks near to the power station had very bright light bulbs, those bulbs burnt out very quickly. The people a few blocks from the power station only had a very dim light from the same bulb types, and although they never burnt out, the light was not enough to be very useful.

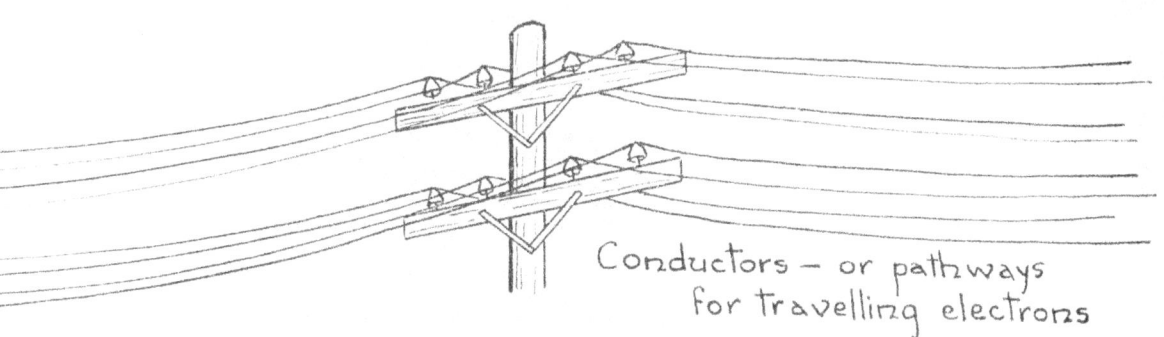
Conductors – or pathways for travelling electrons

The reason for this problem is that as the electrons tried to travel along the wires to those more distant houses, they would dawdle, held up everywhere by the electrons and atoms and metal grains of the wire itself. This resistance to the flow of electrons is, naturally enough, called 'resistance', and the only way to reduce the effects of this resistance would be to make the wires strung up on the telephone poles enormously thick, or to have power stations every couple of blocks. Neither of these ideas was very practical, as you can imagine.

The trick we use today is rather amazing, and it allows long, thin wires to carry the power for entire cities. If you imagine a turbine being powered by a jet of water from a hose, you could either have a very wide stream of water at low pressure gushing onto the turbine blades, or a narrow stream of water jetting out from a very high-pressure hose. Either method would yield enough power to move those turbine blades; low pressure but lots of water flow, or high pressure with only a little water flow.

It's the same with electricity; if we have high pressure, we don't need a lot of electron flow. We can have the same power going through those small wires at high voltage, but the wire's resistance is not so much of a problem since the electron flow is so small. When a power station generates electric power, it sends it out at high voltage, and the higher the voltage the further the electricity can be sent, even across half of a continent like Australia.

I think you can see a problem here, if you have been travelling and noticed those wires looping across the countryside from power stations to cities. With that big voltage, you have big insulators, as long as your arm, to hold those wires. And if you go close to them, you can often hear a crackling noise in your radio or even in your ears.

I wonder if you're thinking this all seems really risky, and not the sort of voltage you would like in your own home. Your feeling would be correct; those high voltages are very hard to control and are extremely dangerous.

So how can we make this electricity useful in our own homes? A method of reducing the voltage is needed, and again Michael Faraday's discoveries lead the way. He invented the very first 'transformer', and it can fairly be said that it transformed the world of electricity.

A transformer can be very tiny, or as big as a house, and it can be made to work in two ways—either increasing or decreasing the electricity's voltage pressure. The huge transformers at power stations

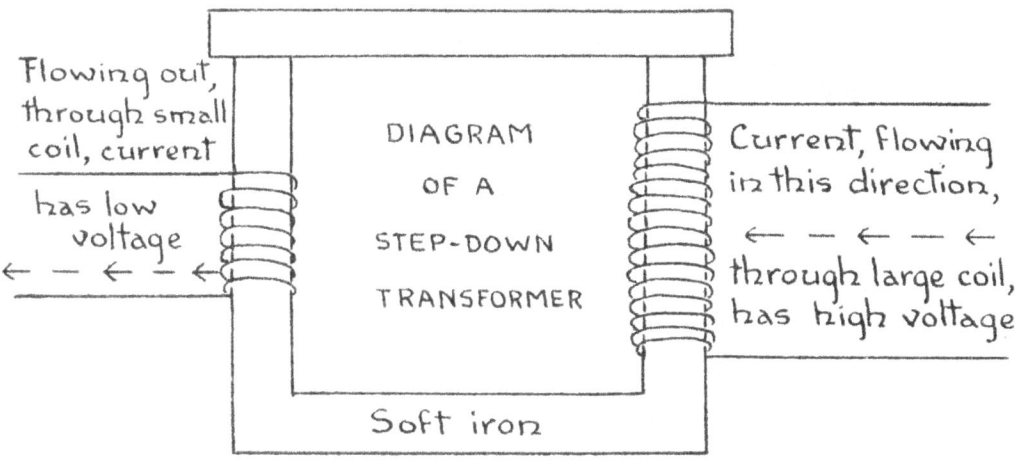

increase voltages for electricity's journey through the wires. We call them step-up transformers, and they step-up the pressure to more than 200,000 volts. Then, when the electric current has come near the end of its journey, it passes through another kind of transformer—a step-down one, which reduces the voltage to an amount which will serve us rather than overpowering us.

Important things don't have to be complicated. In fact they are often very simple—and a transformer is one of these. What makes it a transformer is simply two coils of wire around a piece of soft iron, one coil with a lot more turns in it than the other. The reason why this works is that—as we have found out—electricity can create magnetism, and vibrating magnetism can create electricity.

A coil with many turns in it will handle a much greater voltage than one with only a few turns. So, in a step-up transformer, a vibrating electric current flows in through the smaller coil. Immediately, the iron becomes a vibrating electromagnet, with vibrating lines of force. These magnetic vibrations in turn work together with the second coil of wire to produce another vibrating electric current. But as this second coil is larger than the first one, the current flowing out of it has a much greater pressure (or voltage) than that which flowed into the first coil.

Then, of course, a step-down transformer is arranged in the opposite way. A small amount of vibrating electric current comes into it through the large coil, with a high voltage—but the large current which comes out through the smaller coil has a lower voltage, and is suitable for us to use.

You may already know what we call this special type of vibrating electricity. It goes from positive to negative, then back to positive again, many times every second; 'AC' or 'Alternating Current'. This makes it clearly distinct from the non-vibrating type of electricity we get from batteries and the like, which is 'DC' or 'Direct Current'.

BATTERIES

Electric power stations are not always a long way from home. We can carry little ones around with us—inside portable radios and torches, for instance. And there is a very important one in every car. These power stations are called batteries, and they produce electricity in a different way from the turbine-and-dynamo ones. Batteries make electricity with chemicals.

They have two opposite poles, the way magnets have, but in batteries they are called plus and minus terminals. One type of battery is shown here. It's called a Leclanché cell, after its inventor in France, dating from way back in 1866. It's still in use today but other types

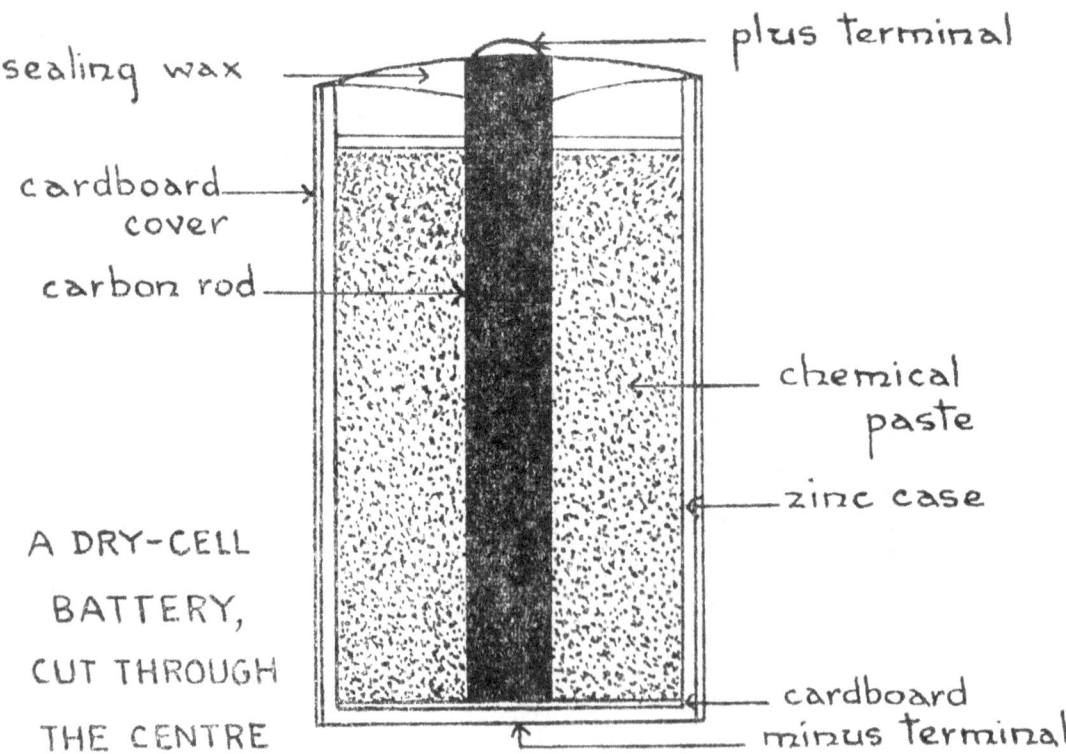

A DRY-CELL BATTERY, CUT THROUGH THE CENTRE

like Alkaline and Lithium cells are starting to take its place. Its plus or positive terminal is a plain rod of carbon down the centre, and the minus or negative terminal is the zinc can around it all. As the battery is used, the chemicals inside react with the zinc case, and use it up to form your electrons.

The batteries in cars are different. Instead of a chemical paste, they have distilled water, a liquid acid and small plates of lead and lead sulphate and lead oxide inside them. The acid is very dangerous, so you want to keep well away from it—but it works together with the lead to produce electricity—and without this, our cars wouldn't start. After the car starts however, a generator driven by the car engine provides electricity to recharge the battery and provide electric power for the car's accessories, so the battery does not have to deliver power while the engine is running.

These days there are all-electric cars that only have a big battery, and no fuel engine. Their battery must be recharged by plugging the car into a power point when it is parked. Other 'hybrid' cars have an intermediate-sized battery, and a small fuel engine. This type of car uses its battery to speed up its car wheels, or uses its wheels to recharge the battery if it needs to slow down. The hybrid car's fuel engine is used for steady running and slowly recharging the battery, which involve much less power than when speeding up or slowing down.

A FEW SAFETY RULES

Chris has loved everything to do with electricity from the time he was quite little. He has explored it, and experimented with it, and made all kinds of interesting things with it. But—most important of all—he has learnt to be very, very careful with it.

For years he used only batteries, which are quite safe—and he quickly learnt all the things that one shouldn't do with light or power. He enjoys telling Tess about these, in a protective big-brother way—and now he has handed me a list of them to tell you, in case I should forget. Here is his list:

DON'T touch any electrical switch with wet hands. (As water is a conductor of electricity, you might get a nasty shock.)

DON'T put anything but a proper plug into a power socket.

DON'T fiddle with frayed electric cords.

DON'T go anywhere near an electric wire if it has come down in a storm or accident.

DON'T stand under a tree during a thunder-and-lightning storm. (The tree might be struck with lightning.)

NEVER do the simplest thing with electricity—like changing a light bulb or pulling a plug out of a socket—without first turning off the light or power.

DO all your experiments with dry-cell batteries, because like that you can learn a great deal about electricity and have lots of fun, without danger. But never place a piece of metal across the battery's two terminals, as in this way you will wear its power out very quickly.

As with so many other things in this world, electricity is a most wonderful friend. But use it carelessly or thoughtlessly, and it becomes a terrible enemy—a real killer. So whatever you do, be very, very careful!

Air and Weather

IF you think back for a moment of all the things that we depend on for our life on this Earth, you will marvel at the fact that we are here at all. We couldn't be here without green plants—and green plants couldn't be here without light. And there couldn't be any of our forms of life without water—and we certainly couldn't be here without air.

We seldom think about air very much. It's another of the many important things that we just take for granted. We know that we breathe it, and that's just about all. Yet if it were not for the thick coating of air around the Earth, we would frizzle to death in the day, and freeze to death at night.

This is because the air—or atmosphere, as it is called—absorbs the fiercest of the sun's rays before they can reach us, during the day. And then at night, it holds down much of the day's warmth, which would otherwise drift off into space, leaving the Earth completely frozen.

Now, what is it made of—this all-important air that does so much for us? It is made up of gases—more than three-quarters nitrogen and about one-fifth oxygen. And although we cannot see it, it presses down on us and on everything else with a great deal of weight. Fortunately our bodies also press outward, against it, since we have the same pressure inside our bodies. If we didn't, we would probably be crushed out of existence by the weight of air.

Just imagine taking a 1kg weight used by for training arm muscles,

Air particles become fewer and farther apart in the higher reaches of our atmosphere — until there are scarcely any of them at all

IONOSPHERE

STRATOSPHERE

TROPOSPHERE

EARTH

and placing that weight onto your skin over a square area only 10mm on a side; you could do it by balancing the weight onto the end of a small stick that rests on your skin. Although I am describing this so that you could do the experiment, I really don't want you to do this. You may take it from me, this would hurt! And yet this is the same pressure that is bearing onto all of our skin surface, day and night, from the weight of the air above us.

Down here on the surface of the Earth, air particles are very plentiful and close together, but up higher they gradually thin out, giving less and less protection against harmful sun-rays and other dangers of outer space. Up there, without any atmosphere, we wouldn't survive for even one minute. But as we will see when we talk about colours that we cannot see, we also would not survive for very long on the surface of the Earth, if we did not have that very thin atmosphere up so high above us.

THE SKY'S COLOURS – THE ONES THAT WE CAN SEE

On a fine summer day, the blue of the sky is one of the purest of all colours. At sunrise and sunset, its glowing reds and yellows are often unbelievably beautiful. And now that you know something about light, you will probably be able to think of some ways that all of this comes about.

You will remember how light travels in a perfectly straight line until it comes to something that it has to pass through—like glass or water. Then it "bends", and sometimes its colours show out separately.

When sunlight strikes against our atmosphere, after its journey through space, we would naturally expect something to happen to it—and it does. Its waves become scattered by the gases that make up the air, and by dust particles. For the most part of the day, the sky looks blue, because blue light waves scatter more easily than red ones.

In the mornings and evenings, though, the sky glows with pink, red and orange colours. This is because the sunlight now comes to us more indirectly—at a greater slant. It has to pass through much more of the atmosphere to reach us, and as it does so, its long red waves are the ones that "survive", whilst its shorter blue waves are scattered

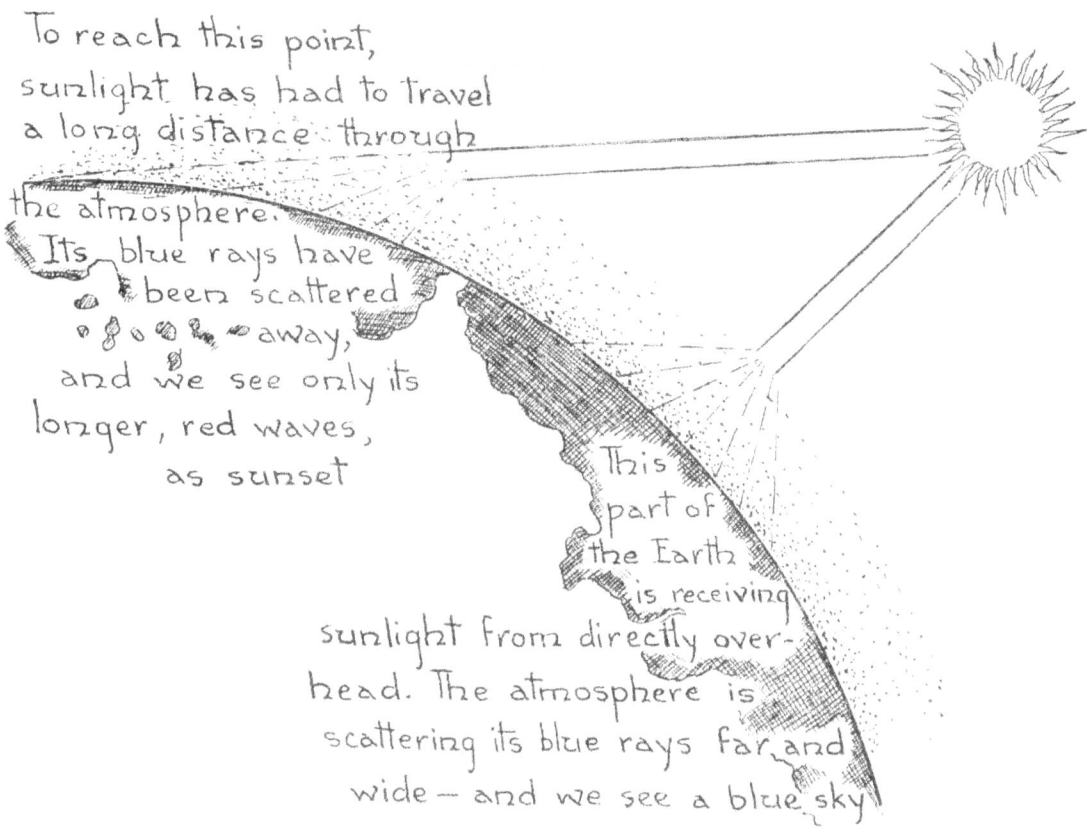

away out of sight. Then, if the sky is filled with clouds so that there is plenty to catch and reflect the red rays, we get a particularly wonderful sunrise or sunset.

The first person to realise why we get a blue noonday sky worked it all out in 1905, more than 100 years ago. You may have heard of him, because he is one of the most amazing and famous scientists; Albert Einstein. And since I am introducing him to you here, I must mention another thing he discovered at the same time; that light can make electrons jump out of atoms and do all of the amazing chemical and electrical things that UV light, chlorophyll in plants, and solar cells can do. Before he told us all about these things, they were a great mystery.

But we must remember that even at midday, our sky isn't blue all the way up. As it grows thinner, higher up, it looks violet—and at 20km height it goes black, since there aren't enough air particles to reflect the sun's light as it travels towards us. Doesn't it seem strange that, with all the light of the sun streaming through outer space, it remains invisible—and space itself black—dark—until something comes along that it can strike against? The Earth, for instance.

Pretty as the sky is when it is blue, we always think it is even prettier when it has clouds in it, because then it seems to be full of stories and pictures.

There are, of course, many different kinds of clouds, but they are all made of the same thing—water droplets. When the sun comes out after a shower of rain, you know how quickly it dries the wet ground. But the wetness on the ground hasn't been destroyed—it has only been changed. Instead of water, it has become water vapour—and when this happens, we say that the water has evaporated.

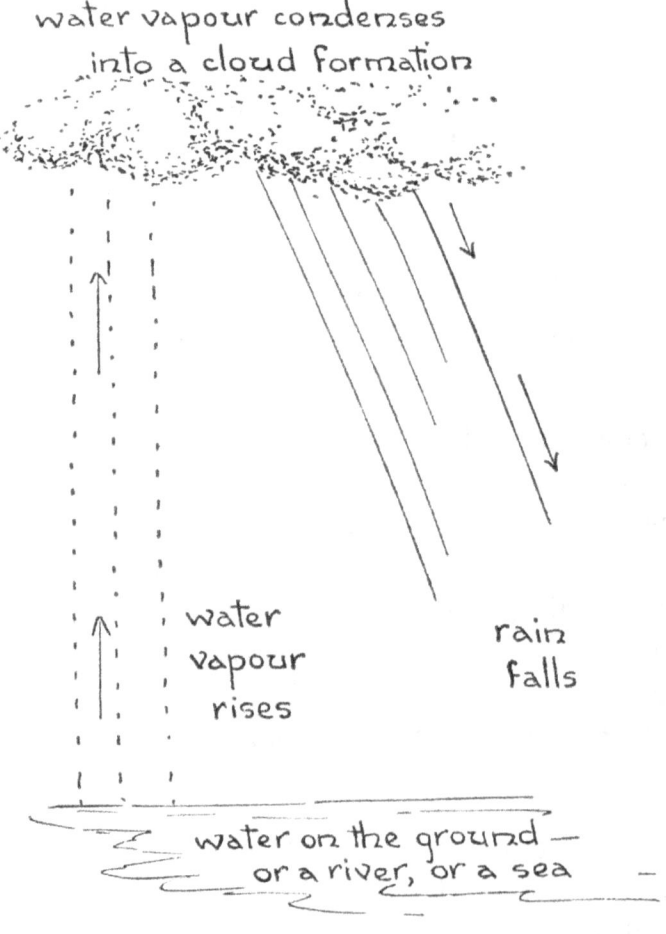

The Comings and Goings of Water

The vapour is very light and warm. It rises higher and higher through the air, and nobody sees it. But then at last, it comes to where the air around it is colder. This cold air changes it back again into water droplets—countless millions of them—and, looking up, we see clouds in the sky. The changing of water vapour into water in this way is what we call condensation. You see the same sort of thing when you pour an icy-cold drink into a glass. Water droplets appear all over the outside of the glass.

Well, after a while those high-riding clouds will probably come down to earth again, in one form or another according to the temperature—perhaps only as dew or rain, but at other times as frost, hail, sleet, or snow.

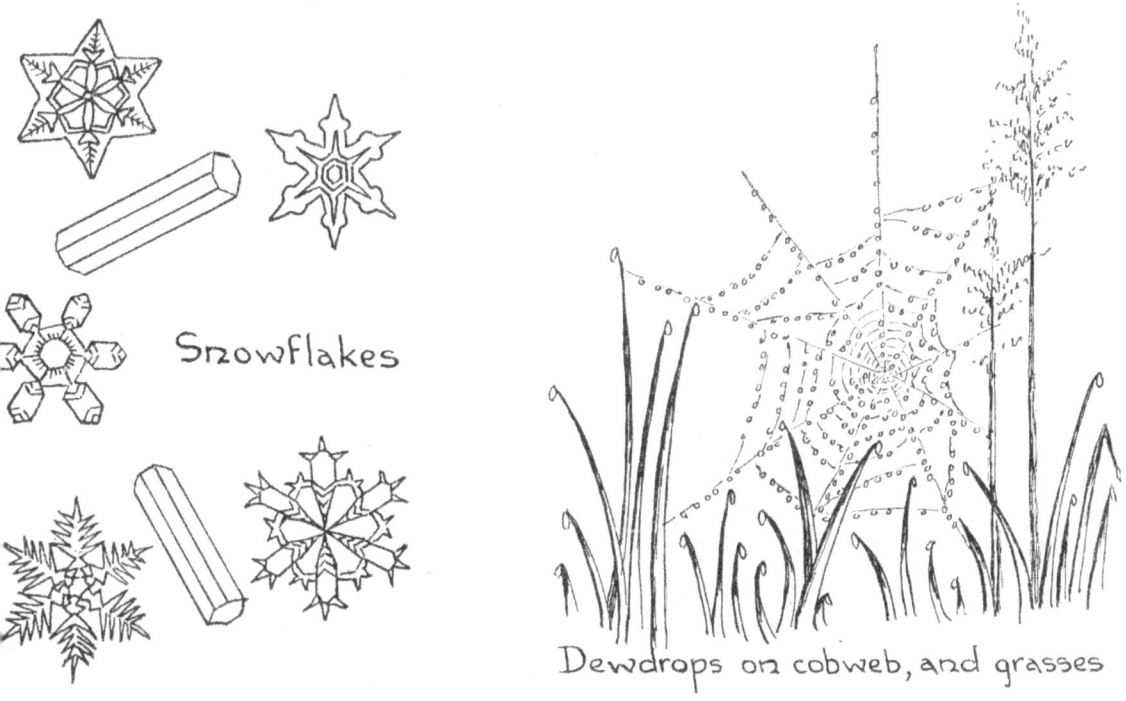

Snowflakes

Dewdrops on cobweb, and grasses

All of this is different from fogs and mists, which are water-vapour "clouds" that form near the ground.

Now, as you know, clouds do not always look the same. This is what makes them so interesting. There are several different kinds, with their own special names. You can have a lot of fun learning about them—then, every time you see a cloud, calling it its right name.

First, there are those big puffy ones, like mounds of white cream. Their name is cumulus. Others form into long, flattish layers, and are called stratus. Those that look like flying strands of hair are cirrus. Piled-up masses of dark thunder clouds are cumulo-nimbus. And the dark, rather ungainly-looking clouds that bring heavy rainfalls are nimbo-stratus.

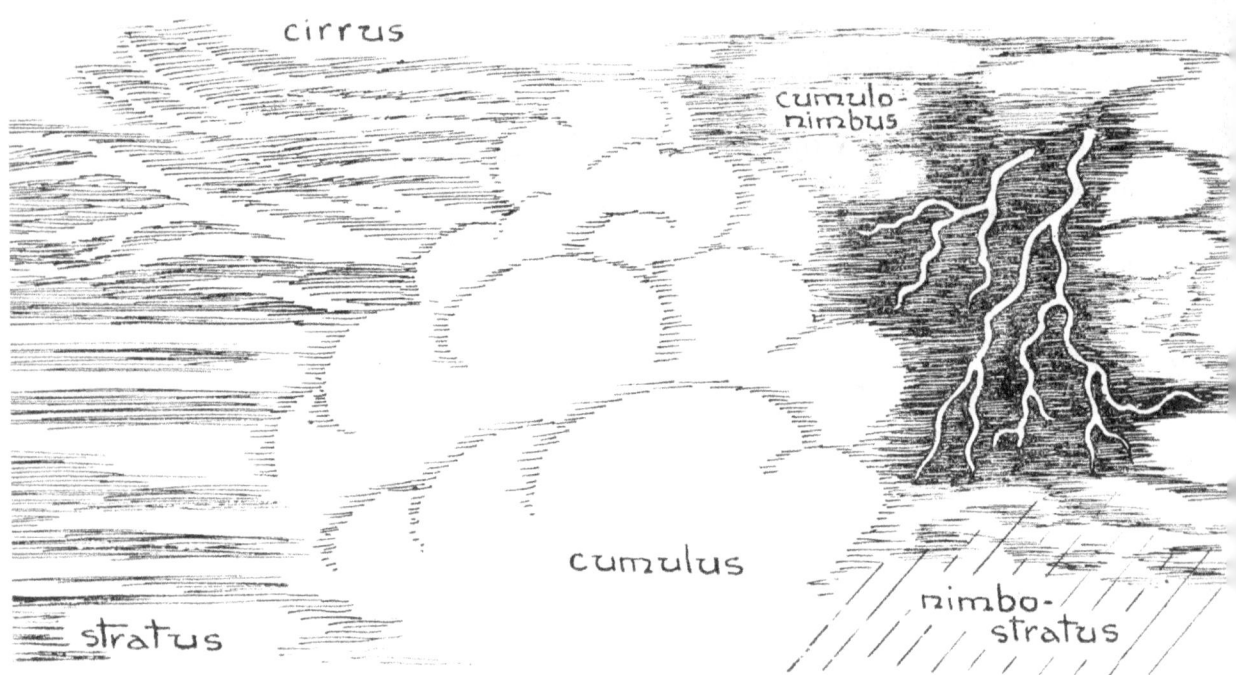

THE ULTRA-VIOLET LIGHT IN THE SKY

By now you know a lot about Ultra-Violet and Infra-Red light, and so you can expect that there is more going on in our atmosphere than just its pretty colours. And the place to start is way up high, where the air is very thin and looks black, 20-40km up. Sunlight is starting to hit our air molecules, after its long trip through outer space. And as you now know, the IR light from the sun, with its low-energy light photons, will not make any chemical changes to the air.

But the UV light, with its higher energy, will certainly try to change the molecules of our air. The oxygen molecules that are normally bound together as two oxygen atoms (O_2) are changed firstly by high-energy UV photons into free and very energetic 'excited' oxygen atoms called oxygen radicals (O^*). These O^* atoms then join up with the regular oxygen O_2 molecules to make a triple-oxygen molecule called ozone (O_3). Of course, once that is done the high-energy UV light photon is all used up.

In the dense atmosphere we live in on Earth's surface, this ozone would quickly decompose, but high up close to outer space, the ozone lives a long time, and has a good chance of being broken if it's hit with another, lower-energy UV photon, so we get the O_2 molecules back again, all ready for more UV light photons to come along and do the same thing all over again.

In this way, our ozone layer, so high up in the sky, stops a range of damaging UV photon energies from ever getting to earth's surface. If we did not have that ozone layer, we would all immediately get sunburnt as soon as we spent even half an hour outside, and our eyes would be all clouded over soon after and we would not be able to see anything. Life on earth would be very different, and—most likely—animals and plants would never have been able to come out of the sea, onto land.

If you have heard about the 'ozone hole', then you already have some knowledge of these matters. We were all very worried about the ozone disappearing from over Antarctica, and the lack of ozone was spreading towards Australia which made everyone get big hats and wear sunglasses at all times outside.

Then in 1985 it was discovered that the 'Freon' chemicals used in refrigerators and air conditioners were causing this ozone hole. These are very stable molecules that are not normally able to be broken down by anything on the Earth's surface, being not from nature, but being entirely one of Man's inventions. However up high in the atmosphere, the sun's UV rays of course are able to break up any chemical, and it happens that these Freon chemicals eat up ozone when they are broken. So all of the world's 197 countries have now agreed to stop making and using these dangerous chemicals, and the ozone hole is slowly getting smaller again.

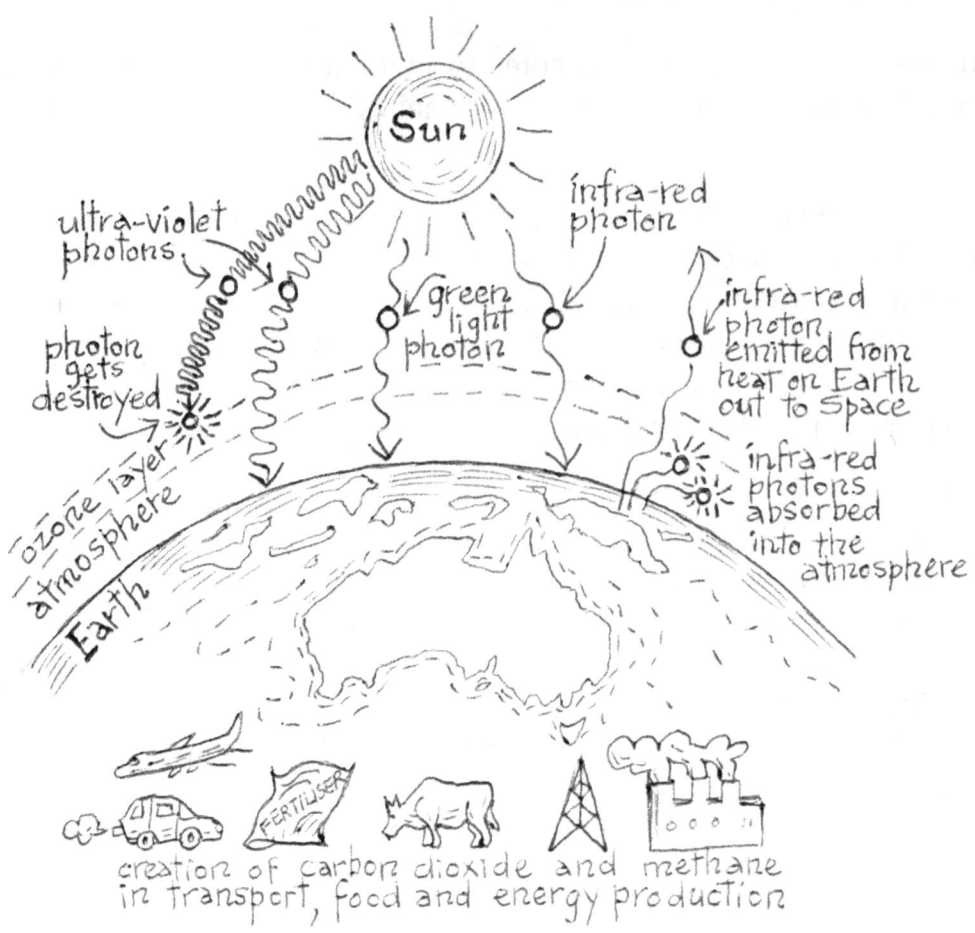

INFRA-RED IN THE SKY – AND THE 'GREENHOUSE EFFECT'

Earth's planet formed 4.5 billion years ago, and over that long period of time there have been many drastic changes in climate, caused by changes in the sizes and shapes of continents and oceans, changes in the intensity of the Sun, variations in Earth's orbit, volcanic eruptions and meteorite impacts.

During the last 8,000 years, which includes most recorded human history, the climate has been fairly stable, enabling people to flourish and build permanent settlements. This has changed since the growth of industry in the 19th century, with our climate growing increasingly warm and scientists finding that glaciers are shrinking, ice sheets are melting, ocean currents are changing due to shifts in ocean temperature, sea levels are rising and dramatic weather events such as cyclones and droughts are increasing.

Let's look at what is happening here with Infra-Red light and the warming of our atmosphere. It's important to know that certain gases, like carbon dioxide and methane, absorb IR radiation and stay up in the air for very many years.

When we breathe in oxygen, we breathe out carbon dioxide. However plants do the reverse; they use carbon dioxide to make sugars and photosynthesise, producing oxygen for us. That is very neat, isn't it, and we call this the 'Carbon Cycle'. This balance has been upset by the burning of oil and gas fuels, and coal in human industry. These substances all emit carbon dioxide when they are burned. This carbon dioxide, sent into the atmosphere, destroys the careful balance of Nature. Another IR-absorbing molecule is methane, which is a compound of carbon and hydrogen. Methane is used as 'natural gas' fuel in cooking stoves. It can leak from wells in the ground that pipe up oil, or from coal mines, from decomposing compost, and is also is a gas that animals give off when they digest their food.

You may have noticed that cloudy nights stay warmer than nights with clear skies. Methane and carbon dioxide act like clouds in our atmosphere, creating a cover over the Earth like a glass greenhouse. These gases in our atmosphere catch the IR photons and get warm, rather than letting the IR go out into space. The amount of these gases has almost doubled today, which is like having more clouds in the sky, every day of the week, trapping the Earth's IR radiation. Our Earth is getting warmer and warmer, every year, creating massive changes in our Earth's environment.

The carbon dioxide is not only building up in our air but also in the oceans and this has a large effect on the sea creatures. Just as the carbon dioxide which makes our drinks fizzy can taste a little bitter, carbon dioxide in the ocean also tastes more bitter to the fish and corals, which then die since they don't like that acidic bitter taste.

The best thing for our planet right now would be to use less energy, to use electric cars and walk more, and to use wind power and solar cells wherever we can.

So think of one of those little steps we can all take. Are all of the light bulbs in your house the new LED types that use tiny amounts of energy, or are they the older incandescent or fluorescent types that often give out more IR than visible light? You may be able to help one of those poor little IR photons get out to run free in outer space, instead of being gobbled up by a carbon dioxide molecule in our atmosphere.

WIND

Sometimes, when you look up at the sky, you may see the clouds in it racing along, blown by strong winds. The winds come down to earth, too, and blow everything about—sometimes gently, other times roughly, and other times again they are raging destroyers called hurricanes. You may ask yourself—as Chris and Tess did when they were littler—"What is wind? Where does it come from? What makes it?"

Air is all the time moving around in one way or another. Warm air, being light and "balloony", tends to rise. Near the coast, when the warm air rises from the land, the cooler air from the sea races in to take its place—and we get a refreshing sea-breeze. At night, the sea keeps its warmth longer than the land does, so the air movement goes the other way.

But as well as calm breezes, there are also great winds which follow a fairly regular pattern. These are caused by the Earth's spinning on its axis, together with the sun's tremendous heat. When air heated by the sun moves upward, and cooler air moves in to take its place, the spinning of the Earth drives it sideways or round in vortex spirals, and a wind is born. In some very hot parts of the world, where huge quantities of air replace each other, this whirling around may go on for days at a great rate, and we get cyclones, hurricanes and tornadoes. Meanwhile the rising warm air, having condensed into water droplets, comes down again as rain—and the wind and rain together make very wild, dangerous weather indeed.

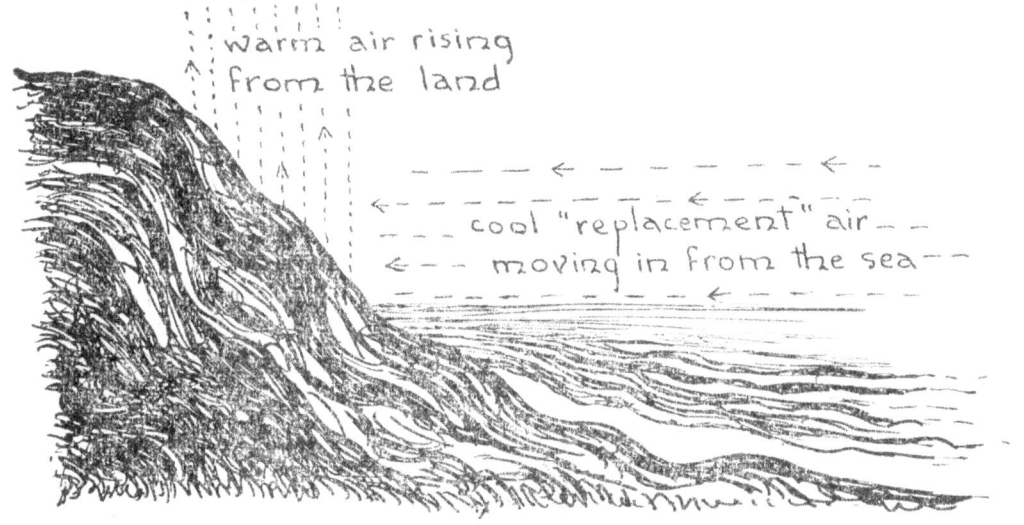

LIGHTNING AND THUNDER

Sometimes, an uprush of wind is so strong that it shatters into tiny fragments the millions of water droplets that are resting high up in the air. This charges both the air and the droplets with electricity—the water with positive electricity, and the air particles with negative electricity. At last these two opposite kinds of electricity rush towards each other with tremendous force and a huge spark flashes across the sky, making a noise like an explosion. The spark is lightning, and the noise is thunder.

WEATHER

All sorts of things are constantly going on in the Earth's atmosphere. Often these activities are so high up that we, down here, are not aware of them. Yet they bring about many changes in our weather—and we are very much aware of *those*. It is by studying conditions in the upper

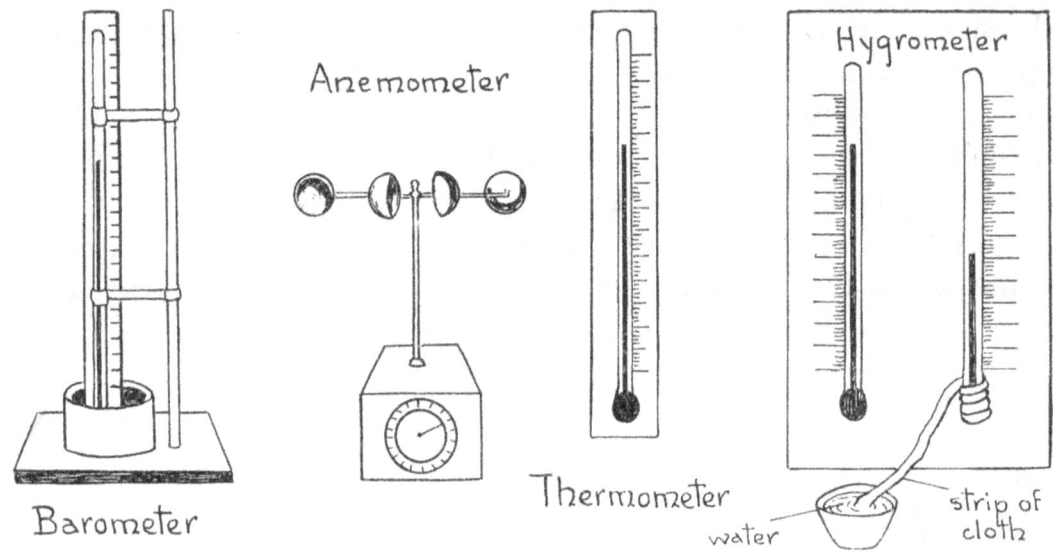

atmosphere, with special instruments, that weather scientists are able to tell us ahead of time, what sort of a day it will be tomorrow, or the next day, or perhaps a much longer way ahead.

Just as there are mountains and valleys on earth, so also there are mountains and valleys in the air. When a mountain of air piles up to form a region of high pressure, it is called a "high". Winds tend to blow out from a high, into parts where the air is less dense. Then, from higher up, more air comes settling in to replace the outgoing air. If you have ever pumped up a bicycle tyre and felt the barrel of the pump get hot, you will know that as you compress air, it gets hotter. The same thing happens when air from high in our atmosphere decides to fall down lower, compressing the air underneath it to make our high pressure region. With that extra warmth in the air, the air molecules move about faster and can hold more water aloft with their constant bouncing around. So clouds do not form—since clouds come from water in the air condensing out as the air chills—and we get fine, warm weather.

But a valley in the air, with low pressure, is called a "low". Winds blow high in the atmosphere, and when two wind currents angle into each other, changing each others' directions, a suction is formed at their impact region, drawing more air into it and causing a real flurry. The air sucked up into that wind vortex rises into colder regions, where its watery humidity condenses into a mistiness, or rain—and we get cold, showery weather.

Weather experts measure air pressure with a barometer and use it to help predict the weather. There are several different kinds of barometers, but a simple one is a thin glass tube with mercury in it, placed upside-down in a dish which also has mercury in it. When the air is heavy it presses on to the surface of the dish mercury, forcing that in the glass tube to rise. This means high pressure and fine weather. But when the air is lighter, the opposite happens, meaning low pressure and unsettled weather.

Another instrument very important to weather scientists is the anemometer. This is to record the speed of winds. It has a series of little cups that spin freely around a central rod. They look rather like soup-ladles, but they are for winds instead of soup. When a wind blows into them, it sends them spinning—and a little gauge attached to them tells how fast the wind is travelling.

A doctor uses a thermometer to take your temperature—and we can also use a thermometer to take the weather's temperature. This is merely a tiny bowl or bulb with liquid mercury or coloured alcohol in it, leading up into a very fine glass tube. Hot weather makes the liquid expand, so that it rises in the tube. Cold weather makes it contract, so that it sinks—and numbers up the side tell us just how hot or cold the temperature is.

Then, the hygrometer measures the amount of moisture in the air, or the humidity. This instrument has two ordinary thermometers, but the bulb of one of them is always kept wet. As this wetness evaporates, we can make a note of the temperature on both thermometers, and the rate of evaporation, and this can then tell us the humidity level.

If it's too hot, we can often do well since our skin sweats, and then the water in sweat evaporates from our skin into the air, cooling us down. The water molecules that have enough energy to escape from our skin take that energy with them, leaving the other cooler molecules on our skin. But if the 'wet bulb temperature' is also high, it means that the air is also humid, so our sweat can't escape as easily into the air, and then we get really hot, with no relief. That's why people often say "it's not the heat, it's the humidity" when we have such weather.

People die if the wet bulb temperature is over 35 degrees C, even if they are right next to a fan. Their temperature keeps rising and they have no way to get rid of that heat. Right now the highest wet-bulb temperatures on Earth have been below 32 degrees in most cases, but this number has been rising lately. Let's hope the Earth does not get three degrees hotter!

Scientists are learning more and more about weather every day not only with these instruments, but also now with satellites which measure winds, rain, clouds, ocean height, mountain height, temperatures everywhere from the ground up through the entire atmosphere, how much green growth is present and what type of crop is growing, and many other things over the entire Earth. It's amazing that a satellite up more than 100km from us can measure the ocean height with an accuracy of better than 10mm, but it can do all of that and more. All of this information is put into some of the biggest computers on Earth to help us predict the weather, including where dangerous storms are likely to go, with better and better accuracy every year.

FIRE AND HEAT

As you know, water and fire do not agree. A fire will blaze away quite happily until water is poured over it. Then it goes out. And we have seen that there is plenty of water in the air, in one form or another, yet without air there could never be fire.

There couldn't be fire without air

You can put out the light of a candle by blowing on it hard, but also you can place a little metal cone over it—and in the "airlessness" of this tiny space, the flame immediately goes out. If we could find some way to cut off the air supply from an area blazing with bushfires, it wouldn't take many minutes to get the flames under control. This is because, for there to be a fire, the particles of the thing being burnt must be able to unite with the oxygen in the air, to form something different. For instance, when coal (or carbon) burns, its atoms unite with those of oxygen to form a gas—carbon dioxide.

Now, imagine a piece of wood that is smouldering. The atoms that make up the wood are coming together with the atoms of oxygen in the air, and as they do this, they move very quickly—ever so much quicker than they move in their ordinary state. This movement, of course, is energy—and energy creates heat. The more vigorously the atoms move, the greater the energy, and the greater the heat. At last, the energy becomes too great to be contained, and some of it explodes into visible light, or flame.

You yourself, on a cold day, will skip or run to get warm. In other words, you set energy to work, and that creates heat. When you rub your hands together you do the same thing, only in a different way—through friction. As they rub against one another, the atoms in your hands move faster and faster until they tingle your hands with warmth throughout.

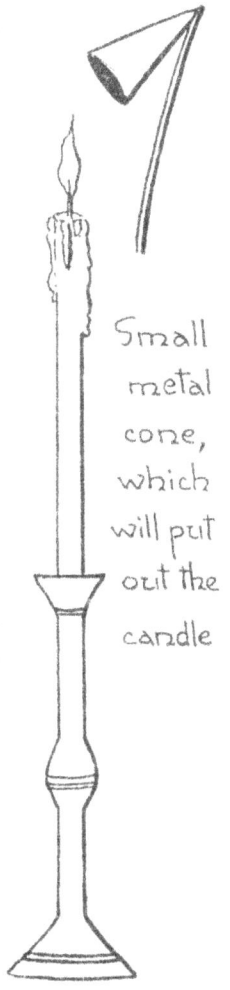

Small metal cone, which will put out the candle

When you strike a match against its box, the friction makes it burst into flame—and many thousands of years ago, people discovered that by striking pieces of flint, or rubbing bits of wood together, they could make fire. This method of starting a fire is still being used today by some primitive tribes—and bush campers are supposed to be able to do it, too, in case they ever get caught without matches.

Of course, one of our most usual ways of creating heat today is with electricity—and, as we have already learnt, electricity is the result of moving electrons. Their energy can be converted to heat. When electricity flows easily, as it does through long highly conducting wires with low resistance that lead from one place to another, it doesn't create much heat. But when it cannot flow easily—as through

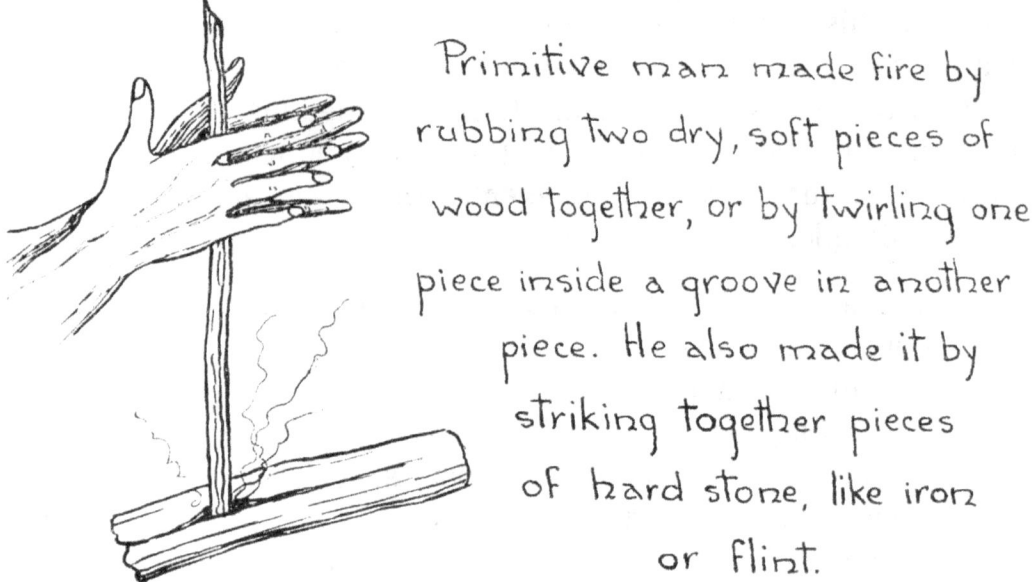

Primitive man made fire by rubbing two dry, soft pieces of wood together, or by twirling one piece inside a groove in another piece. He also made it by striking together pieces of hard stone, like iron or flint.

the specially made poorly-conducting wires in electric toasters, irons, radiators, and so on—the electrons exert a tremendous effort to get through, and naturally this makes a great deal of heat.

☆   ☆   ☆

You see, we started off talking about air—that invisible "nothingness" which people seldom bother to think about—and look at all that it has led to! Perhaps we won't take air quite so much for granted, ever again.

The Wonderful Story of Rocks

IT sometimes seems that Tess enjoys collecting stones and fossils almost more than anything else. Whenever we get out of the car in an interesting spot, the first thing she does is look around for odd shapes and pretty colours among the pebbles.

One day when she was doing this, Chris looked down and smiled at her in an important, older-brother way, and said, "That's all very well, Tess, but do you know what a mineral really *is*?"

"Why yes, it's a stone," she answered.

"Only sometimes, Tess. It isn't always a stone, is it, Mummie?"

"It's anything that isn't an animal or a vegetable," I told them.

But Chris wasn't satisfied with that. He wanted to show off his knowledge. He said, "A mineral has never been alive—so it's called inorganic, Tess. And of course it's made up of chemicals. And different chemicals combined together make different minerals. And different minerals together make rocks. And sometimes a rock can be soft, and sometimes it can even be liquid."

Tess was sure that he was making this up, about rocks sometimes being soft, or liquid, so I came to the rescue and assured her that they *could* be.

You see, to those who study these things, mud and sand are rocks—and they are certainly soft enough. And oil is a kind of rock, too, liquid though it is. As for water—you can see *its* "rockiness" quite clearly as soon as it turns to ice.

But the whole story of rocks and minerals is older than the Earth itself, and today, scientists think that it started something like this:

Countless ages ago, there was a huge body of gas whirling around in space. As you know, gravity is a force that attracts objects together, and over countless millions of years, gravity slowly brought parts of that body of gas together. As these parts became larger, they developed a stronger gravity pull, so the biggest parts became even bigger, faster and faster.

So now you can imagine what happened; the very biggest of these lumps of material became our sun, attracting more and more material. Its gravity was getting so strong, it was able to attract even the fastest atoms around, which smaller lumps could not. So very light atoms such as hydrogen and helium got snapped up by this biggest lump, with smaller amounts of these light atoms going to the smaller lumps. As more and more material fell inwards towards that growing sun, the energy from that falling was all deposited into the sun, making it hotter and hotter, and it began to glow. In its centre it got hot and dense enough to start making its atomic parts congeal into bigger and bigger pieces of atoms, giving out enormous amounts of additional heat.

This process is called 'atomic fusion', and people have tried to do this on Earth, but the heat and pressure inside a sun are really difficult to reproduce in our tiny laboratories. So we have been able to make fusion happen for short periods, but the sun remains supreme in its ability to generate heat in this way.

But what about the other parts, that did not fall into the growing sun? These continued to circle around, collecting more and more material, until they became the planets that we know of today as our 'solar system', and our Earth is of course one of those planets, circling constantly around our sun. Some parts never got to attract each other sufficiently to form planets, and these became moons around the planets, or became a part of the asteroid belt between Jupiter and Mars, or part of the much larger and heavier Kuiper Belt which is beyond Neptune, and includes Pluto. There are many other free-roaming asteroids, some of them circling the sun quite close to Earth. Our own moon shows signs of being hit by many of these asteroids, with its many craters.

The enormous force of gravity pulled our own planet Earth into a tight ball of "rock"—a job made easier by the fact of all of those pieces dumping all of their energy into the growing Earth, keeping it hot, even enough to keep the rocks molten, in a stiff kind of liquid.

Just as our sun is continuing to generate heat by fusing atoms together to make heavier atoms, our own Earth is continuing to generate heat in its very core by changing atoms to new ones. But our Earth uses a different method of keeping hot, deep inside. Since Earth ended up with less of the light atoms and more of the heavy ones than the sun, it got plenty of some of the heaviest atoms in nature. These heavy atoms are so big that they feel unstable, and want to reduce in weight. When another small atomic part called a 'neutron' happens along to tickle it and encourage it to lose weight, that big atom decides to split apart into smaller fragments, and gives out other neutrons that can do the same job for another overweight atom. This process is called 'atomic fission', and it really is the reverse of the fusion process in the sun; but both processes give out enormous heat.

The fission process has been called 'Radio-Activity', from more than 100 years ago, but it has nothing to do with radios. Both names come from the Latin 'radius', meaning a beam that comes from a central source; so if you have the radius of a circle, that is the distance from the centre to the circle's outside; and if you have a ray of radiation from an antenna, it is sending photons of radio waves out to your radio; and if you have some neutrons radiating out from a fissioning centre… you get the idea, I am sure.

Fission is easier than fusion for us to do on Earth for ourselves, and we use fission to make heat in atomic reactors for generating hot steam, and then we make electricity, using that steam. Fission – and for very short instants, fusion as well – are the basis of nastier things; the atomic bomb and the hydrogen bomb. The atomic bomb has been used to cause unimaginable amounts of damage at the end of World War II, in Japan.

Just to continue the historical story of how we came to understand how fusion and fission work; do you remember Albert Einstein, the scientist who showed why the sky is blue, and why photons do their jobs so well, way back in 1905, more than 100 years ago? He also showed how his idea of 'relativity' explained that light is the fastest thing in the universe, and how that made atomic fission and fusion give out masses of heat when they occur. Just how the speed of light explains the energy in atoms is something that you may want to understand yourself, one day. It's a fascinating adventure.

And what year did Einstein explain that to the world? In the very same year, 1905. That's why scientists call that year "annus mirabilis", which is Latin for 'miraculous year'. Other earlier years had been called that; for example when Isaac Newton explained how gravity explains the workings of the sun and planets, and many other things besides. But Einstein's 1905 is the very latest one. So many mysteries of nature got explained all at once, and we became able to adventure in entirely new areas of knowledge.

So it is radio-activity keeping the core of the Earth—which is almost as hot as the surface of the sun—partly liquid, even though the very centre of it is more solid.

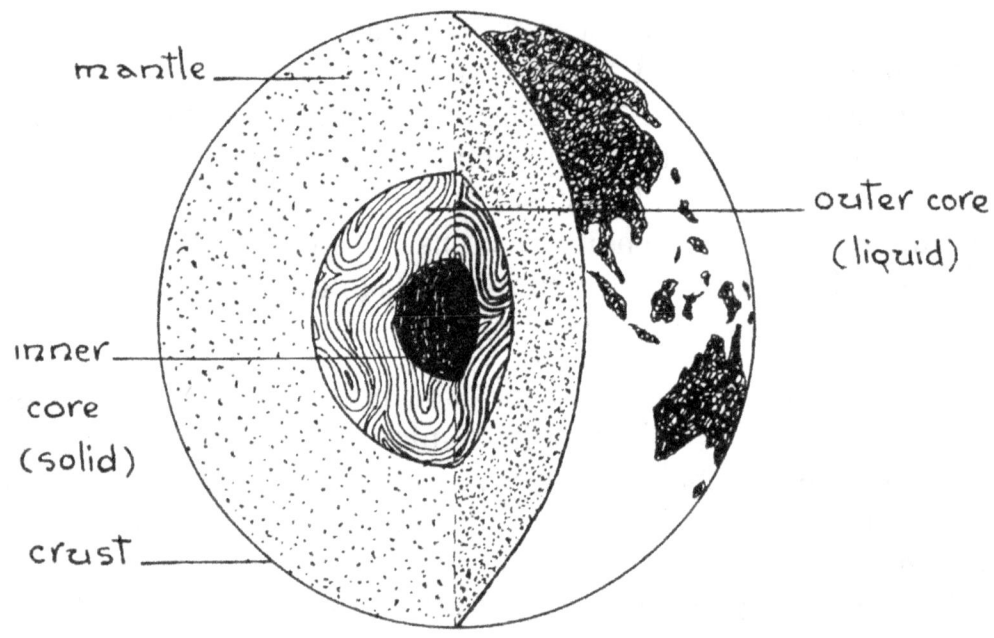

Our Earth is thus made up of a hot core with a central solid sphere 1200km thick, and an outer core of lower-density liquid rock about 2200km thick. Surrounding the core is a layer of rock about 2300-2600km thick, called the mantle, which is much less dense than the core. This mantle has a couple of regions; the outermost one is even less dense, and merges with the thin crust on top. Surrounding the mantle is the Earth's outermost layer, called the crust, only about 30km thick—and it is here on that rather cool crust that we all live.

Now, it seems as if things stay very much the same up here on the crust, year in and year out. The countries and oceans seem to stay in the same places, and so do the mountains and valleys. But that is just because none of us lives here long enough to observe the great changes that are forever taking place—slowly but surely. It is only when one of the changes happens suddenly—like an earthquake, or a landslide, or the action of a volcano—that we can actually see it in a lifetime.

Although that famous author Jules Verne wrote an exciting story about a 'Journey to the Centre of the Earth', nobody has ever made such a journey except in imagination, and even scientific instruments have not penetrated much deeper than 12km, whereas they would have to go down over 6000km to reach the centre. But even in a deep mine, you will find it much hotter than on the Earth's surface, showing that the deeper you go, the hotter it becomes.

Down in the mantle, it must be very hot indeed, and the rocks there, although solid enough, can melt into molten masses called magma. This may happen as a result of radio-activity, or great pressures.

Naturally, if there is any outlet at all for this molten rock, leading up toward the crust, these substances find their way into it. If they manage to burst right through to the surface, we have a volcano, pouring rocks and molten rock lava out over a helpless countryside. Then the lava, as it cools, solidifies into rock. It solidifies very quickly, and we get hard, smooth rocks like basalt and obsidian.

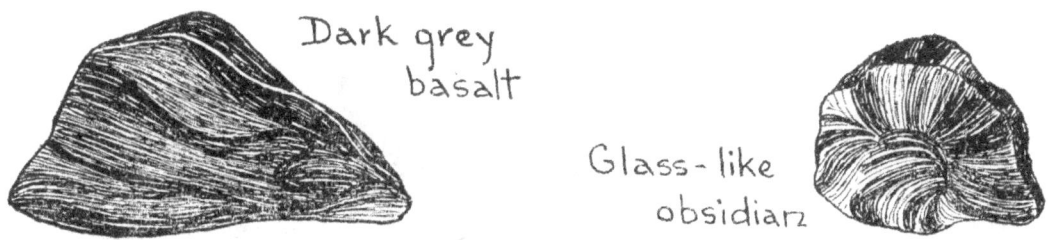

Basalt is that dark grey rock which you often see crushed up for use in road making. But if it is left to Nature, it breaks down gradually with the help of lichens and fungi into wonderful chocolate-coloured earth—that "volcanic soil" in which plants grow so well.

Obsidian is shiny and glass-like. Sometimes we have found pieces—black or dark smoky-grey-which looked so much like bits of broken jars that we could scarcely tell the difference. In fact, you can really think of obsidian as glass made by Nature instead of people.

Just as waves froth and foam as they come thundering up on to the beach or against rocks, so lava froths as it comes pouring out from the craters of volcanoes. As this froth cools and hardens, it also becomes rock—but a very strange kind of rock, filled with little holes, whitish in colour, and so light that it floats in water. This is pumice, often crushed down into grinding powders—and you'll often find a piece of it in people's bathrooms, too.

If the molten rock moves in very slow rivers from a volcano, it can develop a cooled hardened crust that forms a tube around further molten rock moving through it, and if it is tilted downhill then the molten river can drain out leaving an empty tunnel. We call these tunnels lava tubes, and sometimes they can be enormous, over 60kms long and up to 15m wide. They are often amazingly coloured, bright green or ochre, and very smooth inside.

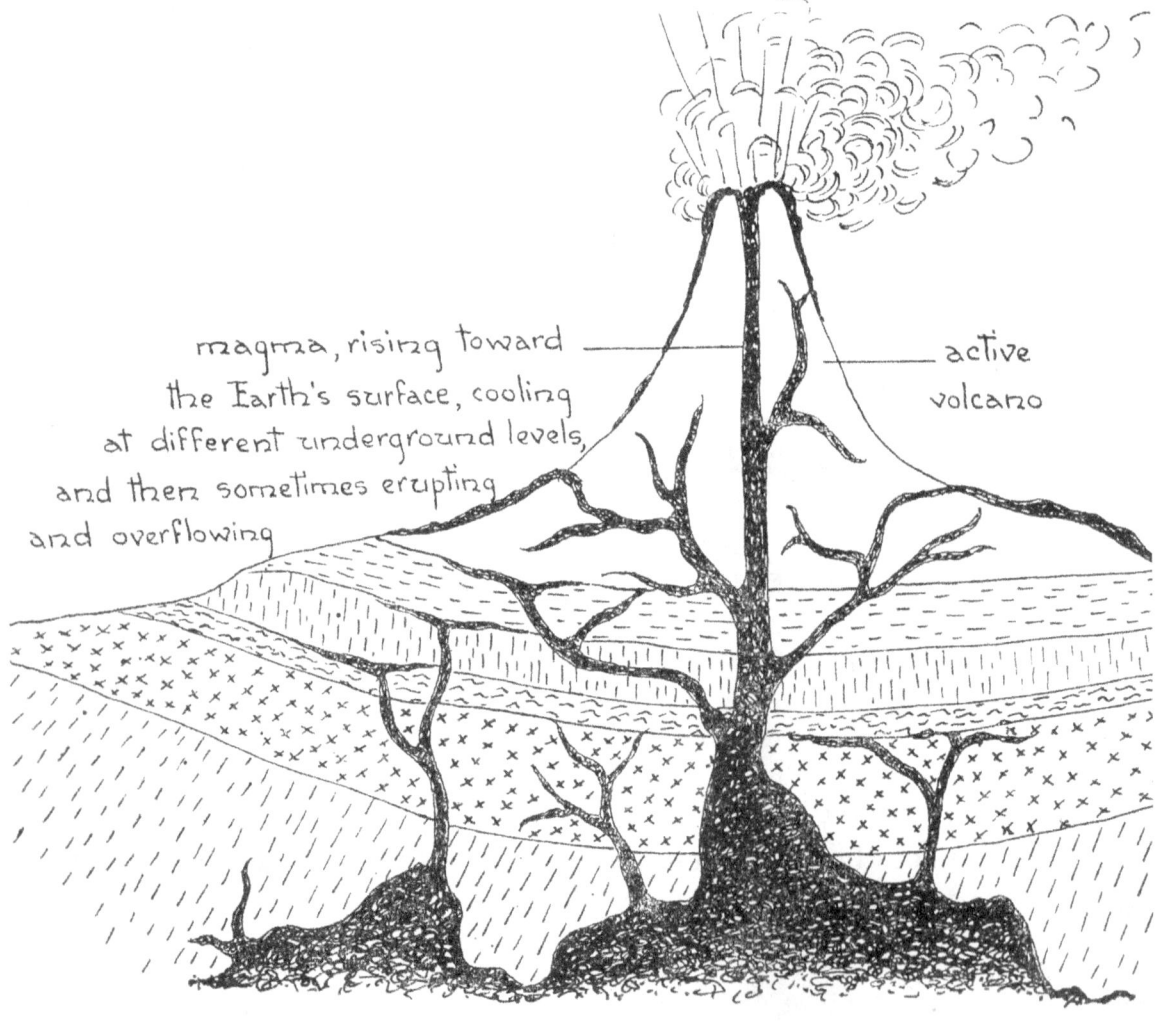

If the molten rock takes longer to cool than basalt or obsidian as it moves up through the Earth's mantle, it has a rougher look because, although the main part of it is smooth, there has been time for the crystals of minerals to form in it. Most of these crystals are small, but some of them grow large if they can cool slower. This kind of rock is called a porphyry—and the different-sized crystals embedded in it make it very pretty.

Then, there are other rocks which cool more slowly still, after they have pushed their way up into the crust of the Earth. These are the granites, and they never come up to the surface of their own accord—not until they are exposed by the wearing away of all the rocks above them. While they are forming, they stay well below the surface—deeper than the porphyrys and other such rocks. And, since they cool more slowly than the porphyrys, the mineral crystals in them are more even in size. So granite is not only a very hard rock, but also a very beautiful one, with a mottled look about it.

Granite is made up of three minerals—white or greyish quartz, black mica, and pink or white feldspar. (You should memorise the names of these three minerals, for you will come across them in ever so many rocks.)

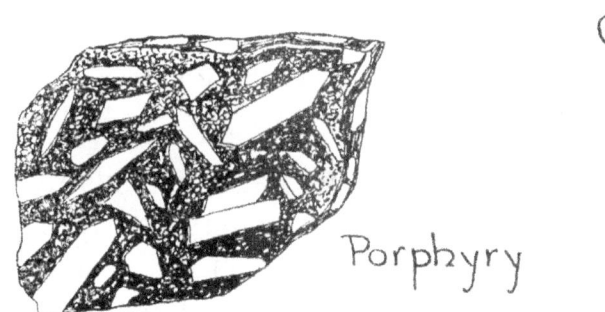
Porphyry

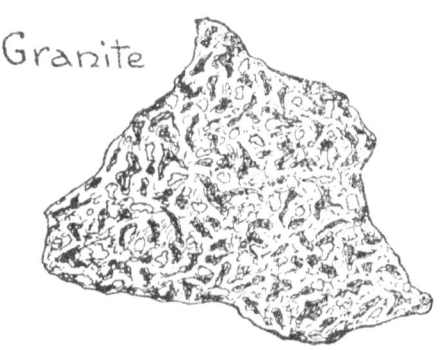
Granite

As we have learnt, quartz is silicon dioxide. This is the third-hardest natural material. Diamond, made of carbon, is the hardest. In between is aluminium oxide, which is known as alumina or ruby or sapphire, and is present in mica also. Feldspar has both of these silicon and aluminium hard oxides in it, as well as other glass-like minerals added.

So granite is a mix of some very hard materials, and only diamond—or our wonderful lichens—can make much of an impression on it.

Here's a little surprise that gives us some amazing kinds of rocks. Granite and quartz can be worn away not only with hard diamonds, or with the persistent pressure and acids of lichens, but with soft and gentle water, especially if the water has some alkaline mineral dissolved in it. It's a very slow process, but as we will see when we talk about fossils, it allows us to see things way back in time that otherwise would have been lost to us forever.

Next time you are near the Sydney Harbour Bridge, have a good look at its pylons, which are made of granite—and keep an eye out for the different coloured granites that you often find in buildings. It's such fun recognising these things, and knowing their names, instead of merely thinking of them as "stone".

We have been talking about three different kinds of rocks formed as a result of heat—those that cool very quickly up on the surface of the Earth, those that cool slower, below the surface, and those that cool slowest of all, still deeper below the surface. But all of them are grouped together under one important name—Igneous Rocks.

Rocks do not always form in this way, though, with heat. Even more of them build up gradually, with layer upon layer of earth or sand, or the remains of plants and animals, or chemicals, or worn-away pieces of other rocks. And these are all grouped together under the next very important name—Sedimentary Rocks.

As we said before, nothing on the face of this Earth remains the same, as the centuries go by. Everything is changing continuously, no matter how slowly. We all know how heavy rains wash soil away—how rivers flowing down mountain-sides and through valleys scoop out channels for themselves, and carry away—bit by bit—the very stuff that the mountains and valleys are made of. We know about dust storms, which happen when strong winds sweep dust or sand up into the air and carry it far away from where they found it. The sand in dust is quartz, and its hardness allows the blowing sand to etch and break down other rocks really quickly. And we know about landslides, which sometimes bring many tonnes of rocks and earth hurtling down a hillside into the valley below.

All of this shifting away of things is known as erosion, and it leads to a wearing down in some parts and a building up in others.

Rivers often carry stones and sand and earth right down into the sea—and if these kept floating around in the water, all of the oceans in the world would look muddy. But of course they don't, because the stones and sand and earth sink to the bottom, and are called sediment—just as coffee-grounds sink to the bottom of a coffee-pot.

After a while, the weight of all this sediment is very great indeed—and the weight of the ocean's water above it is also very great. With so much weight pressing on to it, the sediment's lower layers gradually pack down into a solid mass. Layer after layer packs down on top of these first ones, until a great depth of rock has been formed. Sometimes, after millions of years, it even rises in an earthquake, or slow pushing of rock plates, above the surface of the ocean to become a new land surface—but the whole thing is, of course, sediment, with sedimentary rock underneath it. And as there tends to be more sand than anything else in this rock, it is called sandstone.

Look around you in the country or at the seashore, and you will be surprised at the huge quantities of sandstone everywhere. Sometimes the different layers show out clearly, with beautiful varieties of colour—white, yellow, red, brown. There's a lot of quartz in sand, and this is white, but when iron comes along dissolved in water, it stains the sand with all those other colours which make its different layers look so pretty.

Something else that often finds its way into sandstone is lime. This comes from the shells of dead molluscs, even from some sea plants which have a limy covering. Sometimes there is so much lime in a sedimentary rock that it is known as limestone.

Millions of years later, there might be a great upheaval in the Earth's crust, and this limestone might become part of its landscape. Then, another kind of limestone may start to grow—the kind that fills underground caves, like those at Jenolan outside Sydney, with some of the most beautiful rock formations in the world. This is how it happens:

Rain falls on the limestone, then seeps down through the earth into underground caves which were scooped out thousands of years ago by the action of rivers. But it doesn't seep through just as rainwater, for some of the lime from the rock has dissolved into it. When, down in the cave, the water evaporates, it leaves the tiniest scrap of lime behind it—so tiny that you couldn't possibly see it without a microscope. Yet gradually, during thousands of years, these tiny bits of lime build up into wonderful shapes, which make the whole caves look like fairy palaces.

Have you ever thought of salt as a rock? Well it is—and it comes about very much the same as cave limestone does. Salt is a chemical dissolved in water. When the water evaporates, the chemical is left as a tiny bit of solid matter—and as hundreds of centuries go by, these tiny bits mount up into huge deposits. Now, you see, whenever you sprinkle salt over your food, you can have the fun of knowing that you are eating a sedimentary rock.

Limestone palaces in underground caves

Most children, when they are little, enjoy nothing quite so much as playing with dirt, especially if it is nice and wet and they can pack it together into mud-pies. Nature also likes playing with mud, but when she packs it together, she makes a sedimentary rock of it, called shale.

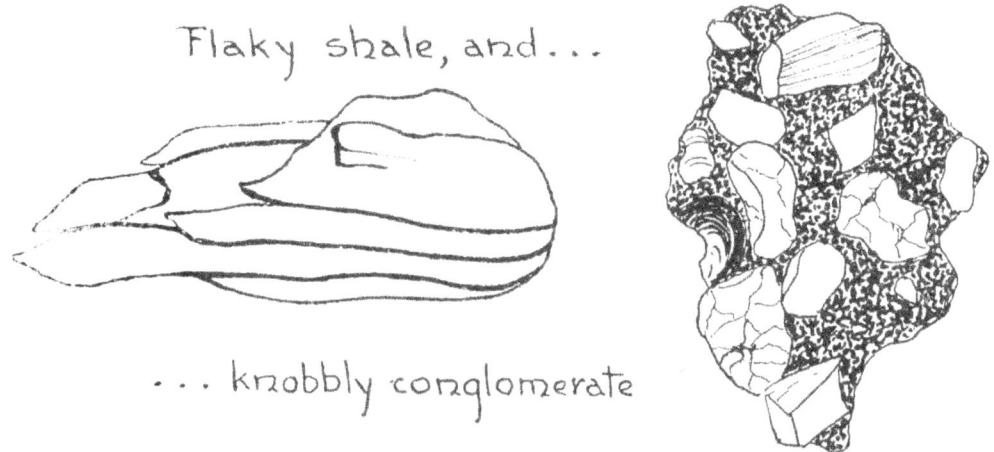

Flaky shale, and...

... knobbly conglomerate

You will find shale everywhere. It is a very soft rock which sometimes breaks at a touch. It does not crumble into grains as sandstone does when it is crushed. It falls apart into flakes, and actually has an earthy smell about it when it is wet. Sometimes it is a dull grey colour, but other times you may find it in beautiful shades of brown, red and yellow. When you go travelling about, just look around and see how many colours there are in different soils—then you will know how many colours you are likely to find in shales.

Now all of the rocks we have talked about so far have been made from materials which were never alive. Even limestone comes from the *shells* of sea creatures—not from their living tissues. But sometimes a sedimentary rock can be formed from living (or organic) matter.

Coal is one of these—untold millions of years old, filled with the remains of prehistoric plants and with the energy that they trapped from the rays of the sun, all those ages ago, just as plants are trapping and using the sun's energy today. Sometimes you can even see the shape of one of those ancient plants impressed in a piece of coal—and of course that is ever so exciting.

As Chris mentioned in the beginning, people who study rocks and minerals sometimes find themselves studying such soft things as soil, and such liquid things as water. Well, a surprising type of sedimentary "rock" is oil, and this, like coal, is formed from the remains of living matter. But with oil, animals as well as plants have gone toward its making. So you see, when you start thinking about sedimentary rocks, you find yourself thinking about a tremendous number of the things on our Earth.

A very pretty kind of sedimentary rock that you often find around creek or river beds is made up of such a mixture of pebbles that it is known as pudding stone, although its proper name is conglomerate. Little bits and pieces of stones are carried downstream, and come to a quiet part at last where they can settle down on the bottom. As time goes by, the river brings down other materials which build up gradually into sandstone or limestone—and the little pebbles already there get mixed in with this rock as it is forming, and become part of it. Now you all know what pretty things pebbles are—the tiny remains of large rocks of all colours, which have broken away and then been rubbed smaller and smoother as the centuries have passed. Well then, you can imagine how pretty a piece of conglomerate can be.

Now that we know a little about two big groups of rocks—igneous and sedimentary—we have only one other big group to talk about: Metamorphic Rocks. That looks like a big, difficult word. But big, difficult words are rather good fun, really. Chris and Tess think so, and I suppose you do, too. Anyway, metamorphic means something that has changed—so metamorphic rocks are rocks that have changed. For some reason they have become different kinds of rocks from the kinds they were to begin with.

Sometimes this happens because of an extra amount of heat, or of pressure. The rock tends to become a lot harder, and new minerals may find their way into it while its whole structure is changing.

When this sort of thing happens to soft flaky shale, it hardens into slate—the kind that is used for roofs, and blackboards. When it happens to some sandstones we get quartzite—a very hard rock indeed, often used in buildings—and when it happens to limestone, we get that glorious rock called marble, filled with beautiful colours and patterns. There is nothing quite so handsome as a building or a statue made of marble, and you can see just as many shapes and pictures in it as you can in the embers and leaping flames of a fire on a winter's night.

☆   ☆   ☆

People do not always know the difference between rocks and minerals. Do you?

As Chris was telling Tess that day, while she fossicked among some particularly lovely pebbles, rocks are *made up* of minerals. So minerals are the ingredients of rocks just as flour, eggs, butter and sugar are the ingredients of cakes. But, unlike flour, eggs, and butter, minerals come in the form of crystals—and the crystals of different minerals have different shapes.

Salt, for instance, has crystals like cubes, whilst those of quartz are sharp, six-sided ones that come up to a point. Mica has neat, flat crystals, asbestos has long thread-like ones (made up of silicon dioxide, again!), and those of feldspar look rather like tiers of shelves.

You cannot always see these different shapes clearly in Nature, for an awful lot of pressing and cramming goes on while rocks are being made, and often the tiny crystals are squashed out of shape. But you can easily make crystals yourself, and see how they form when they are *not* interfered with.

If you dissolve some salt in a little warm water, then set this aside in a big flat dish, the water will all evaporate in two or three days, and you will have perfect little cube-shaped salt crystals in its place.

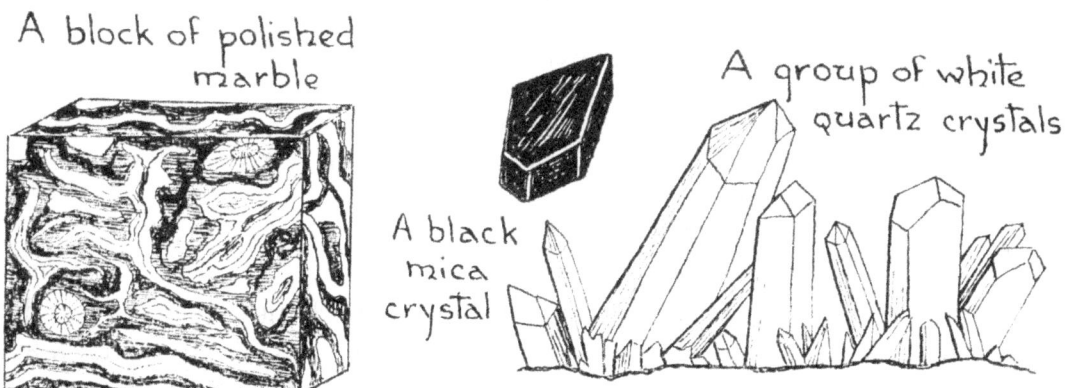

Minerals, then, are very important in the making of rocks, but many of them are important in other ways as well. Think of mica, for instance, which does not burn, and which is used all over the world in the making of irons, toasters and other electrical things. Then think of asbestos, which also resists heat, and which used to be made into firefighters' clothing. A firefighter wearing an asbestos suit could walk right into the midst of flames without getting burnt. Asbestos also used to be used to insulate houses, holding a good inside temperature when the weather is unpleasant. Have you heard of "Mr. Fluffy" houses? They had fluffy white pads of asbestos put into them for that reason.

But these days, we don't want to use asbestos in anything. Remember that quartz can be dissolved in water, very slowly? Asbestos can thus be dissolved, which you may think is just fine, since firefighters don't usually take baths in their clothing. But if those very small particles of silicon dioxide—which are in asbestos, sand, or smashed rock—get into your lungs with a deep breath or two, they stick into the cells inside us and half-dissolve, forming themselves into a permanent irritant for the cells. This can cause all kinds of cancerous diseases, as well as blocking lung airflow. So these days we use other materials to be fireproof or insulate houses.

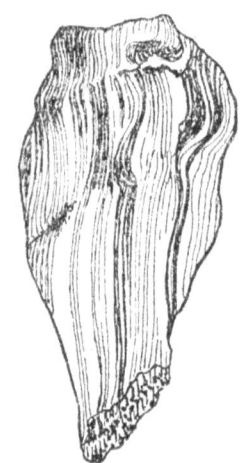

The long, thread-like crystals of asbestos

An arrowhead carved out of flint by some Stone Age man

Flint is another very important mineral, which people have used since the far-away Stone Age. Actually it is a type of quartz which does not come in crystals but in a particularly hard, smooth form, perfect for chipping into various shapes. Primitive man learnt how to carve it into tools, and arrowheads. Also, pieces of it can be struck together to make the sparks that would start a fire. Even "civilised" man, before the days of matches, would strike flint against steel to make a spark. Today we are still using this same idea of friction—in some types of gas-lighter, for instance—only our "flints" are now a mixture of iron and a metal called cerium.

But the usefulness of rocks and minerals to us is almost endless. Look around you—in your city, your home, among the things you use—and you will be surprised to realise how much of it all has been taken from the earth in one form or another. Think of the colourful gems we love to gaze upon—and the gold, silver, copper, iron, zinc, tin, lead and aluminium metals that we use. Whatever they might look like now, all of them were taken out of the earth, to start with, as part of rocks.

And now, just as I was writing this, Tess came into my room with a few little pebbles out of her collection. "You know, Mummie," she said, "I don't really think you could get anything prettier than these." And she showed me a small, colourful piece of conglomerate, and a group of white quartz crystals, a bit of smooth red-and-yellow shale, and a little grey-brown stone with a network of white veins running through it.

Ever so long ago, her grey-brown stone was probably part of a huge boulder somewhere, with cracks in it. Hot liquid quartz, rising up through the Earth's mantle, found its way into the cracks, and then

A pebble, with veins of quartz

cooled into a solid. And today, after all the changes and weathering through thousands of years, here was a little broken-off piece of it in our hands—and to Tess, it was more precious than gold.

Of course, this does not mean that she wouldn't be thrilled if she ever really *found* a tiny piece of gold in all her fossicking, for it is always exciting to come upon something prized and rare—as you will see in the next story.

Opal—and Other Treasures in Australia

JUST imagine if someone could wave a magic wand and show us, right away, all the treasures that lie beneath the surface of the earth—all the gem stones, and colourful ores, and precious minerals! People have been mining many of these and using them for thousands of years—yet if that wand were waved today, we would see a whole vast fairyland of them. It really does seem that there is no end to the treasures of the earth.

Here in Australia—the oldest land in the world, least-touched by earthquakes, volcanoes, and drifting rock plates—there are many riches that people have known about for a long time, and many others which perhaps will *never* be discovered. But those that come to our minds right away are gold, silver and opals. So much so that we tend to forget the others, like tin, lead, zinc, iron, copper, bauxite, uranium, and many lovely gems apart from opal—even diamonds.

URANIUM

There has been quite a lot of attention given to Australia's uranium, because this mineral is important as a source of atomic energy—and we are living, for better or for worse, in the atomic age. Uranium atoms are very easily fissioned, and they do this a little bit all the time by themselves, changing into other types of atoms which are less heavy than uranium.

People usually think of uranium as very rare and special, yet actually it is quite common in the rocks of our Earth. It is about a thousand times more plentiful than gold. The trouble is that it is scattered in such tiny amounts over such large areas that it cannot easily be gathered together and used. Only very seldom can you find large amounts of it all in the one place—and this is what makes it rare as far as human beings are concerned.

Of course, you do not find it just on its own, but mixed in with certain rocks, the way most other minerals are. Rocks that hold important minerals are called ores—and the most common ores of uranium are uraninite and pitchblende. (You may already know something about pitchblende. You may remember the wonderful story of how Marie

A uranium ore, weathering, and showing its telltale powderiness, of orange or yellow

and Pierre Curie discovered radium, and of how in 1902—after years of the hardest work—they separated a tiny fragment of it from many tons of pitchblende.) Yet, in itself, this rock looks quite uninteresting—just heavy and black. If you were thinking of making a collection of "stones", you probably wouldn't look twice at it.

On the other hand, out in the open, when it begins to "weather", it sometimes gets a powdery coating of orange or yellow, and this is very pretty, as well as showing that there might be a fair bit of uranium there.

Most of Australia's uranium has been found in Rum Jungle, high up north towards Darwin, and at Mary Kathleen in Queensland.

BAUXITE - COPPER - TIN

Also in Queensland—at Weipa—a great deal of bauxite has been found. Although this doesn't look a very interesting rock either—rather like lumps of reddish clay—it is from bauxite that we get aluminium, by passing electric currents through it.

Of course, we all know how nice aluminium looks in our kitchens, as shiny pots and pans, but today it is being used for many other very important things, too, like building materials, and aeroplane parts.

Here and there all the way down the Great Dividing Range, copper may be found, and its ores—pyrites, malachite and azurite—are beautiful indeed. Malachite is a rich green, and azurite a rich blue. The pyrites are a bright yellow, but when they tarnish, they often take on so many brilliant colours that they are called peacock ore. Sometimes, also, copper is found in nuggets, and it is a very important metal in anything to do with electricity, as well as in many other ways.

Green malachite, with lovely "ribbon" markings, and...

...some shiny-black crystals of cassiterite

Somewhere in every State except South Australia, a shiny black mineral called cassiterite may be found—and, amazingly, it is from this that we get our bright, "silvery" tin.

Have you, I wonder, ever called something a "rusty old tin"? If so, I hope you never will again, because tin just does *not* rust. It is iron that rusts—and the "tins" we use for so many things were actually made of iron, with the thinnest possible coating of tin to keep them from rusting. While this coating remained, all was well, but when it began to wear off, the iron underneath it began to rust immediately. These days 'tins' are mostly coated with a layer of plastic, which also stops the iron from rusting, at least for a while.

Tin these days is often used in solders, which are metal alloys with a low melting point. If you look inside some of your electronics such as a microwave oven, radio, or mobile phone, you will see this solder attaching tiny electronic parts onto a circuit board that carries electrons to and fro through copper patterns. As solder melts, it forms a further alloy with the electronic part and the circuit board copper, forming a mixture of metals at the joint and a good electric connection. If you have ever heard of a 'dry joint', it refers to the case where the alloying of metals has not happened correctly, and the connection will be unreliable. To avoid this, people use 'flux', which is a mild acid that eats away any metal oxides on the metal surfaces, and makes sure that alloying can occur. Of course that acid can't remain to slowly destroy the electronics, so it is removed after the joint is made.

SILVER

Then, there is silver—and the moment we think of this, we also think of Broken Hill, out in the hot dry west of New South Wales; one of the richest silver mines in the world. Even after 130 years, this precious metal is still being found there.

Sometimes it comes in delicate ferny, flaky or wiry forms, and is called native silver, but mostly it is mixed in with certain ores, and then it is rather a nuisance, for it does not separate easily. In any case, it never looks really "silvery" in Nature, because it tarnishes to a blackish colour, and must be scratched before it shows its gleaming whiteness.

Two different forms of native silver — branching, and flaky

And it is such a soft metal that it is not very useful until it is mixed with some other metal, like nickel or copper. "Sterling" silver, for instance, has a small amount of copper in it, and our "silver" coins are a mixture of silver, copper, nickel and zinc.

GOLD

Of course, the most precious metal of all, for nearly everyone, is gold. The very word itself has come to mean the noblest and best. And here in Australia, our whole history has been bound up with it. If it hadn't been for the gold-rushes, from the middle of last century, our country would probably have developed much more slowly. As it was, when the news spread that gold had been found here, people came from far and wide to "try their luck", and soon the country was really opening up.

Like uranium, gold is surprisingly common throughout the world. Traces of it may be found in almost all rocks and soils—but again, it becomes valuable only when fairly large amounts of it are found in the one place.

There are many ways in which it may come—as exciting, chunky nuggets... or mingled with quartz in "veins" that flow branching out and squeezing their way between rocks... or scattered through rocks as the tiniest particles... or washed on to beaches or along river beds by moving water.

This last kind is called alluvial gold, and it comes about when the quartz in which it has formed is worn away by streams or rivers, freeing the fragments of gold to drift off in the water.

There are many old deserted gold diggings in Australia, and mostly you will find a few hopeful searchers pottering around there, "panning" for gold along the river courses. They swirl quantities of sand, dirt and water around in large dishes—and if they are lucky, they might find a few specks of gold in this way, or even a small nugget or two.

Recently, Chris, Tess and I made a short visit to Hill End—a little town filled with quaint old houses, and dreams and memories. Quiet and hidden-away though it is, it is one of the most famous "gold" towns in the world, for it was here, nearly a hundred years ago, that a man named Bernard Holterman came upon the largest nugget of gold that has ever been found on Earth. Just imagine how he must have felt when he first set eyes on it, after months of seeing just tiny specks in quartz or on river beds! It stood 1.5m high, was 840mm wide, and 100mm thick. Quite apart from its value in money, how beautiful it must have looked! For gold never tarnishes, and its colour is so exciting.

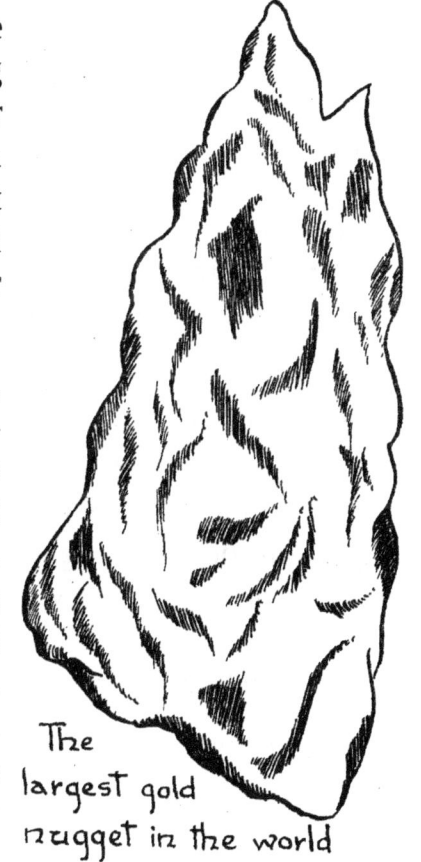

The largest gold nugget in the world

Way back in the ancient world, people prized gold for its beauty, and—realising how soft it was, and easy to work—they moulded it into wonderful jewellery and ornaments. It is, in fact, *too* soft to stand up to hard wear, so you will find that in jewellery, it is mixed with some other metal, mostly silver. This is expressed by the word "carat". Pure gold is 24 carat, so when you see something marked "18 carat", you know that it has 18 parts of gold out of 24.

OPAL

When we visited Hill End, we couldn't spend as much time there as we would have liked, because we were just on our way home after a few days of another great adventure—a trip to Lightning Ridge. This is where the most famous of Australia's opal comes from—the "black" opal that is surely one of the Earth's most beautiful treasures, glowing with pinpoints or streaks or flashes of "fire" whichever way you look at it.

Turn it one way, and it is the brightest green, another way and it seems to be filled with red flames. Sometimes it is the blue of butterfly wings, or the yellow of gold. There isn't a colour in the rainbow that does not find its way into opal at one time or another. So of course, our trip to the home of this extra-special gem was very exciting indeed.

After hundreds of miles, we came to the top of a small rise—and there, spread out before us, was a whole dug-up world—Lightning Ridge itself. There were mounds of earth everywhere, and beside them the deep holes or shafts from which they had been dug. In some of these shafts, miners had found glorious gems filled with flashing "fire", but in others there had been only potch.

Potch is a *kind* of opal, but it has no value. It is mostly greyish in colour, and can be beautifully patterned, so it is a great pity that people think nothing of it. The only thought they give to it is that, where there is potch, there may also be *real* opal, so they go on digging and chipping away, always hoping.

First, a miner will dig down a certain distance, then starts scooping out little passages sideways. Then the miner may go down farther, and dig out more passages. And wherever one goes, with pick and shovel and candle, one goes very carefully. This is one of the most interesting things about opal mining—that today, when everything is done with machinery and electricity, people still dig their own way down for opal—ever so carefully, so as not to shatter what might be a lovely gem—and then they look for it with candlelight.

Tess and Chris will never forget their own adventures down an opal mine—how exciting it was to climb deep down on a rickety ladder made of tied-together branches, and then scramble into little narrow

Entrance to one of the quaint little "home-made" opal mines at Lightning Ridge

passageways, almost like rabbit burrows, with a pick and a candle. Although this was an old mine which had been thoroughly explored already, its owner told them that they might easily loosen a bit of rock or soil, down there, and find a valuable gem—because, you see, this is how opal behaves. Nobody can tell where it will be found. It follows no regular seam or pattern—just crops up willy-nilly wherever it likes. And its colours are just as chancey.

Until recently, no one had been able to explain this wonderful play of colours—so different from what happens with any other gem. Then, some years ago, opal got partly dissolved in acid, and then looked at with an electron microscope which can see many small things, smaller than a light microscope can see. And then an amazing scene appeared, so beautiful and regular. The opal is actually made up of thousands of millions of tiny balls of quartz mixed with a little water, with the clay-like potch material in between. After etching away this potch with acid, these balls remained in stacks, layer after layer, all looking perfectly regular like a castle of tiny spheres.

When light hits onto this stack of balls with a photon wavelength that fits exactly from ball to ball as it reflects, then you see those photons coming from the opal. At another angle, a different photon wavelength will make a match, and so that colour will show. In this way, all of the colours in the rainbow can come out of the reflections from one tiny piece of opal as the angle is changed.

This is called 'diffraction', which scientists use to study materials. X-rays are a form of light which can 'see' atoms in crystals using diffraction, and electrons and neutrons also can form diffraction patterns. Opal is very special; very few other things in nature can do this diffraction to get a rainbow of colours for us to see.

Mostly, nature gets rainbows by another trick called 'interference', and you can see its effects in the feathers of the rainbow lorikeet, or of the peacock, or on some beetle or fly wings. You can see the effect of interference also if a little oil slick floats on water; the many colours you see are due to the different oil layer thicknesses reflecting those photons that fit their waves exactly as they reflect to your eyes. So interference and diffraction work in a similar way, but one uses thin layers while the other uses crystalline arrays of balls or atoms or other small objects.

Of course, none of this worried us in the least while we were pottering around the endless diggings at Lightning Ridge. We thought only of the special and almost magical beauty of opal... and we made friends with two or three of the older miners, who had wonderful stories to tell... and we were enormously excited whenever we found the tiniest piece of opal colour among the heaps of earth and rock which form the landscape of the Ridge. And there was something else that we really pondered over—but this belongs with our next story.

The landscape of Lightning Ridge — all dug up, wherever you look

Pictures in Stone

THE most wonderful thing about drawing and writing is that, from the time people learnt how to express themselves in these ways, they were able to put on record all the things that were happening around them, all of their achievements, discoveries and ideas. Future generations studied these, and learnt from them, and then went on to make further discoveries and to think more advanced thoughts.

Before we discovered how to draw, we could leave no records of the way in which we lived, or of our thoughts. But from the time we began to make drawings on the inside walls of caves, we were able at least to give some idea of our surroundings and of the things we were most interested in. Then, many centuries later, when we learnt how to write, we could make very excellent records indeed.

Yet millions of years before people even appeared on Earth, records were already being made far and wide, all over the world.

These took the form of pictures and mouldings in stone—created by Nature throughout the endlessness of time. Our name for them is fossils, and they form perhaps the most exciting part in our whole study of rocks, for they are, in reality, the Earth's first recorded history.

Try to imagine millions and millions of years ago. The seas were filled with living creatures—plants and animals. Many of them would look very strange to us if we saw them today, because they belonged to types which no longer exist. They have become extinct. Others have gone on, generation after generation, to the present day, looking almost the same as they did then. But as each individual one died, it would sink to the floor of the ocean.

There, it might easily have been covered by a drift of sand and silt, under which the soft parts of its body would slowly rot away, leaving the hard skeleton or shell. More sand and silt would settle over it, and gradually minerals would work through into it.

As centuries passed, the sand and other sediments would pack down heavily into rock—and embedded in that rock would be the remains of the little sea creature which had fallen to the bottom of the ocean so long ago. But by now, many other sea creatures would also be embedded in the rock.

A pretty little bivalve shell

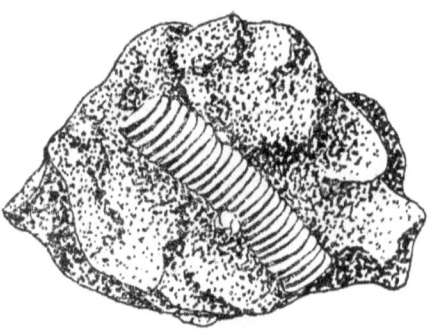
Stem of a sea lily

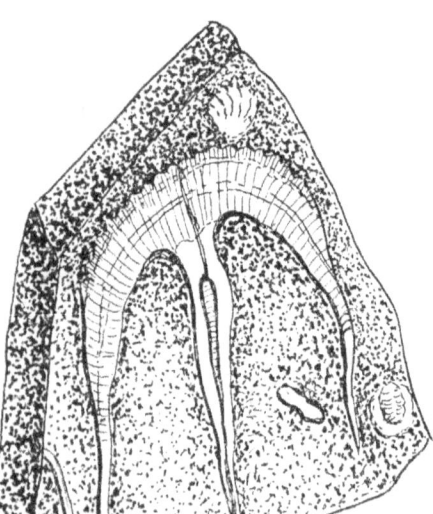
Section of a very ancient type of bivalve — a lamp shell

A heart urchin

Dainty fragments of coral

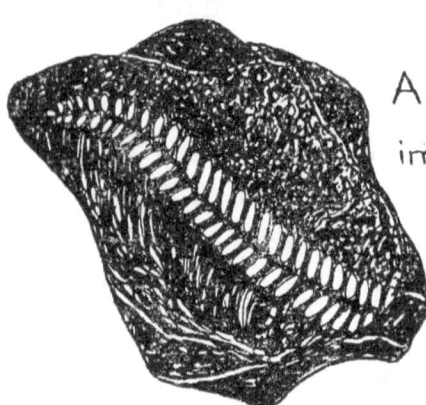
A fern-leaf impression in a piece of coal

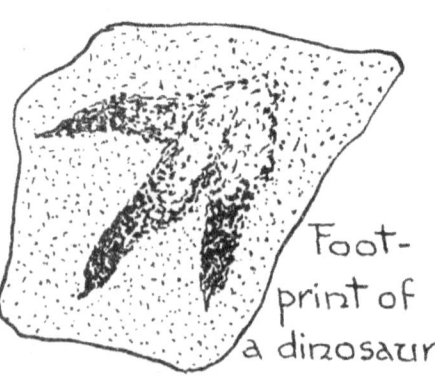
Footprint of a dinosaur

Thousands or millions of years later, a great upheaval might thrust this underwater rock up into a hill, or even a high mountain. In the upheaval it would crack in many parts. Great boulders would fall away from it, and go thundering down until they found a resting place. Many of them are in these same resting places still. We ourselves might come across them some day, on an outing, and might happen to notice on them the perfect shapes of those little beings which roamed through the seas when life on Earth was very new.

In a lump of coal we might easily find the impressions made by way-back prehistoric plants, for those are what coal is so largely made of.

Limestone is often filled with the fossils of corals, shells, ancient sea lilies, and so on. Sea lilies, in spite of their name, were not plants, but beautiful flower-like animals with swaying "stems", anchored on to underwater rocks.

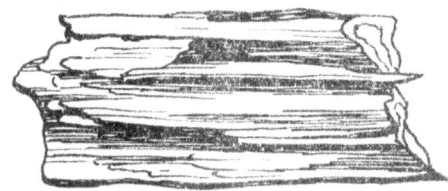

A piece of petrified wood

Sometimes even giant trees which once fell into the mud became transformed into fossils. As they lay buried, water seeped through their tissues, gradually replacing these with minerals. Today, although they look exactly like ordinary tree-trunks, they are actually solid rock, called petrified wood. And this, when polished, is one of the most beautiful of stones.

Remember when we were looking at granite and quartz, and the way they can be dissolved, ever so slowly, in water? Now if we imagine that water with quartz in it, flowing over a fallen tree or animal or plant, seeping into all of its pores and leaving a little of its quartz behind, you can see how something living can be slowly turned into a quartz stone.

Sometimes actual bones and shells themselves are preserved, deep inside the rocks which have formed around them. This often happened when certain resins rolled down tree-trunks, imprisoning insects on their way. The resins quickly solidified—then, through the centuries, became fossilised into lovely golden amber, with the actual bodies of some of the Earth's earliest insects entombed within them.

But other times the actual bodies—even the bony parts of them—rotted away, leaving only the impression of their shapes. If new material settled over this, the impression became a mould. The new material filled into it, and took on the exact rounded shape of the original shell, bone, or whatever it was. We ourselves do the same today, when we fill moulds with clay or metal to make all sorts of pretty or useful things.

A very exciting thing to find in sandstone is the footprint of a dinosaur—one of those huge reptiles which roamed the prehistoric Earth. (When you tread on firm mud or wet concrete, you are doing exactly what those dinosaurs once did, so many ages ago.) Then, perhaps, the mud in which they had trodden became dry and hard, and at last turned into rock, with their footprints still clearly marked in it.

Three times, in our own little trips of exploration, we have come upon parts rich in fossils, and there is nothing quite so exciting—in a deep, quiet way. It is a tremendous experience to take up a stone and see in it the actual shapes of plants and animals as they were when life first awakened on Earth.

We think a great deal—and rightly so—of the glories of our own older civilisations, in Egypt, China, Crete and Greece. But what of the quiet glory of these rocks, and of the records that they hold, going back hundreds of millions of years?

We can look around us today and find that our world is filled with an endless number of wonderful things. But even more wonderful is what we learn from the fossil stories in our rocks—that the world was already filled with the miracle of life countless eons ago—just as it will also be, with ever-increasing marvels and varieties, countless eons from now.

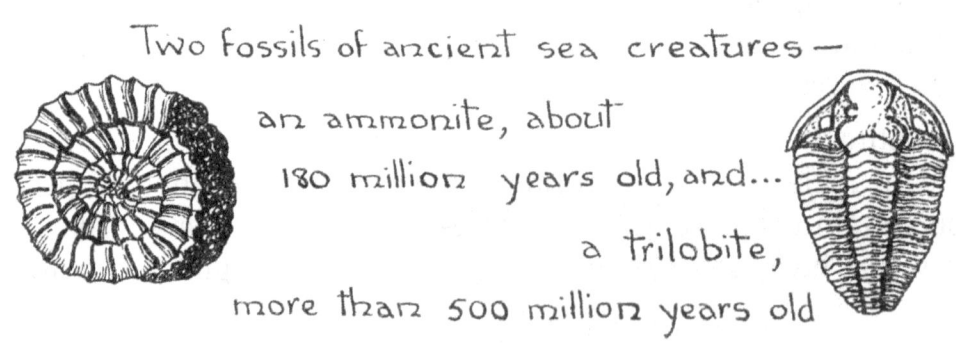

Two fossils of ancient sea creatures — an ammonite, about 180 million years old, and... a trilobite, more than 500 million years old

While this book has been in preparation, the interest, encouragement and assistance of many people have been invaluable to me. In particular, I should like to thank

MR. TOM IREDALE, whose encyclopaedic knowledge of seashore life, and generous giving of time, have helped enormously...

MR. C. E. CHADWICK, who has spared no effort in the solving of many an insect problem...

MR. P. HADLINGTON, with whom it has been so helpful to "compare notes", especially about trees, and...

ANDREW SIMAN, who has most generously shared his specimens and findings.

Finally, a very special thank-you to MISS IDA KELLETT, whose idea it was that this book should be written... and also to her 2A class of 1963, in Peakhurst West Infants' School.

A few of the earlier stories and their illustrations were tried out on this class—and the children's response to them was overwhelmingly warm. This, added to the fascination of the subjects themselves, has made the whole production of the book a joyful experience indeed.

NURI MASS

January, 1964

INDEX

Abdomen, 7
Acid, 152, 259, 295, 299
Air, 225, 232, 234-7, 253, 261-276
Alcohol, 149
Alga(e), 123, 142, 150, 152, 153, 155, 222
Alkalai, 284
Alloys, 241, 295
Alluvial (gold), 297
Alternating Current, 258
Aluminium, 228, 255, 283, 291, 294
Amazon ants, 36
Amber, 248, 304
Ammonite, 304
Anemometer, 273
Angel's wing shell, 209
Animals, 7-139, 175, 288, 301, 303-4
"annus mirabilis", 279
Ant lion, 46, 54-6
Antenna, 7
Ants, 21, 28-36, 86, 87; —and aphids, 25-7, 30, 33; —and lacewings, 55-7
Aphids, 25-7; —and ants, 25-7, 28, 30, 33; —and ladybirds, 10; —and lacewings, 55-56
Ark shells, 205, 206
Army ants, 35-6
Asbestos, 289, 290
Atmosphere, 261-76
Atomic energy, 293
Atoms, 224-5, 227, 232, 235, 240, 242, 247, 249-50, 253, 255-6, 263, 266-7, 275, 278-9
Azurite, 294

Bacteria, 147, 150-2
Ball-rolling beetle, 49
Barnacles, 216-7, 220
Barometer, 272-3
Barrier Reef, 196, 202, 204, 220
Basalt, 281
Battery, 246, 254, 258-9, 260
Bauxite, 293, 294
Bees, 21, 61, 73-9, 86, 227, 228; —and pollination, 78, 167, 169
Beetles, 9, 10, 44-50, 51, 52, 80
Bidgee-widgees, 178
Bivalves, 195, 200, 205, 208, 211
Bladderworts, 191-2
Blue Triangle butterfly, 109-11
Bombardier beetle, 48
Bossiaea, 183, 184-5
Bracken fern, 157, 159
Bracket fungi, 144
Brain, 235
Breathing holes, 128, 154
Broken Hill, 295
Bubble shells, 201
Bugs, 9, 51-4
Bull-oak, 183
Bulldog ant, 28
Burrs, 178, 179

Butterflies, 9, 52, 64, 72, 109-19
Byssus, 209
Cactus, 184
Calcium, 195
Calyx, 165
Capsules, 155
Carat, 297
Carbon, 253, 259, 269, 275, 283
"carbon cycle", 269
Carbon dioxide, 253, 269, 275
Cars, 259, 269
Cart-rut shell, 201
Case moths, 51, 94-6
Cassiterite, 295
Cassytha, 188
Castings, 138
Caterpillars, 60, 65, 87-90, 91-3, 94-6, 180 (See also Moths, Butterflies)
Cat's-eyes, 199
Caves, 285-6
Centipede, 126, 216
Cephalopods, 195, 196, 213-4, 216
Cerium, 291
Chemicals, 68, 75-6, 80, 253, 258-9, 263, 266-7, 277, 284, 286
Cherry and pear slug, 83
Chiton, 195, 212, 217
Chlorophyll, 181, 253, 263
Christmas beetles, 44-5, 61
Chrysalis, 9 (See also Butterflies)
Cicada, 15-18, 41, 89
Cirrus, 266
Clams, 211
Clematis, 177
Click beetles, 49-50
Climate change, 268
Clouds, 250, 263-6, 269, 270, 272, 274
Coal, 250, 269, 275, 287-8, 303
Cobalt, 241
Cockles, 207
Cockroaches, 84-5
Coconuts, 176
Cocoon, 9, 33, 34, 35, 91-3, 100, 107-8, 139 (See also Moths)
Colours, of light, 225-8; —of opal, 298, 300; —of sky, 262-9
Column (in flowers), 169
Compass, 244-5
Concave, 231
Condensation, 265
Conductors, 255
Cone shells, 202
Cone-bearing plants, 142, 160-5
Cones, 142, 160-4, 165-6, 171, 177
Conglomerate, 288, 291
Conifers, 162
Convex, 231
Copper, 255, 291, 293, 294-5, 296
Coral, 145, 202, 204, 217, 219-21, 269, 303
Corallines, 221
Core (of Earth), 280
Cornea, 231

Corolla, 165
Cotyledon, 160, 171-3
Cowboy beetle, 45
Cowries, 201-2, 203-4
Crabs, 180, 216
Crane flies, 58, 59
Crayfish, 216
Crickets, 41-3
Crown (of leaves), 162
Crusader bug, 51-2
Crust (of Earth), 280
Crystals, 283, 289-91, 300
Cumulo-nimbus, 266
Cumulus, 266
Cup moths, 100-1
Curie, Marie and Pierre, 293-4
Curl-grubs, 45
Current (electric), 218, 246-7, 250, 254, 257-8, 294
Current; alternating—, 258; direct—, 258
Cuttlefish, 129, 195, 214
Cyano-bacteria, 147, 150-2
Cycads, 162-4
Cyclone, 268
Cypresses, 162

Dams, 252
Damsel-fly, 70
Dance (of bees), 79
Dandelion, 170, 177-8
Dew, 265
Diamond beetle, 48
Diamonds, 253, 283-4, 293
Diffraction, 300
Digestive juices, 190
Dingy Swallowtail butterfly, 112-14
Dinosaur, footprints of, 304
Direct Current, 258
Dog whelk, 200
Dragonflies, 61, 70-2
Drones, 77, 78
Dry-cell batteries, 258, 260
Dust, 262; —storms, 284
Dynamo, 250, 251, 252, 258

Ear-drum, 235, 238
Ear shells, 197-8
Earth, composition of, 279-81; —as magnet, 245; spinning of—, 270-1
Echo, 237-8, 279-81
Eggs, 92; —of ants, 30, 31; —of aphids, 25, 27; —of cicadas, 16, 17; —of white ants, 19-20
Einstein, Albert, 263, 279, 280
Electricity, 224, 245-6, 248-59, 260, 271, 275, 279, 294, 298
Electromagnets, 241-2, 245-7, 251
Electron clouds, 225
Electrons, 224, 225-6, 240, 242-3, 249-50, 253-4, 255-6, 259, 263, 295
Elm, 177
Embryo, 160

Energy, 227-8, 253, 266-7, 269, 273, 275, 278-9, 287, 293
Erosion, 150, 285
Evaporation, 264, 273, 286, 289
Eyes, of frog 123-4; —of humans, 228, 231 —of snail, 128; —of worm, 138; —of viper, 228

Faraday, Michael, 250, 256
Feldspar, 283, 289
Ferns, 142, 153-4, 157-9, 160
File shells, 208
Fingernail shell, 205-6
Fire, 224, 274-6
Fish, 123, 218
Fission, 279
Flame, 275; —dog cockle, 208
Flannel flower, 184-5
Flies, 58-62, 64, 70, 80, 82, 83, 125
Flint, 275, 290-1
Flowers, 142, 155, 160, 162, 165-74, 183-5, 213
Focus, 231
Fog, 265
Foot (of molluscs), 127, 128, 194-6, 206
Fossils, 164, 194, 284, 301-5
Freon, 267
Frilled Venus shell, 208
Friction, 275-6
Frog, 122-5, 180
Fronds, 157, 159, 162, 222
Frost, 265
Fruit fly, 59
Fungus(i), 27, 142, 143-9, 150, 153, 155, 160, 181, 188
Funnel-web spider, 132
Fusion, 278, 279

Galls, 79-83
Gases, 261, 262, 268-9
Gems, 291, 293, 298-300
Generator, 251-2
Geometer moth, 102-3
Germination, 160
Gills, 123, 147
Girdle, of chitons, 195; —of worms, 139
Glass, 226, 228-31, 232-3, 241, 248-9, 255, 262, 265
Global Warming, 268
Gold, 291-2, 293, 296-7
Granite, 284, 303
Grasses, 173-4, 176
Grasshoppers, 9, 37-41
Gravity, 249, 277-8, 280
Green plants, 143, 150, 180-1, 188, 233, 261
Green tree ants, 33-4
Greenhood orchid, 169
'Greenhouse Effect', 268-269
Gum Emperor moth, 106-8
Gumtrees, 178; seed-boxes of—, 178

Hail, 265
Harvester ants, 35
Hawk moths, 97-9

Heat, 270, 274-6, 278-9, 284
Helmet shells, 202-3
Hercules Club whelk, 200-1
"High", 272
Hill End, 297
Hinge (in shells), 205
Holterman, Bernard, 297
Honey, 74-6, 78, 86
Honeypot ants, 34-5
Host (of parasites), 186-8
Hover flies, 59
Humidity, 272
Humming-birds, 98
Hurricane, 270-1
Hygrometer, 273
Hyphae, 147, 152

Ice, 277
Ichneumon 64-5
Igneous rocks, 284, 288
Inflorescence, 170-2
Infra-red, 227, 228, 238, 254, 266-7, 269
Insects, 7-120, 216, 227, 303; —eaten by plants, 189-92; —and pollination, 167-9; singing of—, 17, 39, 41-3
Inorganic, 277
Insulators, 253, 255-6
Interference, 300
Ionosphere, 261
Iron, 241, 243-4, 246-7, 250, 257, 285, 291, 293, 295

Jacaranda, 176, 177, 179
Jewel beetles, 45, 46
Jingle shells, 207
Jumping spider, 132-3

Keel (petals), 169-70
Kelp shells, 199-200
Kurrajong leaf-rollers, 104-5

Labellum, 169
Lacewings, 54-7
Ladybird, 10-11, 44, 45
Land, 270
Landslides, 281
Larva(e), 8, 9 (See also Ants, Bees, Beetles, Butterflies, Flies, Galls, Ichneumons, Lacewings, Ladybird, Moths, Wasps, White Ants)
Lava, 281-2
Lead, 259, 293
Leaf-rolling spider, 136-7
Leaf-rollers, Kurrajong, 104-5
Leaves, 157-9, 222; —and food-making, 180-1; shapes of—, 157, 162; spore-bearing—, 157-9; veins of—, 171-4; —and water loss, 181-5
Lens, 228, 229-31
Lichens, 27, 153-4, 160, 284
Life cycle, 8, 9
Light, 175, 224-33, 234, 235, 261, 262, 274-5, 279, 300
Lightning, 235, 250, 260, 271; —

Ridge, 298-300
Lime, 221, 285-6
Limestone, 285-6, 287, 288, 303
Limpets, 197, 212
Lines of force, 243-4, 257
Liquids, 235, 279-80
Liverworts, 142, 153-4, 155
Locusts, 40-1
Lodestone, 241
"Low", 272
Lungs, 123, 290

Maggot, 59, 60
Magma, 281, 282
Magnetic field, 243-4; —poles, 244-5
Magnetism, 240-7, 248, 250-2, 257
Magnets, 240-7, 248, 250-2, 257
Magnetite, 241-2
Maidenhair fern, 157-8
Malachite, 294
Mangrove, 176, 178-9, 201
Mantids (mantis), 9, 12-14
Mantle, of Earth, 280-1, 283, 291; —of molluscs, 194-6, 204, 206, 210-11
Maples, 176
Marble, 288-9
March flies, 58
Marriage flight, of ants, 29-30; —of bees, 78; of white ants, 21
Mask (of dragonflies), 70
Mason wasps, 88-9
Mercury, 273
Metals, 240, 248, 254-5, 260, 295-7
Metamorphic rocks, 288
Methane, 269
Mica, 283, 289
Microscope(s), 231, 299
Migrating (of butterflies). 116-8
"Milking" (of aphids), 25-7
Minerals, 277, 283, 284, 288, 289, 290, 291, 293, 295, 301, 303
Mirrors, 226, 227, 228-31, 232-3, 237
Mist, 265, 271
Mistletoe. 178, 186-8
Mole crickets, 42
Molecules, 235
Molluscs, 127, 129, 194-215, 216, 217, 218, 219, 220, 285
Monarch butterfly (or Wanderer), 115-9
Moon shells, 200
Mosquitoes, 62-3, 70, 124
Mosses, 142, 153, 155-6
Mother-of-pearl, 210
Moths, 9, 52, 63, 72, 91-108, 180
Motor, 247
Mountain-devils, 176
Mountains, 280, 284, 303; —of air, 272-3
Mud, 201, 272, 287, 303; —dauber wasps, 88-9; —whelk, 201
Mulberry shell, 201
Mushrooms, 147-9; —and ants, 31, 35; —and white ants, 22
Mussels, 209-210

Mycelium(a), 147, 149

Native (silver), 295-6
Nautilus, 214-5
Nectar, 75, 78, 79, 166-7
Needle-bushes, 176, 184
"Needles" (pine), 162
Negative electricity, 248-50, 254, 258, 259, 271
Neritas, 199, 200
Neutron, 279
Newton, Isaac, 280
Nickel, 241, 296
Nimbo-stratus, 266
Nitrogen, 147, 150, 152, 164, 192, 261
Nucleus, 224, 240, 242, 249
Nuggets, 294, 295, 296
Nymph, 9 (See also Bugs, Cicada, Cockroaches, Crickets, Dragonflies, Grasshoppers, Mantis)

Obsidian, 281
Oceans, 213, 285, 301
Octopus, 195, 213
Oil, 57, 269, 277
Opal, 293, 298-300
Orbits, 224
Orchids, 27, 169, 174
Ores, 293, 294, 295
Organic, 287
Ovary, 165-6
Ovules, 165-6, 167
Oxygen, 241, 253, 261, 266-7, 269, 275
Oysters, 195, 201, 209-10, 220
Ozone, 267, 269
"ozone hole", 267

Paper, 86, 87; —and wasps, 86-8
Parasites, 60, 65, 112, 144, 186-8
Parasitic flies, 60
Pea family, 169, 170, 178
Peacock ore. 294
Pearl shells, 210
Pearls, 210
Pebbles, 277, 288, 289, 291
Pen (of squid), 214
Periscope, 229-30
Periwinkles, 195, 199
Petals, 165-7, 169, 170, 171
Petrified wood, 303
Phasmids, 66-9
Pheasant shells, 199
Photon, 225, 254, 266, 267, 269, 279
Pig's face, 184
Pin-oak, 186
Pines, 160-2
Pipi, 205
Pistil, 165-6, 169, 170, 171, 183
Pitch (of sound), 238
Pitchblende, 293-4
Pitcher plants, 190-2
Pittosporum, 81, 82, 178
Planets, 224, 230, 249, 278
Plants, 142-92, 261, 263, 267, 269, 281, 284, 287, 288, 301, 303-4
Plastic, 246, 246, 249, 250, 255, 295
Platter shells, 207, 208
Polar bear, 180
Poles, 241-5, 248, 255
Pollen, 74, 75, 76, 78, 79, 155, 162, 165-7, 167-9
Pollination, by insects, 78, 167-9; —by wind, 162, 166
Polyps, 219
Poppy, 178
Porphyry, 282, 283
Positive electricity, 248-50, 254, 258, 259, 271
Potch, 298-9
Powder-post beetles, 46, 47
Power, 251-2, 260; —station, 255, 256
Praying mantis, 12-14
Precious wentletrap, 201
Pressure, 272-3, 278, 281, 284, 288
Prickly Pear, 184
Prism, 225, 226
Pudding stone, 288
Puff-balls, 145
Pumice, 282
Pupa, 8, 9 (See also Ants, Bees, Beetles, Butterflies, Flies, Galls, Ichneumons, Lacewings, Ladybird, Moths, Wasps, White Ants)
Pyrites, 294

Quartz, 253, 283-5, 288, 289-81, 296-7, 299, 303
Quartzite, 288
Queen, of ants, 29, 30; —of bees, 74, 76, 77-8; —of paper wasps 87-8; of white ants, 51-2

Raceme, 170-2
Radio, 228, 240, 242, 258, 279; —activity, 279, 280, 281
Radium, 294
Rain, 264-5, 271, 272, 274, 284, 285
Rainbow, 226, 233
Ram's horn shell, 213
Redback spider, 132
Reflecting (of light), 225-8
Refraction (of light), 232-3, 299-300
Relativity, 279
Resins, 303
Resistance, 256
Retina, 207, 231
Rhinoceros beetle, 48, 49
Rivers, 282, 284
Robber flies, 61
Rock whelks, 200
Rocks, 224, 277-304
"Roly-poly", 176
Root, 178-9, 185, 222; —hairs 188
"root forest", 178
Royal jelly, 74, 77

Rubber, 255
"Rust", 149
Rusting (of iron), 295

St. Andrew's Cross spider, 134-5
Salt, 286, 289
Salvia, 167-9
Sand 196, 204, 206, 210, 241, 253, 277, 284, 285, 290; —snails, 191-2, 200
Sandstone, 285, 287, 288, 304
Satellite, 274
Sawfly, 83
Scale insect galls, 80-2
Scales (in cones), 160-2
Scallop shells, 205, 206, 207
Scarabs, 44, 45
Sea, 270; —anemone, 23, 217-18; —eggs, 219; life in—, 194-222; —lilies, 303; —reptiles, 304; —urchins, 219, 304
Seaweed, 180, 199, 201, 219, 220, 221
Sediment, 284, 301
Sedimentary rocks, 284-8
Seed-boxes, 158, 165, 175, 178, 184
Seeds, 144, 159, 160-4, 165-6, 167, 169, 186, 188; how travel, 175-9
Semiconductor, 253, 254
Sepals, 165-6, 171
Shale, 287, 288, 291
She-oak, 176, 183-4
Shells, 127, 129, 194-222, 285, 287; fossilised—, 301-3
Shrimps, 216
Silicon, 253, 254, 255, 283
Silkworm, 107
Silver, 228, 250, 291, 293, 295-6
Silverfish, 9, 23-4
Singing (of insects), 17, 39, 41-3
Slate, 288
Sleet, 265
Slug, 129
Snails, 127-9, 195
Snow, 265, 266
Soft iron, 246-7, 257
Soil, 147, 152, 281, 287-8; —and plants, 150, 155; —and worms, 138
Solar cell, 252-4, 263, 269
Solar system, 224, 278
Solder, 295
Soldier flies, 58, 59-60
Solids, 235, 280
Sound, 226, 234-9
Spiders, 87, 88, 89, 90, 126, 130-7, 209
Spirula, 129, 213, 214
Sponges, 222
Spores, 144, 145, 146, 147, 149, 150, 154, 155, 157, 160
Squid, 129, 213, 214
Stamens, 165, 166, 167, 169, 170, 171, 183
Standard (petal), 169, 170
Starch, 181, 188

Starfish, 180, 219-20
Stars, 225, 230
Static electricity, 248
Steam, 251-2
Steel, 241, 246, 291
Stems, 157-9, 181, 183-5, 221-2
Sterling silver, 296
Stick insects, 66-9, 180
Stigma, 165-6, 167, 169
Stomate, 181, 185
Stomatella, 198
Stone Age, 290
Stones, 277-304
Stratosphere, 261
Stratus, 266
Style, 165-6
Sucker, 186, 188
Sugar, 181, 188, 253, 269
Sun, 224, 225, 233, 249, 254, 261, 262, 263, 264, 266, 267, 268, 269, 270, 271, 278, 279, 280, 287
Sundew, 190
Sunflower, 170
Swallowtail butterflies, 109-14
"Swarming", 77
Sweet pea, 169-70
Sycamores, 176

Tadpoles, 122-4
Tapestry shells, 208
Teeth, of shells, 203; —of snails, 128
Telephone, 236-7
Telescopes, 230
Tentacles, 129, 195-6, 213, 218
Terminals, 246, 254, 258, 259
Termitarium, 20, 21-2
Termites, 19-22, 29, 31, 87
Thermometer, 273

Thorax, 7
Thrip, 80
Thunder, 235, 260, 266, 271
Tiger beetles, 46, 47
Tin, 294, 295
Toadstools, 146-9
Torch, 232, 237, 258
Tornado, 271
Transformer, 256-7
Trap-door spider, 126, 132, 192
Trigger plant, 169
Trilobite, 304
Tritons, 201
Trochus, 198
Troposphere, 261
Trough shells, 205
Tube feet, 219, 220
Turbines, 252, 256
Tusk shells, 195, 196

Ultra-violet, 227, 238, 253, 263, 266-7, 269
Univalves, 195, 197, 199-204
Universe, 225
Uraninite, 293
Uranium, 293-4, 296

Vacuum, 232, 235, 236
Valleys, 280, 284; —of air, 272-3
Vapour, 264-6
Vegetable bug, 52-3
Venus shells, 208
Vibrations, 226, 228, 238, 257
Vinci, Leonardo da, 229
Volcano, 281-2
Voltage, 255-7
Vortices/Vortex, 177, 271, 272

Wanderer butterfly, 115-8, 180
Waratahs, 175, 176

Wasps, 64-5, 80, 86-90
Water, 225-6, 232-3, 235, 236, 251-2, 253, 256, 259, 260, 261, 262, 264-5, 271, 272-3, 274, 277, 282, 284-6, 288, 289-90, 297, 303; distilled—, 259; —tiger, 49
Wattles, 175, 178, 182, 186
Wave lengths, 226-8 (See also Waves, Light, Sound)
Waves (of light and sound), 224, 226-7, 234-5, 237-8, 262
Weather, 271-4
Web (of spiders), 130-3, 134-5, 136
Wedge shell, 205
Weevils, 46-8, 82
Wentletraps, 201
"wet bulb temperature", 273
Whelks, 200-1
Whirligig beetle, 49, 50
White ants, 19-22, 23
Wind, 178, 270-1, 272-3, 274; — and pollination, 162, 166
Wings (petals), 169-70; —on seeds, 169, 170, 175, 176-8 (See also Insects)
Wire, 246, 248, 250-1, 252-4, 255-8, 275-6; —fern, 157; —worm, 49
Wood, 235, 256, 269, 275-6; —petrified, 303
Worm shell, 203
Worms, 138-9
"Wrigglers", 62

X-rays, 300

Yeast, 149-152

Zinc, 259, 291, 293, 296

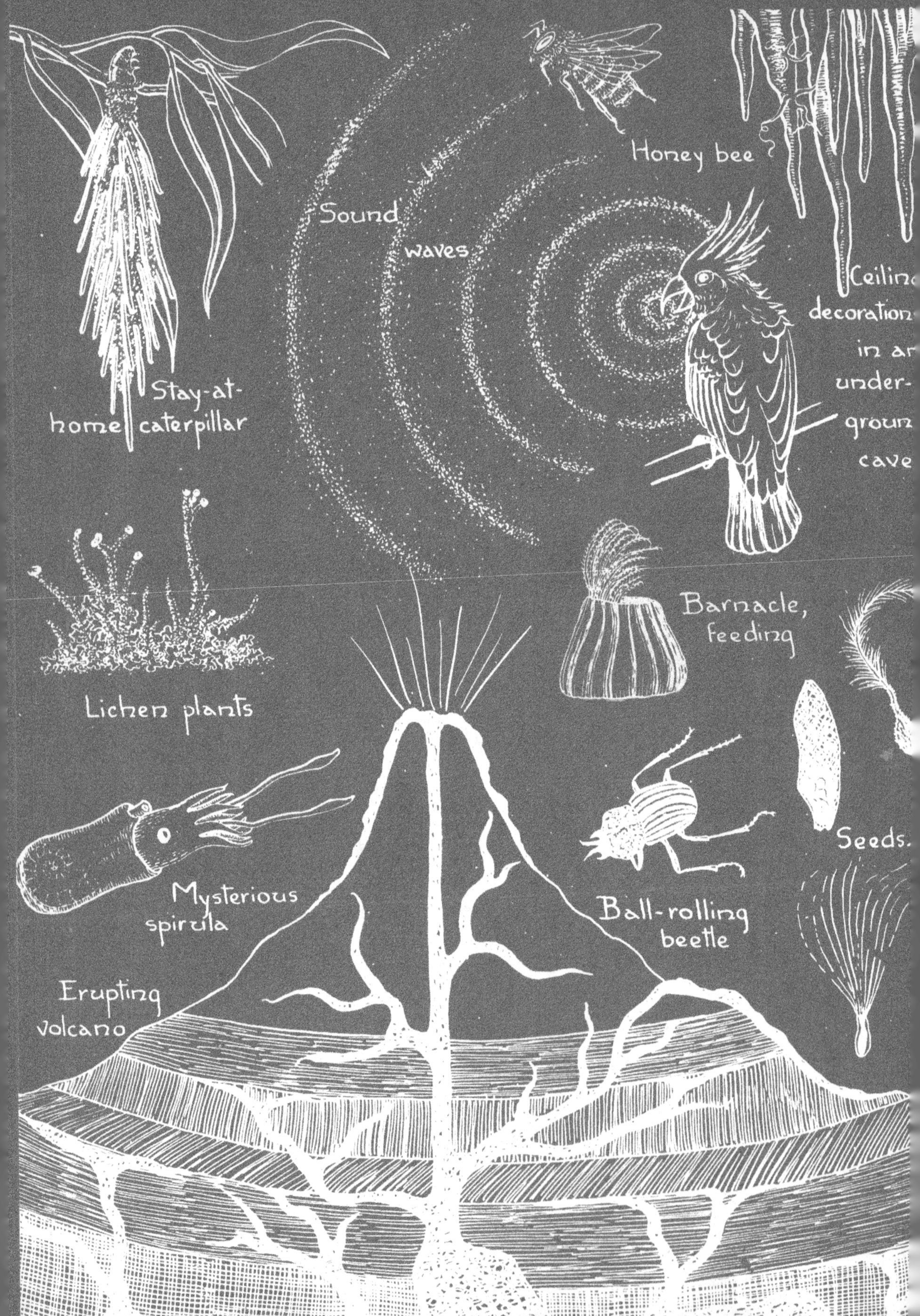

Stay-at-home caterpillar

Sound waves

Honey bee

Ceiling decorations in an underground cave

Lichen plants

Barnacle, feeding

Mysterious spirula

Ball-rolling beetle

Seeds.

Erupting volcano

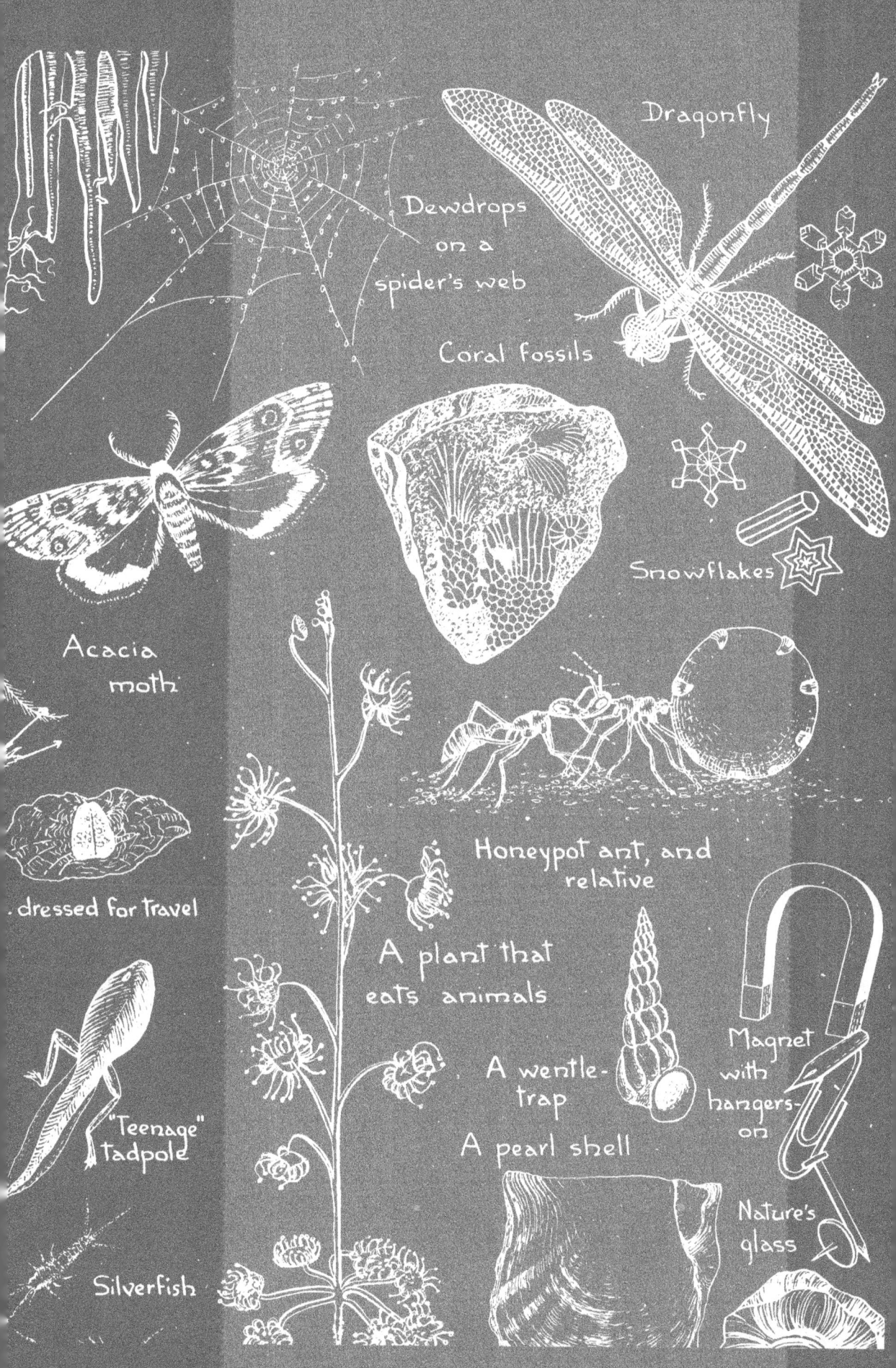

www.ingramcontent.com/pod-product-compliance
Lightning Source LLC
Chambersburg PA
CBHW080213040426
42333CB00044B/2652